AMERICA'S COLD WARRIOR

AMERICA'S COLD WARRIOR

PAUL NITZE AND NATIONAL SECURITY
FROM ROOSEVELT TO REAGAN

JAMES GRAHAM WILSON

CORNELL UNIVERSITY PRESS
Ithaca and London

First published 2024 by Cornell University Press

Printed in the United States of America

Library of Congress Cataloging-in-Publication Data

Names: Wilson, James Graham, 1980– author.
Title: America's cold warrior : Paul Nitze and national security from Roosevelt to Reagan / James Graham Wilson.
Other titles: Paul Nitze and national security from Roosevelt to Reagan
Description: Ithaca : Cornell University Press, 2024. | Includes bibliographical references and index.
Identifiers: LCCN 2023044264 (print) | LCCN 2023044265 (ebook) | ISBN 9781501776076 (hardcover) | ISBN 9781501776090 (epub) | ISBN 9781501776083 (pdf)
Subjects: LCSH: Nitze, Paul H., 1907–2004. | National security—United States—History—20th century. | Cold War. | Nuclear weapons—Government policy—United States. | United States—Officials and employees—Biography. | United States—Military relations—Soviet Union. | Soviet Union—Military relations—United States. | United States—Foreign relations—1945–1989.
Classification: LCC E748.N49 W55 2024 (print) | LCC E748.N49 (ebook) | DDC 327.730092 [B]—dc23/eng/20231108
LC record available at https://lccn.loc.gov/2023044264
LC ebook record available at https://lccn.loc.gov/2023044265

For Remy

Contents

Acknowledgments   ix

List of Abbreviations   xi

Note on Sources   xiii

Introduction   1

1. Men of Action   15

2. The Levers of Influence   32

3. Cold Warrior   49

4. NSC-68   64

5. No Exile   81

6. Nuclear Crises, 1961–1963   104

7. Preponderance Lost   127

8. Negotiating from Weakness, 1969–1975   146

9. The Nitze Scenario   171

10. A Walk in the Woods, 1981–1984   192

11. The Strategic Concept   212

12. No Retirement, 1989–2004   238

Conclusion   263

Notes   269

Bibliography   299

Index   307

ACKNOWLEDGMENTS

I am indebted to those individuals who encouraged and assisted me with this book amid the masked bewilderment of the COVID-19 era. Joshua Botts, Hal Brands, Seth Center, Charles Edel, Francis Gavin, and William Inboden each motivated me to start and finish this book. My colleagues Paul Pitman and Kathleen Rasmussen read large portions of the manuscript; Elizabeth Charles and Kristin Ahlberg offered vital support. James Cameron and David Milne did as well.

I have had the great fortune to get to know stalwarts of the arms control community who shared memories of working with Paul Nitze in some capacity. These include James Goodby, Thomas Graham Jr., and Stan Riveles, who read an early draft manuscript in its entirety and offered helpful feedback. Adene and Richard Wilson read a later version. My mentor and friend Melvyn Leffler also read a draft manuscript. I thank Frank Costigliola and Richard Immerman for their encouragement.

I am grateful to Sarah Grossman, Jacqulyn Teoh, and Mary Kate Murphy at Cornell University Press, and Michael McGandy, who advocated for this book. I thank Abigail Michaud for serving as the production editor and Vickie Jacobs for preparing the index.

I am exceedingly thankful to Mary Barton, my love. And to our son Remy, a young man of action.

ABBREVIATIONS

ABM	anti-ballistic missile
ACDA	Arms Control and Disarmament Agency
ALCM	air-launched cruise missile
C³+I	command, control, communications, and intelligence
CIA	Central Intelligence Agency
CPD	Committee on the Present Danger
CTBT	Comprehensive Test Ban Treaty
DC	District of Columbia
DST	Defense and Space Talks
ExComm	Executive Committee of the National Security Council
FBI	Federal Bureau of Investigation
FDR	Franklin D. Roosevelt
FPR	Washington Center of Foreign Policy Research
ICBM	intercontinental ballistic missile
IDA	Institute for Defense Analysis
INF	Intermediate-Range Nuclear Forces
ISA	international security affairs
JFK	John F. Kennedy
LBJ	Lyndon Baines Johnson
MAD	mutual assured destruction
MIRVs	multiple independent reentry vehicles
MX	Missile Experimental
NATO	North Atlantic Treaty Organization
NPT	Nuclear Non-Proliferation Treaty
NSC	National Security Council
NSC-68	"United States Objectives and Programs for National Security"
NSDD	National Security Decision Directive
NSPG	National Security Planning Group
NSSD	National Security Study Directive
NST	Nuclear and Space Arms Talks
RFK	Robert F. Kennedy

RISOP	Red Integrated Strategic Offensive Plan
RV	reentry vehicle
SAIS	School of Advanced International Studies
SALT	Strategic Arms Limitation Talks
SALT I	Interim Agreement Between the United States and USSR (1972)
SALT II	Treaty Between the United States and USSR (1979)
SAM	surface-to-air missile
SDI	Strategic Defense Initiative
SIOP	Single Integrated Operations Plan
SLBM	submarine-launched ballistic missile
SLCM	submarine-launched cruise missile
SS	surface-to-surface missile (e.g., SS-9)
START	Strategic Arms Reduction Treaty
UN	United Nations
USSBS	US Strategic Bombing Survey
USSR	Union of Soviet Socialist Republics

NOTE ON SOURCES

The views expressed here do not necessarily reflect those of the Department of State or the US government. This book is based on declassified and publicly available sources.

AMERICA'S COLD WARRIOR

Introduction

In the summer of 1914, when Paul Nitze was a young boy, his family vacationed in Tyrol, a bucolic region inside what was then the Austro-Hungarian Empire. As the Nitzes climbed a mountain, a villager gave Paul and his sister glasses of milk straight from her cow. While passing her house on the descent, the family discovered the woman in tears. Her husband had just been summoned for duty in the Austro-Hungarian Army. Emperor Franz Joseph—who had succeeded to the throne in 1848—mobilized the country a few weeks after an assassin gunned down his nephew and presumptive heir, Archduke Franz Ferdinand.[1] On July 28, 1914, Austria declared war on Serbia, commencing World War I.

When Paul Nitze was an older man, he was set to meet with the national security adviser, Condoleezza Rice, on a late fall afternoon at the Paul Nitze School of Advanced International Studies (SAIS) in Washington, DC. Rice intended to deliver a speech extolling the merits of ballistic missile defense to protect the US homeland from attack.[2] Neither event happened. On the morning of that Tuesday, September 11, 2001, terrorists flew two planes into the World Trade Center in downtown Manhattan and another one into the Pentagon. Passengers on United Airlines Flight 93—believed to be headed to Washington, DC—overcame the hijackers, and the plane crashed into a field in Shanksville, Pennsylvania.

Between Europe's last summer and the United States' darkest day, Nitze attended the nation's most elite academic institutions, prospered on Wall Street, and devoted himself to the practice of US national security from 1940 onward. He worked for the White House, Department of State, Department of Defense, and the Arms Control and Disarmament Agency. He was detailed to the US Air Force and Department of Treasury and consulted for the Central Intelligence Agency (CIA) and Senate Foreign Relations Committee. Even outside his service to eight presidential administrations, as President Jimmy Carter learned the hard way, Nitze remained vital in framing and influencing debates about US nuclear policies.

This book is a political biography of Paul Henry Nitze. A good part of his story will be told in his own words. No other American in the twentieth century contributed to high policy as much as he did for as long as he did in both Democratic and Republican administrations. The diplomat and writer George Kennan has garnered more fame, yet from 1950 onward Kennan played no role in shaping high policy. In contrast, Paul Nitze commanded presidential attention and catalyzed action from 1940 to 1989. His career connects the Cold War to the post-9/11 era and the challenges of the 2020s, where the United States finds itself locked in geopolitical competition with the People's Republic of China and the Russian Federation.

Nitze crafted a new type of career: national security professional. Unlike his mentors and near-peers, he never returned to his pre-World War II occupation as an investment banker. The early days of the Cold War demanded generalists with competence in multiple areas—economics, military strategy, intelligence, diplomacy—and the know-how to achieve results, whether in the private sector, academia, or government bureaucracies. Nitze met that demand. Supremely confident in his abilities, he devoted himself to protecting the American way of life. Financial comfort afforded him the opportunity to take risks. Getting fired from a political appointment in government—or simply running afoul of the powers that be—would not imperil his ability to provide for his family.

Paul Nitze remained relevant for so long because he was independent enough to make career decisions on the basis of expected policy impact, not partisan or financial upside. Financial and political independence allowed him to focus on the concept of "tension between opposites." He subscribed to democracy. And the document with which he is most closely associated, NSC-68, recapitulated America's foundational texts—the Declaration of Independence and the Constitution—using the vocabulary of Cold War threats. Yet he distrusted party politics. He was convinced that the American people could pay much more in taxes to guarantee their survival against communism. He believed the two- and four-year election cycles were unhelpful to the cause of preserving US nuclear and conventional superiority. He regarded himself as a nonpartisan expert. "The test of a first-rate intelligence is the ability to hold two opposed ideas in mind at the same time and still retain the ability to function." Nitze enjoyed repeating this quote from F. Scott Fitzgerald.[3] When it came to democracy versus elitism in the crafting of national security policy, Nitze passed Fitzgerald's test. He did not get bogged down in hesitation.

Nitze's longevity also allowed him to gather comprehensive knowledge about nuclear weapons from 1949 onward. He became a leading authority in the emerging field of strategic studies, even though he never published a book-length work. He divined the political implications of weapons of mass destruction short of their actual use. And he was *as qualified* as anyone else to weigh in on how the nuclear-armed United States and the nuclear-armed Soviet Union would interact in a nuclear crisis—especially since he had been in the room with the president during the Berlin Crisis of 1961 and the Cuban Missile Crisis of 1962, which were the only two genuine nuclear crises of the Cold War. When the United States and Soviet Union finally commenced serious negotiations to limit and reduce existing nuclear weapons in 1969, Nitze was outspoken in arguing for those approaches he thought might work. Employing logic chains and a forceful demeanor, he drew upon all his knowledge of atomic matters to overwhelm anyone with whom he disagreed. Nitze's view of the world—that the United States needed to achieve and sustain strategic superiority—remained constant as the country lost that strategic superiority following the Cuban Missile Crisis. He did not predict or expect the end of the Cold War in 1989–91, convinced as he was that the Soviets retained strategic superiority. Nevertheless, he played a critical role in the Ronald Reagan administration in establishing a concept for integrating strategic defenses and reducing strategic offensive arms.

Furthermore, Nitze's career and ideas about national security directly influenced the George W. Bush administration. Nitze developed a theory of strategic superiority that made sense to decision makers throughout the Cold War and after. In his "Nitze Scenario" from the 1970s, the Soviets might preemptively take out US land-based nuclear forces while leaving US cities intact. The president could then order US nuclear submarines to retaliate against Soviet cities—however, Soviet missiles kept in reserve would then rain on US cities. In this scenario, the president would be forced to choose between surrender and tens of millions of US lives. In this scenario, an adversary's capabilities could neutralize the anticipated value of the US deterrent. A democratically elected president would not choose to sacrifice even one US city. US leaders could be forced to be deterred from projecting the power needed to sustain critical geopolitical commitments. After the Cold War ended, the prospect of an unconventional attack from a "rogue regime" replaced the threat of Soviet strategic forces. The terrible events of September 11 hammered home the message that Iraq, Iran, Libya, and North Korea could all blackmail the United States.

The Life of Paul Nitze

Memory shapes history, and Paul Nitze never forgot the summer of 1914 and being with his family in Austria-Hungary—and then Germany—during the outbreak of World War I. Likewise, he always remembered the high-minded but futile debates among his father's colleagues on the faculty at the University of Chicago during the Paris Peace Conference of 1919. After that, he resolved to become a man of action who could shape world events.

After graduating from Harvard in 1928 and flourishing on Wall Street in the 1930s, Nitze arrived in Washington, DC, in 1940 to assist the Franklin Roosevelt administration in preparing for the United States' potential entry into World War II. He stayed in government from Imperial Japan's attack on Pearl Harbor, on December 7, 1941, to the collapse of the wartime alliance between the United States and the Soviet Union in 1946 and the subsequent formulation of the Marshall Plan to rebuild Western Europe as well as the North Atlantic Treaty Organization (NATO) to defend it. In early 1950, after taking a lead role in the study that prompted the decision to build the hydrogen bomb, he oversaw the completion of NSC-68. This US national security strategy called for tripling annual defense spending and placed the country on a war footing. In November 1957, he drafted the Gaither Report, which warned of dire consequences if the Soviets launched a nuclear attack on the US homeland. He called on the Eisenhower administration to take drastic actions to reduce US strategic vulnerabilities.

Following the 1960 presidential campaign in which the candidates sparred over a purported "missile gap" favoring the Soviets, Nitze served on the John F. Kennedy administration's Executive Committee of the National Security Council (ExComm) during the October 1962 Cuban Missile Crisis when the United States and Soviet Union very nearly went to nuclear war. He was the Pentagon's number two official during the tumultuous year of 1968, when the Vietnam War led President Lyndon B. Johnson to decline to seek reelection. Finally, he found himself in the Richard Nixon administration advising the delegation that crafted the SALT I (Strategic Arms Limitation Talks) agreement and Anti-Ballistic Missile (ABM) Treaty in May 1972. He later participated in the Team B alternative National Intelligence Estimate, the findings of which excoriated the US intelligence community for misunderstating Soviet capabilities.

Still later, during a June 1982 "walk in the woods" with a Soviet counterpart outside Geneva, Nitze attempted to craft a grand compromise on the numbers and types of intermediate-range nuclear forces. In January 1985, he presented an even more ambitious approach to President Ronald Reagan—a phased plan, over fifteen years, to reduce substantially the number of long-range ballistic missiles while pursuing research on defenses against them—that became the US position at the Reykjavik Summit with Soviet leader Mikhail Gorbachev in October 1986. Finally, in Washington in December 1987, Nitze led the US team in negotiations that finalized the Intermediate-Range Nuclear Forces (INF) Treaty, which eliminated intermediate-range nuclear weapons and established the formula for the Strategic Arms Reduction Treaty (START), which the US and Soviet leaders would ultimately sign in the summer of 1991. That treaty was the precursor for the 2011 New START agreement between the United States and Russia that President Joseph Biden and Russian leader Vladimir Putin extended in January 2021. As of January 2024, the START agreement that Nitze helped craft is the only remaining arms control regime currently in force from the end of the Cold War.

Whether he testified before Congress, spoke at the Council on Foreign Relations, or wrote an opinion piece in the *Washington Post*, Nitze formulated his words to precipitate action. Behind them was the constant refrain: the United States needed to restore its strength. He retained the cachet of the Truman administration and stayed in Washington long enough for a Republican administration—Ronald Reagan—to embrace Truman and him. Paul Nitze will always be most closely associated with NSC-68, which Truman signed in 1950. His most significant contribution to US peace and security came in the painstaking work during the period 1982–88 to negotiate successful treaties with the Soviets to reduce nuclear weapons while simultaneously deflecting skeptics within the most conservative US presidential administration of the second half of the twentieth century.

In and out of government, Paul Nitze remained an influential figure in US foreign policy from 1945 until the early months of 1989. Even after Secretary of State James Baker dismissed him at that point, Nitze refused to relocate from Washington, DC. Instead, he returned to Massachusetts Avenue and set up shop in an office in a building with his name on it. There he hosted former Cold War interlocuters and kept tabs on the George H. W. Bush administration's efforts to establish a new world order. Spite against Baker animated him. In 1991, at age eighty-four years, he nearly came out against ratification of

START I, the agreement he had helped formulate and negotiate with his Soviet counterpart, Marshal Sergei Akhromeyev, while in the Reagan administration.

Nitze never retired. In September 1993, he delivered an address to the National War College titled "The Grand Strategy of NSC-68," in which he sketched out a blueprint based on the successful waging of the Cold War, which he thought could help the United States overcome fundamental security questions.[4] Subsequently, he called for eliminating nuclear weapons, a significant reversal from his professional days of helping build up the United States' nuclear arsenal. He did so not because of regretting past decisions, but because he thought that weaponry did not mitigate the threats of the post-Cold War era; conventional "smart weapons" did. He also advocated mobilizing US economic might and political will to combat what he regarded as the most severe national security threat following the end of the Cold War: global climate change.

When Paul Nitze died in 2004 at ninety-seven years old, friends and associates gathered at the National Cathedral to pay tribute. They included Secretary of Defense Donald Rumsfeld, who had once attempted to torpedo his nomination to be secretary of the navy, and Deputy Secretary of Defense Paul Wolfowitz, who had once worked for him and later served as dean of the rechristened Paul Nitze School of Advanced International Studies. Following the attacks of September 11, 2001, and the US invasion of Iraq in March 2003, US foreign policy since the end of the Cold War had gone in a much different direction than Nitze had wanted.

National Security as a Profession

In establishing his own professional trajectory, Nitze acted on his ideas. He did not serve in military uniform and was not a lawyer, professor, captain of industry, scientist, or foreign service officer. Rather, he formulated his theories about history and relations between states while pursuing professional opportunities on his own terms. Along with his wartime District of Columbia (DC) roommate, future secretary of state Christian Herter, he cofounded a university, the School of Advanced International Studies, originally intended to train business executives in foreign affairs. While working for the US Strategic Bombing Survey, assisting with the Marshall Plan and broader postwar economic recovery of Europe, and then leading the State Department's Office of Policy Planning, Nitze interacted with the world's leading physical and social scientists. Both inside and outside government, he absorbed as much knowledge as possible and "emerged as perhaps the most important intellectual middleman of the Cold War period," as one scholar noted.[5]

"Intellectual middleman" minimizes Nitze's contributions. There is no question that *he* would have balked at the depiction. It aggravated Nitze not to be taken seriously as a scholar in his own right, and he regarded most scholars as ignorant of how the world actually worked. Nor did he tolerate any criticism of the policies he crafted. He was indignant, in later years, at "revisionists" who took an interest in such matters as the origins of the Cold War yet did not accept his recollections as gospel. In later years, he published *Tension between Opposites*, a book he hoped would achieve his longtime ambition to articulate a unifying theory about international politics.[6] It has not found a place in the political science canon.

Many aspiring national security professionals, however, follow in Paul Nitze's footsteps. "National security policy encompasses the decisions and actions deemed imperative to protect domestic core values from external threats," as defined by the preeminent scholar of this concept.[7] For Nitze, working on national security policy meant identifying a threat, proposing a solution, and advocating for it over alternative ones. Unlike a "merit-based" civil servant, whose profession was formalized in the 1883 Pendleton Civil Service Reform Act, Nitze chose the terms of his employment. Onward assignments depended on his cultivating relationships and demonstrating utility to employers. While he was loathe to admit it, Nitze served at the whim of politicians. This allowed him to gain insight into how the world worked through observing powerful men such as Clarence Dillon, James Forrestal, George Marshall, Will Clayton, and Dean Acheson. He sometimes disappointed these older figures, yet he never fell out with them. He always felt at home at Harvard, on Wall Street, and in the elite corridors of power and social clubs of Washington, DC.[8]

Nitze was wealthy—but not ostentatiously so. Yet his financial security was a key component to his career. His wife's grandfather had helped John D. Rockefeller establish the Standard Oil company, and her inheritance included the farm in Maryland where Nitze entertained friends, colleagues, and foreign diplomats. He drew income from a propitious real estate investment with his wealthy brother-in-law in Aspen, Colorado. He wrote reports for the government through SAIS and later a contracting firm, the System Planning Corporation. After 1966, when Revlon purchased a pharmaceutical company in which he was a significant shareholder, Nitze became wealthy enough not to depend on a government salary (though he still drew one).[9] In 1977, he made a very brief foray into the world of corporate raiders when 20th Century Fox used the profits from *Star Wars* to acquire the Aspen Corporation. From a seat on the board of directors, Nitze participated in a failed effort to take the movie studio private; this was a momentary diversion, and Nitze was soon back at the fore of national security debates. "In and Outer" is a term for someone who alternates between the public and private sector, usually at an executive level. After World War II, Paul Nitze never went out.

Demands imposed on the foreign policy establishment from 1945 onward required generalists who knew something about economics and military strategy, intelligence and diplomacy, metallurgy and supply chains, and how to get things done, whether in the private sector, academia, or government. Nitze fit the bill. His life is an index to the establishment of institutions and means of power that have long outlasted the fall of the Berlin Wall in November 1989 and the collapse of the Soviet Union in December 1991.

Tension between Opposites

In his embrace of "tension between opposites," Nitze sought to delineate a theory of everything. While books about history, economics, and sociology inspired him, he believed that political science and international relations distorted reality. So when it seemed in the 1970s that his government career might end, he embarked upon an elaborate book project that would fuse his personal story with broader ideas about statecraft—along the lines of Henry Kissinger's multivolume memoirs. Ultimately, he published a single memoir in 1989 and then the shorter, *Tension between Opposites*, in 1993. The latter summed up his pursuit of harmony based on tensions and his observations about how men he admired had taught him to do so.

"No one can act on the complex and important policy issues at the forward edge of emerging history without having formed some rough simplifying approaches to such issues," Nitze wrote.[10] To do so required a set of guidelines. Policy makers seldom articulated these guidelines, and so could not understand why they failed or succeeded. Nitze hoped that identifying procedures based on his experiences would enhance the prospects for better outcomes. He was entranced by a passage from the great German writer Johann Wolfgang von Goethe, who defined duty: "What the day demands."[11] Duty required action. "It is by action—in my terms, by the practice of politics—that theory . . . can be kept in touch with reality," Nitze summed up. Only through action could one ascertain "the opportunities and risks of the future."[12] Theory and practice, to Nitze, "constituted harmonic aspects of one whole."[13]

Here and elsewhere, Nitze zeroed in on the assertion attributed to the Greek philosopher Heraclitus that "truth and beauty were to be found in the tension between opposites." He loved recounting Heraclitus's examples of the bow and the lyre. "The power of the bow comes from the tension between the two arms of the bow and its directed release," Nitze wrote. "[T]he harmony and beauty of the tones of the lyre come from the varying tensions of its strings."[14]

When he delivered the commencement address to his son's class at the Groton School in 1953, Nitze applied "tension between opposites" to the challenges of the atomic age and the Cold War struggle between East and West. "In each case, the answer is to be found not in the elimination of one of the opposites or any basic compromise between them but in striving for a harmony in the tension between opposites."[15] Forty years later, Nitze looked back on the speech with pride. He went on to elaborate on four principal elements for building a theory of politics: (1) political structure; (2) value system; (3) situation; and (4) viewpoint.[16]

The key takeaway was that more than theory was needed. Theory could sharpen the mind and lead to a more robust set of guidelines that would simplify the myriad information that confronted a policy maker. By Nitze's terms, it could reinforce concepts of values and ethics. However, theory needed to be accompanied by a set of actions leading to material change—no amount of pure reasoning would ever suffice, most especially to one serving in government.

Consequently, people who merely wrote about power underwhelmed him. "It is my view that most of what has been written and taught under the heading of 'political science' by Americans since World War II has been contrary to experience and common sense," Nitze asserted.[17] Political science had been "of limited value"—and at times "counterproductive, as a guide to the actual conduct of policy."[18] Every situation was different, and no single independent variable stood out. Good policy making required modest expectations. "The best that we can strive for is a judgment that is more apt to be right than wrong; it can rarely produce certainties."[19]

In Nitze's terms, true learning required persistent action. That meant staying involved in political debates in government and being able to set the terms of those political debates or shift their focus. It meant focusing on matters of war and peace. During the Cold War, that meant preventing nuclear war and configuring the strategic (i.e., nuclear) and conventional (i.e., nonnuclear) balance between the United States and the Soviet Union so that the US side would retain its freedom of action. There was no greater tension between opposites than preparation to wage nuclear war and the aspiration that adequate preparation would prevent it from happening.

Expertise on Nuclear Weapons in World Politics

As George Kennan's successor as director of the Policy Planning Staff, as of January 1, 1950, Nitze took on the burden of rebuilding Western Europe, East Asia, and nearly everywhere else in the world following the destruction brought on by World War II. Then there was the improved manner by which the United States responded to Soviet actions. While he was intimately involved in the Truman administration's decision to pursue the hydrogen bomb, nuclear matters were only one of several key areas in his purview. Over the course of the 1950s and 1960s, Nitze's attention narrowed to focus nearly exclusively on how to stabilize the nuclear balance. By 1969, when he joined the US delegation to the SALT, it had absorbed all of his attention and, for twenty-five years, that remained the case.

During the Nixon administration, when Nitze was flying to Helsinki and Geneva for SALT, Secretary of Defense James Schlesinger tasked the director of the Office of Net Assessment Andrew Marshall with producing a history of the strategic arms competition since 1945, a project that Marshall outsourced to Harvard Professor Ernest May, Brookings Institution scholar John Steinbruner, and the RAND Corporation's Thomas Wolfe. The purpose of that project was to understand better why policy makers in Washington and Moscow built their force structures and then to derive lessons from history to create a more stable nuclear balance. Unfortunately, when this highly classified project was completed in 1981, few policy makers read it.

Paul Nitze did not need to. He had been involved in nearly every US decision about nuclear weapons in the study and had seen all of the Soviet intelligence. A select few people enjoyed his level of access to the technical information—whether ingested by reading classified material or meeting with the scientists—in addition to briefing policy makers and engaging with outside academics. Nitze retained privileged access and fully grasped as many policies and theories as anyone. He may not have captured them *better* or more imaginatively; he got them well enough to answer the president's most difficult questions confidently. During the 1960s, the commander-in-chief called on him—far more so than nuclear theorists—to figure out how to reduce the prospects of nuclear war.

During the 1970s and 1980s, Nitze strove for a blockbuster agreement to restrain offensive and defensive capabilities to stabilize the strategic arms competition between the United States and the Soviet Union. After a decade and a half working on SALT I, SALT II (and then becoming its chief critic), and on INF, Nitze's aspirations dovetailed with those of an idealistic US leader. In early 1985, President Ronald Reagan adopted Nitze's "Monday Package," which laid out phases by which Washington and Moscow could incrementally achieve dramatic reductions in nuclear arsenals while shifting the emphasis from assured destruction to assured protection. Nitze's ambitious package fit together nuclear weapons, strategic defense, and arms control in a way that appealed to the president's predilections. This was no paper for the annual meeting of the American Political Science Association; it was official US policy by the time of the Reykjavik Summit in October 1986. In crafting it, Nitze drew upon a careful study of the literature on security studies and practical experience in and out of government. He advocated for his positions without the protection of tenure.

As with other scholars in strategic studies, Nitze's beliefs were grounded partially in nuclear "theology"—a set of untestable predictions about how leaders in Moscow and Washington would behave in the event of a crisis leading one side to use nuclear weapons and how the other side would respond. There has only ever been one example of the use of nuclear weapons in wartime—Hiroshima and Nagasaki. Nitze visited both cities after the war while working for the Strategic Bombing Survey Commission and had encountered, firsthand, burn victims from the atomic attacks. And, from the theory perspective, that was against a nonnuclear power—Japan.

Moreover, there were only two genuine crises between two nuclear powers during the Cold War—the Berlin Crisis of 1961 and the Cuban Missile Crisis of 1962. And, very significantly, US strategic forces vastly outnumbered those of the Soviet Union during both of them—a ratio that would rapidly evaporate, complicating any models of what would happen should another crisis emerge. In coming up with contingency plans for what to do in the summer of 1961 and fall of 1962, Nitze was more helpful than academics such as Thomas Schelling, who advocated for signaling US intentions to Moscow through limited nuclear strikes. Such purported expertise delved too far into the world of nuclear theology with little emphasis on what happens in rooms in the White House, State Department, and Pentagon during periods of crisis.

Nitze opposed limited nuclear war. He was also against total nuclear war—though in both instances, he believed that Soviet (and some US) policy makers did not share his position. The overriding policy objective, from his perspective, was to avoid scenarios where maintaining vital US interests required a president to face the choice of whether or not to launch a nuclear attack. Paradoxically, the credibility of the US nuclear deterrent relied on minimizing the likelihood of those moments in which a US president likely would not give the order to launch because the consequences would be too devastating.

The answer was simple: only the projection of decisive US strength could avert that scenario. The Soviets had backed down over Cuba in October 1962.

Nitze attributed their acquiescence to a US margin of superiority that was in fact fleeting. For much of Nitze's career, US credibility was premised on restoring nuclear supremacy and extending to Western European allies its ability to deter. The value being protected was US freedom to act in regional conflicts, and there was little daylight, in his mind, between US sufficiency and clear superiority.

In the 1970s and 1980s, while Nitze lamented the loss of such superiority, he wrote about strategic stability—wherein both sides had smaller, mobile, and invulnerable land-based nuclear forces—that did not necessarily require a US advantage. The logic of strategic stability dictated that neither side ought to have any incentive to strike first. Among its elusive qualities were the assumptions that the American people could understand why they needed thousands of small missiles and that the Soviets would never give up their biggest ones.

In the aftermath of the Cuban Missile Crisis, while Secretary of Defense Robert McNamara and most Americans accepted mutual assured destruction (MAD), Nitze rejected that concept. The arms race continued, even after the United States capped its production of Minuteman missiles at one thousand. Meanwhile, the Soviet Union overcame the United States' numerical advantage by the 1970s. It continued to build more significant stockpiles of huge, land-based nuclear missiles and very accurate missiles that could hit all of the capitals of NATO allies. Catching up with the West in strategic capabilities did not moderate the behavior of the Soviets abroad. Nor did it stop them from building up a quantitative advantage. From Nitze's perspective, the strategic balance was *less stable* after that moment because Soviet leaders figured that their US counterparts would back down in a crisis.

As the eminent political scientist Robert Jervis later articulated, the theory of the nuclear revolution held that so long as one side possessed a "secure second-strike capability," it did not matter how many warheads the other side deployed. Nitze had little regard for such a theory, which he saw as having no practical advice for the challenges that policy makers encountered. In Jervis's account, MAD was a "fact of life," not a policy.[20] Nitze dismissed that. More importantly, it was not a "fact of life" to inhabitants of the White House during the Cold War. No US president could expect to be reelected on accepting Soviet nuclear superiority simply because academics had devised a theory that rendered nuclear war impossible.

Nitze's lesson of history, again based on his personal experiences and readings, was that preparedness mattered. The United States had been provocatively weak in the late 1930s, leading Germany and Japan to have their way with the free world. Twenty years later, the Soviet nuclear arms buildup had commenced under Nikita Khrushchev even before the Cuban Missile Crisis, Nitze was sure of this. And, very importantly, it did not stop with the advent of perestroika and glasnost in 1985. When Mikhail Gorbachev ascended to power that year, two new systems of Soviet missiles—SS-24s and SS-25s (i.e., surface-to-surface)—were coming online. Nitze distrusted Gorbachev and contended that the Soviets maintained nuclear superiority even as the new leader in the Kremlin spoke of new thinking at home and abroad. Nitze had long warned of the scenario in which the US leadership would have to choose between surrender or destruction. During the 1970s, that vulnerability became real, and at least several critical officials within the US government knew it. Presidential Directive 58, which President Carter signed on June 30, 1980, fit with a series of initiatives intended to shore up US "Doomsday" capabilities. It established a program by which the president could "survive a nuclear attack, even one which involves repeated attacks over a long period."[21]

Strategic vulnerability meant that during a crisis, the Soviets would press their advantage so that a US leader would back down, retreat from strained commitments, and perhaps even abandon its allies. Confidence in that prospect emboldened the Soviets to take risks. In the mid-1970s, Nitze laid out an even more dire scenario. Amid a crisis, the Soviets would launch a "counterforce" nuclear first strike that could take out the entire US Minuteman fleet while minimizing civilian casualties. The US president would then face ordering "second-strike" forces to retaliate against the Soviet Union or spare one hundred million lives by surrendering.

Nitze pursued two main policy objectives during the second half of the Cold War: first, for the United States to restore the situations of strength that had allowed it to prevail during the Cuban Missile Crisis; and, second, to make sure that the restoration of power did not provoke Moscow to build other systems that the United States, a democracy, could not easily match. But, unfortunately, strategic stability was fiendishly difficult to achieve, and Paul Nitze did not believe that the country had done so—even as the Cold War ended in 1989–91.

America's Cold Warrior

"Despite the United States' preponderance of power throughout the Cold War," two very distinguished scholars have written, "the proverbial Martian, if it had landed in Washington at any time between 1945 and the early 1980s and had tuned in to US political debate, would have concluded that America was in a life-and-death struggle with an implacable, ruthless, and fundamentally evil force and that it was on the verge of losing this epic struggle—or, at best, that the two titans were evenly matched."[22]

When it came to the nuclear and conventional military balance, the United States did not possess a "preponderance of power throughout the Cold War." The outcome of the Cuban Missile Crisis ensured that the Soviet Union would never again tolerate such a US advantage. Nitze—who employed the term "preponderance of power"—remained in Washington nearly the entire time between 1945 and the 1980s. His analysis of the Soviet threat was not motivated by party politics. Once they had caught up with the West, Soviets leaders *knew* that US counterparts would back down in a crisis, Nitze was sure. Confidence in that knowledge meant they could afford to take more significant risks. While it ultimately turned out to be a strategic disaster, the Soviet invasion of Afghanistan in 1979 crystallized fears that perceived US weakness increased such appetites for risk. In his gloomy assessments in the 1970s and 1980s, Nitze erred in lacking sufficient confidence that the inherent economic advantages of the US system would eventually prevail—in contrast to his boss during the second Reagan administration, Secretary of State George Shultz, who remained optimistic.

Throughout the Cold War, Nitze's objective was to not go to war with the Soviet Union. Instead, he shared Kennan's lifelong view that the US objective should be to reach an accord through measures short of war while never jettisoning his early opinion that Soviet counters were virtually impervious to reason. "Only under the most extraordinary circumstances can one expect to cause Soviet negotiators to change their position by fact or logic," as Nitze put it after the Reykjavik Summit.[23] However, he never stopped fighting for a grand bargain. When Kennan spoke in Iowa on February 1, 1984, he lamented the "extreme militarization not only of our thought but of our lives," citing the growing power of the military–industrial complex and US disdain for diplomacy with adversaries, and said that the US statesman was "more concerned for the domestic political effects of what he is saying or doing than about their actual effects on our relations with countries."[24]

Throughout that month and year, three decades after George Kennan last participated in the crafting of US foreign policy or grand strategy, Nitze, a registered Democrat in a conservative Republican administration, strove to revive nuclear arms negotiations with Soviet negotiators, even after they had stormed out of the INF negotiations in Geneva the previous fall. At the end of his last government assignment, Nitze believed he had failed to achieve that to which he aspired. Yet he stayed at it. He was America's Cold Warrior. Thirty years after the collapse of the Soviet Union, Nitze's legacy continues to shape the practice of national security, even though the priorities he embraced in the post-Cold War era—above all, eliminating nuclear weapons and combating global climate change—were not those priorities of post-Cold War presidents.

CHAPTER 1

Men of Action

Paul Nitze valued the distinction between people who generated ideas and those who took action. The son of a prestigious University of Chicago professor, he grew up in comfort amid an environment of bright minds. Working on Wall Street in the 1930s, he lived well even as much of the country suffered through the Great Depression. Ennui led him back to his alma mater Harvard to pursue a doctoral degree in sociology. Dropping out after two semesters, Nitze retained a complicated relationship with academia. In subsequent years, he bemoaned its insularity yet also wanted to be accepted as a strategic thinker with a unique understanding of the "real world."

A key figure during Paul Nitze's formative years was Clarence Dillon, the Wall Street titan who cofounded the New York investment firm Dillon, Read & Co. Nitze respected Dillon as a man who took action. Unlike professors, "action men" such as Dillon bore responsibility for the significant decisions of war and peace. Accordingly, Nitze aspired to gain proximity to them and gain their approval. Forged in the era of the Great Depression and then the outbreak of World War II, Nitze's worldview was that great people made big decisions that shaped history.

Nitzes and Hilkens; Baltimore and Chicago

From an ancestral home outside Magdeburg, Germany, Charles Nitze—Paul's grandfather—came to the United States for a "grand tour" shortly after the American Civil War ended in 1865. Settling in Baltimore, Maryland, Charles became general manager of Robert Garrett and Sons, an investment bank that financed the Baltimore and Ohio (B&O) Railroad.[1]

The year 1876 saw the one-hundredth anniversary of the Declaration of Independence, the birth of Charles and his wife Elizabeth's son, William A. Nitze, and the founding of Johns Hopkins University, an institution with which the Nitze family would become associated. Eighteen years later, William Nitze graduated from Johns Hopkins with a focus on early French literature, receiving his PhD from Columbia University three years after that. In 1901, William Nitze married Anina Sophia Hilken, whose family also traced its roots back to Germany.

On January 16, 1907, Anina gave birth to Paul Henry Nitze. "The name Nitze is inherently a Slavic name, not a Germanic name," Paul much later recalled, and a name his father claimed was derived from "Nike," which meant victory.[2] A Russian nurse attended to Nitze and taught him German—he would later recall having learned to speak German before English.[3] Besides the numerous German relatives, Nitze's family tree included a great uncle who attained the rank of general for the Confederacy during the Civil War.

In 1909, Professor William Nitze became head of Romance languages and literature at the University of Chicago, which the industrialist John D. Rockefeller had established a decade and a half after the founding of Johns Hopkins. The Nitzes lived at 1220 East 56th Street, two blocks north of the campus. In recollections of his youth, Paul seldom touched upon his relationship with his father.[4] Instead, he cherished the relationship with his mother, Anina, who was "by far the greatest influence in my life" and "loved me beyond any normal maternal love." Mother and son kept regular and candid correspondence as the latter grew older.[5]

City and country taught Paul about life. He relished the memory of how his mother dressed him up in Russian suits that a friend in Riga, Latvia, had sent her and how, after getting beat up on the way to school, he joined a local gang for protection.[6] While the streets of Chicago in the 1910s provided an introduction to "power politics," the woods of Colorado, where the family bought a ranch and spent summers, led Nitze to appreciate nature's restorative qualities. To help Paul's sister Elizabeth recover from an illness, William and Anina took the family to the pristine area near what would become Aspen.

When Paul Nitze was seven, his father took the family to Austria for a summer vacation that coincided with the immediate aftermath of the assassination of Archduke Ferdinand in Sarajevo on June 28, 1914, a shocking event that nevertheless did not merit the cancellation of travel plans. After mountain climbing in Tyrol, the Nitzes headed to Germany.[7] Upon their arrival in Munich, where a bomb had just exploded at the train station, the family took up lodging only to learn that Germany had declared war on Russia. From a hotel window, Paul watched as onlookers cheered on German troops marching in the street.[8] The family was in Munich when England declared war on Germany on August 4 and spent the rest of the month in Frankfurt with relatives of Anina.[9] Not until September 1914 could William Nitze book a trip on a Dutch steamship back to the United States.

Paul Nitze always remembered spending time at the Lake Surrick Club in Chicago shortly after returning home from Europe at the start of World War I.[10] The club's members included distinguished professors from the University of Chicago—several of whom had already won a Nobel Prize—and representatives of the wealthiest families of the Windy City. "And the thing I couldn't get over was the fact that there was a group that I thought was the most admirable men one could imagine, and they were having no impact upon the things that were going on in the world that seemed to be the most tragic and the most important," Nitze later recalled. "And at that point, I rather felt that I didn't want to follow in the footsteps of those people, admirable as I thought they were, because they did not have a real impact upon affairs."[11] Nitze had grander ambitions than replicating his father's career and social circle. "I wanted to get into some other field where one could be closer to the levers of power, to put it frankly, the levers of influence."[12]

In sixth grade at the prestigious Chicago Lab School, Paul Nitze played, in a school production, the role of future German foreign minister Walther Rathenau lamenting the terms of the Versailles Treaty.[13] With this impersonation, he achieved the same outcome as the academics of his father's circle, who discussed the flaws of the postwar settlement. "They were, in my estimation, as distinguished a group of scholars as had ever been brought together, but it was evident that they were powerless to influence events."[14] Nitze took pride in what he regarded as his rebellious streak. He also benefited from the stimulating intellectual community around the University of Chicago. His neighbor and best friend was Professor Robert Millikan's son, Max Millikan, who would eventually serve as assistant director of the CIA and director of the MIT Center for International Studies.[15]

Outside the classroom and his school-age friends, Paul Nitze saw glimpses of the busy social world his parents and sister inhabited. His outspoken mother befriended Clarence Darrow, the renowned lawyer who defended controversial clients such as Nathan Leopold and Richard Loeb, a classmate of Nitze. She enjoyed the music of Richard Strauss and passed on to Nitze a lifelong appreciation for Johann Sebastian Bach. In 1922, Nitze's sister, Elizabeth Hilken, married Walter Paepcke, a businessman of German heritage who would go on to found the Container Corporation of America. Around that time, fifteen-year-old Paul Nitze passed the college entrance exams and decided to enroll at the University of Chicago. His father discouraged the idea because of his age and not wanting his peer group to pigeonhole him as the son of a professor.[16]

Hotchkiss and Harvard

Nitze did not become (possibly) the youngest undergraduate at the University of Chicago. Instead, he headed to Hotchkiss, the elite boarding school in Connecticut, where his classmates included future deputy secretary of defense Roswell "Ros" Gilpatric. The entry for the second football team in the 1923 yearbook listed Nitze as 5 feet, 8 inches tall, weighing 143 lbs, and headed to Yale, which Paepcke had attended. Having already covered much of the schoolwork, Nitze focused on extracurricular activities. "The main thing on my mind was my peers and having fun with them and getting along with them," as he later put it.[17] The cocky teenager started the "sequester club" for those students who had received demerits. In addition, he pursued physical acts of daring, such as ski jumping, and once knocked himself unconscious.[18] According to the 1924 yearbook, Nitze played for the second football and class baseball teams and also participated in the St. Luke's and Pythian Societies, the Literary Board, the Opera Club, the Dramatic Association, the Mandolin Club, the Banjo Club, the Musical Association, the choir, and the Debating Union.

Nitze possessed confidence and ambition. "Think of the vast multitude of stars, of their tremendous size, of their inconceivable age, and the possibility of life on some of their planets," he wrote in an article for a student publication during his time at Hotchkiss. Such thoughts could easily lead one to feel insignificant and ask: "what difference can the actions of a single human being make in the period of a lifetime?" The answer offered by the sixteen-year-old Nitze was to "keep in mind that for us the world is everything and that each one of us is the center of his small universe [and] not such an unimportant thing after all."[19] Making "the most of his life, he may accomplish things which will not only bring him his reward but which will be given an infinite amount of happiness and comfort to the rest of the world."[20]

Such musings from an angst-ridden teenager are hardly a sign of genius. From a young age, however, Nitze strove to achieve. He was fixated on breaking out from his inherited habitat and playing against type as a professor's son. "I finally got the feeling that all this life that I had been part of in Chicago and Hotchkiss was in a way artificial and separated from the real world," he would later put it, "and that what I really wanted to do was to get away from all this and dive into the real world."[21]

Through Henry Hilken, his grandfather in Baltimore, Nitze got a summer job on the SS *Lutzo*, a German freighter that French forces had captured during World War I and had only recently returned to the North German Lloyd shipping line.[22] Young Nitze, yearning for a world outside of a cloistered academic setting, found it helping take apart the ship's engine while the vessel idled in the middle of the Atlantic Ocean or swimming in the bilge water to retrieve a dropped bolt.[23] For this seventeen-year-old, the experiences of Nobel Prize laureates on the faculty of the University of Chicago could not have compared to those of the ship's fourth engineer, Otto Knocke, who shared tales of escaping from a French prisoner of war camp, inventing a new kind of textile machine, and then losing a fortune during the hyperinflation of 1921–23.[24]

After deboarding at the end of the summer, Nitze prepared for undergraduate education in the Ivy League. While most of his Hotchkiss friends went to Yale, where Nitze had been expected to wind up, he chose Harvard—not "wholly satisfied with the lack of true intellectual interest" on the part of his peer group bound for New Haven.[25] Whatever expectations Nitze had for Harvard, the faculty apparently underwhelmed him. "I couldn't have been more bored with the mercantilists and all this kind of nonsense that bore nothing on today's economic world," he later described the course he took on the history of economic thought. "And so I didn't do much of the reading, and I didn't attend any of the lectures, and I didn't attend any of the section meetings, and the most beautiful girl had suggested that I go down to Newport for the weekend on the day of the final examination, and I did that rather than taking this final examination, so I didn't take the final examination."[26] Nitze received a zero for the course.

After forays into mathematics and physics and then history and literature, Nitze gravitated back to economics. Again, it came back to "some bearing upon the levers of influence." The "economic area" got at "what makes men tick . . . [a]nd not only really just in the business world but beyond that. It has a bearing on how people behave and why."[27] The zero in the history of economic thought notwithstanding, Nitze improved his grades and wound up fine academically. He wrote a senior paper on the theory of rate regulation of public utilities and earned the distinction summa cum laude.[28] In the oral examination, according to Nitze's recounting, the professor knocked down his final grade to a cum laude (from magna cum laude) because Nitze refused to back down on the point of disagreement. Such a moment—whether apocryphal or not—captures the self-assuredness with which he approached everyone.

Nitze pursued extracurricular activities with vigor. He played half back on the football team and rowed crew. His crew pals included Frederick "Freddie" Winthrop Jr., a descendant of John Winthrop, the first governor of Massachusetts.[29] When it came time to be asked to join the elite Porcellian eating club, which had famously recruited Theodore Roosevelt and rejected Franklin Roosevelt, Winthrop insisted that he would only participate if Nitze were also selected.[30] In meetings of the Porcellian, Nitze dined with alums such as a future senator and the incumbent Speaker of the House of Representatives. He also made a lifelong friend in Charles "Chip" Bohlen, who, after college would join the foreign service and go on to serve in ambassadorships to the Soviet Union and France. Nitze had planned to follow friends to do graduate work in England. Yet his efforts to make up for the zero in the history of economic thought led him to physical exhaustion during his senior year when he was hospitalized for infectious jaundice.[31] He came down with hepatitis after he and Winthrop canoed from Boston to New York in April.

A presence in Nitze's life during subsequent months of recovery and college graduation was his first serious girlfriend, Mary Ames, a member of a prominent Boston family. In November 1928, Nitze was driving Ames from her parents' house in downtown Boston to a party in Back Bay. When crossing from Beacon Street to Charlesgate West, he slammed on the brakes—but not soon enough to avoid hitting a couple walking across the street. The man suffered a broken leg, and the woman died a few hours later. At the cost of a lump sum, Nitze avoided prosecution. He broke up with Mary Ames shortly after graduation.[32] His life could have gone differently: he might have been imprisoned. Instead, he felt he had successfully managed a crisis.

Europe and Wall Street

Nitze decided to leave Boston. Walter Paepcke set him up with a job with the Philadelphia branch of the Container Corporation of America. Nitze soon left that position to work for a new box factory in Bridgeport, Connecticut.[33] He initially enjoyed learning about cost accounting but quickly grew bored.[34] "Bridgeport was not exactly my kind of town. . . . It was time to move on."[35] At this moment, he rejected the notion of an ordinary existence of relative comfort. A supervisor told him that he might one day become the company's vice president. Nitze professed horror at this prospect for his life.

Drawing again on family connections—this time his father, William—Nitze received an introduction to William Bacon, a Chicago banker who, based solely on the understanding that Nitze spoke German, sponsored him to go to Germany in the spring of 1929. Given the high valuation of the US stock market, Bacon wondered whether Germany had better buying opportunities. En route to Europe, Nitze stopped in New York City to meet with Clarence Dillon.

Dillon took Nitze to lunch at a private dining room where one of his proteges, James Forrestal, interrupted them to describe plans for a megamerger to counter a deal in the works by rivals at the much larger J.P. Morgan.[36] "This introduction to Forrestal left a deep impression upon me," Nitze later recounted. "I saw him as a man who understood the world of Wall Street and its power politics, was quick to understand what needed to be done next, and was prepared to do it." It was Nitze's "first exposure to a man of action . . . a man fully engaged in the 'practice' rather than the theory of politics."[37] Dillon and Forrestal proved to be indispensable to Nitze in the long term. After this first meeting, Dillon gave Nitze letters of introduction to the banking houses of Germany, including Oppenheim and Company, in Cologne.

In Europe during the summer of 1929, Nitze enjoyed an abbreviated version of the expatriate experience. On the street in Paris, he encountered a friend from Chicago who brought him into a circle of other Americans living there. These included Pat Morgan and his wife, the writer Whitney Cromwell, who had known James Joyce and Ernest Hemingway in the fabled setting of Paris in the 1920s. Nitze moved in with Morgan and Cromwell and assisted them in producing a new American opera. During this time, he briefly considered becoming an art dealer.

Nitze left his bohemian friends after a few weeks and arrived in Germany, where the twenty-two-year-old relied on his letters of introduction from Clarence Dillon to gain entrée into elite circles.[38] In preparing his report on economic conditions—the ostensible purpose of his European journey—Nitze cultivated a professor of labor relations at the University of Berlin, traveled throughout the Ruhr Valley to see German industry up close, went to East Pomerania to learn about its agriculture, and inspected textile mills in Saxony. In Berlin, he attended sculpture exhibitions. Reconnecting with his Paris friends in the Netherlands, upon finishing up in Germany, Nitze was denied a visa to the Soviet Union on the grounds that he was not an artist.

Upon his return to the United States later on in 1929, Nitze met again with Dillon, who was gloomier than before and insistent that an economic depression—not just a recession—lay on the horizon. In response (and, again, with no sense of obligation to the firm in Chicago that sponsored his trip), Nitze showed Dillon his report concluding that Germany was overextended and highly vulnerable to an economic downturn. Dillon invited Nitze to join him at his weekend home in New Jersey, to which a chauffeur drove them in Dillon's Rolls Royce.

A few days after Nitze returned to Chicago and started work for William Bacon (who showed little interest in his report), he received a telegram from Dillon offering him a job. Nitze "was likely the last man hired on Wall Street for many years thereafter," he would quip later.[39] The ensuing stock market crash and Great Depression must have conveyed to Nitze that Dillon—as opposed to the professors he had observed from afar at the University of Chicago and then in the classroom at Harvard—understood the world. Dillon had already reduced the size of his workforce from four thousand to fifty—in preparation for the upcoming crash—and then hired him as employee fifty-one to commence work on October 1, 1929. Young Nitze's ego could hardly have suffered.

Nitze's first test in his new position came three weeks later. On that "Black Tuesday," October 29, Dillon ordered him to close out the firm's position in the Aluminum Company of America and absorb a steep loss. "This was the first of many opportunities I had to witness Clarence Dillon's keen, analytical mind combined with a radical and brutal decisiveness in taking the course of action from his analysts," Nitze later recounted. "When faced with a particular problem, he would be very objective, almost leisurely, about gathering information that might be pertinent." However, when he had determined "the important logic chain involved in the situation, he would suddenly switch from being an analyst to a man of action who would execute his decision without hesitation and with no looking back."[40] These practices—in particular, objective analysis followed by decisive action—were ones that Nitze sought to emulate throughout his career. Deciding to settle in New York City, he stayed at the Harvard Club and then in an apartment on East 43rd Street.[41]

Nitze represented Dillon, Read to maximize returns on new and ongoing investments. In one case involving the transfer of two investment trusts from New York to New Jersey to avoid paying a new state tax, Dillon appointed Nitze as secretary of both of them. In this capacity, Nitze kept minutes for board meetings that included financiers ranging from Frederick Ecker, the respected head of the Metropolitan Life Insurance Company, to Charles Edwin Mitchell, the director of National City Bank, who would later be convicted of tax evasion and whose encouragement of speculative practices may well have contributed to the great crash of 1929.[42]

"As I look back at the people on those two boards—there must have been a combined membership of seventy-five—perhaps a third of them were wise, competent, and honorable men," by Nitze's account, and "another third were basically incompetent, and the remaining third were crooks or barely within the law."[43] Nevertheless, the experience was "quite an education for a young man to be exposed to the machinations of the barons and wizards of Wall Street," and one that left him with "little awe and more confidence in my own abilities and judgment."[44]

Buoyed by this confidence the headstrong Nitze did not immediately endear himself to the firm's older associates and partners. "I soon become Mr. Dillon's fair-haired boy and he would often ask me to check out the carefully constructed negotiations and plans of a partner to give him my recommendation before he would give his approval," Nitze later recalled. "As far as Dillon was concerned, I could do no wrong. As far as the partners were concerned, I was the most objectionable young whippersnapper on Wall Street."[45]

Dillon appointed Nitze a director in a handful of companies he sought to pool together to construct a transcontinental railroad to surpass the achievements of the titans of nineteenth-century US industry. Nitze was twenty-four years old when all these companies went bankrupt in 1931. That same year—by which his "confidence knew few bounds"—Nitze attempted to broker a deal in which Dillon, Read would wrest control of the United Light and Railways Company (a forerunner of the Maryland Transit Administration) away from another financier, Cyrus Eaton.[46] But, unfortunately, that deal fell apart when Secretary of the Treasury Andrew Mellon intervened to protect Chase National Bank, whose largest shareholder was John D. Rockefeller.

"I went in to see Mr. Dillon and reported to him what had happened to my brilliant idea," Nitze later recalled. "He listened to what I had to say but said nothing. From that moment on I was a non-person. He no longer recognized my face, he didn't know my name. For three years I was a non-person at Dillon Read as far as the old man Dillon was concerned."[47] However, with this initiation of the old man's disappointment, Nitze saw his standing with the rest of the firm improve. The other partners had all experienced such treatment by Dillon and took him on as one of their own. Nitze now looked to James Forrestal as his primary mentor. Dillon never actually cast Nitze off. As with the other associates in the firm, he put aside memories of past failures when associates made money for the firm.

Neither failed deals nor the worsening of the Great Depression curtailed Nitze's ambition and good cheer about his surroundings. "I notice some people are gayer now than they have been," he wrote his mother in the spring of 1931. "There seems to be more of a Berlin atmosphere about. Things are just about so bad that they have ceased to worry."[48] While Nitze worried about "rioting and general unpleasantness" within the year, should the downturn continue, he was personally thriving. In July, he formed an independent venture with two partners to use a British machine called the "aquarator" to compete with large beverage companies. Nitze and his partners concocted an elaborate campaign alleging that CO_2 caused stomach problems and temporary sterility—and that consumers should purchase an "aquarator" instead of Coke or Pepsi. They soon conceded defeat.[49]

In 1932, Nitze started dating Phyllis Pratt, with whom he "was immediately smitten, for she was lovely, gay, and blessed with a sunny smile that would light the darkest corners."[50] When she first invited him over to dinner with her parents, Nitze debated the causes of the Great Depression with a family friend of the Pratts who turned out to be a governor of the Bank of England.[51] "Overproduction is not the problem," Nitze explained to Sir Montagu Norman, whom the *Wall Street Journal* had once called "the currency dictator of Europe."[52] "The world needs much more than is being produced," the headstrong younger man went on to say. "The problem is lack of ability to pay because of a worldwide competitive search for economic security through excessive banking liquidity."[53] No harmful consequences ensued from that exchange. Phyllis married him in December.

One month earlier, Phyllis's mother, Republican congresswoman Ruth Pratt, lost in a general election in which New York governor Franklin Delano Roosevelt defeated President Herbert Hoover. Roosevelt's New Deal drew scorn on Wall Street. "The character of my work at Dillon, Read changed somewhat after the passage of the Securities Act in 1933," Nitze acknowledged.[54] That legislation saddled companies with liability for putting out statements featuring material misstatements of facts. As an investment bank that placed securities and bonds, Dillon, Read needed to ascertain that everything listed on the offering was true. While that may seem a reasonable expectation, in the case of an offering for Cleveland Electric, a deal Nitze had worked on, investors did not seem to care about having complete transparency.[55] When it came to the Skelly Oil Company, the Securities Act meant that Dillon, Read needed to figure out which assets belonged to the head of the company and which belonged to the company itself.[56] The Securities Act, it seemed, required a modest amount of due diligence and honesty in financial transactions and thereby created more work for bankers like Nitze. This came at the expense of profit-making activities.

New Dealers treated Nitze and his Wall Street cohort as a political punching bag. In the fall of 1933, the Senate Committee on Banking and Currency called on Dillon, Read to testify about stock exchange practices as part of hearings featuring its hard-charging chief counsel, Ferdinand Pecora. Choosing to forget the United Light and Railways Company fiasco two years earlier, Dillon took Nitze to Washington, DC, and tasked him with assembling a black book full of "issue" papers covering each transaction that might come under scrutiny.[57] As it turned out, the two transactions about which Pecora hammered the firm were ones for which Nitze had not prepared because he saw no evidence of potential malfeasance—suggesting that there were other cases where there was—and leading him to regard the whole endeavor as political grandstanding. "I haven't had so much fun since Freddy and I canoed from Boston to New York," Nitze wrote his mother afterward.[58]

"In two weeks of investigation I learned more about banking, senators, newspaper men, and human nature than in any average year," Nitze would later put it. "We had an entire floor at the Carlton with nine lawyers, eight stenographers and . . . worked late into every night with many differences of opinions and a good deal of feeling being shown at times. It is amazing how a couple of weeks working together brings everyone together."[59] He clearly relished the experience of going up against a hostile congress and came back unscathed.

Nitze worked on at least one deal with James Forrestal that had global implications. Upon its discovery of oil in Bahrain, Standard Oil of California obtained a concession from Saudi Arabia to drill in that kingdom—even though oil had not yet been discovered there. In these early stages, neither venture turned a profit. A competitor, Texaco, had built up a marketing network in Africa and Asia, yet it was expensive to ship petroleum from the United States. With Nitze by his side, Forrestal concocted a plan by which the two oil behemoths would pool their resources "east of Suez" through a joint venture, the California-Texas Company. The terms included equal stakes in the California Arabian Standard Oil Company, which would later become the mammoth Arabian American Oil Company.[60]

Nitze also worked closely with Dillon, Read associate William Draper on public bond offerings for infrastructure projects that significantly changed the landscape of the modern United States. These included collaborating with New York powerbroker Robert Moses in the financing of the Triborough Bridge, the Whitestone Bridge, the Queens–Midtown Tunnel, as well as with local officials in California in the construction of the Golden Gate Bridge and San Francisco–Oakland Bay Bridge.[61]

By 1936, Nitze, twenty-nine years old, was making $25,000, the equivalent of $541,079.14 in 2023.[62] He occasionally invested some of his wife's money in bond offerings.[63] In 1935, he invested in a lab for two French scientists to develop a vitamin–mineral product in exchange for exclusive distribution rights in the United States. The first product, Visynerall, proved to be a financial success. A diabetes pill followed. In 1966, Nitze and fellow investors would sell their stake to cosmetics giant Revlon in a deal valued at $100 million.[64]

Nitze made deals at Dillon, Read. He had an appetite for risk and never suffered any long-term damage. He and others in his immediate circle risked losing high sums of money and even running afoul of the law. When it came to who got caught, politics clouded legal jurisdictions. Prosecutors and judges tended to be elected—or at least appointed—by democratically elected officials. Nitze had a somewhat jaundiced view of all this. The United States presented boundless opportunities to succeed, fail, and start all over. Government intervention seemed to depend on how politicians thought they could best get reelected. Or, in the case of Andrew Mellon, to protect his friend John D. Rockefeller—one titan helping another. "Men of action" knew more about growing businesses and building bridges and highways than purported experts who wrote books that occasionally got it right. John Maynard Keynes's *General Theory*, published in 1936, signified that academics had caught up in understanding what Nitze and his friends were sure that they already understood about the causes of the Great Depression.[65]

Return to Europe, Harvard, and Wall Street

In 1937, Paul, Phyllis, and their children set sail for Germany. In Hamburg, they picked up a Ford and drove it to Berlin. There Nitze was supposed to meet up with an old business associate whom the Gestapo had hauled off and shaken down. In Munich, the Nitzes stayed for six weeks with their old friends, the Duke of Leuchtenberg (a relative of the late Tsar Nicholas II), and his wife, the daughter of a Russian provincial governor before 1917. During this stay, the Nitzes saw Hitler deliver a speech in Rothenburg, the medieval Bavarian town that the Nazis put forward as a model German community.

"I never saw anybody who scared me more than those young Germans being trained in the Jungendkorps," so Nitze recalled the youth brigades encouraged by the Nazis to make pilgrimages into the town. "They were thin, arrogant, disdainful looking."[66] His hosts, the Leuchtenbergs, mocked the Führer and regarded him as a temporary aberration. Nitze professed to take the Nazis more seriously. Gone were the unemployment and defeatism from earlier in the decade. "Germany was an entirely different country. It was humming, and I believe that a majority of the Germans were fully behind Hitler . . . it was scary."[67]

Sometime after the Nitze family returned from Germany, Nitze reevaluated his professional aspirations. His visit to Germany and rereading of Oswald Spengler's *The Decline of the West* led him "to feel an inadequate understanding of the world social and political scene and felt myself confused and inadequate in trying to estimate what was apt to happen in the future."[68]

The "scariness" of Nazism notwithstanding, he seemed more interested in understanding the grand ideological experiments of the 1930s than in combating them. Nitze also believed he had demonstrated on Wall Street that he could do the job well—even though he claimed not to have made "any real money for myself."

Nitze made the equivalent of half a million dollars a year. His wife stood to inherit a modest fortune. Fascism was rising in Europe, and the Great Depression lingered at home. At the start of the fourth decade of Nitze's life, he sounded bored. Dillon, Read made him a vice president in 1937, a year that saw a sharp contraction (the so-called Roosevelt Recession) in which business slowed. It is plausible that Nitze and his colleagues saw opportunities dwindle amid an economic downturn during the second term of a president who beat up on Wall Street.

In the fall of 1937, Nitze reenrolled in Harvard, this time as a graduate student in sociology. He became entranced by a professor named Pitirim Sorokin, a Russian exile who detested communism.[69] He also reread Spengler's magnum opus, which he considered a great book with misguided conclusions—even though he could not fully articulate why they were wrong. He enrolled in classes on Plato and comparative religions.[70] While Nitze had not cared much—at least up to that point—about distinguishing himself as a scholar and receiving academic accolades, he set a challenge that would sustain his attention through the rest of his life: to come up with an original idea that would impress academics.

During his fall and spring semester at Harvard, in which he took seven graduate courses and wrote papers for four, Nitze kept at least a finger in Wall Street. He got involved in enterprises that he had seeded while at Dillon, Read, but that the firm neglected to nurture during his absence. After he unceremoniously abandoned the pursuit of a PhD and returned to New York City in the summer of 1938, he formed Paul Nitze and Company, setting up a small shop with one partner and one secretary. Specializing in public utilities, he dealt with Secretary of the Interior Harold Ickes on matters of rural electrification. Such business brought him to Washington to testify before Congress to justify why he commanded such high consulting fees for deals that split up or combined public utilities, at least some of which US taxpayers had subsidized. His business affairs also brought him back into collaboration with James Forrestal—by this point the president of Dillon, Read—and Clarence Dillon, who remained the firm's chairman.

Nitze worked himself to exhaustion. In 1939 he came down with a streptococcus infection and took the family to Florida for a summer of recuperation. Upon his return to New York, Nitze asked if he could rejoin Dillon, Read to work directly for Forrestal. When Hitler's Germany invaded Poland on September 1, the Nitzes were visiting William and Anina's Colorado ranch high up in the Rocky Mountains.[71] Paul hurried back eastward and resumed his activities at the firm. He did not then see World War II as the United States' fight. At a dinner party in New York City, he allegedly stated that Hitler's Germany was no more rapacious than the British Empire. That assertion—so clearly consistent with Nitze's affinity for verbal jousting—would come back to haunt him.

While the United States maintained its neutrality during this first year of the war in Europe, President Roosevelt sought to assist the United Kingdom within the strictures of the neutrality acts and the limits of public opinion. To pull off such feats as the destroyers-for-bases deal, he needed to bury the hatchet with Wall Street. In June 1940, FDR sent an intermediary to meet with Paul Nitze to determine whether James Forrestal would agree to join his administration as a special administrative assistant to the president. To Forrestal, Nitze appealed as much to logic as patriotism. If the job worked out, Forrestal would find himself in a position of considerable influence—a "can-do" man for the president. If it did not, he would return to Dillon, Read. Forrestal agreed to go to work for FDR. A few weeks later, while in Louisiana putting together a gas deal, Nitze received a telegram: "Be in Washington Monday morning. Forrestal."[72]

Nitze obeyed this order. He arrived the next day to seek out Forrestal's office in the building next to the White House. It was then called the State–War–Navy Building; today it's the Old Executive Office Building, home to the offices of the National Security Council (NSC) staff. Forrestal put Nitze to work. "The government could not pay me, so I was to remain on the payroll of Dillon, Read," as Nitze put it in his memoir. "In this wholly illegal fashion my career in Washington began."[73]

Washington, DC

Nitze was hardly a "millionaire" by the terms of the era, and he needed the salary. But, more to the point, the government would not pay him until it could run a thorough background investigation. A reasonable person involved in that process might well have posed questions about his family history. His uncle and namesake, Paul Hilken, had been an accomplice in the German plot responsible for the July 1916 Black Tom explosion in New York Harbor—the most significant act of industrial sabotage in US history.[74]

Nitze lived with Forrestal and worked directly for him until August 1940, when he became undersecretary of the navy and Nitze briefly returned to New York City. Then, summoned again to Washington by another Dillon, Read, partner, William Draper, Nitze went to work on the Selective Service Act of 1940.[75] Meanwhile—and omitted in Nitze's memoir—he was undergoing a background investigation for government employment. According to a November 5, 1940, letter from Federal Bureau of Investigation (FBI) director J. Edgar Hoover, Coordinator of Inter-American Affairs Nelson Rockefeller had requested the investigation into Nitze for a position on the Advisory Commission to the Council of National Defense.

A preliminary report cited a "reliable confidential informant who has furnished valuable information to [the FBI] in the past," which claimed, "Since the beginning of the Nazi regime [Nitze's] political thoughts have been leaning more and more along those lines and he has expressed feelings of admiration for totalitarianism and considerable contempt for the processes of democracy." In addition, the source described a secondhand (if not thirdhand) account of the New York City dinner party incident. "It seems that he expressed himself so forcefully, although not under the influence of drink," on that occasion, "that a somewhat unpleasant impression was left with the others who were present."[76]

The final report, which Hoover sent Rockefeller on January 16, 1941, included testimony from Forrestal on Nitze's behalf. Nitze was "a highly intelligent individual" and "an exceedingly able and energetic business man," who was also "aggressive [and] the 'pusher' type," according to Forrestal. He was also "100% American." Nitze had confided in Forrestal his uncle's role in the Black Tom affair yet had also affirmed that, should the United States find itself at war with Germany, he, Nitze, "would be willing to fight for the United States." Forrestal professed awareness of the dinner party incident, yet insisted that Nitze's remarks had been misconstrued.[77] Along with a report on Forrestal's interview, Hoover included a summary of the endorsement of the US attorney for the Southern District of New York, John T. Cahill, who "considered Nitze a brilliant individual [who] possessed a good background, his only fault being that he is inclined to be argumentative at times."[78]

Such testimony from elite figures paved the way for Nitze's joining the team coalescing around President Roosevelt as the United States prepared to enter World War II. The FBI investigation also opened the door to troubling insinuations about his parents. Whether or not Nitze was fully aware of statements given about them, he would later encounter suspicions about holding lingering sympathies toward Germany.

At no point in his memoir did Nitze mention any controversy surrounding himself or his parents as he took up roots in Washington. Indeed, he admitted to having been a strict neutralist and an "America Firster." Given his self-assuredness and enthusiasm to put forward his "logic chains" and never back down, it is reasonable to assume that he indeed raised the case of Germany versus England at a dinner party in the late 1930s. He did not travel to the United Kingdom during his ventures abroad in the 1920s and 1930s—though he lamented how many of his classmates had been able to study at Oxford while he recuperated from physical ailments of his own making—yet it is impossible to conclude that not spending time there made him "anti-British."

Nitze's View of the World

Nitze was pro-United States and also pro-European. Politicians failed to impress him. Neither did many academics or titans of industry that others held in high regard. Clarence Dillon and James Forrestal did, and it did not hurt Nitze's estimation of them that they took him on as a protégé. He was nominally a Democrat. But, as mentioned above, his mother-in-law, Ruth Pratt, was a two-term Republican congresswoman who lost in the election of 1932 that sent FDR to the White House. "I also supported Roosevelt," Nitze contended in his memoir. "I had come to the conclusion that Herbert Hoover and his economic advisers lacked understanding of the way the domestic economy—and its relation with the international economy—worked."[79] Fairly or not, he blamed the Hoover administration for turning the 1929 Wall Street crash into a worldwide depression.

Nitze remained a registered Democrat until 1937 when he became a Republican. Nitze's accounting for this switch—his principled objection to FDR's court-packing—meshed with his early impressions of Franklin Roosevelt, whom he had previously encountered on Wall Street and considered a lousy investment banker. Nitze's disdain for party machines was apparent in Connecticut as well as New York City. He had no real political allegiance—though it is unfair to conclude, in the end, that he was anything other than a patriotic American.

Paul Nitze believed in democracy. For him, the United States—with its existing institutions of popular sovereignty, freedom of expression, and free enterprise—was a better place to live than in a totalitarian regime. And Nitze had little reason to complain. He was an elite white male who could walk through any door and whose fortunes rose whether or not a Republican or Democrat resided in the White House. He had grown up in comfort and received a first-class education. Between his father's affiliation with the University of Chicago and the alumni network of Harvard University, Nitze never found himself more than one step removed from the most critical person in a particular field or enterprise. His networks facilitated his European adventures and connected him to Clarence Dillon, who set him on a course to prosperity. Paul thrived during the Great Depression and could not say that capitalism had failed him. At the same time, he was dubious about how democracy played out in practice. His interactions with grandstanding politicians during the 1930s failed to inspire confidence in him that they could make a positive difference in the lives of ordinary US citizens.

Power matched with the United States' ideals could overcome all challenges, he was led to believe. "Paul, you are overly discouraged," Dillon told Nitze after France fell to Nazi Germany in June 1940. "The situation is extremely serious but not hopeless. Let us analyze it together. In this war, modern technology, as exemplified in the tank and the airplane, is of enormous importance. In the long run, Detroit can outproduce the Ruhr. The question then is one of time." So long as the French fleet did not fall into the hands of Nazi Germany, Dillon went on to say, Great Britain would prevail. That was precisely why Dillon had just called his friend Lord Beaverbrook to beseech Prime Minister Winston Churchill to bomb the French fleet at Mers el-Kebir, Algeria. Which was precisely what British forces did. Was Dillon responsible for this action? Probably not. However, Nitze's read of the situation was that this was how significant matters of war and peace got decided.[80]

To Nitze, the distinction between men of action and ineffectual academics could not have been more apparent. He set upon a formula: go somewhere, see for yourself, assess and analyze and devise a plan for individuals in power. Repeat this sequence until power comes to you.

CHAPTER 2

The Levers of Influence

Paul Nitze spent the bulk of World War II in Washington, DC, safe from enemy bombs. But he did travel, under the auspices of the US Strategic Bombing Survey, to Nazi Germany during active combat—placing him in some physical danger. He went to Imperial Japan only after its surrender. As with a number of Wall Streeters and captains of industry, he held administrative posts vital to achieving victory for the United States and its allies. Nitze socialized with well-off colleagues, living for a time in Nelson Rockefeller's mansion.[1] He also oversaw several hundred people. "The war years were an important transition period for me," in his words, during which he went "from an analyst to an executive."[2] During this time, he achieved his goal: to become a man of action who wielded levers of influence.

Washington, 1940–1941

President Franklin Roosevelt had reoriented his fundamental approach to US national security before Paul Nitze arrived in Washington. Back in 1933, when FDR had undermined the London Economic Conference by announcing that the United States would go its way, his focus was on unilateral US recovery from the Great Depression. The Munich Conference of 1938 changed his mind. "FDR insisted with growing fervor that, in the age of airborne warfare, the world could and did threaten America," as one historian has emphasized, "and that only in a world in which American values reigned supreme could the United States feel secure."[3] Despite the isolationist mood and neutrality acts that Congress had foisted on him, FDR prepared for inevitable conflict and attempted to educate the American people about the nature of the threat to the American way of life. Yes, the United States ought to shore up the Western hemisphere. No, it should not precipitously intervene in Europe and Asia. However, the implications of totalitarian control of the resources of the Eurasian landmass would make the forces of fascism all the more formidable once they set eyes on North America. Moreover, long-range bombing meant that the Atlantic Ocean no longer made the US homeland invulnerable to attack.

The president courted James Forrestal in the spring of 1940, tasking him to build a national security team that could convert the United States' economic potential into military strength. After the fall of France in June 1940, he assembled a wartime cabinet that included two prominent Republicans: Secretary of War Henry Stimson and Secretary of the Navy Frank Knox. The president gave fifty destroyers to the United Kingdom and pressed Congress to reinstate the draft. Running for an unprecedented third term, he promised to keep the United States out of foreign wars. No sooner had FDR won re-election the chief of naval operations, Harold Stark, submitted to him the much-heralded "Plan Dog" memo laying out the basic strategic concept to challenge Nazi Germany. Forrestal enlisted Nitze to assist in that effort.

Nitze lived with Forrestal in a house near the State, War, and Navy Building (now the Old Executive Office Building) adjacent to the White House. He lunched at the nearby Metropolitan Club and spent weekends at the homes of other transplants from New York or with Forrestal and other members of FDR's inner circle. From Nitze's perspective, there was "a sense of crisis, but not of real danger to the United States except in the very long run."[4] He dined in Georgetown, played tennis with Nelson Rockefeller, and got to know Henry Wallace, who played the piano and threw boomerangs at parties.[5] "Intellectually, it was a stimulating atmosphere."[6]

Much would later be made of the "Wise Men"—Dean Acheson, Charles Bohlen, Averell Harriman, George Kennan, Robert Lovett, John McCloy, and others—whose careers intersected in Washington during the 1940s.[7] They took charge amid the unpreparedness of US federal institutions to contend with World War II. Nitze interacted with them as a subordinate who clearly stood out. Demand for talent outweighed supply. The president's July 1940 appointment of Henry Stimson as secretary of war—a position he had first held in the William Howard Taft administration three decades earlier—came off as a shrewd act of bipartisanship. Yet there were few other highly qualified candidates.

Selective Service and the Office of Inter-American Affairs, 1940–1942

In the summer of 1940, Forrestal and Nitze focused on shoring up South America and the Caribbean to defend the region from Nazi penetration. Immigration from Germany and Italy to Latin America in the years following World War I had created thriving local businesses whose owners sometimes pledged allegiance to fascist regimes. "With much of Europe now under German occupation," Nitze figured, "the export markets on which several Latin American states had depended were effectively under the control of Berlin," through the use of "economic, psychological, and other pressures."[8] Washington also needed to be prepared to repel a direct military incursion. Here Forrestal and Nitze worked quietly with executives from Pan American Airways—then a leading US airline—to construct airfields in the Caribbean that could be quickly converted for military use.

"No one agency in the government was clearly in charge of addressing the problem [of preparedness]," according to Nitze. Concerning overall US foreign and defense policies, three strong-willed cabinet members vied for FDR's attention. Secretary of Agriculture Henry Wallace pressed for accommodation with leftists; Secretary of the Treasury Henry Morgenthau called for preemptive action in Europe; and Secretary of State Cordell Hull advocated for reducing trade barriers to lessen the chances of war. FDR assigned Forrestal the task of harmonizing these views.[9] Neither Forrestal nor Nitze put much stock in career diplomats to make sense of things. "Most of the people in the State Department at the time had been brought up in the school of diplomacy that emphasized reporting; few were oriented toward the formulation and execution of strategic policy per se," Nitze later recounted. "We concluded that the State Department was inadequately staffed and not intellectually equipped to deal with the radically new situation brought about by the war."[10]

What exactly was the "radically new situation"? In short, the threat to the United States' fundamental values and interests was acute even without an imminent declaration of war. Hemispheric defense—tending solely to North and South America—would not suffice when it came to protecting the American way of life in an era of long-range bombing. No longer did Fortress America offer protection. Nazi Germany might someday insist that the United States surrender in advance of an imminent attack. For Forrestal and Nitze, national security encompassed foreign policy, defense strategy, economic planning, interagency coordination, and the clout to drive private actors into action. President Roosevelt strove to educate the American people, showing how such a threat both affected them and merited their potential sacrifice. This, at the same time he was figuring it all out for himself.[11] Acting upon Forrestal and Nitze's recommendation in August 1940, FDR signed off on the creation of the Office of the Coordinator of Inter-American Affairs under the leadership of Nelson Rockefeller and his deputy, Will Clayton, the Texas cotton trader who would play a critical role in the wartime and postwar US economic policies.

When FDR nominated Forrestal to be undersecretary of the navy shortly after that, Nitze returned to New York where he stayed only briefly until his Dillon, Read colleague William Draper called him back to work on the Draft Act for the chief of staff of the US Army, George Marshall. Considered a "math" expert for having worked with Robert Moses on bond offerings for New York City bridges, Nitze determined the fate of millions of US citizens at a time when the majority of them *opposed* intervention in World War II. Ultimately, FDR signed the Selective Service Act into law on September 16, 1940, after Congress passed it by one vote.

Working on the Draft Act proved to be a pivotal assignment for Nitze. Just as FDR attempted to educate the American people on internationalism during this period, career public servants taught Nitze about American civics. "For those of us who spent most of our lives on Wall Street where the important thing is to think the problem through clearly and find a solution to a complicated problem, and think it through fast," Nitze later recounted, "we weren't really that much interested in the democratic process." George Marshall broadened Nitze's horizons. "Marshall's view was that if we were to get into a war, then we would need a vast number of men, and if there were any suspicion that this thing was not wholly democratic and equitable, it would cause a back reaction which would be terribly serious." In a democratic system, it was a "traumatic kind of thing" to set up a draft; unless it was done absolutely right, it was never going to work.[12]

"Up to that point I had looked at two aspects of the political scene—that of the world's cultural and political position as a whole and that of me, the I, trying to do something personally, trying to get something done, to succeed, to participate, to make things better," Nitze wrote four decades later. He looked upon this experience from the perspective of his efforts to formulate a theory that would reconcile contemplation with action or, in this case, nationalism and internationalism through the mediation of his ego. "It was the experience of working with General Marshall which impressed upon me the importance of the national 'we' as an intermediary between the 'I' and the world culture. I found the perspectives and standards of behavior associated with loyalty to the United States as a nation morally and ethically superior to a purely individualistic viewpoint, and far more effective than the soft and ambiguous generalities that so often flowed from looking only at humanity as a whole."[13] In short, George Marshall fired up Paul Nitze's sense of patriotism.

Leadership mattered. "When a high official makes a public statement, the thing that counts is not the fine print," Secretary of War Stimson told his lawyers during this period. "[T]he thing that counts is the billboard effect. If this is understandable to the people, what comes through is the main point; it isn't these little minor caveats."[14] Stimson's tutorial made the rounds within Washington's burgeoning national security community. When it came to policy pronouncements, legalese would not suffice. Nitze discerned that appealing to the nation required a different approach than pitching a business proposal to a board of New York City trustees. The average US citizen would not conduct due diligence by poring over the details of a bid. Instead, they would react based on a tagline that could produce an emotional wallop. Declaratory policy—which was not necessarily the actual policy—had to be based on that reality.

The declaratory policy of the United States under Roosevelt during 1940–41 was to keep the United States out of the war by preparing to wage it. This was a rough approximation of the actual policy. FDR hoped he could deter the Axis powers and keep the United States out of the war, yet achieving this was an unlikely outcome. The president was simultaneously preparing for the eventuality that the United States would enter World War II on the side of the Allies.[15] According to Nitze, "it was perfectly clear, what we were trying to do was to . . . prepare for a situation in which Hitler had perhaps gotten down to Dakar [Senegal, the westernmost point of Africa] and was threatening South America, and that the real threat was to the Western Hemisphere from Europe which was dominated by Hitler."[16] Under those circumstances, the United States would inevitably have to fight to defend itself.

In the summer of 1941, Nitze became Rockefeller's assistant for financial matters in the Office of the Coordinator of Inter-American Affairs. He also moved into Rockefeller's Washington estate at 2500 Foxhall Road in Northwest DC. Following a split between Rockefeller and Wallace—a case of clashed egos—Nitze then worked for Wallace on a broad portfolio still covering Latin American economic affairs. When the Japanese attacked Pearl Harbor on December 7, 1941, Nitze was on assignment in Asuncion, Paraguay. His later recollections of that moment focused less on the sneak attack in Hawaii than the strategic disaster that befell US forces in the Philippines. Nevertheless, Nitze's memory of that day accorded with his overall worldview. In his mind, Japan had no choice but to attack, given the oil embargo that the United States had placed on it. Their perception of the unpreparedness of US forces led the imperial leaders to believe their attack could succeed. Nitze would return to the overriding importance of preparedness in the closing days of World War II; it would loom large in his thoughts about how to advance US national security in the postwar era.

Chief, Metals and Minerals Branch, Board of Economic Warfare

Adolf Hitler's declaration of war against the United States on December 11, 1941, turned the United States into a formal belligerent in the Atlantic and Pacific theaters.[17] On April 13, 1942, FDR issued an executive order to expand the role of the Bureau of Economic Warfare (which had replaced the Economic Defense Board) to oversee the control of imports. Still working under Henry Wallace, Nitze took charge of procuring metals and minerals—including mica, quartz crystals, and beryllium—that proved essential to the overall war effort.[18]

Procuring strategic minerals introduced Nitze to the world outside the United States and Europe. He learned by doing and coming up with penetrating questions. Put in charge of a field about which he knew very little, he called upon those whom he immediately identified as the experts in the area. He asked them the most challenging questions he could think of in the hope of hiring the best people. Nearly all of the geologists he hired were Republicans.[19] Party allegiances meant nothing to Nitze. Moreover, the national security team FDR assembled after 1939 was not dug into political tracks. At the level of the so-called wise men, it mattered little that Robert Lovett and John McCloy were Republicans working for Secretary of War Stimson, who was himself an éminence grise of the party that had vigorously opposed FDR (or that Secretary of the Navy Frank Knox had been the Republican vice-presidential nominee in 1936).

However, party allegiance mattered greatly at the staffing level in which Nitze operated. The disdain for political patronage and shenanigans that Nitze had felt during his brief time in Connecticut and New York grew after he relocated to Washington. His basic approach was meritocratic: surround yourself with the best people. Acknowledge partisan concerns on the part of politics, but do not let that determine the right decision. Do not get hung up on titles; get the job done.

The stakes were too high to worry about political purity tests for political appointees. Instead, obtaining the right minerals could determine the difference between victory and defeat. At the Battle of Kasserine Pass in February 1943, German forces led by Erwin Rommel intercepted Allied radio communications, which relied on only two frequencies because of the scarcity of quartz-based oscillator plates.[20] So Nitze led a team of forty geologists to Brazil, where they rode around on horseback searching for a fresh supply of quartz.[21]

Back in Washington, Nitze negotiated contracts to procure copper and lead and admired the can-do attitude of titans of industry who joined the war effort and cut through bureaucratic red tape. For example, former General Motors president William S. Knudsen impressed Nitze in a meeting of the War Production Board about where tank plants would be located. "I'm afraid I have done a dreadful thing," he admitted. "I thought it was important to get these tanks produced as rapidly as possible."[22] So he had already signed the contracts.

Nitze enjoyed tracking supply to fit demand, dealing with foreign actors, and maximizing efficiency. However, political appointees frustrated him. In September 1943, the Foreign Economic Administration superseded the Office of Economic Warfare. Leo Crowley, a prominent Democrat from Wisconsin, led the new Foreign Economic Administration and regarded Nitze as expendable. "I found Crowley a thoroughly incompetent and corrupt individual," Nitze later put it.[23] With tens of thousands of carloads of ores and metals stuck at the Mexican border, Crowley refused to sign off on an order of entry into the United States, admitting to Nitze that he wanted to get Will Clayton fired and take over his job.[24]

When Nitze quit out of disgust, Crowley told him he would never again work in a Democratic administration. Following this dustup, Nitze took a cab to the newly constructed Pentagon in Arlington, Virginia, to see Colonel Guido Perera, an old Boston friend who had recently suggested that he join a study of how the strategic bombing affected the German war economy.[25] Secretary of War Stimson signed off on the project on November 3, 1944, in response to a directive from FDR himself.

Nitze began a new phase in his career. Rather than figuring out how to procure strategic resources in the war mobilization effort, he now tackled the problem of how best to employ arms to defeat the enemy. His experience in corporate boardrooms made him a natural addition to the US Strategic Bombing Survey (USSBS). The USSBS was no academic project. Chief of the Army Air Forces General Henry "Hap" Arnold supported it as Allied forces were making their way toward Berlin, hoping to make strategic bombing more effective in the pursuit of victory. Chairman Franklin D'Olier, the president of the Prudential Life Insurance Company, and vice chairman, J.P. Morgan vice president Henry Alexander, were no ivory-tower types.

Here, then, were action-oriented men. The USSBS was precisely the type of research project that had eluded Nitze during his foray into graduate school in 1937. And it was eminently well suited to Nitze's relentless drive toward gathering different strands of information and rendering confident judgment.

USSBS (Germany)

The USSBS was an endeavor unique to the United States at war. It was a near-real-time historical project that involved a staff of a thousand—yet, unlike US official histories of World War II, employed no professionally trained historians—to derive lessons that senior military leaders could quickly apply to an ongoing military campaign. Early losses in the air war were considerable. The attrition rate reached 9 percent and receded only after the Allies sent bombers to flush out German fighters to shoot them down, an innovation that led to the establishment of Allied air supremacy. Even with a safer path to reach industrial and population centers, it was unclear how Allied strategic bombing of those targets could defeat Nazi Germany.

"One of the fundamental purposes of the survey is to determine whether the results obtained were commensurate with expenditures of men and materiel," Franklin D'Olier was told in October 1944.[26] Chairman D'Olier instructed his staff in December: "we shall proceed in an open-minded manner, without prejudice, without any preconceived theories, to gather the facts."[27] "We have no intention, nor should we at this stage, of commending or criticizing any individual, group, or organization in any way except as the final facts the real truth might so require."[28] In the final reports and their subsequent recollections, participants rendered candid assessments. The sharp-tongued economist John Kenneth Galbraith cited statistics showing that levels of production in Hamburg rebounded and increased almost immediately after the city was firebombed—suggesting utter futility.

Nitze assessed the impact of strategic bombing on the German production of ball bearings, which reduced friction on loads and were essential to heavy industry. He studied the Allied bombing campaign that started in August 1943 in and around Schweinfurt. The overall summary drew upon Nitze's study to describe how the pause in bombing led the Germans, under a newly appointed local production czar, to rebuild and disperse the ball-bearing industry to restore production to preraid levels by the fall of 1944—and that there was "no evidence that the attacks on the ball-bearing industry had any measurable effect on essential war production."[29] "The Germans were far more concerned over attacks on one or more of their basic industries and services—their oil, chemical, or steel industries or their power or transportation network—than they were over attacks on their armament industry or the city areas," the survey's summary concluded.[30] This judgment relied on reams of captured records, the wartime gathering of which cost the lives of several survey members and briefly put Nitze in physical danger.

Following the death of Franklin Roosevelt on April 12, 1945, Harry S. Truman took over as commander-in-chief. On May 7, Germany surrendered. In July, Truman and his team assembled in Potsdam to meet with Soviet leader Joseph Stalin to discuss postwar Europe and efforts to defeat Japan. Nitze found himself nearby looking for a man named Rolf Wagenfuhr, who had headed an economic and planning section for Albert Speer. Amid rumors that Wagenfuhr sought terms of surrender to the Soviets, Nitze hoped to get to him first to procure his records.[31] Such was Nitze's objective at a time when both sides were more famously tracking down Nazi scientists who might contribute to research into nuclear weapons.

The real prize was Speer, whom Nitze had just spent ten days interviewing. Two years older than Nitze, Speer drew his keen interest. They were on different sides yet had tackled several related problems concerning wartime production. "The speed with which [Robert] Moses built the massive Triborough Bridge filled Nitze with envy," one biographer said. "He wanted to get things done in the way that Moses got things done."[32] A similar sentiment probably animated Nitze's interactions with the architect of the Nazi war economy. "If the military decided they wanted so and so many more tanks, somebody would have to estimate what the steel requirement was for those tanks and then that would have to be taken into account and take that steel away from some other project," as Nitze later wrote. All sides had attempted to use primitive computers to rationalize the inputs of raw materials and outputs of tanks and airplanes to maximize efficiency. "The Germans finally turned to a different scheme in which Speer created a ring of representatives of all the chief companies in a given sphere of production and take not the heads of the companies, but those who were the senior people in the companies dealing with production."[33] Such topics excited Nitze in his conversations with Speer, who had helped build the destructive forces that had ravaged Europe.

Nitze's lack of revulsion toward Speer unsettled his colleagues. Nevertheless, Nitze remained unapologetic about acknowledging Speer's achievements even though they supported a terrible cause. "Speer, who had been an architect before the war, had demonstrated a phenomenal versatility and power of mind in developing and maintaining German war production despite the force of allied bombing and the stupidities of Hitler's interference," Nitze would later tell the 1953 Groton graduating class, which included his son Peter. "I have rarely met a more powerful intellect."[34] "I think you are too soft on Speer," Nitze's editor told him in a session on the draft manuscript of his memoir three and a half decades after that. "I wanted to portray Speer as I saw him," Nitze responded. "He was a criminal, yes, but he was eminently more successful and effective than we were at running a war economy."[35]

USSBS (Japan)

When they returned to Washington, Nitze and the rest of the USSBS received instructions to apply lessons learned from the analysis of the strategic bombing of Nazi Germany to the ongoing campaign against Imperial Japan. He spent the Fourth of July weekend at Jones Beach on Long Island with Phyllis and the children. There he formulated, on long sheets of yellow paper, a way to win the war in the Pacific.[36] General Hap Arnold invited Nitze to present his plan in competition with that of a General Sampson in front of a board led by General Carl Spaatz. That plan's mandate was to synthesize elements from each one into a new air campaign set to go into effect on August 1.

Nitze anticipated that Japan could hold out only until March 1946. He made this prediction based on his grasp of the history of Germany's air power. With any luck, surrender would come well before that. Effective use of air power would forestall the need for a US ground invasion, a prospect that Nitze maintained would be catastrophic. "We weren't going to accomplish a damn thing by a ground invasion," he asserted forty-nine years later. "These fellows were going to fight to the last man and if we were against that kind of thing, fighting to the last man on the ground, I thought the estimate of 500,000 US casualties was a gross underestimate."[37]

Less than four years after the attack on Pearl Harbor, Nitze had meaningfully contributed to plans to coerce Japan into surrender, based on his newly acquired expertise on the grim military science of strategic bombing. He drew upon economics, sociology, political science—all of the topics he had dabbled in throughout his twenties and thirties. Nitze presumed that this expertise was transferrable from one country (Germany) to another (Japan). Racial and cultural considerations did not come into play. German war planners "were of the opinion that it would have been absolutely vital for them to disperse either their chemical or oil plants or their power facilities or their steel or their transportation," Nitze had told the Joint Strategic Target Selection Board.[38] Attacking transportation hubs had stopped the shipment of coal, an act that had shut down three-quarters of the rest of German industry. According to Nitze, logic dictated that a similar approach to Japan would shorten the path to victory.

The use of the atomic bomb disrupted these plans. "What's this all for?" Nitze had asked, some months earlier, when told to procure forty thousand flasks of mercury and two thousand tons of graphite, along with zirconium and beryllium.[39] In the spring of 1945, Nitze probably knew as much—or as little—about the atomic bomb project as did the new president, Harry S. Truman, prior to FDR's death. Never again would Nitze allow himself to be so out of the loop about a significant US military program in development.

After the United States dropped the atomic bomb on Hiroshima on August 6 and Nagasaki on August 9, and Japan's subsequent surrender, on August 15, 1945, President Truman asked the Strategic Bombing Survey to continue their work. He tasked its members not only to conduct studies on all uses of air power in Japan but also to consider the physical effects of the atomic bombs, identify the key moments leading up to Japan's defeat, and make recommendations for the postwar organization of US forces.[40] At that moment, most of the other members left the USSBS and returned to the jobs they had held prior to the war. With the cessation of hostilities, there was no compelling reason for them to continue their government service. Mediating between the army and navy in how they depicted their role in getting to Victory over Japan Day was a fruitless enterprise to most of the staffers. And there was more money to be made in the private sector.

Nitze saw things differently. Promoted to vice chair upon the departure of Henry Alexander, he took on even more responsibilities in this second phase of the USSBS, traveling to Japan in September 1945 in what became his first visit to Asia.

"I remember flying in over Tokyo Harbor on a most beautiful kind of a pale blue day light clouds, a small island rising out of the harbor supporting very Japanese looking pine trees, Fujiyama on the left and coming to the conclusion this was the most beautiful country I'd ever seen," Nitze later recalled. "Then we got down to the airfield, and close to it we could see all these figures. I thought it was the most beautiful island populated by the most hateful of all people." As with "all Americans" in 1945, he conceded, he felt deep "anti-Japanese prejudices as a result of Pearl Harbor."[41] This broad-brushed depiction of the defeated foe went beyond anything Nitze said about Germans—he was disturbed by political developments in Nazi Germany, but never *hated* Germans. It probably reflected a then-widespread sentiment among Americans that they considered the Japanese even less human than the Germans.[42] In his coldly rational way, Nitze did not regard ethnic or racial distinctions as inputs when it came to the statistics-driven Strategic Bombing Survey. The success or failure of allied bombing campaigns were numerically measurable independent of whatever prejudices Nitze or anyone else held.

Shortly after his arrival in Tokyo, Nitze reported to Allied Supreme Commander General Douglas MacArthur, who lectured him on the role of air power in the lead-up to Japan's surrender and ordered him not to cause trouble during his stay. Establishing an office in the Dai Ichi building, where MacArthur had his general headquarters, Nitze led daily operations of the USSBS in Japan even though D'Olier retained the title of chair. The objective, as Nitze explained to the staff, was to finish up interviews and fieldwork by December 1, 1945, and return home by Christmas. With a team of interpreters, Nitze interviewed top Japanese officials, including Prince Konoye, the former prime minister who had resigned in October 1941 after purportedly failing to convince the rest of his government to avoid going to war with the United States.

In this interview and others, Nitze attempted to modulate the aggressive style of questioning that had worked for him on Wall Street—in other words, he learned diplomacy on the job. When questioning Marquis Kido, the Lord Keeper of the Privy Seal, on what led Japan to surrender, Nitze followed the advice of his interpreter: "I would phrase the question by saying, 'Marquis Kido, when did it first occur to you that the Will of Heaven demanded that the Emperor seek a different course?'" It pleased Nitze to learn from Kido that he regarded the Battle of Saipan in 1944 as a turning point that led him to pursue plans for peace with the United States. This depiction comported Nitze's own previous view that a reconfiguration of the air campaign would have produced a victory without a ground invasion. Nitze paid no mind to the fact that Kido and others had strong incentives to portray themselves as voices of moderation amid the fanatical members of the war cabinet who had been ready to fight to the end. In Hiroshima, where Nitze walked through the ashes, he found a city that was flattened. As he would observe—infamously—the destruction was not that much worse than that of other Japanese cities where conventional air attacks had taken a devasting toll.

Nitze wrote much of the *Summary Report (Pacific War)*, which was published in July 1946. It concluded that Japan was likely to have surrendered by the end of 1945 even without the bombing of Hiroshima and Nagasaki. In subsequent years, that conclusion has become a Rorschach test for scholars and anyone else interested in Truman's use of the atomic bomb against Japan. Critics of the decision point to this official account of the US government, which strongly suggested that it was unnecessary to achieve victory. Critics of Nitze, in turn, point to his equating of the atomic bomb at Hiroshima and Nagasaki to 210 B-29s and 120 B-29s respectively, and to the matter-of-fact statement in the summary: "Trains were running through Hiroshima 48 hours after the dropping of the atomic bomb on that city."[43]

This was a coldly clinical assessment of what was unimaginable horror for anyone trapped inside the city. Reference to the trains ought to be considered in the context of Nitze's staunch advocacy for changing the overall war plan, at the start of the summer of 1945, along with this sentence earlier on in the same paragraph in the Pacific War summary report: "The railroad system had not yet been subjected to substantial attack and remained in reasonably good operating condition at the time of surrender."

Convinced as he was that the implementation of his own plan at the start of the summer would have forced Japan to surrender, it is not surprising that Nitze concluded that the atomic bombing was unnecessary. The kilo tonnage of both conventional and atomic bombs *was measurable*; Nitze's lack of sentimentally at the horror of the aftermath of Hiroshima and Nagasaki did not change that basic fact. His assertions about redundancy of the atomic attacks came not from Nitze's empathy for the victims but rather his stubborn conviction that his own strategy was better. In interviews with Japanese leaders that fall, he pressed them to get the answers he sought. The testimony itself, according to one historian, showed "only Kido supporting [it] and everyone else stating that Japan would have fought on indefinitely. When would Japan have surrendered without the bomb and the Russians? The *only* credible answer is that given by Robert Butow when Freeman Dyson asked him about it: 'The Japanese leaders themselves do not know the answer to that question.'"[44]

As the de facto head of the Strategic Bombing Survey, and one of the few who stayed on past January 1, 1946, Nitze made sure that his view came through in the chairman's reports. This does not necessarily mean he was wrong; it merely suggests that he had gone through the logic chains and arrived at the conclusions before he landed in Japan. From Nitze's perspective, he was writing the survey not so that it could wind up in a university library to be pored over by scholars at some later point. Rather, it was to precipitate action in the real world following the end of World War II. Nitze's accounting for the start of the war, as laid out in the Pacific summary report, said as much about US national security policies—past, present, and future—as it did about Japan.

"December 7, 1941, found the United States and its Allies provocatively weak in the Pacific, particularly in land and carrier-based air power," according to the summary. Japanese leaders who clamored for an attack figured that it would take eighteen months for the United States to mobilize sufficient strength to counter imperial forces in the Pacific, after which the US political system would not have the wherewithal to fight the kind of war its own leaders would encounter. "The weakness of the United States as a democracy would make it impossible for her to continue all-out offensive action in the face of the losses which would be imposed by fanatically resisting Japanese soldiers, sailors, and airmen, and the elimination of its Allies." Wartime United States, Japanese leaders figured prior to December 1941, would ultimately seek accommodation that would allow Tokyo to retain much of its territorial gains.[45]

The United States had wrecked Japan's plans by unexpectedly mobilizing rapidly—thanks to the work of men such as Forrestal, Draper, Rockefeller, Wallace, Clayton, and Knudsen—and deploying forces in the Pacific, where the adversary "never fully appreciated the importance of adequate maintenance, logistic support, communications and control, and air fields and bases adequately prepared to handle large numbers of planes."[46] And, "along with all other military powers prior to the war, the Japanese had failed fully to appreciate the strategic revolution brought about by the increased capabilities of air power."[47] Control of the air was not considered a requirement for their basic war strategy. "Had this basic requirement been well understood it is difficult to conceive that they would have undertaken a war of limited objectives in the first place."[48] Nitze believed that a clear-eyed understanding of the opponent could deter aggression and lead to restraint.

Miscalculations on the part of Japanese leadership could not excuse what the summary identified as clear US failures leading up to December 1941. "Prior to Pearl Harbor it had been decided that, in the event of war, Germany would have to be eliminated first, and that our initial role in the Pacific would, in large measure, be defensive."[49] This prioritization had clearly underestimated Japan's offensive capabilities, as events would demonstrate. "To have implemented an adequate plan in December 1941 would have required better intelligence regarding Japanese intentions and capabilities, an earlier understanding of the predominant and indispensable role of air strength and full public support for the necessary appropriations, well before the actual outbreak of war."[50]

Along with this judgment, the summary offered additional lessons in hindsight about preparedness—both in its deterrent effect and necessity should deterrence fail. "One thousand planes in the Philippines, at least equal in performance to the best then available to the Japanese, including types effective against shipping, well-manned, equipped and supplied, and dispersed on some 50 airfields," it concluded, "would have seriously impeded the original Japanese advances if knowledge of their existence had not entirely dissuaded the Japanese from making the attempt."[51] The lack of prewar economic intelligence had handicapped US target selection on Japanese home islands and, according to the summary, had obscured the case for focusing strategic bombing on the railroad system, which was, again, a key part of Nitze's plan in the early summer of 1945.[52]

The atomic bomb had raised the stakes of air warfare, but it had *not* fundamentally transformed it, the Pacific summary report went on to say. "The threat of immediate retaliation with a striking force of our own should deter any aggressor from attacking," it stated. "If we are not to be overwhelmed out of hand, in the event we are nevertheless attacked, we must reduce materially our vulnerability to such attack."[53] That meant the dispersal of US military forces, especially as they related to components used to construct atomic weapons, as well as setting up forward operating bases. Above all, it meant sustained expenditures in peacetime, noting that the United States had afforded Japan a head start on the torpedo and other technologies. "This type of work has become so complex that expenditures for research and development in the order of one billion dollars annually may be required to assure an acceptable degree of national security."[54]

"The Survey's report on the European war stated that the great lesson to be learned in the battered cities of England and ruined cities of Germany is that the best way to win a war is to prevent it from occurring," the Pacific summary concluded. "This is fully supported by the example of the devastated cities of Japan and their unhappy and hungry surviving inhabitants."[55] The objective of maintaining peace was supported by preserving the strength and security of the United States, which was based "upon principles of tolerance, freedom, and good will."[56] Strength based on these principles was no threat to world peace, and the prevention of war could not be furthered by the neglect of that strength. "As one of the great powers we must be prepared to act in defense of law and to do our share in assuring that other nations live up to their covenant," the summary concluded. "The United States must have the will and the strength to be a force for peace."[57] For the United States to be weak was to invite an attack on the nation.

Nitze's Wartime Conclusions

In the span of twelve months, from the fall of 1944 to that of 1945, Nitze went from working for a political hack to briefing generals and then issuing orders to them upon the cessation of hostilities. Four years in Washington before that prepared him to delegate responsibilities, manage upward, and mediate the considerable friction among different military services. The five years he spent for the government's wartime effort gained him no permanent status or tenure. Unlike in the military or foreign or civil service, he was outside an established career track. The practice of national security came from learning and doing. It upended hierarchies. As the lethargy of US prewar institutions clearly demonstrated, upending was necessary.

From his wartime experiences, Nitze drew several key lessons. First, he was as good a strategist as anyone he encountered. While he shrewdly placed conditions on accepting General Douglas MacArthur's offer to make him head of Japan's postwar economy—and then turned it down when the general refused—Nitze undoubtedly regarded the offer as validation of his abilities and strategic acumen. World War II reinforced Nitze's confidence that he could stand his ground in a debate with anyone. He believed that he had come up with a plan that applied the lessons of air power in Germany to Japan. There would have been no need for the use of the atomic bomb had only the generals and the president accepted his plan to apply the lessons of air power in Germany to Japan. Nitze's motivation was not humanitarian impulse (i.e., sparing Japanese civilians) but the cold, hard logic of weighing evidence and drawing conclusions. "The survey's task was to measure as precisely as possible the exact effects of the two bombs," as he later described the Strategic Bombing Survey, or, "to put calipers on the problem so that people back home would have a factual frame of reference within which to draw conclusions about the bomb's true capabilities as well as its limitations."[58]

Nitze also took from the wartime experience the possibility of generating answers to big questions. Why did the Japanese go to war with the United States? He attempted to figure that out in the period after Japan's surrender. Such questions were answerable, he believed, and the answers could help determine policy prescriptions. Nitze was also writing the report, which would be published on July 1, 1946, amid early developments in the Cold War such as Joseph Stalin's "Election Speech" on February 9, 1946, in which the Soviet leader blamed World War II on a crisis of the capitalist system of the world economy. Nitze surely had an eye on the collapse of the wartime alliance between the United States and the Soviet Union.

What, then, was the lesson to take from the recent conflict in terms of the rising danger of Soviet power? The key takeaway was that the United States, having failed to mobilize its strength on the eve of its entry into World War II, could not afford again to let down its guard. The battleships lost at Pearl Harbor could just as well have been scrapped anyway. Fortunately, from the United States' perspective, the carriers were out to sea. Yet the United States had failed to prepare adequately for a naval war with Japan. As the Strategic Bombing Survey noted, a small force of airplanes in the Philippines would have gone a long way in the opening days of war following December 7, 1941. "Larger overall appropriations to the armed forces, beginning at the time of Japanese occupation of Manchuria when the threat to peace in the Far East became evident," the survey went on to conclude, "might have made war unnecessary and would have paid for itself many times over in reduced casualties and expenditures had war still been unavoidable."[59] Whether or not Nitze drafted that particular sentence, he certainly endorsed this point. Only military preparedness could deter potential enemies, he was certain. In the long run, it was the least expensive way to protect US lives.

"I became convinced therefore that any postwar reorganization of the armed forces should include provision for, first, a vigorous research and development program, to assure the optimum exploitation of science and technology for national defense; second, a vastly improved system of intelligence gathering and analysis to avoid a repetition of the Pearl Harbor disaster; and lastly, closer coordination of the armed forces under an integrated department of defense oriented toward weapons systems based upon modern technology," Nitze later recalled. An ideal organization, as Nitze saw it, was for a "Department of Strategic Forces" responsible for "deep strategic attack against an enemy's heartland and the defense of our heartland against such an attack by an enemy" as well as "to achieve general control of the air through the progressive destruction of enemy air forces."[60]

The National Security Act of 1947 would later fulfill each of these provisions, establishing the Department of Defense, CIA, and United States Air Force. However, it did not establish a cadre of individuals who could maneuver between the fields of defense policy, intelligence, grand strategy, and diplomacy. Nitze set an example that others would replicate. In his capacity working on matters of national security during the war, Nitze operated outside any military chain of command and did not join the professional civil service. He had obtained tremendous knowledge and on-the-job training, and there was a clear demand for his abilities. He was not prepared to move away from Washington, DC, and never would.

Chapter 3

Cold Warrior

Paul Nitze had no onward assignment when World War II ended. Military and foreign service officers could advance in rank, yet Nitze lacked an established trajectory. Most corporate lawyers and bankers who served in wartime executive roles left Washington after 1945. Briefly tempted by an offer to run a New York investment firm, Nitze decided to remain in the capital. He was enticed by Under Secretary of State for Economic Affairs Will Clayton's offer of the position of deputy director of the Office of International Trade Policy at the State Department. His mentor James Forrestal had remained as secretary of the navy; while another Dillon, Read pal, William Draper, led the economics section of the Allied Control Council for Germany. With these key personal connections, in the spring of 1946, the thirty-nine-year-old Nitze joined the State Department.

Economics Portfolio, Will Clayton, and the Marshall Plan

Nitze brought considerable practical experience to postwar US foreign economic policy. He could do business with representatives from the private sector and other countries. Few things brought him more satisfaction than tackling complex and significant problems. And no problem was more urgent than restoring the devastated economies of Europe. When it came to supplying Europe with oil, which was essential to recovery, that meant mediating between US and international firms and governments. Traditionally, this had been the purview of State Department consular officers. Postwar circumstances called for individuals of greater stature to broker deals with chief executive officers and government leaders. Nitze's experiences made him a formidable negotiator. What he lacked in diplomatic adroitness, he made up for with the self-confidence gained from interacting with powerful men at Hotchkiss, Harvard, on Wall Street, and in wartime Washington.

Nitze's first year at the State Department was momentous. The awful winter of 1946 sapped Great Britain of the strength to preserve political stability in Greece and Turkey—gateways from East to West. In March 1947, President Truman requested from Congress $400 million in emergency assistance to those countries and declared, "I believe we must assist free peoples to work out their destinies in their own way." Head of Near Eastern Affairs Bureau Loy Henderson asked Nitze to help implement that assistance package. Dealing with allies was no easy task. As the United States was taking over the geopolitical responsibilities of a crumbling British Empire, Nitze and Will Clayton encountered stiff resistance from the United Kingdom and Australia in their efforts to harmonize tariffs on wool in the spring of 1947.[1]

Meanwhile, Nitze-as-diplomat remained a work in progress. Meeting with Dag Hammarskjöld, the Swedish government official who later served as United Nations (UN) Secretary-General, Nitze could not abide the Swede's modesty. He had calculated how to reduce the US–Swedish trade imbalance, and his number was significantly higher than Hammarskjöld's. Once he determined its accuracy, a Nitze figure became nonnegotiable, with no give and take. Effectively, Nitze dictated to Hammarskjöld what his position ought to be.[2]

Here and elsewhere, Nitze regarded problems as manageable and solutions as quantifiable. Regarding Germans suffering in the aftermath of World War II, caloric intake overrode all other factors. At 1,700 calories a day, food was all a person thought about. However, 2,700 calories a day meant a person would be full of "political energy." The objective ought to be to keep caloric intake somewhere between the floor (desperation might make communism attractive) and the ceiling (free will could also lead in that direction).[3] While none of this pseudopolitical science made it into Nitze's memoir, it is emblematic of his quantitative approach to a qualitative problem: hunger. Whether it was the terms of a Wall Street deal—or, as it would be later, the ratio of warheads on missiles to targets—he thought it was possible to apply formulas and calculate precise figures to explain why people and states acted as they did, and thus what they ought instead to do. Logic could surely prevail. Whether in formulating US high policy or negotiating with allies or adversaries, Nitze regarded his role as apprising his interlocutors of paths to logical outcomes.

Nitze's approach to human needs may have been coldly rational. The context was a widespread skepticism about the State Department's ability to think strategically. Returning from the March 1947 Moscow ministerial conference, Secretary of State George Marshall lamented the quality of the preparatory staff work (i.e., an analysis of a problem and options for what to do about it) on the US side compared to that of other countries. In his charge to George Kennan to set up a Policy Planning Staff to report directly to him, Marshall exhorted him to "avoid trivia." Kennan initially asked Nitze to serve as his deputy. However, Under Secretary of State Dean Acheson nixed this appointment. Not without evidence, Acheson blamed Nitze for circumventing the State Department during World War II. "George, you don't want Nitze," he told Kennan. "He's not a long-range thinker, he's a Wall Street operator."[4]

This was neither the first nor last time that Nitze found himself passed over. Kennan set to work writing papers; Acheson returned to Covington & Burling. Nitze stayed close to Will Clayton, who spearheaded the effort that became the Marshall Plan. On May 19, 1947, Clayton convened a meeting at the Metropolitan Club, where he assessed that Europe stood on the brink of disaster and needed immediate intervention. "It is now obvious that we grossly underestimated the destruction to the European economy by the war," he wrote a few days later. Millions faced starvation. "Without further prompt and substantial aid from the United States, economic, social, and political disintegration will overwhelm Europe," Clayton continued. "Aside from the awful implications which this would have for the future peace and security of the world, the immediate effects on our domestic economy would be disastrous: markets for our surplus production gone, unemployment, depression, a heavily unbalanced budget on the background of a mountainous war debt." He summed up: *"These things must not happen."*[5]

Clayton asserted that the United States needed to provide up to $6 or $7 billion a year to prevent European citizens from starving. "Canada, Argentina, Brazil, Australia, New Zealand, and Union of South Africa could all help with their surplus food and raw materials," Clayton wrote, "but we must avoid getting into another UNRRA [United Nations Relief and Rehabilitation Administration]. The United States must run this show."[6] As in past instances in Nitze's career, a determined figure set aside hesitation, cut through red tape, and took command.[7]

In a speech at Harvard on June 5, 1947, Secretary of State George Marshall outlined the plan for assisting the economic recovery of Europe. Afterward, Nitze and colleagues threw themselves into generating congressional support for what became known as the Marshall Plan. Nitze crunched the numbers for precisely what each recipient country needed. According to Clayton, he knew "more about the Marshall Plan than perhaps any other individual."[8] In a more stressful testimony than his 1933 appearance before the Senate Committee on Banking and Currency, Nitze endured several weeks of hostile questioning before Congress and lost fifteen pounds.[9]

In discussions in Paris from August 4–6, Nitze stressed to allies that economic assistance was not charity. The vitality of US trade relied on preserving a European way of life. Since $10 billion in previous assistance had failed to restore Europe, the scrutiny of further US expenditures promised to be intense. In a coldly rational way—while acknowledging its self-interest—the United States had to help the Europeans help themselves. Congress should appropriate money on a declining scale to create "a self-sustaining Europe at the end of three or four years."[10] No matter which justification the administration prioritized to obtain the money from Congress, there was little daylight between the twin objectives of preventing starvation and fending off communist penetration of Western Europe. "Our goal was to revive Europe economically and spiritually and make it thrive again," Nitze would later recall: "theirs [the Soviets] was to perpetuate squalor and chaos in the hope that eventually all Europe would fall to Communist control."[11]

The National Security Act of 1947

Nitze's work on selling the Marshall Plan overlapped with the creation of the modern US national security apparatus. On July 26, 1947, President Truman signed the National Security Act, which created the Department of Defense, CIA, Joint Chiefs of Staff, and the NSC. The measure took effect on September 18. Nitze's Dillon, Read mentor James Forrestal became the nation's first secretary of defense. Admiral Sidney Souers served as executive secretary of the NSC, which employed only a handful of staffers. While some State Department officials remained in the old State, War, and Navy Building, most moved into the department's current home at 2201 C Street in what had been called Foggy Bottom since the late eighteenth century.

One thing that the 1947 National Security Act did not do was set up a pipeline for training national security professionals. Future army officers would continue to be recruited from West Point; foreign service officers—and, now, CIA aspirants—would come mainly from Ivy League institutions. "Pale, Male, and Yale" prevailed at the State Department. Nitze himself added no diversity. Given the skills that he brought to the table—generalist experiences in economics, military, diplomacy, and an ability to work with Congress—he was supremely qualified.

Elitism certainly informed his worldview. So did the cause of defending democracy. He was skeptical about popular opinion and doubted whether democratic institutions could act efficiently or effectively reward merit. More trustworthy were the actions of great men who rose to the top. For the lead, Nitze looked to Marshall and Clayton and others—not to the so-called common man or congregations thereof. Women and non-whites were virtually nonexistent in positions of authority. Just "getting by" was an alien concept to the residents of Northwest DC with whom Nitze associated.

Did Nitze think of himself as "one of the great men"? Or "a great man in the making"? Neither seems likely, as the nature of his ambition was down to earth: aspirations that were practical and results driven. He savored verbal, as well as physical, competition, in the same way one might seek to play tennis against someone better. Perseverance prevailed when innate talents went unrecognized. He was willing to do tedious staff work and weather disappointment. For instance, General Lauris Norstad recommended to President Truman that Nitze become the first secretary of the air force, a position which the National Security Act had created out of the United States Army Air Forces. After apparently discovering that Nitze was a registered Republican, Truman nominated his fellow Missourian, Stuart Symington. "Symington doesn't know anything about the Air Force, the air business, at all," according to Norstad. "Would you be willing to work with him and help him get started in this job?" Without resentment, he did as Norstad asked and spent the next six weeks in an adjacent office assisting Symington.[12]

The Division of Europe, the "Loss" of China, and the United States' Economic Policy

On April 3, 1948, President Truman signed the Economic Recovery Act (the Marshall Plan) and appointed the former president of the car company Studebaker, Paul Hoffman, as head of the Economic Cooperation Administration, overseeing the dispersal of funds to rebuild Europe. Will Clayton recommended Nitze to be Hoffman's deputy. Yet Hoffman rejected him in favor of Nitze's friend, Richard Bissell, the son of the president of the Hartford Insurance Company and a graduate of Groton and Yale. As with previous slights, this one made Nitze work only harder. Tremendous obstacles remained in terms of getting Congress to authorize the funds, and Nitze intended to overcome them. In seeking votes on the Hill, Nitze continued to be dazzled by the political acumen of George Marshall. On one occasion, the secretary of state refused Nitze's offer to prepare an opening statement for his testimony so that he could declare he had come from a memorial service for a fellow retired general and tell committee members he had no prepared statement to read.[13]

Nitze's own political acumen rested on an ability to avoid getting pinned down on any particular issue. This was a time when many of his peers found themselves in the crossfire of the House Un-American Activities Committee. As deputy assistant secretary for economic affairs, he worked in a functional bureau and held a global portfolio that included China. In August 1948, Nitze wrote memos on currency reforms in that country. And, while he later acknowledged that Chiang Kai-shek's government was hopelessly corrupt, he refrained from stating that on the record at the time.[14] Unlike foreign service officers such as John Paton Davies, Nitze evaded blame for the so-called Loss of China the following year.

NSC 20/4 (November 23, 1948)

On November 2, 1948, President Truman pulled off his surprise victory over former New York governor Thomas Dewey and two other candidates. In his campaign, Truman trumpeted the passage of the Marshall Plan and other foreign policy achievements while promising a "Fair Deal" for the American people to include increased civil rights and expanded health insurance coverage while also balancing the budget. Pursuing these domestic priorities amid financial solvency was premised on restricting the defense budget in the hope that European recovery—and the US atomic monopoly—would obviate the need for significant rearmament.

Three weeks later, the NSC presented the president with a report, NSC 20/4, which Kennan had drafted, titled "On US Objectives with Respect to the USSR [Union of Soviet Socialist Republics] to Counter Soviet Threats to US Security." "The will and ability of the leaders of the USSR to pursue policies which threaten the security of the United States constitute the greatest single danger to the US within the foreseeable future," it read. However, Moscow's ambitions did not stop there. "Communist ideology and Soviet behavior clearly demonstrate that the ultimate objective of the leaders of the USSR is the domination of the world."[15]

NSC 20/4 warned of stark dangers. "The present Soviet ability to threaten US security by measures short of war" would soon become even more fearsome, it stated. "Present estimates indicate that the current Soviet capabilities . . . will progressively increase and that by no later than 1955 the USSR will probably be capable of serious air attacks against the United States with atomic, biological and chemical weapons, of more extensive submarine operations (including the launching of short-range guided missiles), and of airborne operations to seize advance bases."[16] To counter that threat, NSC 20/4 listed two primary objectives: (1) "To reduce the power and influence of the USSR to limits which no longer constitute a threat to the peace, national independence and stability of the world family of nations," and (2) "To bring about a basic change in the conduct of international relations by the government in power in Russia, to conform with the purposes and principles set forth in the UN charter." In so doing, the United States and its allies needed to proceed without "permanently impairing our economy and the fundamental values and institutions inherent in our way of life." Doing so required a series of steps, laid out in sections 21 A–F of the directive. In the event of war, military aims were laid out in sections 22 A–E.

Perceptions of threat and proposed policy responses in Kennan's Long Telegram and Mr. X article had guided US policy makers during 1946–48. With Truman on the verge of a new four-year term, they now constituted US policy. Implementing this policy required people to make hard choices that were bound to be politically costly. Left unclear were such matters as funding or potential tradeoffs occasioned by the ambitious domestic agenda that Truman and the Democrats had in mind. The state of US abilities to combat communism— whether in measures short of war or in actual war—also remained unclear. So too were such questions as: Might it be possible for the Soviet Union ever to abide by the Charter of the United Nations? Did not others in the "world family of nations" threaten peace? How long could the American people expect the conflict with the Soviets to last? And, how many dollars should they be expected to contribute? The Truman administration expected a budget surplus for fiscal years 1948 and 1949, as balancing the budget in future years was then considered practically a moral responsibility of US representatives.

On December 1, 1948, Secretary of Defense Forrestal submitted to Truman a proposed increase in the defense budget, recommending a figure between the $23 billion requested by the Joint Chiefs of Staff and the $14.4 billion the president had previously insisted was the ceiling. He wrote that a $16.9 billion budget "will furnish the strength necessary for our national defense under present international conditions"—even though the Joint Chiefs disagreed.[17] Truman rejected Forrestal's request. On March 2, 1949, Forrestal submitted his letter of resignation. His successor, Louis Johnson, promised to keep the defense budget under $13 billion. Meanwhile, Forrestal's physical and mental health rapidly deteriorated. He committed suicide on May 22, 1949.

Nitze grieved for his mentor. If he took umbrage at how Truman treated Forrestal, however, he kept that to himself. Nitze certainly held new secretary of defense Johnson in open contempt—an assessment he shared with Dean Acheson, who became secretary of state on January 21, 1949. Nitze held no grudge toward Acheson, who had previously rebuffed his warnings of Soviet aggression and scuttled his appointment as deputy director of policy planning. The State Department's top priority in the first half of 1949 was to restore the economic strength of Western European nations and build up their forces to defend themselves. In the lead-up to the signing of the North Atlantic Treaty, on April 4, 1949, and the formulation of the 1949 Mutual Defense Assistance Act, Nitze contributed much of the staff work and must have impressed Acheson more than on previous occasions. In the founding of NATO, to whose cohesion Nitze was committed forever thereafter, Acheson was the man of action.

S/P, the Prospect of War, and the H-Bomb Debate

On August 1, 1949, Kennan elevated Nitze to deputy director of policy planning with the expectation that he would eventually succeed him as director. This time, Acheson supported Nitze. On August 10, Truman endorsed an amendment to the National Security Act that upgraded the position of secretary of defense by placing him above the unified services, a move that strengthened Louis Johnson's hand in his efforts to restrain defense spending. Even more consequentially, on August 29, 1949, US intelligence detected that the Soviet Union had successfully tested an atomic device. The Truman administration now had to decide whether to pursue a hydrogen bomb, a then-hypothetical weapon consisting of fusion triggered by fission. A hydrogen bomb could potentially be a thousand times more powerful than the atomic bombs used over Hiroshima and Nagasaki in the summer of 1945.

The fall of 1949 thrust Nitze into the field that would define much of the rest of his career: atomic and nuclear strategy. Although Nitze had witnessed the effects of the atomic bombs in Japan, his main objective in the Pacific War summary report had been to assert that air power strategy—as he conceived it at the beach in the summer of 1945—could have ended the war without the use of the atomic bomb. Never before had he (or anyone else) had to contend with two atomic states locked in opposition with each other. Nitze set about getting up to speed on the technical details while also assisting Kennan and Acheson in dealing with other setbacks in what were an awful ninety days for US foreign policy. In September, the sterling crisis further imperiled the United

Kingdom's ability to protect its once-mighty empire against communist encroachment. And, on October 1, Mao Zedong declared communist victory in the Chinese Civil War. These events were not organically connected with each other. Yet it would have been impossible for anyone in government to disentangle the Soviet acquisition of an atomic bomb from a perception that it empowered communist advancements everywhere.

The implications of nuclear weapons for the reconstitution of Western Europe came up in a meeting of the Policy Planning Staff on October 11, 1949, where Secretary Acheson "suggested that unless we face up to what we want, decide on how to get it, and take the necessary action, the whole structure of the Western World could fall apart in 1952."[18] One of the challenges, at least from Kennan's perspective, was figuring out how the United States could "swallow its own surpluses." To Nitze, the solution was calculable: "we may not have to spend $5 billion a year abroad but we probably will have to spend something." Helping Western Europe to restore its strength, however, required more specificity about what was required. Implicitly acknowledging one of the omissions of NSC 20/4, Kennan "stated his belief that there is no clear-cut Government concept of what our objectives would be if we got into a war with Russia."[19]

Acheson, Kennan, and Nitze speculated that Soviet possession of the atomic bomb might deter the United States from using atomic weapons against an overwhelming conventional attack. Again, for Nitze, Soviet possession of the bomb "might make conventional armaments and their possession by the Western European nations, as well as by ourselves, all the more important." And, that it would require European countries to devote 20 percent rather than 5 percent of their economies toward defense. Consequently, it might be necessary "to lower rather than to raise civilian standards of living in order to produce arms as against consumer goods"; promoting this objective would require a "different propaganda approach than the one we were presently using."[20] In other words, the Americans would have to figure out how to convince the Europeans to rearm.

On this last point, Acheson reminded Nitze "that we must examine these problems from the point of view of what peoples and governments *will* do rather than what they *can* do." An exchange toward the end of this meeting presaged debates about atomic deterrence that played out in some variant for the next forty years. "The Secretary said that it was his feeling that we should look first at the general implications of the Russian possession of the atomic bomb and then proceed to the examination of the problem of international control of atomic energy," according to the minutes. Nitze responded that US "effective civilian defense against atomic warfare" might deter the enemy.

Acheson went on to reject any agreement of "no-use" of atomic weapons was "to deprive yourself of the effect on the enemy of the fear of retaliation by atomic bombing against orthodox aggression."[21] In other words, discussions about the role of nuclear weapons in deterring the other side would inevitably be hypothetical, and arguments about it were unwinnable so long as countries possessing atomic weapons refrained from attacking one another using such weapons.

Regarding the hydrogen bomb debate, a fundamental question was whether the Soviets could build one. The failure of US intelligence to detect the Soviet atom bomb project, in advance of August 1949—not to mention the failure of US counterintelligence to uncover Soviet spies in the Manhattan Project—strengthened the argument for taking a worst-case approach to Soviet capabilities. "In discussing the pros and cons of the advantage to us of developing the super-bomb," according to the minutes of a November 3, 1949, meeting of the Policy Planning Staff, "the only complete agreement was that we would have to start with the assumption that the Russians were working on it also." Members reached no conclusion on whether Moscow could successfully build a hydrogen bomb while also weaponizing its atomic capabilities. "There were no final conclusions as to whether the Russians would be able to develop it and the atomic bomb at the same time. Nor is it known how much effort it would require for us to develop both."[22] In his opinion, Nitze "felt that the burden of proof should fall on those who say that there would be no power advantages to the country developing it; but further study obviously is called for on the answers to the Secretary's question as to whether we would really be at a disadvantage if they developed it and we did not and why."[23]

On November 19, 1949, Truman placed the hydrogen bomb decision in the hands of a Special Committee of the National Security Commission, which consisted of the secretaries of state and defense as well as Atomic Energy Commission chairman David Lilienthal. Acheson, Johnson, and Lilienthal deputized members of their staff to come up with an agency recommendation. Acheson selected Nitze.[24]

Nitze threw himself into a study of all the technical components of the potential hydrogen bomb. He called in physicist Edward Teller, a Hungarian émigré who had urged the pursuit of fusion even before the success of the Trinity Test on July 16, 1945.[25] Nitze delighted in standing at the chalkboard with Teller and going through complex equations that he purported to grasp. He also received briefings from Robert Oppenheimer, who was exceedingly pessimistic about the future. "Dr. Oppenheimer said that if one is honest the most probable view of the future is that of war, exploding atomic bombs, death, and the end of most freedom."[26] Ten years prior, Nitze had been enamored of Spengler, whose warnings seemed justified given the horrors of World War II. Sentimentality was, however, of no matter to the task at hand. Nitze paid no deference to Oppenheimer, whose political opinions he considered to be steeped in remorse and quite distinct from his technological prowess. When it came to determining how the US government should proceed, logic should always trump emotion. When it came to debating US national security, neither past achievements nor rank could overcome faulty judgments.

The primary task, as Nitze saw it, was to determine whether it was possible to build the hydrogen bomb. "I agreed with the judgment that Oppie [Oppenheimer] and others who opposed trying to build the 'super' bomb that the world's future prospects would be better if it proved beyond the power of technology to build such a weapon," Nitze later recalled. "But I also suspected that Oppenheimer was not being totally straightforward with me on other arguments—that he was letting his political views cloud his scientific judgment."[27] Again, according to Nitze, the scientist felt that it was simply too dangerous for one side to have such a powerful weapon. Nitze regarded such a judgment as outside the writ of his assignment, which was to determine the *feasibility*, and then move on to how to prepare for a world in which the hydrogen bomb existed. Moreover, he saw nothing at all wrong with the US possession of overwhelming strength. The lack of US preponderance had invited Japan to attack Pearl Harbor.

Consistent with the findings of the Strategic Air Survey for the Pacific, preparedness was the paramount consideration. Preparedness could deter; it was inseparable from preponderance. Needless to say, the consequences were enormous, and it was a choice between two undesirable outcomes. "I believe that the Secretary thinks the military position will probably be that it cannot afford to take any risk of finding itself without this weapon if others have it," Undersecretary of State James Webb, who had succeeded Robert Lovett, wrote to Nitze and the two other members of the State Department's working group on December 3, 1949. "I believe, also, he is troubled about the possibility that a decision to go ahead would be interpreted all over the world as a decision that war is inevitable and that we have reached this decision, with all its implications and effects on all types of future decisions." [28]

At a December 16, 1949, meeting of the Policy Planning Staff, Nitze suggested that US objectives "must be examined in the light of the risks." Among these risks "a total war started deliberately by the Soviets is a tertiary risk." Rather than "deliberately start a total war themselves," the Soviets were "more apt to get the satellites involved with the West, as they have gotten the Chinese communists to do their dirty work in the Far East."[29] Kennan agreed with Nitze and Soviet expert Llewellyn E. "Tommy" Thompson that the Kremlin preferred "to intervene cheaply in someone else's war, their ideal being a to-tal conflict between 'imperialists.'" Still, the United States needed to commit to preventing Western Europe from being overrun.[30] In other words, "tertiary risk" hardly diminished the need to rebuild US and allied strength to prevent Moscow from orchestrating attacks on the free world.

On December 19, Nitze advised Acheson that the State Department sup-port going ahead with research on the hydrogen bomb. While he estimated a 50 percent probability of success, the bottom line was that there was more "to be feared from a growing fission bomb capability and a possible thermo-nuclear capability on the part of the USSR than is to be gained from the addi-tion of a thermonuclear possibility to our growing stockpile of fission bombs."[31] Emphasis "on the possible employment of weapons of mass de-struction, in the event of a hot war" would be "detrimental to the position of the US in the cold war." He recommended to Acheson that President Truman tell the Atomic Energy Council to "proceed with an accelerated program to test the possibility of a thermonuclear reaction," and that further decisions be deferred until it was proven possible. During the course of the research and testing, there should be no public deliberation of the topic.[32] Left unstated was the fact that Americans could hardly be expected to understand this convo-luted approach. Needless to say, there would be no public referendum on this decision to proceed with a weapon that could destroy cities.

On January 1, 1950, Secretary of State Acheson appointed Nitze director of the Policy Planning Staff, while keeping George Kennan on as counselor of the department. Three years earlier, George Marshall had given Kennan little instruction apart from "avoid trivia." Acheson provided more clarity. "Congressional support is essential but judging whether it is adequate or not isn't your job; that is the President's and my job," Acheson told Nitze about one idea. "What we want from you and the Policy Planning Staff is your con-sidered judgment on the issue, based on national-security and foreign policy grounds, not on the degree to which public or congressional opinion favors a given stand." The president and secretary of state would have to compromise and make concessions to congressional and public opinion—but "we don't want these concessions made twice, first by you and then by us."[33]

In other words, Nitze's Policy Planning Staff was to provide clinical advice, as would a doctor. The president would face Congress and the public. His political party's fortunes would be on the line every two years. As a foreign service officer in charge of policy planning, Kennan worked within an exist-ing framework of assignment—in that case, a capstone to his undeniably im-pressive diplomatic career in wartime Germany and Russia prior to and after World War II. As his successor, Nitze was a political appointee with the ex-

FIGURE 3.1.   Paul Nitze, January 1950. He received news of his promotion to director of the Policy Planning Staff while vacationing in Aspen, Colorado. Photo by Floyd H. McCall/*Denver Post* via Getty Images.

plicit charge to avoid politics. He was a registered Republican in a Democratic administration. The men he admired—e.g., Marshall and Clayton—had little use for politics, though the elected officials who chose them had political use for them. Nitze acted with confidence and intellectual agility, yet he had no stature with Congress. The staff work he provided helped triage the problems and summarize the potential ways forward. While he did not offer pithy quotes as did Kennan, Acheson did not need help on that front. He and the president would make the decisions. They were accountable to the American people. Nitze was not.

In a January 31, 1950, meeting of the Special Committee, Truman resolved the debate over the US pursuit of the hydrogen bomb. "Can the Russians do it?" he asked. Yes, the committee responded. In retrospect, no alternative could have advanced US interests.

The Soviets were not only capable of building the hydrogen bomb they were close to achieving it. This was because of a combination of spies from Los Alamos and their own independent efforts led by physicist Andrei Sakharov. George Kennan and Robert Oppenheimer opposed going ahead with the hydrogen bomb, warning that the Soviets would have no choice but to reciprocate. We know today it was *not* the US decision to proceed with the hydrogen bomb that led the Soviets down the path toward building one; they were already on it. Nitze was correct, but not necessarily for the reasons he figured. Nitze's aspirations to get up to speed on the science behind fusion were broadly irrelevant to the outcome of the debate. Truman still would have cut through the details with the simple question: *Can the Russians do it?* The answer was yes. Simply put, capabilities outweighed intentions.

Meanwhile, George Kennan retreated to his farm in Princeton. He remained the counselor of the department for a short time, yet that title was transitory and mattered little because Acheson did not seek his counsel. Though he would return to the department in 1952 to serve a disastrous ambassadorship to the Soviet Union, never again would Kennan persuade the president or secretary of state to make an important decision. To put it another way, Kennan retired from Cold War policy making in 1949 and embarked on a successful career as a nonfiction writer. His histories of Russia were first rate; his introspection exquisite. His contribution to the Cold War had been to put forward the idea that the United States could ultimately win it without outright war with the Soviet Union. It stopped after that.

This fundamental concept—winning without war—required a cadre of people who could stay involved and guide US policy makers throughout it. National security became a practice, just as law or medicine. All this was new to the United States after World War II ended. The country needed people like Nitze to meet the challenges of the postwar era. It needed generalists who would stay on and lend expertise to challenges that oftentimes resembled ones from World War II. The upside was that policy makers could apply history to make better outcomes. The downside was that history never actually repeats itself. A historical sensibility could help to solve problems, evaluate threats, and advocate for ways to address them. Cultivating and sustaining relationships made Nitze an action man close to the levers of power. While not fabulously wealthy, he did not need to rely on seeking positions of increasing salary levels. For Nitze, there was no leaving DC. For him, the practice of national security meant a life in the Cold War—however long that would last.

Chapter 4

NSC-68

"United States Objectives and Programs for National Security," or NSC-68, will forever be linked to Paul Nitze. He did not write all of it. Yet he oversaw drafting the seventy-page paper, which he hoped the president would declassify to stimulate domestic support for increased defense spending. Nitze vigorously fought for NSC-68 to become an official US strategy, something Harry Truman did not do on April 7, 1950, when he first received it. The outbreak of the Korean War that June—and Truman's decision to intervene in that conflict—led the president finally to sign off on it. That decision was to triple the US defense budget for the next fiscal year.

NSC-68 drew upon the United States' founding documents—the Declaration of Independence and the Constitution—and repurposed them as part of a global struggle between freedom and slavery. It proclaimed victory over communism as the nation's objective and destiny. Left unanswered were fundamental questions about US war aims toward the Soviet Union should deterrence fail. Nitze grappled with these in an unfinished strategy paper, NSC-79. Only through sustained personal involvement in Cold War decision making could Nitze follow through on the objectives that NSC-68 laid out. Perceptions of threat were constantly changing. Inherent in them was a tension between the US public and those entrusted with preserving its national security. Nitze was one such individual. He served for six months under President Dwight Eisenhower and would otherwise have stayed on much longer had not partisan politics intervened. A diminution of perceived threats would give the appearance that strength was no longer needed. As Nitze conceived national security practice, the sustainment of US strength was essential.

The Drafting of NSC-68

On January 17, 1950, Director of Policy Planning Paul Nitze sent Secretary of State Dean Acheson a long memorandum stitching together his thoughts about the research and employment of atomic weapons and the potential implications of moving toward an era of thermonuclear weaponry. He advocated for "go[ing] into such a study [about the consequences of pursuing a hydrogen bomb] with a preliminary presumption in favor of such a revision of our strategic plans as would permit of a use policy restricted to retaliation against prior use by an enemy."[1] Two days after Nitze's memorandum, Acheson spoke to Admiral Sidney Souers—no longer the NSC's executive secretary yet still a consultant—and mentioned a paper in development that would revisit fundamental assumptions about the new era and reconcile its challenges with US values.[2] That project became "United States Objectives and Programs for National Security," with the designation NSC-68.[3]

On January 31, 1950, following their White House conversation, President Truman wrote Acheson affirming his support for pursuing the feasibility of a hydrogen bomb and stating his intention to announce this publicly. The president also called for a "reexamination of our objectives in peace and war and of the effect of these objectives on our strategic plans, in the light of the probable fission bomb capability and possible thermonuclear bomb capability of the Soviet Union."[4]

As the nucleus of strategic planning during the early days of the Cold War, the State Department's Policy Planning Staff took up this endeavor. NSC executive secretary James Lay had taken over from Admiral Souers in 1949 and retained only a skeletal staff. There was no influential national security adviser with a team of bright minds working directly for them. And the parameters of the assignment lay outside the traditional role of the State Department as the custodian of US diplomacy. With a free hand from Secretary of State George Marshall, whom no one challenged, George Kennan had turned the office into a policy clearinghouse. The absence of a "national security" cadre under the terms of the 1947 National Security Act meant that the portfolio was up for grabs. During the challenging fall of 1949, Acheson turned to Nitze. Unelected and accountable only to the secretary and the president, he fulfilled one of the central roles of the modern-day national security adviser: crafting a national security strategy.

From February through April 1950, when the final report went to the NSC, Nitze led a team that included John Paton Davies, a China specialist, and Louis Halle, an academic. Nitze commenced drafting NSC-68 when Acheson trusted him most and when the latter commanded Truman's attention. This was no time for prolonged reflection. Nitze regarded the prospect of war as "considerably greater" than the previous fall, which saw the Soviets detonate an atomic device and the Chinese Communist Party prevail against the nationalists. Unstated in meetings—yet present—was the fraught domestic political context. Alger Hiss was convicted of perjury. On February 9, 1950, Senator Joseph McCarthy delivered a speech in Wheeling, West Virginia, where he alleged that 205 communists were working in the State Department.

The moment demanded action, and Nitze savored the challenge. NSC-68 allowed him to apply the full scope of his talents and persuade action men wielding the levers of influence. In addition, he benefited from the presence of a bureaucratic foil—Secretary of Defense Louis Johnson, a Democratic politician and aspirant to succeed Harry Truman. Johnson had elbowed out his predecessor, James Forrestal, whom Nitze revered. In short, he encapsulated everything Nitze despised.

As Nitze recounted to the Policy Planning Staff following a meeting with Acheson on February 2, 1950, "there are an increasing number of signs of toughness on the part of the Kremlin," and "the informal opinion of the Joint Chiefs now is that the Soviet Union could begin a major attack from a standing start so that the usual signs of mobilization and preparation would be lacking." Moreover, there were "increasing indications that some of the basic elements of Communist dogma no longer hold" and that the Kremlin, no longer patient to sit back and watch the capitalist world collapse, would take a more active role in achieving that objective.[5] It is not entirely clear what those signals were. Nevertheless, the secretary and everyone on the policy planning team shared a sense of urgency.

On February 8, Nitze distributed to State Department principals a study titled "Recent Soviet Moves," in which he made sure that they recalled Joseph Stalin's February 1946 speech—"an open declaration of hostility"—and concluded that "since that time the USSR has given every sign that it neither intends to abandon the struggle, other than on its own terms, nor pause in its prosecution." Instead, expediency guided the actions of Soviet leaders. "As the USSR has already committed itself to the defeat of the US," Nitze continued,

"Soviet policy is guided by the simple consideration of weakening the world power position of the US."[6]

This did not mean that Moscow was plotting a surprise attack. Instead, Soviet leaders were demonstrating a greater tolerance of risk—bordering on recklessness—based on calculations that US power was evaporating and that the communist world could weaken it further. Its actions suggested "a greater willingness than in the past to undertake a course of action, including a possible use of force in local areas, which might lead to an accidental outbreak of general military conflict." The "chance of war through miscalculation" had thus gone up at the same time that both sides in the Cold War had added atomic bombs to their stockpiles. Soviet acquisition of atomic technology had increased the chances of accidental war by emboldening the Kremlin to take more significant risks.

"In assuming the risks involved in exploiting its present opportunities and in dealing with its imperial problems," Nitze went on to say, "Moscow appears to be animated by a general sense of confidence." He considered that confidence to be justified. "[Moscow] has developed an A-bomb; it has achieved the prewar level of production and other solid economic successes; it has made progress in consolidating its control over the European satellites; and it has apparently effected an increase in the prestige of the Communist Party among the Russian people." Moreover, leaders in the Kremlin interpreted the economic travails of Western Europe through the lens of Marxist–Leninist ideology, which predicted a coming crisis within the capitalist world, one in which nations would turn on each other. "Moscow's faith in the inevitable disintegration of capitalism is not a passive faith in automatic historical evolution," according to Nitze. "Instead, it is a messianic faith that not only spurs the USSR to assist the transformation of the Marxist blueprint into a reality, but also gives the Soviet leaders a sense of confidence that in whatever particular course they follow they are riding the wave of the future."[7] It was entirely plausible that Kremlin leaders would decide that "the wave of the future" meant jettisoning patience that capitalism would collapse on its own.

The best way to counter Soviet leaders' expectations to capitalize on divisions within the Western world, according to Nitze, was to convince them to weigh the relative gains as a result of their actions against the relative costs. In the near term, US policy makers could expect that Soviet leaders would test US resolve in areas such as Indochina, Berlin, Austria, the UN, and the Korean peninsula—this last being outside the US defensive perimeter, as Secretary Acheson had publicly stated on January 12.[8] Intent on establishing and maintaining effective Soviet control in China, Kremlin leaders looked to focus on

Southeast Asia and tighten rules over indigenous communist parties every-where. And Nitze was confident that US leaders could demonstrate that the costs of Soviet aggression would outweigh the gains.

Nitze summed up his response to Truman's January 31 directive: the United States needed to restore its strength. Preparedness lay at the heart of deter-ring Soviet aggression. Deterrence in peacetime necessitated acquiring the means to prevail in wartime. Nitze had arrived at similar conclusions in the *Summary Report (Pacific War)*. Pearl Harbor was the great negative example in the leadup to US involvement in World War II—never again could something like that be allowed to occur. In overseeing NSC-68, a collective enterprise in which Nitze claimed no sole authorship, the central theme was restoring US strength to preserve the core values on which the nation was founded. No con-stitutional scholar, Nitze based his understanding on the words of the found-ing documents and his conclusion that in 1941 US weakness had provoked the Japanese attack.

How would the Soviets respond to the restoration of US strength? Accord-ing to the model of the "security dilemma" in the academic field of interna-tional relations, a state can sometimes take actions to enhance its security such that a rival state perceives those seemingly defensive measures as threatening. Nitze rejected the notion that the United States and the Soviet Union shared culpability for the outbreak of the Cold War. In his view, Soviet probing and risk-taking had commenced when the United States had rapidly demobilized after Japan's surrender in the summer of 1945. In February and March 1950, he brought distinguished consultants who entertained variations of the secu-rity dilemma (though they did not call it such) in meetings at the State De-partment. These included Oppenheimer, Harvard University president James Conant, former under secretary of state (and future secretary of defense) Rob-ert Lovett, and nuclear physicist Ernest Lawrence. Nevertheless, no one could assuage Nitze's conviction that the prudent way forward could be any-thing less than to build US and allied military capabilities to a level previously unprecedented in peacetime.[9]

Nitze gathered support from key allies to co-opt or neutralize potential crit-ics of increased defense spending. He did so in the same way as brokering a Wall Street deal: this required discretion, tact, and guile.[10] The drafting of NSC-68 culminated with a contentious interagency meeting held in the Policy Planning Staff's conference room on March 22. In a memorandum to Ache-son earlier that day, Nitze choreographed the anticipated showdown between the secretaries of state and defense. He encouraged Acheson to lead off by stressing that the White House had initiated the study. He would then turn the meeting over to Nitze and air force general, and former commander of

US Air Forces in Europe, Truman Landon, who would present NSC-68 to the assembled group as a unified front on behalf of the president.[11] In preparation, Nitze had worked assiduously with representatives of the military services to isolate Secretary of Defense Johnson from the call to increase military spending. Johnson had pledged to Truman that he would keep costs down. As he had displayed in corporate board rooms and during briefings to the strategic targeting committee in the summer of 1945, Nitze possessed supreme confidence in his ability to advocate for his cause. And the prospect of confrontation did not faze him.

As might have been expected, the meeting went poorly. Johnson said that neither he nor the chairman of the Joint Chiefs of Staff, Omar Bradley, had read the draft of NSC-68. The secretary of defense had become aware of it only that morning and would sign off on no part of it. "Mr. Nitze started to outline the working group's tentative conclusions," according to the meeting minutes, "but was interrupted by Mr. Johnson, who said that he did not want to hear what the conclusions were."[12] Secretary of State Acheson purportedly replied to Johnson: "You and I are supposed to deliver this report and these are the people we've appointed to do the staff work for us. I can't understand why you won't let yourself be briefed on what they've done. After all, the report is going to be yours and mine, not theirs. We're the ones who are going to have to sign this document."[13] Secretary of Defense Johnson stormed out of the room.

The Content of NSC-68

"The objectives of a free society are determined by its fundamental values and by the necessity for maintaining the material environment in which they flourish," stated the finished version of NSC-68. "Thus we must make ourselves strong, both in the way in which we affirm our values in the conduct of our national life, and in the development of our military and economic strength," was the first objective Nitze and his team put forward. "We must lead in building a successfully functioning political and economic system in the free world," was the second objective. "It is only by practical affirmation, abroad as well as at home, of our essential values, that we can preserve our own integrity, in which lies the real frustration of the Kremlin design."[14] "But beyond thus affirming our values our policy and actions must be such as to foster a fundamental change in the nature of the Soviet system, a change toward which the frustration of the design is the first and perhaps the most important step," according to the third objective. "Clearly it will not only be less costly but more effective if this change occurs to a maximum extent as a result of internal forces in Soviet society."[15] Restoring US strength and revitalizing its values were necessary but not sufficient factors in waging the Cold War; winning it meant achieving a fundamental change in the nature of the Soviet system without fighting a war. There was nothing especially controversial about this part, which accorded with Kennan's NSC 20/4.

NSC-68 drew distinctions between "Soviet" and "Russian" (as well as US short-term versus long-term objectives). Unlike Kennan, Nitze took no particular interest in Russia's history or what drove its people. "By practically demonstrating the integrity and vitality of our system the free world widens the area of possible agreement and thus can hope gradually to bring about a Soviet acknowledgement of realities which in sum will eventually constitute a frustration of the Soviet design." Short of that, "it might be possible to create a situation which will induce the Soviet Union to accommodate itself, with or without the conscious abandonment of its design, to coexistence on tolerable terms with the non-Soviet world." That outcome would constitute "a triumph for the idea of freedom and democracy, [and] must be an immediate objective of United States policy."[16] Short of precipitating a short-term Soviet collapse, the immediate restoration of US strength would compel Moscow to accept long-term "coexistence" with the West.

NSC-68 acknowledged the prospect that World War III might happen. However, in the ghastly event of war with the Soviet Union—with both sides in possession of atomic weapons—there was no reason "to alter our overall objectives . . . [which] do not include unconditional surrender, the subjugation of the Russian peoples or a Russia shorn of its economic potential. Such a course would irrevocably unite the Russian people behind the regime which enslaves them." Instead, US strategic aims would focus on "Soviet acceptance of the specific and limited conditions requisite to an international environment in which free institutions can flourish, and in which the Russian peoples will have a new chance to work out their own destiny. If we can make the Russian people our allies in the enterprise we will obviously have made our task easier and victory more certain."[17]

Here and elsewhere, NSC-68 contained ideas that Nitze had previously proposed but still needed to get traction for. For example, he had earlier failed to achieve an increase in spending to build up regional powers' defenses and shift US attention's focus from Kennan's five centers of power to a global orientation. Emboldened by his successful staff work on the H-bomb decision, Nitze seized the opportunity that NSC-68 afforded him to revive previous recommendations. His work led to a general increase in perception of threats versus pre-1945.

Much about NSC-68 has been shrouded in mythology. The basic premise—acknowledging an existential campaign between capitalism and communism—hardly constituted a revolution. NSC-68 prescribed no secret formula for winning the Cold War and revealed no sensitive military secrets. While Nitze classified it as top secret and made portions of it "Restricted Data"—particularly the handling of sensitive material about the design of atomic weapons—he did so to limit distribution during its drafting; and, above all, keep it away from the desk of the secretary of defense. NSC-68's attitude toward the possible use of atomic weapons did not differ from what was already a well-established part of US war plans to repel any potential Soviet invasion of Western Europe. Nor did NSC-68 take the line that the United States needed to build a vast nuclear arsenal to cow the Soviets into submission. Truman's writ set two premises: pursue hydrogen bomb research and prepare for a scenario where the Soviets had expanded their atomic arsenal and made headway on their hydrogen bomb. This is what Nitze did.

"When we were going through NSC 68 we came to the conclusion that the order of magnitude of the—not only of the defense, but the general security effort which was necessary, was of the order of magnitude of fifty billion dollars a year for the United States, and that this should be adopted right off the bat, and should be continued for a number of years," Nitze acknowledged in one of Dean Acheson's Princeton Seminars in 1953.[18] No such actual figures appeared in NSC-68 itself. "If we had put this kind of figure in the paper, we never would have gotten the concurrences that we did get on the paper."

Nitze's objective for NSC-68, as he acknowledged in that seminar (after he and Acheson had left office), was to commence a political campaign to get increased funding for defense. The grandiose language in NSC-68—the appeals to democratic traditions and freedom versus slavery—was intended to convince Congress and the American people to go along with higher defense budgets. "Only one percent of the information in NSC 68 was secure information," Nitze admitted in 1953. That was on purpose. It did no good for the cause of getting to $50 billion if broad swaths of NSC-68 could not be released to the public.

Moreover, Nitze did not believe that the Joint Chiefs of Staff could make their own judgments about how much money they needed. Just as he dismissed Dag Hammarskjöld's effort to redress Sweden's trade imbalance after World War II, Nitze had complete confidence that he alone could figure out the sum. Offer the military services a number, he reasoned, and they could figure out what forces they needed.

NSC-68 was simultaneously a strategy statement and a political document. It remained closely held and would not be declassified until 1975; yet the contents were not particularly sensitive. While it did not constitute a revolution in US foreign policy, it accentuated the fact that the Cold War needed to be waged globally and that the long-term US objective in that conflict should be *victory*. In the December 16, 1949, meeting Soviet expert Tommy Thompson had stated: "we have two objectives, a short-term and a long-term, the first being to win the cold war and the second to prepare for a hot war." As NSC-68 made clear a few months later, whatever the nature of the conflict between the United States and the Soviet Union, it could genuinely be over only with the victory of the United States—however long that took. It did not specify what success would look like in a hot war with the Soviets. Everyone who worked on it surely hoped that would never happen.

The Korean War

Events soon made unnecessary the political campaign that Nitze hoped NSC-68 would allow Truman to wage on behalf of higher defense spending. The Nitzes were camping in Canada in June 1950 when word came that North Korean forces had crossed the thirty-eighth parallel and were streaming into South Korea. Nitze quickly rushed to the airport to fly back to Washington. "Because I thought militarily that we did not have the assets to do it," he initially deemed it a bad idea to intervene militarily. However, by the time he had arrived in the nation's capital Truman had decided to do just that.[19] For Nitze and everyone else in the Truman administration, the North Korean invasion conjured up memories of Nazi Germany's invasion of Poland in 1939. Despite the creation of the CIA as part of the National Security Act of 1947, analysts provided little forewarning about what to expect. "The best our intelligence community could provide was an estimate saying that while the Soviets were likely to attack anywhere at any moment, such attacks might not necessarily take place," as Nitze later recounted. "No doubt Mr. Truman found this assessment as unenlightening as we did in the Policy Planning Staff."[20]

Neither Truman nor Acheson asked Nitze his opinion on how the United States ought to respond to Korea. Following the decision that the United States would lead a coalition of forces under the auspices of the UN to turn back the North Koreans, Nitze threw himself into the work of preparing for mobilizing US forces for war in Asia and potentially again in Europe. In July and August, he participated in meetings about whether to cross the thirty-eighth parallel should allied forces under General Douglas MacArthur's command successfully reverse the tide of the war (as they ultimately would do after MacArthur's daring Inchon landing in September).[21]

The Korean crisis led to a revision of timetables on military outlays—or future expenditures—a process that Nitze oversaw.[22] Secretary of Defense Johnson approved increasing army personnel from 630,000 to 834,000. At the same time, President Truman asked Congress for an additional $10 billion to support that action while also boosting navy combatant ships from 238 to 282 and air force wings from 48 to 58. Truman requested an additional $4 billion in military assistance, most of which would go to NATO countries.[23] Korea provided the political impetus finally to shore up European defenses.

On September 30, 1950, two weeks after the Inchon landing, Truman signed off on NSC-68. The previous day, Secretary of Defense George Marshall, who had succeeded Louis Johnson, gave MacArthur permission to go north of the thirty-eighth parallel. Even as the tide appeared to turn in Korea, none of the other Cold War challenges abated. Nitze redoubled his efforts to figure out a viable conventional defense of Europe in planning for a potential global conflagration stemming from the Korean War. This required economic and military planning as well as diplomatic finesse. On September 9, Truman committed to increased US strength in Europe yet dodged the thorny question of German rearmament. Along with Acheson and Marshall, Nitze participated in subsequent planning sessions for the defense of Europe.[24]

When, in October 1950, Chinese forces entered the war in Korea, Nitze expressed concerns about the intentions of General MacArthur, whom he had come to know (and turned down a job from) in Japan five years earlier. "I learned, from intercepts of cable traffic coming across my desk, that MacArthur's real aim was to expand the war into China, overthrow Mao Tse-tung, and restore Chiang Kai-shek to power," Nitze revealed later.[25] Given the prospect of a wider campaign, on November 4, 1950, Nitze summoned General Herbert Loper, the Pentagon's assistant for atomic energy, to discuss the potential use of atomic bombs in Korea.[26] One year after Acheson handed him the atomic research portfolio, Nitze now found himself considering active employment plans in an actual war.

The consequences were predictable when it came to atomic weapons and the Korean War. The United States' first use of atomic weapons in Korea would indeed cause opinion in East Asia to sour against Americans, who had already used the bomb against the Japanese in 1945.[27] And the Soviets would be compelled to respond. Nevertheless, Nitze approached all this dispassionately. He did not consider with ashen horror the prospect of using atomic bombs, nor did he feel it inimical to the US way of war. Instead, he evaluated possible scenarios and options and ultimately concluded that the drawbacks of using atomic weapons in Korea outweighed any potential advantages. A key element in his thinking was that US troops in Korea were part of a UN force; UN authorization of an atomic attack would be a nonstarter.

NSC-79

On August 22, 1950, the Joint Chiefs of Staff sent a memorandum to the secretary of defense asking for "clear-cut United States objectives in the event of [global] war," stating that neither NSC 20/4 nor NSC-68 had adequately laid these out.[28] The tasking wound up on Nitze's desk. The paper he oversaw, NSC-79, laid out three options for essential US aims in a global war with the Soviet Union: Pax Americana, world government, and a balance of power. After reworkings from Policy Planning staffers, John Paton Davis, Charles Burton Marshall, and Louis Halle, a draft went to Acheson, who shut down further work. Were the president to approve such a plan, according to the secretary of state, word of it would get out, and the results would be as catastrophic as Keynes's *Economic Consequences of the Peace* had been for the settlement of World War I at Versailles.[29]

Acheson presumably meant that Keynes's evisceration of Allied leaders in Paris in 1919 had sapped public confidence in the peace settlement of World War I. Similarly, the prospect of *planning* for a global war would come off as a precursor to *waging* war just as the United States was fighting a limited war in Korea to preserve a broader postwar peace in Europe and Asia. At home and abroad, critics could seize on NSC-79 eroding public confidence in that entire enterprise. Moreover, each of the three potential outcomes of a war with the Soviet Union diverged from President Truman's declarations to support free people to select their form of government. Pax Americana, world government, and balance of power were all inimical to the objectives of his administration. A remarkable thing about Acheson's statement is that it was okay to declare America's intention to win the Cold War, but not okay to deliberate about what victory constituted.

By December 1950, a US Cold War victory was nowhere on the horizon. Gone were Truman's aspirations to contain communism on the cheap. That month, the president asked for an additional $16.8 billion for the Department of Defense and a rough doubling of army troops, navy combatant ships, and air force wings, as compared to June 1950. "It would not be too much," Acheson said at an NSC meeting on December 14, "if we had all the troops that the military wants. If we had all of the things that our European allies want it would not be too much. If we had the equipment to call out the reserves it would not be too much. If we had a system for full mobilization it would not be too much."[30] By the end of 1950, the spirit of "it would not be too much" was now guiding the Truman administration's approach to the defense. On December 16, the president declared the existence of a national emergency.

Iran and NSC-141

Korea in 1950 did not turn out to be Poland in 1939. The conflict ground to a stalemate. Meanwhile, another crisis emerged. From 1951 to 1952, Nitze spent considerable time working on Iran, where the new prime minister, Mohammad Mosaddegh, sought better terms from the British, who held a controlling hand in the Anglo-Persian Oil Company (which would later become British Petroleum or BP). Nitze got to know Mosaddegh and, unlike many of his peers, considered him a wily and underestimated figure. Still, Nitze was involved in crafting a policy that would culminate in the overthrow of Mosaddegh's government in 1953.

Nitze was also involved in US efforts to square the circle of US interests and ideals regarding South Africa. "As a practical matter, the intervention of the U.N. in such a question as the racial policy of the South African Government will not solve the problem," he wrote in a memorandum of November 3, 1952. While NSC-68 had framed the contest between the Kremlin and Washington as one between slavery and freedom, the sovereignty of Iran and the enactment of apartheid in South Africa existed (at least then and to Nitze) outside of the basic Cold War paradigm. One day after this memo, Eisenhower defeated Adlai Stevenson.

Nitze appreciated Truman's achievements with a proviso: despite tens of billions of dollars added to the defense budget, the level of preparedness that he hoped NSC-68 would instigate had not come about. As he made clear in a memorandum accompanying NSC-141, one of the last papers he drafted during the Truman administration, Nitze had misgivings about the administration's national security policies. He was profoundly dissatisfied and disappointed with the status of the United States and allied conventional forces, the poor state of which would shorten the path of escalation toward nuclear war in the event of a crisis.[31]

"Our national security programs have never actually been consistent with our objectives as these objectives have been repeatedly stated in NSC papers (20/4, 68, 114, and most recently 135/3)," he wrote. "This became clear in the course of the work on this project when the Defense representatives stated time and again, in answer to the point that the defense program would not produce the situation of strength defined in NSC 135/3, that the defense program had never been designed to produce any such situation of strength." The fundamental choice came down to whether the United States could feel secure as "a sort of hedge-hog, unattractive to attack," or do "what is necessary to give us some chance of seeing these objectives attained."[32]

On January 12, 1953, Nitze wrote Acheson a gloomy memorandum on the outstanding vulnerabilities that Truman was handing off to Eisenhower.[33] Better conventional forces were needed to prevent overreliance on nuclear, even where nuclear remained an option. Nitze never viewed atomic bombs to be "ordinary" weapons. To his mind, the effects of their actual use were—indeed—measurable. But the psychological impact of their existence shaped the geopolitical landscape. Only sufficient US and allied strength could discourage Soviet risk-taking.

Unlike Kennan and Oppenheimer, Nitze did not agonize over whether to pursue "The Super." That did not mean he took the matter lightly. The only prudent option was to pursue research on the hydrogen bomb. The consequences of the Soviets building one, after the United States had forgone it, would have been disastrous. As has been said, Nitze thought perceptions of strength and resolve determined geopolitics. That was the key takeaway from the *Summary Report (Pacific War)*, in which Japan's conception of US weakness had provoked the attack on Pearl Harbor in December 1941. A decade later, in Europe, Asia, Africa, Latin America—and pretty much everywhere else in the world—the prospect of a Soviet monopoly on the hydrogen bomb would broadcast the message that Washington would either surrender to Moscow's demands or accept that World War III was inevitable. This was hardly an academic debate: men of action made decisions that shaped the free world's future. In the nearly decade and a half that Nitze had resided in Washington, he had already proven himself to be one of them.

The Eisenhower Transition

On November 1, 1952, three days before a presidential election, the United States exploded a hydrogen bomb on the island of Elugelab in the Enewetak Atoll, far out in the Pacific Ocean. President Harry Truman resisted exploiting this development in support of Democratic candidate Adlai Stevenson. Meeting with Truman on December 30, Paul Nitze "expressed the view that the State of the Union Message would appear to be the most appropriate vehicle for any Presidential comment, for then such comment would appear in a suitable context."[34] "Since Alamogordo [where the United States tested the first atomic bomb, on July 16, 1945] we have developed atomic weapons with many times the explosive force of the early models, and we have produced them in substantial quantities," Truman informed the American people on January 7, 1953: "And recently, in the thermonuclear tests at Eniwetok [sic], we have entered another stage in the world-shaking development of atomic energy."[35]

Nitze presumed he would stay in government for this new stage. He saw much unfinished business from his tenure at the State Department including his sense that the Truman administration had not fully implemented the recommendations contained in NSC-68, or resolved the matters of NSC-79, "Basic War Aims." It remained unclear how countries in Western Europe could contribute to their continued economic revival and, at the same time, assume their share of the burden of supporting NATO. Germany remained divided. The Cold War was heating up in the third world—especially in French Indochina. There was also considerable uncertainty about the future of oil-rich Iran, where Nitze remained in negotiations throughout the presidential transition from Truman to Eisenhower.

Still concerned about the strength of both US atomic and conventional forces, Nitze saw no resolution to the overall threat that Moscow posed to the American way of life. "It has been estimated that if the Soviet Union should drop 500 or more atomic bombs on targets in the United States, our ability to recover from the attack would be destroyed," Nitze wrote (along with Carlton Savage, a colleague on the Policy Planning Staff) in a draft paper the week after Eisenhower defeated Stevenson. "In a few years the Soviet Union will have enough atomic bombs and the means to deliver them to launch such an attack," they claimed without elaborating on the provenance of that estimate.[36] Nor did they offer specificity to back up the phrase: "it has been estimated that." Instead, in a proposal that led nowhere, Nitze and Savage called for constructing an early warning system and a civil defense network at an annual cost of some $250 million.

The transfer of power from Truman to Eisenhower had extraordinary features. It took place with the country at war on the Korean Peninsula. Republicans would now control the executive branch for the first time in twenty years. President-elect Eisenhower and secretary-of-state-designate John Foster Dulles pilloried their predecessors even though they had themselves served in substantive foreign policy roles during the Truman administration. Dulles had negotiated the peace treaty with Japan; Eisenhower served as NATO supreme commander and then, while president of Columbia University, commuted to Washington, DC, to serve as de facto chairman of the Joint Chiefs of Staff. Once in power, Dulles privately admitted to Acheson that he had supported most of the outgoing man's policies. In this context, it was not outlandish for Nitze to presume that he could stay on.

There was also the matter of a scarcity of national security professionals. Dulles considered himself eminently prepared to be secretary of state—a position his uncle and grandfather had both held—yet he had few top advisers and no cadre from which to staff midlevel national security positions. Soviet specialists and Europeanists abounded in the State Department's geographic bureaus and the CIA. Yet no team of advisers stood poised to help Dulles wage a global Cold War. As might be true in a later era, no cluster of DC think tanks set to work equipping the new administration with desired policy statements.

"Paul, you know, I have greatly admired the work that has been done by the Policy Planning Staff under your leadership, but you know it really doesn't deal with foreign affairs," Nitze remembered Dulles telling him just after he arrived as secretary of state. "It deals with security strategy or national security policy as much as it does just for the conduct of foreign affairs." That charge was hard to rebut. Nitze and his predecessor George Kennan had carved out a niche for policy planning apart from traditional State Department activities. An evocative example was the March 1950 meeting when Nitze convened the secretary of defense, secretary of state, and Joint Chiefs of Staff to meet in his conference room. Instead, Dulles thought "that work ought to be done in the NSC, not in the State Department"—and he, Dulles, intended to spend 95 percent of his time in the Old Executive Office Building with the NSC staff and only 5 percent of his time at the State Department, leaving Deputy Secretary of State Walter Bedell Smith in charge of Foggy Bottom.[37] Dulles would find another position for Nitze. He could not remain director of policy planning.

Nothing compelled Dulles to keep Nitze. The former must have seen value in the latter. A proud generalist not lacking in confidence, Nitze was becoming closely linked to the policy implications of nuclear weapons and the sustainment of US alliances. Whether at Policy Planning Staff or elsewhere, he kept working on these topics. Where Kennan had proven himself as a "Russia" specialist, given his study of the language and the country's history as well his affinity for its people and culture, it was considerably easier for Nitze to proclaim expertise about nuclear policies. The subject was too new and untested. With his security clearances, proximity to the highest level of government, and self-assuredness in business, government, and academia, Nitze proceeded to teach himself about the intricacies of nuclear designs, production chains, and deployment prospects. He had debated towering figures such as Robert Oppenheimer from an equal standing (even without formal training). He weighed in on whether the United States could use nuclear weapons to win the Korean War. However, "Policy Planning"—unlike, say, "the Office of Soviet Affairs"—had no clearly understood meaning apart from whatever relations existed between the director of policy planning and the secretary of state.

Nitze got off to an inauspicious start with President Eisenhower. Summoned to the White House, he opened the wrong door and found Ike in his underwear. Notwithstanding this encounter—which amused the First Lady (who was also there, clothed) more than Eisenhower himself—Nitze participated in a substantive meeting with the president once it commenced in another room down the hall.

International Security Affairs (Briefly)

As this first meeting concluded, Dulles recommended that Nitze work on a speech taking up an idea from the incoming secretary of defense, Charles Wilson, who, in February 1953, urged Eisenhower to appeal for peace directly to the Soviet people. The urgency of such an appeal increased upon the death of Stalin on March 5, 1953. Eisenhower approved the participation of Nitze, who worked on it with his old Harvard friend, Charles Bohlen.[38] As he and Bohlen were drafting Eisenhower's "Chance for Peace" speech, Dulles offered Nitze the job of assistant secretary of defense for international security affairs (ISA). Even ahead of the required Senate confirmation, Nitze reported for work at the Pentagon.

Politics intervened. Because he needed an eminently qualified Soviet expert for the post, President Eisenhower nominated Bohlen as ambassador to the Soviet Union. Now in the majority for the first time in two decades, Senate Republicans declared Bohlen to be the last holdover from the Acheson State Department that they would confirm. Before a potential Nitze confirmation hearing, a newspaper supporting Senator Joseph McCarthy dredged up his uncle's association with the notorious Black Tom explosion during World War I. (Here was the first time that Nitze's familial connection to German sabotage became known outside the circle of his supporters.)

Dulles and Eisenhower withdrew Nitze's nomination. Still occupying the position of director of policy planning, Nitze returned to the State Department where he continued his work on matters related to mutual security assistance planning, the continued prospect of whether to use the atomic bomb in the Korean War, what to do about the potential collapse of French Indochina, and whether to build a continental defense against Soviet bombers.[39] These were hardly trivial matters. In a candid April memo to Dulles, he predicted unfavorable outcomes in East Asia should the administration follow through on Eisenhower's campaign pledge to cut the defense budget.[40]

The United States was the wealthiest society in history, Nitze told Dulles. Americans could easily afford to pay more for security against the twin menaces of communism and nuclear peril. There was no good reason to cut defense spending and taxes. Higher taxes were needed to support more lavish defense spending. These were not things that Dulles wanted to hear. Neither Dulles nor anyone else at the highest level of the Republican ranks was about to jettison President Eisenhower's commitment to lower taxes and a balanced budget. Although it would take a year before the new administration fully articulated its plans, Dulles and Eisenhower had already indicated their intent to take a "new look" when it came to nuclear weapons, a change in strategic posture that they believed would allow them to cut billions of dollars from the defense budget.

In 1952, Nitze had switched his registration from Republican back to Democrat. He later attributed this to the Eisenhower campaign's nasty insinuations about the Truman administration. Yet the timing was puzzling, given that he had spent nearly a decade working for Democratic administrations and that Eisenhower was the clear favorite to win in the upcoming general election. After Ike won, Nitze tried to have it both ways. Just as he had been a registered Republican working in Democratic administrations, he saw no reason why he could not be a Democrat in a Republican administration.

Moreover, Nitze had unfinished business. He did not regard NSC-68 as sufficient for waging the Cold War. It was a living document to be amended, and the version that probably mattered more was NSC-68/4, the revised version of the original that Truman approved in December 1950. The Korean War had forced the president's hand, and the fighting was ongoing. It had triggered internal demand for NSC-79—on US basic war aims in a global military conflict with the Soviet Union—and Nitze did not relish leaving that assignment unfinished.

The Cold War was already Nitze's life's work. As with the strategic bombing surveys, NSC-68 and follow-on papers were collective efforts in which Nitze may have drafted only parts yet exercised control over all their content. The main ideas were consistent with those he had expressed since his time in Japan. The difference was the shrinking proximity between Nitze's pen and President Harry Truman's. Nitze grew to admire Truman, about whom he had been dubious before 1945. The "guiding light" of Truman's drive, according to Nitze, was "to recognize that he was a small, average American, but the whole theory of the United States was that a small, average American could be President and could be a good President and he was determined to be a good President."[41] Despite his personal admiration for this average American, Nitze remained disappointed at Truman's failure to fund such conventional forces as he believed necessary to achieve victory in an enduring Cold War.

CHAPTER 5

No Exile

Paul Nitze remained director of the State Department's Policy Planning Staff until June 1953—nearly half a year into the Dwight Eisenhower administration. He then left to set up shop at SAIS, which he had cofounded in 1943 with his wife's cousin, Christian Herter. Under Nitze's guidance, SAIS added an early example of a policy think tank and expanded its mission to train aspiring national security practitioners.

At SAIS, Nitze constructed a de facto policy planning staff in exile comprising former State Department officials. Retaining his connection to former secretary of state Dean Acheson—and with an eye on the 1956 and 1960 presidential elections—he kept his security clearances, worked on classified projects for the government, and seldom found himself more than one degree away from national security decisions made at the highest level. Secretary of State John Foster Dulles called on Nitze throughout the Eisenhower years despite the disdain the two men held for each other.

Nitze also resumed his quest to formulate a unified theory of politics. He spoke and wrote about topics such as US grand strategy, specific foreign policy challenges, intelligence matters, and the efficacy of government institutions. The geopolitical implications of thermonuclear weapons consumed the bulk of his attention. Notably, he believed that his criticisms of Eisenhower's nuclear policies eventually led to change. Paul Nitze showed during the period

1953–60 that a man of action could wield quite a few levers of influence without needing a government appointment.

Tension between Opposites

Shortly after he departed the State Department, Nitze traveled to Massachusetts to give the Commencement Address at the Groton School, from which his son Peter was set to graduate. Paul focused on "tension between opposites," a leitmotif for the rest of his career (although he called it "tension of opposites" that day). Invoking the Greek philosopher Heraclitus, Nitze spoke about how the bow and lyre created beautiful music out of physical tension. This principle applied to the work of atomic scientists Robert Oppenheimer and Niels Bohr. As Nitze put it, the behavior of light could only be understood by perceiving it in "two opposite concepts—that of the wave and that of the particle." He identified a tension of opposites in the broader world of 1953: "individual versus society, change versus continuing order, force versus consent, the East versus the West, power versus responsibility." Graduates ought to remember the bow and lyre and not ignore the one for the other—they should strive "for a harmony in the tension between the opposites."[1]

Nitze proceeded to give a sort of accolade to himself. "In the field of foreign affairs, for instance, it is not those who have taken the specialized courses in international affairs who make the real contribution," he opined. "[I]t is those who combine a truly humanistic background with a sense for relevant facts and an intense care for the significant details who are invaluable." Follow in his footsteps, he was saying: approach problems head-on, seek ever-wider portfolios, and risk failure. In order "to carry responsibility in important matters, it is essential to have gained experience through trial and error in handling responsibility in smaller matters." Not until one overcame failure was it possible to develop "the stamina and courage to become a participant and molder of history—not merely an object of history." These were lofty expectations for sixteen-year-old Peter, whose father was implicitly chiding his own father and the rest of the scholars at the University of Chicago who failed to turn thought into action.

Nitze concluded by stressing the importance of preserving US strength. Before World War II, a rough balance of power had existed outside the Western hemisphere. The destruction of Nazi Germany and Imperial Japan and the rise of Soviet power created a bipolar era. Sustaining US power was the minimum requirement for opposing Soviet designs because no alliance could stand up to the Kremlin without a strong United States. The global engagement was a responsibility, not a choice. "We can no longer choose when to throw in our influence," Nitze told the assembly of teenagers. "Our influence is continually necessary."

To his young audience, he had to admit: the future was as precarious as ever. The combination of the "ruthless and implacable hostility of the U.S.S.R." and the range and power of nuclear weapons meant it was clear: "We now find ourselves living in a situation in which most of the other great powers of history continually lived." He defended the actions of the Truman administration while not omitting a certain sense of satisfaction with his own tenure of office. "Future historians may well judge that the United States moved toward a preliminary adjustment to this new situation with remarkable speed and adaptability, and that it made this preliminary adjustment in a manner consistent with its basic principles."[2]

Nitze intended in his peroration to invite the graduating class to seize the "opportunity to participate in the growth of the human spirit." He pointed to himself as the model. This was hardly outlandish, given that his elite background and education at Hotchkiss and Harvard had opened up many opportunities and he had tried to make the most of them. This advice was aimed at those Groton classmates, including Peter, who were headed for Harvard—and such places.

Nitze spent the summer of 1953 with his family at their farm in Maryland. As he had previously discovered, the outdoors restored his physical and mental energies. He entered a horse race and briefly considered running for the House of Representatives (though it turned out that it was his wife, the daughter of a former representative, Ruth Baker Pratt, on whom Democratic Party leaders had their eye).

SAIS

Following this summer respite—his first since before World War II—Nitze devoted himself to the one institution to which he would remain forever loyal: SAIS. Born out of a conversation between Nitze and Herter in the summer of 1943, SAIS was supposed to be "an institution in Washington that would be outside the government but close enough to it to exploit the knowledge and wisdom of those in it, with ties to business, labor, and the media, and with an academic core to give it continuity and depth."[3] All of the "real-world experience" that Nitze saw as lacking in his education he intended to make up for in SAIS. The most prestigious comparable school of that time was the Fletcher School at Tufts University in Boston. Nitze and Herter scored a coup in poaching the founding dean of Fletcher School, Halford Hoskins, to come to Washington to be the first director of this new institution.

When Nitze and Herter failed to attract a university affiliation for SAIS, they set up the Foreign Service Educational Foundation to oversee the school's curriculum and finances. Its charter included the mission of furthering "the education and training of persons in the fields of government, business, international economic relations, international law, and such related fields as may fit them for better service in the foreign interest of this country at home or abroad."[4] Service did not necessarily mean formal government employment. Instead, Herter and Nitze hoped that corporations would send employees to the school to equip them better to conduct business abroad (and, in so doing, promote US values of democratic principles and entrepreneurialism). Finding this to be a profitable investment, they hoped, firms would then underwrite the school's long-term financial stability.[5] While that aspiration fell short—it was more advantageous for corporations to hire fresh SAIS graduates than to give up their best employees for a year or two—SAIS stayed afloat with the implementation of the Servicemen's Readjustment Act of 1944 (better known as the GI Bill), which supported the tuition of returning veterans. Most students during these early years went on to work for the State Department, the CIA, and multinational oil companies.[6] And Nitze saw each career as a form of foreign service.

SAIS remained afloat but needed to be financially self-sustaining. Still lacking an endowment, the Foreign Service Educational Foundation took up an offer from the Carnegie Foundation to accept $60,000 on the condition that SAIS affiliate itself with an established academic institution. Based in Baltimore, Johns Hopkins University already had an international relations school, the Page School; yet that school's endowment had suffered during the stock market crash of 1929. Throughout the latter half of the 1940s and into the 1950s, the Page School had been under the direction of Owen Lattimore, the Asia specialist whom Senator Joseph McCarthy pilloried for his alleged role in the "loss of China" to the communists in 1949. SAIS prevailed. In 1950, the Foreign Service Educational Foundation approved its integration with Johns Hopkins. SAIS technically remained a separate entity from the university (an hour away by train), but the president of Johns Hopkins would serve on the board overseeing the school.[7]

In the fall of 1953, Nitze took over as the Foreign Service Educational Foundation president. In addition to teaching a course, "Concepts of Foreign Policy," he became chairman of the SAIS Advisory Committee in 1954. With Herter ensconced in the governor's mansion in Boston, SAIS was now Nitze's to guide. (They would switch places again in 1960, when Herter, having become secretary of state following the death of John Foster Dulles in 1959, returned to SAIS, and Nitze joined the Kennedy administration.)

In early attempts to raise funds, Nitze insisted that he was not trying to create a "Policy Planning Staff in exile." But—in actuality—he was. Early faculty included his close friend Charles Burton Marshall, who had served on Nitze's Policy Planning Staff and would later become the school's first "Paul Nitze Professor." Against the advice of Marshall, who figured that overt partisanship would diminish Nitze's—and, perhaps, Marshall's—"usefulness to policy" while the Republicans were in office, Nitze stayed closely aligned with the Democratic Party. Since it was clear that Eisenhower and Dulles would never bring him on full time, his best bet was to position himself for office in a future Democratic administration.[8] In 1954, Nitze joined former secretary of the air force Thomas Finletter in a foreign policy discussion group in New York City. Finletter held considerable clout in Democratic circles and had political aspirations of his own (he would attempt a run for the Senate in 1958). In New York, Nitze also attended luncheons at the Council on Foreign Relations, which was becoming a nexus between business, government, and academic elites.

Opposing "Massive Retaliation"

On January 12, 1954, Secretary of State John Foster Dulles unveiled the Eisenhower administration's "New Look" defense policy at one such luncheon. He could not resist castigating the Truman administration for the foreign policy messes he and the president had inherited. To the threat of communist penetration anywhere in the world, Dulles said the United States would respond to Soviet aggression "at a time and place of its choosing" using all weapons at its disposal. This prospect would soon become known as "massive retaliation."[9]

Sitting at a table with former colleagues from the Truman administration, Nitze was flabbergasted. He wrote up his objections in a private memo he circulated to friends—including the once and future Democratic presidential nominee Adlai Stevenson, who drew from its points in his own subsequent public criticism. "It is interesting but probably irrelevant that the decision to withdraw our troops from Korea was made on the basis of a recommendation of the Joint Chiefs of Staff transmitted over the signature of General Eisenhower," Nitze wrote, referring to Truman's pullback of forces that domestic critics alleged had "invited" North Korean aggression in June 1950. In other words, Eisenhower had advised Truman to do the very thing Dulles now criticized as having invited aggression. Moreover, Nitze believed that massive retaliation took the wrong lessons from the outbreak of the Korean War. The

United States had held a practical monopoly in deliverable atomic bombs at the start of the war. That had not stopped Stalin from giving the green light to Kim Il-sung to attack South Korea. A blanket threat of nuclear attack defied credulity and diverted resources and attention from a conventional deterrent. "If we are to attain victory, or peace with justice and without defeat," Nitze wrote in his critique of Dulles's speech, "we must attain it with non-atomic means while deterring an atomic war."[10]

Nitze was convinced that it was foolhardy to set an arbitrary ceiling on defense spending. Focusing on "atomic deterrents to general war cannot be expected to give us the flexibility required for success in achieving peace with justice against the rising power of the Kremlin and its satellites." Nitze warned of growing Russian and Chinese capabilities, pointing to ongoing trends and citing the coming years 1958 and 1960 as especially dangerous in the absence of drastic and timely action on the part of the Eisenhower administration. He urged "no exaggerated view" but rather the "coldest, soberest view that our experts are able to give us." No doubt Nitze meant experts such as himself.

In his January 1954 speech to the Council on Foreign Relations, Dulles charged the Truman administration with being at the mercy of Soviet initiatives. On that occasion and elsewhere, Dulles described the problem with containment as being fundamentally *reactive*, not proactive. Feeling otherwise, Nitze thought the problem was not with US containment policies but instead that the United States was devoting insufficient resources to tackling the problem that the Soviets posed to the free world. "Clearly it would be desirable to have[,] together with our allies, such a preponderance of power, military, political, and economic, that it is the Soviets who would primarily be engaged in adjusting their policy to ours." Unfortunately, that required far more money than what either the Eisenhower administration or the Truman administration was prepared to spend.[11]

In justifying massive retaliation, Dulles quoted Lenin's pursuit of the "practicable bankruptcy" of the United States—a line that Eisenhower himself repeated to warn against the nation's spending itself into oblivion. Nitze considered all this to be nonsense. Americans were "living better than any people on earth have ever lived," in an economy with significant agricultural surpluses and steel plants at 75 percent of capacity.[12] They could afford more in taxes. By Dulles's logic, "one cannot afford an adequate police force to deal individually with criminals, [and so] it is good enough to have the capability of burning the entire town down."[13] From Nitze's perspective, it was fundamentally dishonest to promise the American people that nuclear weapons would reduce the financial burden of defense also deterring Soviet and potentially Chinese aggression.

Associating with the Democratic Party

While he initially distributed his critique privately, the public debate over massive retaliation proved a boon for Nitze's career. Criticizing it put his name on the minds of future Democratic candidates. Not only that, he came at it from the perspective of toughness—precisely what the party needed to counter Republicans' charges of softness on communism and defense of traitors such as Alger Hiss. Nitze claimed that Dulles's flawed logic made the United States weak and harmed US relations with adversaries and allies alike—wording intended to help Democrats on the stump. "Whether we can destroy the Russians a little more thoroughly than the Russians can destroy us, while everyone else is getting destroyed in the process, is of little interest to most of the peoples of the world." "Can one really believe that a policy of political, economic, and military withdrawal, announced with a tone of condescension to our allies, friends and potential friends can give a platform for success?"[14]

In April 1954, Nitze gave a speech in Boulder, Colorado, titled: "History and Our Democratic Tradition in the Formulation of United States Foreign Policy." Beating a path through the ideas of Thomas Jefferson, George Wilhelm Friedrich Hegel, Karl Marx, Niccolo Machiavelli, and recent headlines, Nitze enumerated the nation's challenges in the 1950s. "The risks with which we are threatened are diverse and interrelated," he averred. "One risk is general, all-out war initiated by the U.S.S.R. either by direct attack on us or on one or more of our principal allies. Another risk is localized communist military aggression. Another is the loss of arms or positions important to the West through internal weakness, intimidation, or subversion. Another is the risk of a general weakening and splitting up of the cohesiveness, will, and power of coordinated action of the free world coalition. And finally there is the domestic risk of loss of fortitude, restraint, and faith in our own institutions." However, the main danger was turning away from "the responsibilities which have fallen to us with respect to the free world coalition."[15]

"It would seem to me that we can do so only if we are prepared gradually to withdraw under pressure to this hemisphere accepting the prospect of Asia, Europe, the Middle East, and possibly Africa, being gradually added to the enemy sphere," Nitze continued, recapitulating the strategic rationale for Franklin Roosevelt's actions in 1940–41 and Harry Truman's in 1946–47. "Then our survival, even as a secondary power, would become contingent on whether or not the Kremlin, unopposed by any power comparable to their own, could successfully coerce and organize the rest of the world." "Cut off from the rest of mankind, subjected to mounting external pressures and humiliations, the time would not be long before domestic faction and dissension destroyed such of our internal freedoms as still remained. We would then have lost that external climate in which our democratic experiment can survive and prosper."[16]

Renouncing US leadership abroad was tantamount to surrender. That was not actually what the Eisenhower administration was doing, but Nitze was in full partisan mode. "The other course, the course of responsible leadership of the free world coalition, is not easy." "It requires that we take no narrow view. It means, above all else, that we must regard the vital interests of those peoples and nations who are members of the coalition as being associated with our own most basic interests. The purposes and policies we pursue must be broad enough to embrace the essential interest of the whole group. The essence of leadership is the successful resolution of problems and the successful attainment of objectives important to those whom one is called upon to lead."[17]

He felt there was no need for a fundamental reconceptualization of US traditions, to which the Truman administration had subscribed in its program of aid to Greece and Turkey, the Marshall Plan, Point Four, networks of alliances, revitalization of the military, the pursuit of the hydrogen bomb, and repulsion of communist aggression in Korea. "In fact it is our belief in truth, in the dignity of the common man, in the consent of the governed, in the independence of nations, in a decent respect to the opinions of mankind, which is the core of our psychological strength and the force which, if backed by adequate material strength, can attract to our leadership nations and peoples all over the world."[18] Such was the essence of NSC-68, the drafting of which Nitze led in 1950—even though that paper remained classified for another two decades.

Uneasy Relationship with Academia

Back in Washington, Nitze developed a "Framework of Theory Useful to the Practice of Politics," which he wrote out in the style of the Enlightenment philosopher Baruch Spinoza in preparation for the seminar he was teaching at SAIS. Despite the encouragement of his SAIS colleague, the acclaimed international relations scholar Arnold Wolfers, he did not turn the framework into a book. While he could lead a large writing project, as he had demonstrated both with the *Summary Report (Pacific Theater)* and NSC-68, he did not possess the same facility for words as George Kennan or academics closely aligned with the Democratic Party such as economist John Kenneth Galbraith and historian Arthur Schlesinger Jr. He was also never comfortable with a discipline like social science; he preferred hands-on policy work.

Emblematic of Nitze's ambivalence toward academia was the fate of his attempt to hire Hans Morgenthau, the author of *Politics among Nations*, who was probably the leading scholar of international relations at the time. Morgenthau came from the University of Chicago to SAIS in 1954, and Nitze must have taken some satisfaction in luring a leading scholar from that particular institution. However, Morgenthau's basic views about the levers of power were incompatible with those of Nitze. "I became thoroughly disillusioned with Hans Morgenthau as being really a rigorous student of the subject," Nitze later recounted. "He had this simplistic idea that the only consideration was the maximization of power on behalf of the State and that's what drove everybody who dealt with foreign policy and this clearly wasn't so. It bore no relationship to the way in which policy was made in the U.S. Government."[19] Realism, in theory, was not the same as realism in practice. Academic models did not adequately account for the frenetic pace by which human beings made decisions based on imperfect information. Morgenthau returned to Chicago.

Lacking a sense of community with leading academics, Nitze took heart in the response of his students. At the end of his one of his seminars, he later recalled with great pride, a student approached him to say that he had not taught them anything new—it was all "just plain common sense." That, to Nitze, was the highest compliment a teacher could receive.[20]

The Cold War in Theory and Practice

Meanwhile, in policy debates, Nitze continued to inveigh against the New Look. In a July 1, 1954, letter to the influential columnist Joseph Alsop, he inserted himself into an exchange between Alsop and Arthur Schlesinger Jr. on the topic of whether to launch a preventive war against the communist world—something that Alsop had proposed following Eisenhower's disinclination to stave off French defeat at Dien Bien Phu, Vietnam, that spring. As someone who had grappled with such topics—especially during the Korean War—Nitze professed to know more than either the journalist or the historian.

Whether or not Eisenhower's inaction in Vietnam could genuinely be "Munich at all costs," as Alsop called it, Nitze wrote that neither the president nor members of the NSC—nor, above all, the American people—supported launching a preventive war that would inevitably lead to the use of nuclear weapons. It was unfair of pundits to argue for something outside the realm of the possible just to have it on record for later on. "It may give you some sense of personal satisfaction later when things go badly to be able to say, if only they had done what I suggested," as Nitze put it, "but that isn't going to help the country one iota." Absent here was any self-reflection on Nitze's part: Was he doing the same thing by claiming that 1958 would mark a deterioration of the United States–Soviet nuclear balance unless Eisenhower heeded his warnings?

Concerning policy makers and the bomb, the gap between theory and practice clearly animated Nitze. Throughout the 1950s, researchers at the RAND Corporation and elsewhere came up with elaborate models that contributed to the emerging field of security studies.[21] These focused on "thinking about the unthinkable" use of nuclear weapons in potential conflicts with the Soviet Union or China. Nitze regarded his calculations and his beloved logic chains as necessary and sufficient to figure out the policies that would avoid nuclear war.

Setting aside the morality and the lack of domestic support for preventive war against the Soviet Union, Nitze contended that the complex strategic calculus of such a war was bleak. The highest amount of damage the United States could anticipate in a first strike would be 50–75 percent of Soviet cities—though these numbers would be likely lower because Soviet citizens would be evacuated before a nuclear exchange—and it could not expect to take out Soviet bombers. The resulting Soviet counterattack would consist of at least 150 atomic weapons reaching targets within the United States. Even taking out 50 percent of incoming Soviet bombers would still lay waste to "a considerable percentage of U.S. centers of population and industry." Nitze asked: Was this scenario—the likely result of preventive war—a better outcome than the present state of affairs? He answered himself: "I can hardly believe that morale would be high in the United States if such an event occurred as a result of policy decision most Americans were wholly against, about which they weren't consulted and, in preparation for which, wholly inadequate measures had been taken."[22]

Implicit in Nitze's closing remarks to Alsop was a question that no president seemed willing to address: What would US and allied "victory" in a general war entail? For instance, would it be a Pax Americana, meaning a peace imposed by the United State upon the rest of the world? In his response to Alsop and Schlesinger, Nitze considered this prospect and cited his inability to obtain final approval of NSC-79, the unfinished "war aims" paper (described in chapter 4) that identified Pax Americana, world government, and balance of power as the three options for a new order following a global war between the United States and Soviet Union. Acheson had declared each potential outcome to be contrary to the fundamental values of the country. That determination emboldened Nitze's conviction that the United States needed sufficient strength to place severe constraints on the Kremlin's appetite for risk-taking. The overriding objective of US strength was to deter war, not initiate it.

RAND scholars such as Herman Kahn dwelled on updating traditional theories of war to fit the nuclear age. Nitze was more practically minded. In his letter to Alsop and Schlesinger, he touched on the geopolitical consequences, based on his wartime experience dealing with allies and the attempt to rebuild Europe from the ashes of World War II. What kind of world would emerge after World War III? It would have to be one that lived up to US values, as demonstrated by how Washington nurtured political and economic coalitions after World War II rather than dictating its will to war-weary people. Pax Americana was decidedly *different from* the approach that the Truman administration took to rebuilding Europe and Asia after 1945: Nitze was convinced—the United States did not count as an empire. "I doubt whether American democracy as we have known it could survive the test" of Pax Americana, he went on to say. "Democracy at home and imperium abroad have rarely mixed well for long."[23]

Nitze yearned for decisive leadership from the White House—as he rather than Alsop envisioned it. "I do not believe leadership consists in advocating a course impracticable by any constitutional standards, dubious as to its outcome if it were practicable, and offensive to all morality, just because it appears neat, bold, and decisive one way or another and all other courses are uncertain, difficult, expensive, and complex." Instead, Nitze wanted Eisenhower and Dulles to increase defense spending and level with the American people that massive retaliation would cost far more money over the long run and make war more likely. "As you know," Nitze wrote Alsop, "I generally felt that the last administration [that of Truman] was doing too little too late . . . The trouble is this administration [that of Eisenhower] is doing less and less beyond issuing empty and misleading statements."[24]

Government Contractor

Nitze's public and private criticisms drew the ire of Secretary of State Dulles, who complained to Vice President Richard Nixon, at a January 13, 1955, meeting of the NSC, about a memorandum to members of Congress criticizing the administration over its proposed mutual defense treaty with Taiwan. This document was written by a "somewhat nebulous group of former members of the State Department" that included Paul Nitze. Dulles thought this one more endeavor "plainly designed to obfuscate the issues and to throw monkey wrenches into the Administration's plans."[25]

There was nothing nebulous about Nitze's connection to the Democratic Party during the Eisenhower era. He stuck with Adlai Stevenson and rallied to the support of Dean Acheson, who remained a bogeyman to the Republican Party but who was also well connected to power brokers in the nation's capital.

What might be said to be nebulous was Nitze's connection to the executive branch of the US government over which Eisenhower presided. Dulles himself had been a consultant to the State Department during the Truman years, while also serving as the top foreign policy aide to the 1944 and 1948 presidential candidate Thomas Dewey. Similarly, from 1954 onward, Paul Nitze served as a consultant to the CIA under the direction of the secretary of state's brother, Allen Dulles. An added layer to Nitze's national security work was that he had set up the Foreign Policy Institute of SAIS to solicit work from the legislative branch.

By 1954, Paul Nitze was working for the US government, advising policy makers of the political party out of power, and castigating the administration in power. With the rise of Federally Funded Research Centers and the proliferation of privately funded think tanks that also accepted government contracts, this would become an increasingly common set of circumstances. However, that would be so a decade later.

In the case of RAND, founded in 1948 to assist the air force, there was not the same fluidity among government, business, and academic circles. Its most prominent figure, Bernard Brodie, remained an academic by profession. His research spoke directly to the concerns of the time, and he invented the discipline of strategic studies as an outgrowth of economics. While Nitze lacked the same level of intellectual depth, he possessed something essential that Brodie lacked: real-life experience in advocating for war plans in front of generals and evaluating the strengths and weaknesses of questions such as whether to pursue the hydrogen bomb and whether or not to use atomic weapons against the enemy during a war. Brodie dazzled other experts who sprang up in the discipline of security studies within this relatively new field of political science. Nitze tended to respect those figures who demonstrated respect for him. After his tenure in the Truman administration, his attitude toward nuclear strategists recalled his reaction to John Maynard Keynes, who published his *General Theory* while Nitze was working on Wall Street: nothing about it added value to what experienced practitioners already knew.

Sometime after 1953, Nitze's old friend Max Millikan, who had gone to MIT to lead the Center for International Studies, invited him to Cambridge for a conference considering how the United States should approach the Soviet Union following the death of Stalin. Participating along with Clyde Kluckhohn (Harvard anthropologist) and Richard Bissell (CIA), Nitze's contribution was to stress the importance of obtaining overhead photography of the USSR as an essential long-term US capability. He took pride in that advice since years later, Bissell, who would become CIA deputy director of plans and then the first head of the National Reconnaissance Office, said that his arguments convinced him to sign off on the U-2 spy plane.[26]

In January 1955, Nitze accepted an invitation from Admiral Norvell Ward and Jerome Wiesner, head of MIT's Research Laboratory of Electronics, to be a consultant for the highly sensitive Project Lamplight, which operated under the auspices of MIT. Its goal was to consider options for the continental air defense of the United States. Nitze tackled the problem of establishing a communications network to link early warning outposts to a central command. He also evaluated a proposal (later called "Texas Towers") to set up a series of giant oil rigs hundreds of miles along the US coast on which radar devices could be placed. These would also pass on early warnings allowing US interceptors to take out incoming Soviet bombers in the event of an attack on the American homeland. On this last project, Nitze pondered how to integrate this ambitious and as-yet untested scientific project with foreign policy and any international legal concerns that were bound to emerge.[27]

Meeting with Wiesner on the MIT campus, Nitze learned about his efforts to harmonize communications from early warning systems in Canada with the newly proposed Pine Tree radar network. As always, Nitze embraced a quest to solve logistical problems. Given the cost of installing landlines to route communications to the radar outposts, Wiesner came up with the idea of bouncing signals off meteor showers using burst transmissions to deny the enemy the opportunity to intercept them. While the project did not finally amount to much, working on it kept Nitze up to speed on the most urgent and highly classified national security concerns. And it compounded his interest in bringing together offensive and defensive capabilities. This pursuit would animate much of his thinking about the evolution of the strategic arms competition between the United States and the Soviet Union. Increasingly, that would focus upon on intercontinental ballistic missiles (ICBMs).

The Soviet Union Up Close

In the summer of 1955, the Nitzes traveled to Moscow, where they met with Ambassador Charles Bohlen and his family. Bohlen had just attended the Geneva summit between the "big four" leaders from the United States, Great Britain, France, and the Soviet Union (with Khrushchev also in attendance).[28] Amidst the new "spirit of Geneva," Nitze's children chided him for his pessimistic view of their destination while marveling at the sites en route from the airport to central Moscow. That scenery failed to impress the elder Nitze. After the family had crossed the Moscow River, "the depressing reality of the city settled around us like a blanket of fog," as he later described it. "Stretches of scarred earth greeted us where buildings had been stopped in mid-construction and abandoned years earlier." The Nitzes eventually arrived at Spaso House, the residence of the US ambassador, which sat in the middle of a slum. Nearby, "A ruined church sagged at one of the squares and pavement was in dire need of repair."[29]

Ambassador Bohlen invited Paul to attend a meeting of the Supreme Soviet. The two men sat together as Nikita Khrushchev and Soviet premier Nikolai Bulganin reported on their recent meeting with President Eisenhower in Geneva. From the diplomatic box, Nitze observed audience members nodding off as Khrushchev and others droned on for hours, and he became fixated on the word *mir*, which he heard repeatedly. Bohlen, who was considered the best Russian speaker in the foreign service, confirmed that *mir* had several meanings—but in this case probably meant victory through socialism. He assessed that the audience responded better to *mir* than to calls for the relaxation of tensions between the superpowers.[30] Nitze's takeaway was that "victory" received more applause than "détente."

After a few days in Moscow, the Nitzes and Bohlens traveled to Leningrad, where the Nitzes visited Peterhof Palace (Peter the Great's architectural attempt to rival Versailles) and wandered around the city. At the Astoria hotel, they were amused to learn that the authorities discouraged dancing. When it came time to depart, the Nitze family flew from Leningrad to Helsinki in a Douglas C-47 Dakota (a modification of the civilian Douglas DC-3 airplane) that the Soviets had received from the Americans as part of Lend-Lease during World War II. Nitze later recalled seeing from the air the starkness of one side of the border between the USSR and Finland and the other. "Everything was shambles on one side, and everything was green and beautifully cared for on the other side." "There was a difference of day and night between looking at Finland from the air and look at the USSR from the air."[31] Even the Nitze children had changed their tune on the Soviet Union, rushing out of the plane when it arrived in Helsinki and exclaiming: "You can feel it, it's free."

The visit to the Soviet Union reinforced Nitze's previously held assumptions. Unlike Bohlen and Kennan, who were deeply steeped in the Russian language and culture, Nitze held no affinity for either. After his thwarted attempt to visit the Soviet Union during his Europe trip after college (as described in chapter 1), he could now tell others he had seen the country up close and that it had lived down to his expectations. Moreover, in assessments of Soviet military capabilities and intentions, he now claimed firsthand expertise. Walking past visible pipes sticking up from the ground near subway stations, Nitze had inquired passers-by about them and was told they were ventilation tubes for the underground civil defense shelters. Some US analysts denied such shelters existed—Nitze would set them straight. In Leningrad, while in between the excursion to Peterhof, and not dancing at the Astoria, Nitze spotted several Chinese individuals who he concluded—though without any hard evidence— were apprenticing in the shipyards and other naval facilities. Such "firsthand" observations only bolstered Nitze's previously held suspicions of close Sino-Soviet cooperation and his conviction that monolithic communism posed a threat to the free world.[32]

"It is quite a different thing to read and argue about a place and actually see it in the flesh," Nitze reported to his friend Charles Burton Marshall in October 1955. "On balance I think I found it somewhat more humane and understandable than I had anticipated but even more worrisome and disturbing," he said. "Basically, it is more of a dump than I had thought but the degree to which they can concentrate on any given objective is really impressive."[33]

The primary Soviet objective was victory, Nitze heard the Supreme Soviet spell that out. Not that the Kremlin intended to wage a nuclear war. Instead, victory meant eroding US strategic and conventional superiority, which would cause US leaders to be deterred from protecting vital interests. "The situation is analogous to a game of chess," as Nitze put it in a January 1956 *Foreign Affairs* article. "The atomic queens may never be brought into play; they may never actually take one of the opponent's pieces. But the position of the atomic queens may still have a decisive bearing on which side can safely advance a limited-war bishop or even a cold-war pawn. The advance of a cold-war pawn may even disclose a check of the opponent's king by a well-positioned atomic queen."[34]

From June to September 1956, Nitze participated in Project Nobska, a summer study organized by Chief of Naval Operations Admiral Arleigh Burke, which called on Nitze, physicist Edward Teller, and other leading physicists and military leaders to come up with ideas for upgrading US anti-submarine warfare. Participants started their deliberations by boarding the USS *Nautilus*, the first US nuclear-powered submarine—so named for the vessel in Jules Verne's *Twenty Thousand Leagues Under the Sea*. Their subsequent discussions laid the foundations for developing the ballistic missile submarine and modernized torpedoes.

Once again, Nitze's involvement was due to his forceful policy advocacy, enthusiasm for improving US technological capabilities, and possession of high-level security clearances—which he retained as a consultant to the CIA. As with the Texas Towers analysis, the expertise he brought to the table relied less on mastery of scientific or military matters than his ability to evaluate the implications of technology through the lens of US national security. "I was asked to translate all this [technology] into the strategic importance of this kind of warfare," as he later wrote. In the ongoing competition between the navy and air force for being at the vanguard of the United States' nuclear arsenal, participants in Project Nobska probably also presumed that Nitze would someday receive some high appointment in a future Democratic presidential administration.

Ike's Reelection and the Establishment of the Center for Foreign Policy Research

Nitze and other Democrats would have to wait. On November 6, 1956, Eisenhower crushed Stevenson in an electoral landslide of 457 to 73. The president's reelection did not fundamentally alter Nitze's professional activities. In 1957, the Rockefeller Foundation, led by Nitze's former State Department colleague (and future secretary of state) Dean Rusk, granted SAIS $300,000 to establish what became the Washington Center of Foreign Policy Research (FPR). Launching such a think tank allowed Nitze to help shape policy debate during the Cold War. "What I tried to do [with FPR] was get a research adjunct to the school, which would deal with the longer-term aspects of current problems that the government, particularly the State Department, the defense establishment, and the Treasury Department, were dealing with."[35]

The establishment of FPR allowed SAIS to attract and retain world-class faculty whose joint appointments would enable them to teach less and write more. Arnold Wolfers could now spend more time on his research, and the university brought on Robert Osgood, another acclaimed realist scholar, who focused on contemporary policy making (and would later serve on the Policy Planning Staff). While Nitze kept his work separate from intelligence, Congress, and other institutions around DC and New York, basic knowledge was fungible. There was nothing "top secret" about rigorous thinking.

Under the auspices of the FPR—and at the behest of the Carnegie Endowment for Peace—Nitze wrote a paper on the prospects of a UN police force. This he sent on to Assistant Secretary for International Organizations Francis Wilcox (who would become dean of SAIS in 1961).[36] This paper recalled work he had overseen back in 1949–53 when he directed the Policy Planning Staff. Whether or not the Eisenhower administration chose to take up his proposals, Nitze was mirroring the internal think tank of the State Department—which itself reflected external think tanks—relying on acquired knowledge from sources inside and outside government. Unlike the Institute for Defense Analysis, which had been established the previous year to be semiautonomous from the Department of Defense, Nitze did not have to worry about someone above him "clearing" his proposals. Thus, by coauthoring papers with

Wolfers or other colleagues, Nitze operated outside the restrictions of government bureaucracy.

Around the same time he set up FPR, Nitze joined Dean Acheson on the Democrats' Advisory Committee on Foreign and Defense Policy. Acheson was a chair with Nitze, the vice chairman. Undeterred by Stevenson's defeat, Nitze reaffirmed his connection to Democratic Party leaders. He lacked passion for a domestic agenda that included bolstering labor unions or advocating for civil rights. His focus remained on national security with an emphasis on external threats. His own politics stemmed from a mixture of personal ambition and realpolitik. The February 24, 1957, issue of *Foreign Policy* included an article by Nitze titled the "'Impossible' Job of Secretary of State." In it, Nitze reveals how he himself might have approached the job.

Introduction to Henry Kissinger

Later in 1957, Nitze joined a Council on Foreign Relations study group to reexamine the impacts of nuclear weapons on foreign affairs. He contributed a pamphlet based on a speech he had previously given, "The Effect of New Weapons Systems on Our Alliances." In this, he contended that nuclear weapons had done little to enhance the security of NATO countries in light of overwhelming Soviet conventional capabilities.[37] The study director, thirty-four-year-old Harvard professor Henry Kissinger, synthesized the work of Nitze and others and then published *Nuclear Weapons and Foreign Policy*, a book that to Kissinger's surprise—and Nitze's chagrin—became a national bestseller.

Nitze and Kissinger were different people. Nitze was not a flatterer. He did not come across as self-deprecating and witty as Kissinger could. Most importantly, Kissinger wrote faster than Nitze. *Nuclear Weapons and Foreign Policy* exposed the fallacy of Eisenhower's stated policy of massive retaliation in the way Nitze might have done following Dulles's 1954 speech had he concentrated his efforts and steadied his aim. Rather than writing a private memorandum to Adlai Stevenson, or a letter to Joe Alsop and Arthur Schlesinger, Nitze might have attempted a Kissinger-type book. But his facility and mastery of the written word did not compare with Kissinger's.

In his review of September 5, 1957, Nitze took Kissinger to task, focusing his criticism on sloppy mathematical calculations related to nuclear yields and other such esoteric matters. He did not write what he believed at the time and afterward: that Kissinger had taken the work of others and published it under his name. Through his writing Kissinger, not Nitze, became the most prominent critic of massive retaliation. Being overshadowed was not new to him.

In his work on the *Summary Report (Pacific Theater)*, Nitze felt he had summed up Stalin's challenge to the United States in the postwar era, drawing on lessons learned from earlier challenges from Nazi Germany and Imperial Japan. He was eclipsed by the more effective writer: George Kennan.

With a similar sense of irony mixed with tragedy, Kissinger could speak about the balance of power in the nineteenth century. Nitze, in contrast, liked to list numbers of nuclear weapons and joust, with neither irony nor tragedy, at nuclear scientists as well as tenured professors. He would explain how such numbers applied to international relations—a project the reading public found less interesting. Thus Kennan and Kissinger became iconic figures of US realism and, consequently, household names. Very few among the Kennan/Kissinger readership cared about the accuracy of nuclear yields.

In an early moment in what became a long-term (and mostly one-sided) rivalry, Kissinger threatened a lawsuit upon reading a draft of Nitze's review of his book. Nitze was surprised by such a response. Kissinger had quickly established himself as an expert on the policy implications of nuclear weapons; by the time Nitze's critical review finally came out, few people noticed. Nitze may have regarded Kissinger as a younger and more aggressive version of himself. Throughout his early career, Nitze had acted audaciously around more senior figures; but he always paid deference to those he believed commanded respect. Although Kissinger generally did likewise, he paid little attention to Nitze. After all, he lacked the academic credentials of Arthur Schlesinger Jr., Kissinger's friend; and he wielded neither the political nor financial clout of Nelson Rockefeller, Kissinger's patron.

The Gaither Report

Nitze and Kissinger found agreement in their low regard for the Eisenhower administration's attitude toward nuclear weapons and its lethargic (as they saw it) responses to imminent national security challenges. Sputnik I, on October 5, 1957, affirmed what they already believed. On that day, the Soviet Union launched into outer space what they called "a traveling companion" the beeping of which could be picked up by radios in households across the United States.

On November 3, Sputnik II delivered a dog named Laika on a one-way trip to the heavens.[38] In the wake of these astounding Soviet achievements, President Eisenhower received a briefing on November 7 from a commission headed by Ford Foundation head Rowan Gaither. This commission, in which Nitze took part, had just published "Deterrence and Survival in the Nuclear Age," also known as the Gaither Report.[39]

Conceived initially as a project to develop ideas meant to strengthen US defenses against a Soviet attack, the Gaither Report expanded into a more comprehensive critique of US preparedness. This was in good part the result of Nitze's participation. "Our early warning radar network could not assure sufficient warning time to our bombers to get them into the air before being destroyed on the ground," Nitze later recounted. "We calculated that ninety percent of our bomber force could be knocked out on the ground by a surprise Soviet bomber attack, let alone an attack by Soviet ICBMs."[40] As a result, the report "emphasized that maintaining an effective second strike force should be our priority. Deterrence . . . was not achieved by the force we had in being during peacetime. Still, by that portion of the force that was capable of surviving a Soviet first strike."[41] When the Gaither Committee met with President Eisenhower on November 7, the president expressed little enthusiasm.

On November 16, Nitze wrote Secretary Dulles a letter expressing his frustration about the Gaither briefing as well as a discussion the day before to which Dulles had summoned Nizte and others. "Finally, assuming that the immediate crisis is surmounted," Nitze wrote Dulles, "I should ask you to consider, in the light of events of recent years, whether there is not some other prominent Republican disposed to exercise the responsibility of the office of Secretary of State in seeking a balance between our capabilities and our unavoidable commitments, equipped to form persuasive policies, and able to secure the confidence and understanding of our allies, whether by direct communication or communication through emissaries."[42] Dulles, asked to find a replacement for himself, took no action.

A few weeks later, Stewart Alsop and Chalmers Roberts wrote about the Gaither Report in the *Washington Post*. The article was written after Roberts had lunched with Nitze, leading one biographer to speculate that Nitze discussed the classified report's details.[43] Evidence neither supports nor rules that out. Nitze was careful to compartmentalize classified and unclassified information, yet he relied on his judgment to determine that distinction. Moreover, the report's gist was consistent with what Nitze had been saying publicly and in his letter to Alsop and Schlesinger about his unsuccessful efforts to sustain increased military spending during the final years of the Truman administration. (Admittedly, in that letter, Nitze took it upon himself to describe details of a classified NSC study.)

Nitze remained plugged into strategic debates for the rest of Eisenhower's second term. In December 1957, he was invited to join the Air Force Advisory Board. Given that both Eisenhower and Dulles regarded Nitze as something of a nuisance, it is unclear whether they realized that he was actually in the employ of their own administration. In a 1958 Senate Foreign Relations study, which he wrote with SAIS professor Arnold Wolfers, Nitze warned of a potential "missile gap" favoring the Soviet Union shortly. Nitze's disdain for Eisenhower and Dulles notwithstanding, he saw his work as impacting their move away from New Look and the doctrine of massive retaliation. He also credited Albert Wohlstetter, who in 1958 published "The Delicate Balance of Terror," a much more influential paper than anything Nitze produced about nuclear weapons. From the perspective of strategic nuclear policy, Nitze considered the second Eisenhower administration to have been better off than the first. He later wrote that the administration "got all the things going which cured the problems which [he] had foreseen in the Gaither Committee," including "the gross vulnerability of our bomber force."[44]

The lesson Nitze took was that his constant barrage of criticism had paid off. No longer did US bombers and tankers lie in close proximity so as to invite a surprise Soviet attack that would cripple US offensive forces. By the end of the second Eisenhower administration, the United States had restored funding for the B-52, placed the first Polaris submarine at sea, and deployed the first Atlas missiles. It had constructed the strategic triad—ICBMs, submarine-launched ballistic missiles (SLBMs), and heavy bombers—that has lasted well into the twenty-first century. In later years, Nitze asserted that US nuclear strength had improved so that "by 1963 we were in strong shape, all that had been gotten underway in the Eisenhower administration so that all the work on improving the accuracy of our bombing and improving the weapons so that they were more accurate . . . was done during the . . . latter part of the Eisenhower administration."[45] The "high priority recommendations" of the Gaither Committee prevailed, in other words, Eisenhower's skepticism notwithstanding. "As a result, the relative strategic position of the United States vis-à-vis the Soviet Union rapidly became both more stable and more favorable to the United States."[46]

Whether or not he acknowledged it, Nitze had internalized the lesson that the threat should be stated in the clearest terms. That had worked—temporarily—with NSC-68 and then again with the Gaither Report. He was convinced that his judgment had been ahead of the curve in both instances. Even as he aspired to obtain a high national security post in the next Democratic administration, he considered himself an analyst who tackled the facts without a partisan filter. Proximity to power was essential. SAIS could not succeed without an apparatus supported by government contracts and foundations run by Nitze's former and future colleagues. While he and Herter initially hoped to train a cadre of business executives in international affairs, and that their companies would then underwrite an endowment for the school, these early aspirations were never realized. SAIS would not have remained in existence without the proximity to power that Nitze nurtured and sustained. On the other side of the coin was Herter, who served for one term as governor of Massachusetts and then became secretary of state following the resignation of John Foster Dulles in 1959.

Years without a full-time appointment in the government placed Nitze in a unique position in the 1950s. "I was very much around [and] probably [knew] more [about] what was going on in the government than I did at any other time," as he later put it, "cause you know more when you're outside the government but still have friends all through it. They'll tell you what's going on. . . . While when you're in a given job you're kind of isolated just to see what's working with the people at your level one echelon above or one echelon below. But you can't get down the bowels of the problem."[47] People told him what they believed was happening, as opposed to what he only "needed to know." While Nitze focused primarily on matters of nuclear and conventional force structures, he had time to travel and learn about new areas of the world. That meant traveling across Africa on a fact-finding trip jointly sponsored by the Council on Foreign Relations and the Carnegie Endowment. Nitze had established himself as an important voice, SAIS provided a base of operations, and there was plenty of money sloshing around.

1960 Campaign and Missile Gap

In 1958, the Eisenhower administration considered using tactical nuclear weapons in response to the People's Republic of China's shelling of the islands of Quemoy and Matsu off the coast of Taiwan. Nitze bet a friend that the off-shore island crisis would blow over. He was pleased when it did, yet also horrified by the reaction of Senator William Fulbright, then the chairman of the Senate Foreign Relations Committee, who confided in him: "You know, Paul, I wish the President had stayed with his decision to use the nuclear weapons . . . it would be terribly interesting to see what would have happened."[48]

Nitze would never have been that cavalier about the potential use of such weapons. At the same time, he was dubious about the prospects of agreements either to limit the testing of nuclear explosions or limit the arsenals of warheads and delivery vehicles. The danger may not yet have arrived, yet it lay on the horizon.

In the spring of 1960, Nitze went to Geneva as a consultant to the US delegation at a UN conference of eight nations on disarmament.[49] The negotiations were "extremely interesting" to him. "The contest between the Russians and ourselves was a contest in establishing which of us was more rigorously

FIGURE 5.1. Nitze and Senator John F. Kennedy at a press conference for the Democratic nominee for president, August 30, 1960. Nitze aspired to obtain a high national security position in Kennedy's administration. Photo by Bettmann/Getty Images.

and absolutely dedicated to the total abolition of nuclear weapons." The Soviets were for the "total and complete abolition of nuclear weapons," while the Americans favored the "phased and complete elimination of nuclear weapons."[50] However, as Nitze saw up close, neither side had any idea of how to achieve its stated objectives.

In the fall of 1960, Nitze contributed material to Democratic presidential nominee John F. Kennedy's foreign policy speeches. A short time after Kennedy defeated Vice President Richard Nixon, President Eisenhower asked his advisers about "what kind of a man Mr. Nitze is"—presuming that he was soon to receive an appointment to high office in the incoming John F. Kennedy administration. Unlike Kissinger, whose nuclear book Eisenhower had assigned subordinates to read, Nitze failed to impress the president with his own criticisms. Nitze "is a very able and dedicated man," responded Under Secretary of the Treasury C. Douglas Dillon (the son of Clarence Dillon), one "extremely embittered against the Republicans because, as a Republican, he was forced to withdraw from consideration for Assistant Secretary of Defense by Senator [William] Knowland early in this administration. He thereupon became a Democrat." Eisenhower's trusted Staff Secretary Andrew Goodpaster "agreed with Mr. Dillon's assessment of Mr. Nitze's capacities. He is very keen and able although he does not have perhaps a personal 'fly wheel' of a size commensurate with his energy and intelligence."[51]

Nitze would have disputed Goodpaster's assessment—although it was probably true. Under two terms of a Republican presidential administration, he had avoided political exile and learned to wield at least some levers of influence. In the United Kingdom, the shadow cabinet comprises senior members of Her (or His) Majesty's Loyal Opposition, usually about twenty in number. The US practice of national security that Nitze established during the Cold War was less formal. Unelected officials spoke for the political party out of power with the expectation of future high appointments. Nitze positioned himself for that opportunity and took full advantage of his current and previous access to classified information. The Atomic Energy Act of 1946, amended in 1954 and 1958, set strict limits on who could access nuclear secrets. As a result, it was exceedingly rare for those outside the military services to obtain them. Paul Nitze could not forget what he had already learned. This made him valuable to Dulles and others in the Eisenhower administration who needed intellectual sounding boards—however much he irked them in person and disparaged them in public.

Nitze's unique accumulation of policy experience was on view at Sunday dinners in Georgetown. These became small interagency meetings where he would encounter such influential journalists as Joseph and Stewart Alsop. He was one of the handful of individuals during the Eisenhower years who understood the challenges of the Cold War. His opinions were informed opinions. He took away from the 1950s the realization that he could shape US national security policy from just outside an administration. No doubt he would have preferred to be fully inside.

CHAPTER 6

Nuclear Crises, 1961–1963

During the 1961 Berlin Crisis and 1962 Cuban Missile Crisis, the United States and the Soviet Union came very close to nuclear war. Paul Nitze would advise President John F. Kennedy throughout. After US planes found evidence of Soviet missiles in Cuba, he served on the storied ExComm. According to Robert F. Kennedy, who crafted a heroic narrative of his brother JFK's role in avoiding precipitous military action, Nitze advocated too strongly for war. The truth is more complicated. Nitze supported more brutal action against Cuba that we now know would have precipitated the use of Soviet nuclear weapons against US forces there. He also opposed limited nuclear options to defend West Berlin—an approach that would have been just as calamitous. Nitze's logic was not that the United States needed to wage war but that the Soviets would back down in light of superior US strategic and conventional forces.

Defusing nuclear crises required careful planning and skillful diplomacy. As assistant secretary of defense for ISA, Nitze engaged in both. Never part of Kennedy's inner circle, Nitze could not play a decisive role in ending the Cuban Missile Crisis. But he did become more confident in his conviction about the need for military strength. Overcoming the prospect of World War III led some policy makers—including President Kennedy himself—to reconsider priorities. Nitze concluded in October 1962 that sustaining US military capabilities and constraining Soviet strength outweighed the cause of preventing nonnuclear states from acquiring nuclear weapons.

President John F. Kennedy

From his position at SAIS at the start of the 1960 Democratic presidential primary, Nitze favored Minnesota senator Hubert Humphrey. His donation to the senator's campaign paid the salary of Humphrey's principal foreign policy adviser, Ernest W. Lefever, a former SAIS postdoctoral fellow. When Humphrey withdrew after losing to JFK in the West Virginia primary, Nitze threw his support behind the senator from Massachusetts. "It was a charmed circle, a charmed group, entitled to the charmed life by virtue of beauty and grace," Nitze later said of the Kennedys and their entourage. "[W]ere they really that beautiful, witty, and graceful?" Forty years later, he was uncertain.[1]

Nitze's esteem for JFK increased when he testified before then-senator John F. Kennedy's Subcommittee on African Affairs in 1959. "I was impressed by John at that first meeting," Nitze later recounted. "He listened carefully, absorbing information and ideas for use when the occasions arose." In addition, JFK was "young, intelligent, attractive, and energetic," and Nitze admired these attributes.[2]

On November 9, 1960, one day after JFK defeated Vice President Richard Nixon in the presidential election, Nitze submitted a report, "Basic Strategic Judgments," which he had coauthored at Kennedy's behest.[3] The portion dealing with nuclear weapons was drawn from a talk he had given in Asilomar, California, in 1960.[4] This report posed the question—one easier to ask than answer—of whether the United States should secure a "win" capability or merely seek to deny the Soviets from achieving that advantage. "Basic Strategic Judgments" also called for a top-level appointee on nuclear matters who would report to the president through the secretary of state. William Foster would come to fill just such a position when Congress authorized the creation of the Arms Control and Disarmament Agency (ACDA) in 1961.

President-elect Kennedy arranged for Nitze to work out of an office in the Department of Treasury and monitor a plunge in the dollar's value. He also tasked Nitze to lead a small team that included the outgoing secretaries of state and defense, Christian Herter and Thomas Gates, to evaluate a proposal for "Missile X," a road-mobile system for intermediate-range missiles that NATO operators would drive on highways in West Germany, Belgium, and Holland. "Mr. Kennedy asked me to hold the hands of Gates and Herter," was how

Nitze remembered the circumstances. "We came to the conclusion that [Missile X] was a bad idea."[5]

Nitze also influenced the selection of JFK's cabinet, a process led by President Harry Truman's fixer Clark Clifford and the highly respected former defense secretary, Robert Lovett, who had supported Nitze during his prior tenure as undersecretary of state. For the position of secretary of state in 1961, Nitze advocated for his friend Dean Rusk, the former assistant secretary of state for Far Eastern affairs. As president of the Rockefeller Foundation during the Eisenhower administration, Rusk had authorized a grant to establish the Foreign Affairs Research Center at SAIS—obviously a Nitze project. Emblematic of the close nexus among policy makers and private foundations, Lovett, the chairman of the board of the Rockefeller Foundation, saw to it that Rusk—who, unlike many of his Cold War peers, grew up poor—received a "generous termination allowance."[6]

President-elect Kennedy initially offered Nitze to choose among the posts of undersecretary of state for economic affairs, national security adviser, or deputy secretary of defense. Nitze rejected the position of undersecretary of state for economic affairs because he held the equivalent office during the Truman administration. He turned down national security adviser, believing it to be a position of little importance (JFK's second choice, McGeorge Bundy, turned it into one of the most influential positions in the US government). Nitze chose deputy secretary of defense. However, when the incoming secretary of defense Robert McNamara insisted that the choice of deputy was his to make, he favored Roswell Gilpatrick. Robert Lovett called Nitze to offer him the consolation prize of assistant secretary of defense for international affairs.

ISA

Nitze seemed unperturbed by this downgrade to the same position that John Foster Dulles had offered him in 1953. (The earlier offer had been withdrawn owing to conservative backlash.) While it undoubtedly displeased Nitze that Lovett—rather than the president-elect—made the phone call, he soldiered on. As always, Nitze stayed close to those wielding the levers of influence. His job title was of less consequence.

The Pentagon's Office of International Security Affairs, or ISA, had gained a reputation as a miniature hybrid of the Departments of State and Defense. Crafting military assistance packages for those countries that the United States deemed susceptible to communist penetration, for instance, required diplomatic engagement with foreign counterparts on top of defense planning and bureaucratic maneuvering. In later years, as the Office of the Secretary of Defense grew even larger, the position would become subordinate to the under secretary of defense for policy, which was created in 1978. In 1961, leading ISA meant that Nitze enjoyed a direct line to McNamara, accompanied him to the White House for meetings of the NSC, and managed a team equivalent in size to that which he had directed on the Policy Planning Staff during the period 1950–53.

Meanwhile, the new holder of Nitze's previous job directing the Policy Planning Staff, MIT professor Walt Rostow, had recently written *The Stages of Economic Growth: A Noncommunist Manifesto* and now set out to write a basic US national security strategy. Though Nitze took pride in his grasp of economic matters, he steered clear of debating. At ISA, he directed his energies toward nuclear policy and its implications for US alliances. But that was not all. Nitze regarded ISA as the focal point of national security policy, following in the lineage of forerunners such as the War Department's Operations and Plans Division during World War II and the Joint Staff and Policy Planning Staff during the early Cold War. This would supplant what Nitze considered to be the "ad hoc" manner of John Foster Dulles, Dwight Eisenhower, and Charles Wilson during the previous eight years.

"During Mr. Kennedy's regime, policy was really made—well, it wasn't made by the Policy Planning Staff at the State Department," Nitze later recounted. "It was not really made by 'Mac' Bundy and the NSC staff, and it was not being made by the [military] services. Therefore—We in the ISA would have to supply the missing component when it was necessary, and we would try to do that by working as closely as we could with people in the State Department, either the Policy Planning Staff or people in the regional bureaus, and with the military—the JCS [Joint Chiefs of Staff], the Joint Staff—the Joint Strategic Survey Committee, and relying on information from the CIA."[7] Nitze answered to no one except his immediate boss, Secretary of Defense McNamara, who, in turn, answered to the president.

Everyone found dealing with McNamara taxing. Nitze once confided to a friend that McNamara caused him to spend a week in the hospital. Nevertheless, they started with similar outlooks. Both had worked the statistics side of US strategic bombing during World War II and shared faith that the rigorous application of logic could solve seemingly intractable problems. In his memoir and elsewhere, Nitze told a story that encapsulates the compatibility of his way of thinking with that of McNamara—whether or not they came to the same conclusions. While attempting to reconcile competing positions on how to set up sensor arrays to monitor nuclear explosions (in support of a potential approach to the Soviets on a test ban treaty), Nitze lamented to McNamara that different scientists were giving him different answers. McNamara recommended that he write down fifty important issues on the back of fifty notecards, gather together every expert on each topic, and then make fifty decisions. Nitze complied. "Policy evolved ineluctably from the decisions on the cards," he would later put it—though he would also admit that a number of the resultant decisions later proved to be wrongheaded.[8]

Nitze's role in national security did not change much from the eight years he spent "outside" of government. He worked on many of the same topics. And because he had participated in many governmental study groups during the Eisenhower administration, he was better prepared than McNamara, Rostow, or Bundy, especially regarding US intelligence and military capabilities. Moreover, he continued to oversee the preparation of reports about threats and opportunities. The main difference was that now he wrote primarily for the president via the secretary of defense.

Nitze never ingratiated himself with the Kennedys. Nor did he become a friend to the chiefs of the armed services who distrusted Kennedy and disliked McNamara. Chief of staff of the US Air Force Curtis LeMay never forgave Nitze for his work on the Strategic Bombing Survey in which he criticized the US air campaign against Japan that LeMay himself had designed. While visiting Strategic Air Command Headquarters in Omaha, Nebraska, Nitze apparently lectured LeMay about Bernard Brodie's central thesis in *The Absolute Weapon*—that atomic weapons would deter wars, not win them.[9] "This fellow Paul Nitze is one of our greatest headaches," stated an "unnamed general"—potentially LeMay—in *Newsweek* a short time later. "He wants to throw the A-bombs out and fight with bayonets. That's what all that limited-war talk is about."[10]

Nitze was not proposing to throw out atomic weapons. US strategic (i.e., nuclear) superiority was, he thought, necessary but not sufficient to waging—and ultimately winning—the Cold War. Only from a position of strength could US presidents repel Soviet efforts to isolate West Berlin, encourage revolutionary nationalism in Africa and Southeast Asia, and—most importantly—create a forward base on the island of Cuba. Building up strength meant sustaining nuclear and nonnuclear capabilities to deter any conceivable form of Soviet risk-taking.

Bay of Pigs

On January 22, 1961, Paul Nitze attended a principals-level meeting about Cuba, where Fidel Castro had seized power in 1959 and later proclaimed himself the leader of a socialist revolution in league with Moscow.[11] Two days later, Nitze met with President Kennedy, National Security Advisor Bundy, and Secretary of State Rusk to discuss the situation in Laos, where the United States was supporting General Nosavan Phoumi's faltering efforts to defeat the communist-led Pathet Lao. (The new president faced the decision of whether the United States should intervene.)[12] Finally, when it came to the Congo, where Patrice Lumumba had been executed on January 17, 1961, the uranium-rich country teetered on the brink of civil war while Moscow and Beijing vied for the support of its left-wing factions. Here Nitze favored strengthening the UN mandate. He endorsed the position of the Joint Chiefs of Staff that the United States could intervene militarily without jeopardizing its commitments to Europe and Asia, and recommended devising a "fall-back position" for measures short of US military involvement.[13]

When it came to Cuba, Nitze supported swift action. CIA officer C. Tracy Barnes relayed to Deputy Director Richard Bissell: "A comment by Paul Nitze to me on 23 February to the effect that as far as he was concerned, we should go ahead and do it."[14] While "it" is unclear, one possibility is the plan that Barnes—who had crafted the Eisenhower administration's successful efforts to topple Guatemalan president Jacobo Árbenz Guzmán in 1954—was developing to overthrow Castro.

Had Nitze reservations about Operation Zapata, codename for the Bay of Pigs invasion, he did not convey them to the president in a meeting on April 4 at which Senator William Fulbright expressed his own skepticism.[15] He later recalled that counterinsurgency expert Edward Landsdale had told him it was "badly organized, poorly prepared, and, on its current course doomed to failure."[16] The infamous effort, which would prove damaging to Kennedy, went ahead on April 17.

Neither Nitze, nor apparently anyone else in the new administration, considered the spectacular failure of the Bay of Pigs invasion to prompt a scaling back of an ongoing campaign to weaken Castro. On April 24, Nitze sent McNamara a memo in response to a series of proposals from Policy Planning director Walter Rostow, among which Nitze supported the following: "(a) to quietly build up the internal capabilities of Latin American countries, (b) to develop all possible intelligence on the Castro regime, (c) to exploit this intelligence, (d) to develop a contingency plan, and (e) to think again before acting in the old grooves."[17] While Nitze opposed making public US intentions toward the island, he was committed to ongoing attempts to degrade or destroy the Castro regime. Asked by the president to chair an interagency task force on Cuba, Nitze submitted a report on May 4 citing the dangers that Castro posed to Central America and evaluating measures to contain Castro or drive him back to the hills whence he came. In an NSC meeting on May 5, Nitze reported to President Kennedy that "the Navy could blockade the island but results would not be immediate but rather long-range, and in the course thereof unfavorable world reaction would probably accrue."[18] As Admiral Arleigh Burke concluded in his readout of that meeting: "It was decided that sooner or later we probably would have to intervene in Cuba, but that now is not the time."[19]

Vienna Summit

When the two men met in Vienna in June 1961, Soviet leader Nikita Khrushchev lambasted President Kennedy for the Bay of Pigs. The Kennedy administration's ongoing attempts to destabilize Castro likely contributed to Khrushchev's sense that he needed to escalate over both Berlin and Cuba—starting with verbal belligerence. In 1958, Khrushchev had triggered the so-called Berlin Crisis by threatening to sign a separate treaty with the German Democratic Republic (East Germany) that would abrogate the rights of the United States, the United Kingdom, and France to maintain troops in West Berlin. When Kennedy met with Khrushchev in Vienna, his thinking was that the United States and its NATO allies could not credibly pledge to defend West Berlin using only conventional forces.

Only the threat of using nuclear weapons could defend Berlin. This reality provided the Soviets with a propaganda advantage—they could legitimately contend that the West would be the first to use nuclear weapons in a potential war. This, in turn, could hamstring US efforts to shore up even its own hemisphere. A key factor behind the indecisiveness over the Bay of Pigs—i.e., whether to provide US air support—was that nearly everyone in the Kennedy administration expected that Khrushchev would respond to a full-out invasion of Cuba by taking action in West Berlin. During a moment that Soviet notetakers purposely left out of the transcripts, Khrushchev dared Kennedy to act: "If the US wants to start a war over Germany, let it be so; perhaps the USSR should sign a peace treaty right away and get it over with."[20]

At the Vienna Summit, Nitze represented the Department of Defense in a meeting between Secretary of State Rusk and the Soviet foreign minister Andrei Gromyko over whether a "troika" of nuclear monitors (the United States, Soviet Union, and one neutral country) could verify an agreement on limiting nuclear testing. Gromyko stonewalled. From witnessing this and picking up on Khrushchev's badgering of Kennedy, Nitze intuited that the Soviets were emboldened to take risks because conventional and nuclear balance trends favored their side. US capabilities had to reinforce Kennedy's stated positions.

When Nitze saw a memorandum of a conversation between Kennedy and Khrushchev, he scribbled next to a reference to US objectives: "This would not be possible if there were a further shift in the balance of power to the Soviet side."[21]

The "further shift" was deliberate. In the first six years of the Eisenhower administration, Nitze witnessed what he considered a capitulation: lax planning for strategic capabilities. He took at least some credit for improvements made in the final two years. This did not mean that the United States had lost its position of strategic superiority: it foretold that the Soviets expected that to happen by the end of the 1960s. While Nitze had made similar assessments in 1946, 1950, and 1957—incorrectly as it turns out—that did not necessarily mean he was wrong in 1961. Nor was he an outlier within an administration led by a president who famously stated in his inaugural address: "only a few generations have been granted the role of defending freedom in its hour of maximum danger."[22]

Nitze welcomed President Kennedy's acknowledgment of the present danger. But he did not, himself, have to face voters. Consistent with his views from earlier years—in which he led the crafting of the *Summary Report (Pacific War)*, NSC-68, and the Gaither Report—Paul Nitze insisted that Americans could and ought to pay *much more* for a defense posture to deter the Soviets from attacking Berlin or anywhere else. Neither tax cuts nor domestic spending on public works or health care resonated with him. As before, Nitze's reports landed on the desks of publicly elected officials who had to stand before their constituents and assure them that their taxes yielded tangible results. After eight years of the Eisenhower administration that built thousands of nuclear weapons and succeeded in balancing the budget and reducing military expenditures, the Kennedy administration passed a large tax cut and asked for more troops to defend West Berlin. The objective was to stimulate economic growth and pivot away from massive retaliation. By Nitze's chains of logic, these measures were wholly inadequate to meet the challenge the Soviet Union posed to the American way of life.

Berlin Crisis

Diplomacy was plausible, but only if the Kennedy administration ruled out any concessions to Soviet negotiators. "My position was that we should go to great lengths to avoid war, general or limited, over Berlin," Nitze later recounted. "But if we were to be routed out of a rightful position, we should not legitimize the act through a negotiated agreement." To back down over

Berlin, under such circumstances: that could hardly be termed a "negotiation," it would be a surrender.[23]

In March 1961, President Kennedy asked former secretary of state Dean Acheson to lead a study of the Berlin situation and develop contingency plans. Acheson relied on Nitze to write the report, which linked US global prestige to the fate of the divided city. If the Soviets drove the Americans (and the United Kingdom and France) out of West Berlin, other European countries would reorient themselves toward Moscow, and it would embolden national liberation movements in Asia and Africa. The message would be that the United States backed down; this would encourage further Soviet probing and propensity to take risks. Based on Nitze's report Acheson recommended that the president call for a large supplemental for the defense budget and declare a national emergency.

Secretary of Defense McNamara tasked Nitze with drafting contingency plans to keep a military conflict over Berlin below the threshold of nuclear war.[24] With vigor, Paul tackled such questions: "If access to Berlin is blocked, do we undertake an airlift? Do we immediately probe? What if the probe is turned back? What is the capability of the military force available?"[25] Meanwhile, on July 15, 1961, he lunched with Soviet ambassador Mikhail Menshikov at the Metropolitan Club and warned him that nuclear war was a real possibility. "The computations were not difficult to make of what would happen to Russia if a thousand megatons were dropped, if 7,000 megatons were dropped, if 10,000 megatons, or even if 20,000 megatons were dropped," Nitze coldly observed to his guest, who was heading home for a month's vacation.[26]

At that moment, President Kennedy's inner circle was more cautious about how tough to get over Berlin. "I believe there is general agreement in the steering group that a national emergency is not now necessary," National Security Advisor McGeorge Bundy wrote JFK, "but a hard wing of the Kohler group [working the Berlin issue], led by Acheson and Nitze, disagrees."[27] When President Kennedy met with the task force on July 26, Nitze and Acheson did not press their case for declaring a national emergency. Later that day, the president announced an additional $3.2 billion in defense spending yet declined to make the giant spectacle that Acheson had recommended and which Nitze supported.[28]

The question of what to do about Berlin was tightly linked to the United States' commitment to extended deterrence within the rest of NATO, which the Federal Republic of Germany (West Germany) joined in 1955. To preserve the alliance, the US president needed to convince his Soviet counterpart that he was willing to use nuclear weapons in the event of an attack on Western European allies. So long as leaders in the Kremlin considered this threat to be credible, it should deter them from launching an attack. And, so long as leaders in NATO countries believed both things, it would keep them from seeking a separate accommodation—as French president Charles de Gaulle seemed to be doing in his overtures to Moscow.[29]

Nitze savored this problem, to which his "tension between opposites" model was clearly applicable. By the logic of extended deterrence, stability rested upon a US commitment to wage nuclear war and invite a counterattack on the US homeland in response to any attack on another country. While such a commitment vastly exceeded anything Woodrow Wilson had proposed at Paris in 1919, Congress had duly ratified the North Atlantic Treaty in 1949, before the advent of hydrogen bombs on ICBMs. To prevent an active conflict over Berlin from escalating to the point where one side used nuclear weapons, Nitze was sure that the United States needed to establish conventional capabilities to deter a conventional Soviet attack—or, should deterrence fail, combat Soviet forces long enough for Kremlin leaders to reconsider their plans. However, building conventional troops strong enough to deter a conventional Soviet attack might *also* broadcast to NATO allies that US leaders were ultimately unwilling to use nuclear weapons to defend them—a prospect that had led the United Kingdom and France (and, by 1961, US and allied leaders were concerned, potentially also West Germany) to pursue their independent arsenals. No such concerns would arise if the United States sustained strategic and conventional superiority.

As Nitze had come to understand during the late 1940s, Europeans expressed even more reticence than Americans regarding increased military spending. The postwar economic recovery that took off after the Marshall Plan and lasted throughout the 1950s had not altered that enduring reality. From the perspective of Nitze and other national security practitioners, the *perception* of détente between East and West often sapped the will of democracies to divert resources from social programs to pay for military capabilities that visibly conveyed toughness and cohesion—even as those capabilities were deemed necessary to induce the Soviets to seek a relaxation of tensions.

Deterrence rested on the credibility of threats. When it came to nuclear weapons, the United States needed a clear plan for how it would employ nuclear weapons in the event of war. In late July 1961, McNamara and Nitze traveled to NATO's Supreme Headquarters to consult with its "Live Oak" unit about plans to maintain access to Berlin in the event of Soviet denial of such access. Supreme Allied Commander, Europe, General Lauris Norstad, expressed understandably grave concerns about what would happen in the event of war. The sequence of planned actions made no sense to Norstad, who considered the Single Integrated Operations Plan (SIOP) useless.

Earlier that month, on July 5, 1961, the acclaimed game theorist Thomas Schelling wrote JFK laying out how the president should respond to a Soviet closure of the allies' access to Berlin. First, the president should send a small force down the autobahn from West Germany to Berlin. Then, should that force meet resistance, the president should escalate by employing "nuclears"—in tandem with simultaneous messages and accompanying restraint—to bargain with Soviet leaders. "It is not likely that the Soviets would allow a precedent for US unilateral use of nuclears," Schelling concluded. "Because time will be short, there must be imaginative advance exploration of what Soviet responses, nuclear and verbal, to anticipate and how to interpret them. (The possibility of Soviet initial selective use in a bargaining strategy must also be explored, so that we can interpret it and respond appropriately.)"[30] According to Bundy's notation, this memo reached Kennedy in Hyannis Port the weekend of July 21 and made a "deep impression" on the president. Deep impression notwithstanding, Schelling's plan offered up more questions than practical answers for how to deal with the problems at hand and how to prepare for ones that could emerge in a war over Berlin.

Neither the doubt expressed by General Norstad nor the game plan proposed by Schelling instilled confidence that the Kennedy administration had good options for responding to Soviet aggression. Meanwhile, Nitze was vacationing with his family on Mount Desert Island in Northeast Harbor, Maine (August 13), when word came that the *Volkspolizei* (East German police) had set up a wall made out of barbed wire and assorted rubble. As with the attack on Pearl Harbor and Korea's outbreak of war, Nitze hurriedly returned to the nation's capital. This time, the president and secretary of defense looked to him for answers.

East German authorities had yet to pour concrete in the first days of the Berlin Wall; allied troops could easily have knocked down the barriers. Such action would have precipitated a likely Soviet response, potentially leading both sides up the escalation ladder. Moreover, intelligence reports indicated that East German and Soviet divisions were surreptitiously moving to encircle Berlin. Nitze took this to mean they were not bluffing. Had the Soviets and East Germans intended merely to intimidate the United States and its NATO allies, he reasoned, they would have made a more public demonstration. Nitze felt that knocking down those temporary barriers was too great a risk.

Nitze acted as both a policy adviser and diplomat during this time. In addition to representing the Department of Defense on the Berlin Task Force, he also led a subgroup on military planning for the Washington Ambassadorial Group, which consisted of the United States, Great Britain, and France. Through the Washington Ambassadorial Group, he discerned the allies' concerns; through the Berlin Task Force, he incorporated these concerns into a practical strategy. The result, "Poodle Blanket," laid out a sequence of graduated responses and applicable procedures to simultaneously de-escalate a military conflict over Berlin and position US and allied forces to respond to additional Soviet escalation.

On October 3, 1961, President Kennedy queried his advisers whether a nuclear war over Berlin would remain limited or lead inexorably to a general nuclear war.[31] The mood was grim. According to Nitze's notes, the usually taciturn secretary of state, Dean Rusk, called for "pulling down the house, because the house is lost anyway."[32] On October 9, Nitze went to the Soviet embassy in Washington to meet with Soviet ambassador Dobrynin. To his claim that the Soviets could destroy Germany within ten minutes, Nitze countered that the United States could just as quickly take out Moscow or Leningrad.[33]

At 11 p.m. on October 10, President Kennedy assembled his national security team in the Cabinet Room to consider Nitze's "Poodle Blanket" paper, at one point asking "whether in fact there was much likelihood that IV. A. and B. could be undertaken without leading to IV. C.," which was general nuclear war. On this, Nitze disagreed with his boss, Robert McNamara, in front of the president, contending that "since IV A. and B. would greatly increase the temptation to the Soviets to initiate a strategic [nuclear] strike of their own, it would be best for us, in moving toward the use of nuclear weapons, to consider most seriously the option of an initial strategic strike of our own." He went on to say "that with such a strike, we could in some real sense be victorious in the series of nuclear exchanges, while we might well lose if we allowed the Soviets to strike first in the strategic battle."[34]

In other words, Nitze was saying that there was no way to wage a successful limited nuclear war: if the United States struck first—which, in the dire scenario of an imminent nuclear war, it should do—it needed to strike hard at Soviet missiles and bombers before they reached US allies in Europe and the American homeland. This is as explicit a conversation in the White House about using nuclear weapons against the Soviets as is on record during the Cold War. In the parlance of nuclear theorists, Nitze advocated for "damage limitation" and "counterforce" as the only alternatives to a conventional defense of West Berlin. Victory was possible in a nuclear exchange only if the United States preempted a Soviet attack with a large wallop of its own. Soviet consideration of US strategic superiority—which was diminishing yet still viable—ought ultimately to lead them to back down.

Khrushchev did back down. On October 17, 1961, the Soviet leader announced that he would no longer seek a separate treaty with East Germany by the end of that year. The Berlin Wall staunched the flow of East Germans fleeing westward, but the matter was hardly resolved. On October 23, President

Kennedy signed off on the approach that Nitze called for in the "Poodle Blanket." National Security Action Memorandum (NSAM) 109, "US Policy on Military Actions in a Berlin Conflict," formalized categories of responses ranging from a naval blockade to selective nuclear strikes to general nuclear war.[35] Four days later, US and Soviet tanks faced each other down after an incident near the Berlin crossing. The prospect of war remained even after Khrushchev ended the immediate crisis he had commenced.

Throughout that fall, Nitze and McNamara prepared a "rationale" paper intended to bring NATO allies on board with NSAM 109. Nitze never ruled out the prospect of the United States using nuclear weapons.[36] He remained vehemently opposed to a limited nuclear strike intended to signal restraint— one of the approaches Schelling had suggested. There was no such thing for Nitze as a limited nuclear war. It was yet another reason for the United States and NATO allies to increase the conventional defenses of Europe. Americans needed to pay more, and Europeans especially needed to pay more. Only the Soviets needed to spend less on defense.

Overall US nuclear superiority may have been one of the factors behind Khrushchev's decision to back down. Yet that advantage was not substantively different from the start of the Berlin Crisis back in 1958. Nor had it changed from the beginning of the summer of 1961, when Khrushchev signed off on the wall's construction. Top scholars of nuclear history continue to ponder these issues. Those who approach the matter of nuclear weapons and politics from a quantitative lens see it as an example of a superior power compelling an inferior nuclear power to back down and thus concede victory to the United States.[37] Others argue that "coding" the resolution of the Berlin Wall as a victory or defeat presumes that it was actually a victory or defeat for one side.[38]

There was no doubt about any of this in Nitze's mind. As he said in a December 1961 speech to the Institute for Strategic Studies in London, the United States and its allies possessed "a definite nuclear superiority." The United States believed "this superiority, particularly when viewed from the Soviet perspective to be strategically important in the equations of deterrence and strategy."[39] US nuclear superiority was the prerequisite for Khrushchev's backing down over Berlin. Demonstrating resolve, the Kennedy administration had impelled Khrushchev to abandon his pursuit of a separate treaty.

Strength and Resolve

The showdown over Berlin led to modest efforts to pursue arms control, and Nitze was skeptical of them. In meetings of the NSC Principals Committee throughout 1962, Nitze opposed formulas that would lock in Soviet advantages. On March 1, he stated that "an across-the-board cut of 30% in all armaments would freeze the inferiority of the United States in conventional armaments," and he "wondered how our allies would react to such a freeze in US conventional inferiority vis-à-vis the Soviet Union."[40]

When the group met with President Kennedy, on March 9, Nitze suggested "a possible alternative proposal in which we would withdraw our offer of a moratorium [on testing] upon treaty signature but would agree to a complete ban without a threshold as soon as elements of the control system became operational." He also "pointed out that this would maintain the laboratories during the period when Soviet intentions to fulfill the treaty were being tested."[41] Unfortunately, in these meetings and subsequent ones, Nitze and the other members of Kennedy's team argued with each other about potential approaches to the Soviets without any urgency or any sense of optimism.

On April 13, 1962, Nitze met with West German chancellor Konrad Adenauer in Bonn and assured him that "Washington would do nothing on Berlin without [Adenauer's] agreement." He said "the US has conducted all of the talks with the Soviets about Berlin along the lines of papers mutually agreed upon among the four powers, without any concessions which deviate from these agreed papers, subject to certain reservations contained in them. The US wants a joint position with the FRG and the UK and, as far as possible, with France."[42] Preserving the Western alliance, in other words, was worth the wait on figuring out a long-term settlement on Berlin.

Far more important—at least from Nitze's perspective—was continuing to build up sufficient conventional forces to deter the Soviets in Berlin and sustain the United States' nuclear advantage that was holding the Kremlin in check. "It seems to me that the resulting position is too weak," Nitze wrote McNamara in June 1962 after the secretary deleted a section of the draft Basic National Security Policy that linked a "stable military environment" to the ability of US strategic forces to leave the Sino-Soviet bloc's forces "worsened drastically as a result of a general nuclear war." "To say that our strategic forces should only be able to worsen the Bloc's power position in a general nuclear war is to set too modest an objective," Nitze asserted. "The ability to worsen the Bloc's power position as the result of a general nuclear war would be easily satisfied in an absolute sense with a much less effective strategic retaliatory force than we provide for in our present 5-year plan." The US ability to "worsen the Bloc's power position" would not suffice the next time Khrushchev tested the resolve of the United States and its allies, whether over Berlin or Cuba or elsewhere. At the heart of the matter was the "concept of the relative strength of the US to that of the Soviet Union."[43]

Preserving US strength was the paramount objective for Nitze as the Kennedy administration undertook arms control initiatives under the auspices of the recently established ACDA. The number of warheads and delivery vehicles that Moscow and Washington controlled was only part of the challenge. "There are indications because of new inventions, that 10, 15, or 20 nations will have a nuclear capacity, including Red China, by the end of the Presidential office in 1964," then-senator Kennedy had stated in one of his presidential debates with Vice President Richard Nixon in 1960. In a July 30, 1962, meeting of now-president Kennedy and his national security team, Nitze "discussed the situation during the next ten years in China, Sweden, India, Japan, Australia and South Africa, including the capabilities of these States to produce nuclear weapons and the restraints involved in their deciding to seek a nuclear capability," and "acknowledged that in Germany and Italy pressure for nuclear capability was very great." The cost of producing nuclear weapons over the next decade would drop drastically if the United States and Soviet Union continued testing and improving their weapons.[44] The best way to address the problem of proliferation was to strike a verifiable deal with the Soviets that preserved US nuclear superiority. The worst way was to allow the Soviets to attain nuclear supremacy.

Meanwhile, Berlin remained unsettled a year after the wall went up. At an NSC meeting on August 29, 1962, JFK and his advisers discussed whether to continue allowing Soviet troops periodic access to the war memorial in the Tiergarten inside West Berlin. "The Soviet Union is pushing the Western Powers out of East Berlin, and at the same time striving to make West Berlin a Four-Power city in which they have an active role," Secretary of State Dean Rusk put it. He continued: "The problem on which we must shortly make a decision is thus whether we should not begin to head off the Soviet efforts to increase their role in West Berlin."[45] Nitze agreed. The issue was whether the United States would "control the terms on which they could come to Berlin." If not, the United States was on a trajectory toward a "Four-Power West Berlin."

Whatever the president decided, Nitze said, "we must be prepared to respond to Soviet refusal to accede to it." He proposed to "block their access to West Berlin if they do not accede to whatever request we think appropriate." The president expressed reluctance to take action over what Secretary Rusk noted was ultimately a "symbolic" matter. Nitze urged immediate action—"it was better to take the risks of action now than to defer them."[46] His views failed to carry the day.

Nitze was concerned that Khrushchev's self-confidence and appetite for risk were intensifying. The previous week, on August 23, Rusk, McNamara, CIA director John McCone, and Chairman of the Joint Chiefs of Staff Lyman Lemnitzer sent the president a joint report on the implications of recent Soviet intelligence estimates. These came from the interagency working group on defense policy led by Nitze. Given what we now know was happening—unbeknownst then to the Americans—ninety miles off the coast of Florida the report's conclusion #3 was playing out. "The Soviets previously were willing to act only with caution on the basis of a capability which they knew existed mainly in their opponents' minds," the report stated. "Their appraisal of risks may change now that their capability has become real and is growing." Still, it was doubtful that Soviet leaders would "abandon caution in Soviet–American confrontations, including Berlin." Ultimately, they "recognize that there are limits to the challenges which they can pose without incurring the risk of military response by the US."[47] Meanwhile, throughout that summer, just as Nitze was growing increasingly impatient with President Kennedy's reluctance to take action over Berlin, the Soviets were shipping medium and intermediate-range nuclear missiles to Cuba.

Cuban Missile Crisis

On August 31, 1962, Senator Frank Keating of New York delivered a speech on the Senate floor alleging that he had been "reliably informed" that the Soviets were constructing missile bases in Cuba. While the Kennedy administration publicly denied these charges—which came from West German intelligence, although Keating's source became a long-standing Cold War mystery—they paid attention to them.[48] On September 14, 1962, Paul Nitze participated in a meeting of the Special Group that included National Security Advisor McGeorge Bundy and Attorney General Robert F. Kennedy. When the conversation turned to Cuban reconnaissance, CIA deputy director Marshall Carter referred to "special efforts . . . to identify certain installations the nature of which is not clear at present."[49] Senator Keating had gotten it right.

On the evening of Monday, October 15, Nitze found himself at the State Department dinner for the West German foreign minister. Secretary of State Rusk took him aside, ushered him onto the eighth-floor terrace overlooking the National Mall, and told him that photos from a US U-2 spy plane showed Soviet missiles in Cuba. Both men knew at the time that US contingency plans for Soviet weapons in Cuba consisted of an air attack and an invasion, and realized that these U-2 images likely portended war.

As part of the effort to keep the news secret, Kennedy administration officials attended their scheduled events, which for Nitze meant speaking in Knoxville, Tennessee, on Tuesday, October 16 (incredibly) on civil defense.

When he returned to Washington, Nitze joined the now-fabled ExComm, at the meetings of which he took copious notes. Apart from JFK and RFK, participants knew nothing about a taping system that the president had installed. But this technology did not catch all relevant conversations. Those held at the State Department, with neither the president nor his brother in attendance, were not recorded.[50] Thus, the "Kennedy Tapes" do not tell the entire story of the US side of the Cuban Missile Crisis nor the Kennedys' role in it.

Nitze was as prepared as anyone on ExComm to deal with a nuclear crisis. While the photos of missiles were clear, other intelligence was murky. CIA director John McCone was abroad. To this emergency, Nitze brought his Korean War experience, where he had had to weigh the possibility of an escalation that might have led to the use of nuclear weapons. He had, as well, a command of the technical components and concepts from his work ranging from the Strategic Bombing Survey to the Gaither Commission. He was the only one in the room at these October 1962 meetings who had visited Hiroshima after the atomic attack. He may or may not have been the only one to have crafted a plan to win World War II without using the atomic bomb.

This is not to say that Nitze had the answers. He knew that someone needed to take command. Initially, JFK did, pressing for a quick invasion. After four days—to Nitze's intense frustration—the president equivocated. Not until the arrival of his old boss, Dean Acheson, did members of the ExComm take action—at least, according to Nitze. Acheson cut through the idle chatter and swatted down the State Department legal adviser's line of argument that international law prohibited cutting off outside access to Cuba.[51] Acheson's proposed blockade—euphemistically called a "quarantine"—galvanized the ExComm and anchored the sequence of events around the speech that JFK planned to give to the American people on Monday, October 22.

While the other ExComm members continued talking, Nitze and Deputy Undersecretary of State for Policy Alexis Johnson took action. S Day (or P Day), named for the president's Monday speech, became the D-day of the Cuban Missile Crisis. Whereas members of ExComm had argued with each other over whether to launch a blockade, bombing campaign, or invasion, JFK's planned announcement of the quarantine "liquidated the conflict between the three because you didn't have to decide," according to Nitze. "You did the minimum one first and then if that didn't work, you did the second, and if that didn't work, you did the third."[52] Johnson and Nitze shared confidence that the Soviets would not "escalate in the face of our nuclear superiority." That power dynamic—and the swiftness with which the US side acted—outweighed all other considerations. "Now the rest of them never consciously came around to the same view that Alexis and I had," Nitze recalled twenty-five years later.

"The logic of the case didn't permit them to take a different view," such as allow-ing the missile installations to become the new status quo. "What were they going to suggest—that we not be prepared to take these missile sites out in the event that the quarantine didn't work and the Russians were in fact getting their weapons in there and were to strike New York?"[53]

The stakes could not have been higher. In Nitze's ISA file is a Standing Com-mittee paper, dated Thursday, October 18, 1962 (four days before President Kennedy's Monday, October 22 speech to the nation), laying out "Attack Plan 3," one that would "almost inevitably escalate into an invasion of Cuba through either attacks by air or sea on US territory, attacks on Guantanamo, or inter-nal uprisings of the Cuban people to which we would be compelled to respond." In the scenario of a full-out US invasion of Cuba, "it would be difficult for the Soviets to resist pressures to retaliate, preferably in kind as in Turkey." US forces would surely kill Soviets in Cuba, "and an attack on Turkish bases is almost sure to involve killing Americans." Such actions would make it "very difficult to avoid an escalation into general nuclear war." Retaliation against Berlin "would be equally difficult to accept." Prospects were grim. "If NATO were forced to choose between defeat in Berlin or disgrace in Turkey on the one hand, or nuclear war on the other, because of 200-sorties against Cuban facilities which might have become a nuclear threat against the US of the sort the Europeans have long lived with, the alliance would be put under serious strain indeed."[54]

On the afternoon of Monday, October 22, a few hours prior to JFK's sched-uled address to the nation, Nitze led a briefing of the president and ExComm in his capacity as head of the Berlin Planning Group. Kennedy was justifiably concerned that the Soviets might respond to the announcement of a quaran-tine around Cuba with similar action encircling West Berlin. Even more wor-risome was the prospect that the quarantine might lead to a shooting war—unintended or intended—and that a subsequent US assault on Cuba would lead the Soviets to launch strikes against US bases armed with Jupiter missiles in Turkey. Finally, in a calamitous scenario, local US commanders in Turkey, upon receiving early warning of incoming Soviet intermediate-range missiles (of the same class as were in Cuba) from somewhere in Eastern Europe, might launch the Jupiters at targets inside the Soviet Union. General nuclear war would therefore have commenced absent any presidential order. This entirely plausible sequence negated anything Tom Schelling or anyone else had to say about nuclear signaling.

During the briefing, Kennedy interrupted Nitze to press him on the point that the Joint Chiefs needed to reiterate orders to local US commanders that no one could launch missiles without specific authorization from the commander-in-chief. JFK's concern followed a frustrating conversation with Curtis Lemay the previous Friday, October 19, in which the air force chief of staff appeared unfazed by the prospect of an unintended thermonuclear war. "Can we take care of that then, Paul? We need a new instruction out," JFK told Nitze, who responded that reminding the Joint Chiefs of the established chain of command was unnecessary. The hint of frustration came from the otherwise unflappable and exceptionally polite JFK: "I don't think we ought to accept the Chiefs' word on that one, Paul." When Nitze continued to argue with the president, stating that he and McNamara had already gone over with "these fellows" not to fire, President Kennedy responded: "Well, let's do it again, Paul."[55] Nitze complied.

This would not be the last awkward interaction between Nitze and the president during the acute phase of the Cuban Missile Crisis, which saw Soviet ships approaching the US quarantine line that Kennedy had announced Monday evening. On Wednesday, October 24, JFK asked the ExComm what would happen if US forces sank a Soviet ship. Answering his own question, the president speculated that the Soviets would respond aggressively in Berlin. Then what? Nitze replied that the logical next step was for the United States to shoot down Soviet planes over Berlin. The president wanted to hear a different answer. Fortunately, several hours after this conversation, word came that the Soviets had turned back their ships—though, unbeknownst to the ExComm, Khrushchev had given the order twenty-four hours before that moment.[56]

Nitze continued to hold meetings of his subcommittee looking at contingency planning on Berlin, yet it was increasingly clear that the ExComm was absorbing all NSC deliberative functions. In a discussion of Nitze's group on Thursday, October 25, the Jupiters in Turkey came up again, this time in the context of Walter Lippmann's proposition in that morning's edition of the *New York Herald Tribune* that Washington and Moscow agree to take out missiles from both Cuba and Turkey. Whether or not Nitze was aware that the proposal was likely a trial balloon originating from JFK or RFK, he was indignant at the idea of withdrawing the Jupiters from Turkey under such conditions. "Not that we love these things," he told Under Secretary of State George Ball in the late afternoon of Friday, October 26. "We wanted to get rid of it before." As he elaborated elsewhere, the problem was that every other NATO country would get the message that the Soviets could take provocative steps. Washington would trade away their security to diffuse a crisis. Only superior US strength and resolve would cause the Soviets to back down. "We take a very dim view," as Nitze put it to Ball. "We have to contemplate now, in this kind of a thing, negotiations apart from Cuba would just ruin us all the way around." Ball said, "The [State] Department is no happier about it than you are."[57]

Over the next thirty-six hours, as is well known, Khrushchev sent a conciliatory letter to Kennedy Friday evening and broadcast a message Saturday morning demanding the removal of the Jupiters on top of a pledge not to invade Cuba. In addition, a surface-to-air missile (SAM) site in Cuba shot down a US U-2 plane on Saturday afternoon. President Kennedy decided to respond to the letter, offering a pledge not to invade Cuba in exchange for the Soviet withdrawal of missiles and permission for UN inspectors to verify the exit. That evening, Attorney General Robert F. Kennedy met with Soviet ambassador Dobrynin and affirmed that the United States would withdraw Jupiters from Turkey but that the Soviets were not allowed to say it was a "quid pro quo" (though it remains unclear what would have happened had they proclaimed it to be so).

With the Cuban Missile Crisis seemingly resolved, media outlets reported Khrushchev's decision. That Sunday morning, the Kennedys attended Mass. Nitze, exhausted as was everyone else on ExComm, received little time to rest. The president called to ask that he fly to India, which China had invaded on October 20. Nitze was to express US support for this neutralist country that sometimes tilted toward Moscow. Nitze's respite from Cuba was to spend twenty hours on a cargo plane only to emerge from the darkness and be greeted by Ambassador John Kenneth Galbraith, with whom he was never close.

When Nitze returned to the United States, he again worked on the matter of Soviet offensive missiles that remained in Cuba. He pondered what pressure the United States could apply on Castro in light of Kennedy's "anti-invasion guarantees" expressed in his October 27 letter to Khrushchev. Continued aerial surveillance, economic forces, propaganda designed to overthrow Cuba, and the return of civilian refugees all appeared to be on the table. Food and supply drops—as well as a "Bay of Pigs-type operation"—were "doubtful," yet not "included" in the anti-invasion guarantee.[58] Continued aerial surveillance was essential since Castro had refused to abide by Khrushchev's pledge to Kennedy to allow UN inspectors to enter Cuba.

While the most dangerous phase of the Cuban Missile Crisis appeared to be over, the worrisome prospect of a shooting war over Soviet missiles in Cuba remained. ExComm persisted in its routine meetings. On November 7, Nitze distributed to its members contingency plans for scenarios where Soviet or Cuban forces downed, or even just shot at, another US plane. He thought President Kennedy, in any case, needed to state the case that the Soviets had not upheld their end of the agreement. Clearly, Soviet weapons "capable of offensive use" remained in Cuba even after the public resolution of the Cuban Missile Crisis.

If a SAM site shot down a U-2, Nitze recommended that US bombers destroy the SAM site—the very thing President Kennedy had declined to do during the so-called Black Saturday (October 27) of the Cuban Missile Crisis.

FIGURE 6.1. (L–R) National Security Advisor McGeorge Bundy, President Kennedy, Assistant Secretary of Defense for International Security Affairs Paul Nitze, chairman of the Joint Chiefs of Staff Maxwell Taylor, and Secretary of Defense Robert McNamara, October 29, 1962. Nitze served as a member of the Executive Committee of the National Security Council yet was frustrated with President Kennedy's handling of the Cuban Missile Crisis. Photo courtesy of the John F. Kennedy Presidential Library.

Likewise, if a MIG fighter shot down a U-2, US fighters should remove the MIG. Suppose subsequent Soviet and Cuban actions failed to acknowledge the gravity of the situation. In that case, the United States should respond by reimposing the quarantine and strengthening it to include petroleum and lubricants.[59] The bottom line was that the United States could expect additional Soviet probing over Cuba, and it was incumbent on US leaders to match that with a forceful response. While the two sides had just gone to the brink of nuclear war, it was no time for the Kennedy administration to go soft. "A combination of carrot and stick pressures should be so played as to force out the offensive weapons and Soviet military presence while weakening the Cuban Communist regime," Nitze wrote to the ExComm on November 14.[60]

Around this time, President Kennedy asked Nitze to devise plans to prevent a rekindling of the Berlin Crisis. Nitze's idea, which went nowhere, was to carve up parts of Germany and exchange them with the Soviets.[61] But, according to Nicholas Thompson, Nitze also wrote a memorandum, "Basis for Substantive Negotiations," in which he proposed limiting NATO and the Warsaw Pact to five hundred nuclear missiles each in exchange for which the Soviet Union would hand over East Germany to West Germany. While that proposal also went nowhere, these early sketches would become relevant later as Nitze realized his ambition to craft a grand bargain on nuclear armaments between East and West.

As 1963 got underway, Nitze worked on creating a Multilateral Force for NATO that would deal with potential West German nuclear aspirations and contribute to Kennedy's redoubled efforts to pursue a limited nuclear test ban treaty with the Soviets. However, he never stopped working on Cuba for as long as he led ISA. Nitze could not accept a status quo that allowed Castro to remain in power and continue his campaign to make the United States look weak. On May 10, 1963, Nitze and Alexis Johnson submitted a contingency study summarizing how the United States could exploit the prospect of Cuba's shooting down a US surveillance plane to nullify the anti-invasion pledge of October 1962.

By this point, the Kennedys had little use for Nitze. On June 10, at American University, the president delivered perhaps the most conciliatory speech of any Cold War leader. On August 5, US and Soviet delegations signed the Treaty Banning Nuclear Weapon Tests in the Atmosphere, Outer Space, and Under Water. The US Senate then ratified this on October 10. Apart from avoiding a nuclear war over Berlin or Cuba, the Partial Test Ban Treaty was the outstanding foreign policy achievement of JFK's presidency, which ended tragically on November 22, 1963.

The Berlin Crisis and the Cuban Missile Crisis served to confirm Nitze's steadfast conviction that the United States needed to possess overriding strength. The Soviets backed down over Berlin because they acknowledged US strategic superiority, and over Cuba in the face of US conventional superiority there and remaining strategic superiority. Handwringing was unnecessary, Nitze was sure, the concessions superfluous. Nothing about his interpretation differed from how he understood the lead-up to Pearl Harbor or the origins of the Cold War.

In later years, Nitze stated that the United States had been "too weak in the Cuban Missile Crisis." Even after Khrushchev had agreed to withdraw the missiles, the Soviet leader did not follow through on all his promises. "We didn't have the sense of follow-up [or] follow-through pursuit," according to Nitze.[62] President Kennedy and top advisers such as Robert McNamara were concerned about the dangers of pushing the Soviets too hard. "I didn't have any worry about that last point," Nitze acknowledged. "I was convinced we ought to push them hard."[63] In his estimation, trading away the Jupiter missiles in Turkey created the very circumstance he had warned against: fear on the part of NATO allies that the United States would ultimately not support them in a crisis. In subsequent years Nitze never departed from this view.

A US invasion of Cuba in October 1962—something Nitze supported—would have been costly. Likely the Soviets would have responded with tactical nuclear weapons against US forces. Even though Kennedy had been briefed on Soviet short-range missiles, the reality did not sink in: that US landing troops would be incinerated on the beaches.[64] The Kennedy administration would have responded to that by obliterating any missile installations in Cuba. A short path followed to general nuclear war. Given the nuclear balance—in sheer terms of the numbers of weapons that could hit military or civilian targets—many more Soviets than Americans would have died under such circumstances. Never again would Soviet leaders tolerate such a disparity. "You'll never do this to us again," a Soviet official informed John McCloy, a member of the ExComm.[65]

"I think the situation was rather similar to that of the British when they really had control of the seas," Nitze later recalled, thinking of the period after October 1962. "The moment anybody started to threaten that control after the Napoleonic wars, they went to great lengths to demonstrate a margin of superiority and maintain it even at great cost." Likewise, the United States could have maintained its margin of superiority concerning the Soviet Union in the nuclear era, but its leaders chose not to. "[W]e began to go downhill, I think right after the Cuban Missile Crisis," Nitze averred. "From that point on the relationship [between the United States and the Soviet Union] deteriorated."[66]

In other words, Nitze's understanding of stability in the US–Soviet relationship rested on a clear mutual recognition of US strategic superiority. Instability resulted from a bipolar nuclear order. As the next chapter will demonstrate, Nitze and McNamara differed over the fundamental meaning of preserving peace in the nuclear age as the nation's focus turned from Berlin and Cuba to the trauma of Vietnam. MAD became synonymous with the nuclear balance during this period. Yet for national security practitioners working on strategic affairs and the emerging field of arms control, it was never simply a fact of life.

CHAPTER 7

Preponderance Lost

Under President Lyndon B. Johnson, Paul Nitze rose to the highest-ranking position he would ever achieve in government: deputy secretary of defense. However, as with President John F. Kennedy, Nitze never penetrated Johnson's inner circle. He spent the first three and a half years of LBJ's presidency in the lesser position of secretary of the navy. During that time, Secretary of Defense Robert McNamara made crucial decisions about the future of US nuclear forces.

McNamara and Nitze interpreted the legacy of the Cuban Missile Crisis in different ways. For McNamara, Soviet leaders realized the stupidity of placing missiles in Cuba; both sides stepped back from the brink of nuclear war, and neither side had any incentive to risk that again. For Nitze, US nuclear superiority and its superior conventional forces surrounding Cuba forced the Soviets to back down. The lesson Nitze took was to continue his quest to sustain US nuclear forces while also building up its conventional capabilities. In other words, nothing about the resolution of the Cuban Missile Crisis (and the Berlin Crisis) challenged the fundamental conclusion that Nitze had drawn from the US experience in the lead-up to Pearl Harbor on December 7, 1941: US weakness invited foreign aggression.

To Nitze, it was evident that drawing the wrong lessons from a crisis would beget failure and create vulnerabilities. Soviet leaders would capitalize on the loss of the US position of strength—especially now in the Middle East, Africa,

Latin America, and Southeast Asia—where they might not have done so other-wise. That, in turn, would lead to the erosion of the ideals of human free-dom and human dignity that NSC-68 propounded in 1950. By 1968, which saw the collapse of the Cold War consensus, these fears appeared to have been well founded. The United States lost the preponderance of power that Nitze was convinced had forced the Soviets to back down in October 1962.

Secretary of the Navy

In the fall of 1963, Nitze reluctantly accepted JFK's offer to be secretary of the navy. Certain senators had expressed reservations about his attaining his pre-ferred post: as successor to Deputy Secretary of Defense Roswell Gilpatrick. He survived a confirmation hearing in which Congressman Donald Rumsfeld and Senator Strom Thurmond accused him of being soft on communism. Sworn in on November 29, 1963, one week after the assassination of the commander-in-chief in Dallas, Nitze faced a dubious staff. The officer corps knew the new secretary had never served in uniform—let alone in the navy— and word spread that in the Pacific Summary of the Strategic Bombing Sur-vey, he had criticized the navy's performance in World War II (he had criticized all the services). Early on, Nitze heard that the chief of navy materiel was slow-walking his policy guidance, and telling staffers, "Secretaries of the Navy come and go." Nitze fired him.[1]

Nitze initially gained a favorable impression of President Lyndon Johnson, about whom Dean Acheson spoke highly.[2] However, summoned to meet with him in the Oval Office, Nitze sat across from Johnson while the latter went about his calls and stole glances at Nitze to see if he was impressed. Paul was not.[3] This was not how Clarence Dillon, Will Clayton, or other great men in Nitze's life acted upon receiving him.

Even though he was no longer routinely attending meetings of the NSC, Nitze worked on nuclear policies and wartime contingencies, such as devel-oping plans for a maritime blockade of the Soviet Union in the event of yet another Berlin Crisis. He savored matters such as anti-submarine warfare, which entailed vast numbers and complexity. Tracking Soviet submarines and formulating plans to repel them presented a quantifiable challenge—one on a grander scale than those Nitze had encountered in bond issuances in the 1930s and the Selective Service and Strategic Bombing Survey in the 1940s.[4]

Anti-submarine warfare spoke directly to one of the fundamental riddles of nuclear weapons in the Cold War: Should the United States unilaterally forego some areas of advantages to assure the Soviets that it was not seeking a "first

FIGURE 7.1.   Secretary of the Navy Nitze peers at Cuba from Naval Station Guantanamo Bay, February 13, 1964. As secretary of the navy, Nitze tackled significant problems and evaded responsibility for escalating the US commitment to Vietnam—yet he yearned for more of a say on nuclear matters. Photo by Keystone/Getty Images.

strike" advantage? So long as Soviet nuclear submarines were "survivable" in the event of a "nuclear exchange," that prospect of a "second strike" would deter any US president from launching an attack on Soviet nuclear forces or cities. The perception that Soviet submarines could be vulnerable, however, could motivate Soviet leaders to fear preemptive US attacks and restore "balance" by compensating elsewhere. After the Cuban Missile Crisis, the Soviets were resolved never again to confront the Americans from a position of weakness.

Nitze downplayed the notion that US unilateral advantages in antisubmarine warfare (or any other category) destabilized the nuclear balance. Such thinking "ignores the point when we had an absolute monopoly of nuclear capability, and we had a stable situation because they are on the political offensive and we are not," he declared at a meeting of the Navy Policy Council on February 18, 1966. He went on: "therefore it does not contribute [to instability] for us to have nuclear superiority."[5] This did not mean that he opposed agreements to restrict testing or limit arms; it simply meant that any deal had to guarantee US superiority, which was for Nitze the most stabilizing influence conceivable.

Nuclear Strategy After the Cuban Missile Crisis

Nitze's statement in February 1966 shows his detachment from crucial developments in the strategic arms competition between the Soviet Union and the United States following the Cuban Missile Crisis in October 1962. In 1963, the Soviets started constructing a missile defense system (Galosh) to protect Moscow. Meanwhile, Washington was also investigating the possibility of a plan to shoot down any incoming ballistic missiles. In his secretary of the navy confirmation hearing, Nitze stated that the development of such a system "should be prosecuted with all urgency, and I believe it is being prosecuted with all urgency."[6] However, going from ISA to the navy kept him out of the loop on such planning.

It is important to note that ABM systems in the 1960s (as well as 1970s) were blunt instruments. They consisted of nuclear-tipped SAMs that one side would launch at incoming missiles based on rough coordinates provided by large radar systems. They could provide either "area defense" of cities or "point defense" of an array of missile silos. It did not comfort residents of New Jersey to hear that the Pentagon was considering installing ABM launchers that would make targets of their neighborhoods and leave a nuclear cloud above New York City.[7]

Even had Nitze become deputy secretary of defense under McNamara, his supposedly airtight logic on ABM would have met the harsh reality of "not in my backyard." As a result, with McNamara as secretary of defense neither the Kennedy nor Johnson administrations moved forward with any urgency. They focused instead on building a US fleet of Minuteman IIIs, which featured three multiple independent reentry vehicles (MIRVs) and were scheduled to be ready in the 1970s. This was meant to overwhelm any potential ABM system that the Soviets fielded.

Nitze and McNamara believed that the United States needed a secure retaliatory capability. Yet, Nitze thought this capability to be potent enough to convince Soviet leaders that the United States would retain strategic superiority even after a Soviet first strike. Such a reserve force, as he later put it, "would be a stronger deterrent to Soviet leaders than the risk of losing large numbers of their population."[8] The Soviets had weathered staggering losses during World War II—some twenty-seven million. Based on Nitze's firsthand 1955 encounter seeing components of the Moscow subway designed to evacuate civilians, he was sure that they would withstand a nuclear attack. "Therefore, it seemed to me that the strongest deterrent to the Kremlin's initiating a nuclear strike was for them to see for themselves that our capabilities were such that the Soviet Union would come out second-best after the initial phases of a nuclear exchange, even if they struck first."[9] On this point (and many others), Nitze's views would remain consistent throughout the 1960s.

McNamara's changed. In 1962, he announced a "no cities" plan. This stressed "counterforce," and it limited targeting to Soviet military infrastructure. But he realized the immense financial costs this would entail. Such a doctrine required large arsenals of very accurate missiles that could penetrate "hardened" (heavily fortified) missile sites and an intelligence apparatus that could identify all of them. Targeting cities—a "counter value" approach—was cheaper. In the aftermath of the Cuban Missile Crisis, McNamara regarded as unlikely the prospect of a direct nuclear confrontation with the Soviets. A central tenet of MAD was that both sides had now glimpsed what nuclear war would entail.

Nitze saw no need to revisit his assumptions based on the Cuban Missile Crisis. He *continued* to believe that the United States required a counterforce capability with which it could preemptively strike Soviet forces before leaders in Moscow could order their launch. Counterforce differed from a "first strike" capability—though the distinctions were sometimes murky. A fundamental asymmetry in the Cold War, at least from Nitze's perspective, was that US presidents would never accept massive losses when it came to American civilians— yet they could have no confidence that Soviet leaders *would not* sacrifice a few of their cities in deciding to launch a first strike. Otherwise, why would Moscow have its own ABM system and elaborate evacuation plans? By this logic, MAD was flawed. The United States should not accept it as policy, as McNamara did. Nor was it a "fact of life," independent of any policy decision—as the eminent political scientist Robert Jervis would later contend.

Neither should it bear upon potential threats outside of the Soviet Union. On May 11, 1963, Nitze wrote McNamara about US nuclear doctrine toward Northeast Asia. While his enclosed paper remains classified, the gist of the covering memo is that the United States needed to approach the use of nuclear weapons in Asia the same way as it would in Europe. In both instances, it ought not to shortchange conventional forces and rely solely on nuclear weapons simply because General Maxwell Taylor said, "we should not permit ourselves to become engaged with the hordes of China." Such weapons needed to stay on the table as the United States contended with a nuclear-aspirant People's Republic of China. There was also no substitute for a robust conventional deterrent. "We can't foretell the exact relationship between Peiping [Beijing] and Moscow that will emerge," wrote Nitze, "but to my mind it is equally doubtful, or more doubtful, that the U.S.S.R. would stand aside while we defeated China with nuclear weapons, than if we did so with non-nuclear weapons." The more salient point was the same critique that Nitze had previously lobbed at John Foster Dulles over massive retaliation: "that the Soviets might have less reason to restrain the Chinese in aggressive action if our only possible response were a nuclear response which the circumstances might make politically difficult for us and thus of dubious credibility."[10] Whether on nuclear or nonnuclear capabilities, the United States needed to maintain its ability to project strength globally.

By Nitze's recollection, McNamara was set on minimizing the prospect of a confrontation with the Soviets after the Cuban Missile Crisis. That meant avoiding decisions about US strategic forces that might appear provocative. Nitze regarded this approach as "in conflict with a policy of maintaining a credible deterrent."[11] He saw no reason to reconfigure the US approach to the Cold War in the wake of the Cuban Missile Crisis. From his perspective, neither McNamara nor Kennedy appreciated long-term strategic planning. "As it was," he recalled in his memoir, "we tended to be in a perpetual state of reaction to one crisis after another rather than working toward long-term goals."[12]

Nitze strove to distinguish himself at navy in the hope that he could return to a position with regular access to the secretary of defense and president. In the fall of 1963, Nitze had worked with Admiral Elmo "Bud" Zumwalt to produce a long paper, "Considerations Involved in a Separable First Stage Disarmament Agreement," which they completed on October 1—shortly before he left ISA. Intended to harmonize the imperatives of safeguarding the United States' primary national security while sketching out an arms control agreement, it was the genesis for Nitze's ambition to incorporate offensive and defensive arms into a deal with the Soviets that would preserve US superiority.[13] Recovering from a hernia operation, Nitze had scribbled a few pages for bilateral arms negotiations aimed not to limit nuclear testing, which had been the focus of prior failed endeavors, but to constrain strategic nuclear delivery vehicles. The starting point for any negotiations should be that Moscow—not Washington—needed a deal. That, in turn, required the United States to sustain high military spending. Pursuing arms control would require additional US strength and its codification.

McNamara did not act on Nitze's collaboration with Zumwalt or scribbled notes. As Vietnam increasingly diverted the Johnson administration's attention and resources, the secretary of defense capped US production of Minuteman missiles at one thousand. Nitze was not part of a team to debate this decision; he merely received notice of it. On May 16, 1964, McNamara wrote Nitze, as well as the secretary of the air force and the chairman of the Joint Chiefs of Staff, that the strategic retaliatory force requirements of the United States should be based on two objectives: (1) "Assured Destruction," or the ability to inflict unacceptable damage to the Soviet Union even after the United States had absorbed a Soviet first strike; and (2) "Damage Limiting," which relied on a counterforce capability that could neutralize enough Soviet forces to reduce the damage to the American homeland in the event of a Soviet attack.[14]

Nitze was convinced that limiting Minuteman III at one thousand was a mistake. In the arms control proposal that he and Admiral Zumwalt had worked up, strategic nuclear delivery vehicles were the "units of account" (i.e., the things each side would agree to limit or reduce). Setting a limit of one thousand—or any other number—made sense only if the Soviets reciprocated by building up to that number and stopping. However, there was no indication that this was their intent. Entering into negotiations might lead them to initiate restraint—even before agreeing to a treaty. In an arms negotiation, however, unilateral restraint upfront provided no incentive for the Soviets to agree to a deal.

Bilateral arms control did not top the Johnson administration's priorities list while Nitze was secretary of the navy. Instead, nonproliferation among nonnuclear states took precedence. The January 21, 1965, "Report by the Committee on Nuclear Proliferation," overseen by former deputy secretary of defense Roswell Gilpatrick, warned of a "tipping point of no return" regarding the spread of nuclear weapons among states that did not already possess them.[15] While the report nominally called for a freeze and reduction of Soviet and US strategic forces, its chief consequence was to set the Johnson administration's push for the 1968 Nuclear Non-Proliferation Treaty (NPT) into motion. Nitze did not work on these matters, and never devoted much energy toward combating the spread of nuclear weapons to other states.

Far more pressing was his concern that the Soviets had embarked on a massive nuclear buildup and US preponderance was lost. Restoring US preponderance was essential to reduce the Soviet propensity to take risks in Cold War hotspots. It was also essential in allowing US policy makers to take risks—notably, by the 1960s, in the so-called periphery of East Asia, Africa, and the Middle East. Only from a position of strength could US leaders hope to bring the Soviets to the table.

However, each component of US strength was essential. Were that not the case, the Soviets understood, the US Congress would not authorize money for it. An enduring dilemma in Nitze's strategic thought during the early and mid-1960s was how to bargain effectively when nothing could be sacrificed at the table. Even when the United States held a nuclear monopoly, and then astounding ratios of nuclear advantage, Soviet leaders would not agree to much of anything. Nitze continued to think that such US strength could be sufficient to compel the Soviets to come to terms.

Vietnam

Nitze's tenure as secretary of the navy placed him outside the room for the Johnson administration's escalation of the United States' military commitment to South Vietnam. When Nitze participated in debates, he claimed it was out of a sense of responsibility either to "his marines" or the crewmembers on surface ships. This is not entirely accurate. He weighed in on Vietnam vigorously, despite never entering LBJ's inner circle, seldom offering plausible alternatives to the policies he criticized. In the summer of 1964, according to one of his sons, Nitze was adamant that the United States not get bogged down in Vietnam. He informed McNamara in June 1964 that the United States could win the war using exclusively air and naval forces. President Johnson and his top advisers were also keen not to get embroiled in Vietnam in the summer of 1964.[16] Had Nitze remained assistant secretary of defense for international security affairs, he might have found more traction for his ideas about Vietnam. Yet it is unlikely they would have had much impact in slowing the United States' ill-fated commitment to South Vietnam.

In June 1965, Nitze visited that country to inspect recently deployed US Marines. When he came home, he told McNamara that it would take another two hundred thousand men to achieve victory and that victory in Vietnam would not be worth the cost to achieve it. McNamara asked Nitze whether the communists would test the United States elsewhere after it pulled out of Vietnam. Nitze said yes. Could he foresee that situation being any more manageable? Nitze admitted: "No, I can't."

In a White House meeting about Vietnam on July 22, 1965, LBJ asked his secretary of the navy, "Paul, what is your view?" Nitze responded that if "we couldn't beat the VC, the shape of the world will change." The perception of a weakened United States would resonate in other Cold War hotspots—emboldening the communists. Citing the Philippines and Greece as recent examples where guerillas had lost, Nitze told the president that only by providing more men to counter insurgents in South Vietnam could the odds of success increase.[17]

In his memoir, Nitze portrayed himself as a Cassandra in Vietnam. He purported to have known from the start that it was a mistake and claimed his only failure was one of imagination. To his answer to McNamara's question—"No, I can't"—he regretted not following up: "But we can come up with contingency plans, just like in Berlin." Elsewhere, Nitze acknowledged that he regarded the situation in Vietnam as dynamic and the conflict ultimately as winnable. "[I]n 1965 when I went out [to Vietnam]," he put it in interviews for the memoir, "I took a very pessimistic view of the situation. Then in 1966 when I went out, I was really very much surprised with the progress that the Marines had made, the Army had made." The tide appeared to be turning. "It was tough work, but we were making much greater progress at it than I had thought in 1965 we would be able to make."[18]

As with Secretary of the Air Force Harold Brown, Nitze was not involved in any of the operational decisions—yet McNamara respected the judgments of both and invited them to offer fresh ideas. "I fully recognize that as service Secretaries you are not in the chain of command with respect to the air operations against North Vietnam," McNamara told them at one point. "But . . . I would like each of you separately to create a small task force of people you have confidence in in your respective services and take an independent look at the air campaign against North Vietnam."[19] Nitze selected a small team and threw himself at the challenge. Crunching numbers, useful in his earlier work on the Strategic Bombing Survey, made him less confident about coming up with a strategy to win expeditiously. "We could compute the number of sorties and the tonnage of ammunition that had to be dropped in relationship to the amount of tonnage on those trains. It turned out that you had to drop four tons of ammunition against those targets for every ton of war materiel you destroyed. You compute the cost of getting a ton of ammunition dropped against the antiaircraft and every other goddamn thing up there to get the figures, and you know it is a mug's game."[20] There was no short-term solution. "With respect to the question of how long it would take to really defeat the Viet Cong and North Vietnamese, I think our estimate was 7 years."

On February 10, 1966, George Kennan delivered a day-long testimony to the Senate in opposition to the Vietnam War. Dapper and widely regarded as the mastermind behind the US containment strategy against communism, Kennan was no hippie. Whatever reservations he expressed, his testimony did not lead to different policy outcomes. Nitze regarded such remonstrations counterproductive. "Certainly in the later days of the Vietnamese war, we had a Congress and public that thoroughly disapproved of our policy in the Vietnamese war, and the upshot was disastrous," as he later put it. "From the standpoint of what happened on the ground in Vietnam, I believe that war could have been won. The thing that made it impossible was, in fact, the lack of domestic support."[21] He singled out newspaper journalists and correspondents such as David Halberstam, whom he accused of ignoring the real story and writing *The Best and the Brightest*—perhaps the most famous book about US policy making and Vietnam—"based on every rumor" he had ever heard about McGeorge Bundy, Robert McNamara, and the rest of Nitze's colleagues in government.

Missile Defense, Nuclear Weapons, and NATO

Paul Nitze was sixty years old on July 1, 1967, when he was finally promoted to the position of deputy secretary of defense. He inherited a more substantive portfolio on Vietnam and oversight of the Pentagon, which, in 2023, is still the largest office building in the world. Later that month, news came that the People's Republic of China—what one scholar has termed the "rogue state" of its era—had tested a hydrogen bomb. US defense planners regarded the leaders of that country as irrational.[22] At least Khrushchev had backed down in the face of superior strength and resolve in October 1962 rather than wage nuclear war; Mao inspired no such confidence that he would do the same. The perceived Chinese threat led McNamara to recommend—and President Johnson to sign off on—a "thin" missile defense system, Sentinel, which would hopefully protect the US homeland from a Chinese nuclear attack.

Soviet armed forces, in their 1967 annual military parade, introduced a missile (the SS-9) more menacingly than anything ever before seen. US intelligence estimated that it could carry a warhead of twenty-five megatons. In subsequent monitoring of Soviet SS-9 tests with tests of their MIRVs, US analysts interpreted the targeting pattern as matching the layout of US Minuteman silos in the US heartland.[23] In other words, the mission of the SS-9 appeared to be taking out the US land-based nuclear deterrent.

The appearance of the SS-9—*not* the narrow avoidance of nuclear war during the Cuban Missile Crisis—led the US side to get serious about bilateral arms control between Washington and Moscow. Throughout 1967, President Johnson attempted to persuade Soviet premier Alexei Kosygin to commence formal negotiations to curb the nuclear arms race. At a summit in Glassboro, New Jersey, that June, Johnson got nowhere by citing the Galosh defensive system around Moscow as an "escalation" in that arms race. Kosygin, who was still jockeying with Leonid Brezhnev for control of the Kremlin following their ouster of Nikita Khrushchev, had little incentive to move forward with arms control.[24]

Nitze opposed reaching out to the Soviets from such a position of weakness. Not only had the United States foregone a strategic advantage but, since the end of the Cuban Missile Crisis, it had also allowed the NATO alliance to deteriorate. Charles de Gaulle had taken France out of its unified command structure. By 1967, other Western European nations could quickly have decided to follow France's example. In a Senior Interagency Group meeting on October 19, 1967, Nitze "stressed the importance of progress in reviewing the strength of the Alliance" and "agreed wholeheartedly with the conclusion . . . that a lack of action in December would be a major failure."[25]

Ultimately, the Harmel Report—so named for former Belgian foreign minister Pierre Harmel—was approved on December 14, 1967. It listed specific guidance for strategic consultations, shared commitments to spend, and initiatives for East–West negotiations such as the Mutual and Balanced Forces Talks. These ingenuities helped sustain NATO over the long term. However, closer to home, the United States' domestic strength was deteriorating. Two days after the Senior Interagency Group on the Harmel Report that October, Nitze found himself with the unlikely task of organizing the defense of the Pentagon against protesters attempting to perform an exorcism, levitate the building, infiltrate it, and incite a violent response that television cameras would capture. On November 29, President Johnson announced that he was nominating McNamara as the next director of the World Bank, effectively firing him as secretary of defense.

The Tumultuous 1968

Nitze regarded himself to be the natural contender to succeed McNamara. His unwillingness to cultivate LBJ made this impossible. On January 19, 1968, President Johnson nominated Clark Clifford for the post. "I could tell that he [Nitze] was exceedingly put out at having been passed over for the job that now fell to me," Clifford later recalled. The new secretary "was all the more impressed by [Nitze's] sense of duty."[26] Clifford's longtime aide, George Elsey, later conceded that Nitze had been the more qualified—the problem was that Johnson did not like him.

Clifford was in for a tough stretch. On January 21, 1968, North Korean Commandos snuck south of the thirty-eighth parallel and attempted to raid the Blue House, the South Korean equivalent of the White House. Two days later, North Korean forces seized the USS *Pueblo*, capturing eighty US sailors and state-of-the-art surveillance equipment. At an NSC meeting that day, McNamara told Clifford, sitting in while awaiting confirmation: "this is what it is like on a typical day. We had an inadvertent intrusion into Cambodia. We lost a B-52 with four H-bombs aboard. We had an intelligence ship captured by the North Koreans."[27]

Nitze had personally approved the ill-fated *Pueblo* mission and was now frantically coming up with options for how to respond. McNamara assured Johnson that Nitze and his team were engaging the problem. Not only was the fate of the US crew members at stake but there was also the prospect that the North Koreans would hand over to the Soviets the KW-7 encryption device onboard the ship. Particularly amid the recent North Korean attempt to decapitate the leadership of South Korea, a military rescue attempt could quickly escalate into a second US intervention on the Korean peninsula.

Nitze regarded North Korea's actions as linked to the broader Cold War. He figured the communists were coordinating efforts to pressure Washington to "take a weaker position on Vietnam negotiations." While the Johnson administration had been pursuing the so-called San Antonio formula that linked bombing pauses to peace overtures, Nitze insisted that US firmness be made clear. "Thus, it might be necessary for us to ask Congress for additional authority to take military action to make clear to the Soviets that they must not misunderstand our attitude toward the *Pueblo incident*."[28]

Thinking it unwise to retaliate directly against the Soviets for something the North Koreans had done, Nitze was willing to risk escalation with North Korea, so long as the United States could present to the world a clear case for which side instigated the affair. The vessel had been operating in international waters, yet it was—after all—a spy ship. He proposed a plan that could justify taking action and was open to instigating a more explicit justification for the action. In an NSC meeting on January 25, Nitze suggested that President Johnson send a destroyer to where the *Pueblo* had thrown overboard its gear, and deploy divers to retrieve it. "This is completely legal and it is possible that the North Koreans would take action against this vessel," he said. "If they did we would be in a good position in the eyes of world opinion to retaliate." At the very least, the United States should take some action to get the ship back, and retaliate for its seizure.[29] Failure to demonstrate resolve in this case would hinder the Johnson administration's ability to do so elsewhere. That would encourage the Soviets and North Vietnamese to take further risks.

While the stakes were not nearly as high as in the Cuban Missile Crisis— even though eighty Americans were being held hostage—the *Pueblo* affair substantiated Nitze's takeaways from October 1962 onward. The United States was now operating from a position of weakness, since it had unilaterally limited production of the mainstay of its nuclear arsenal, the Minuteman, and was attempting (unsuccessfully) to extricate itself from a seemingly unwinnable war in Vietnam. (It is clear that he felt no personal responsibility for the *Pueblo* incident.) The *Pueblo* affair dragged on for nearly a year, when US servicemen were released (and the ship remains, to this day, in North Korea). It was not even the administration's most tremendous headache by the end of that week in January 1968. On January 31, North Vietnamese and Vietcong forces launched, in the midst of their Lunar New Year, the "Tet Offensive." While this turned out to be a military defeat for them, the sheer scale of the offensive was shocking, raising expectations of further coordinated offensives.

FIGURE 7.2.   (L–R) President Lyndon Johnson, outgoing secretary of defense Robert McNamara, and Deputy Secretary of Defense Nitze, February 7, 1968. Nitze never ingratiated himself with LBJ. He remained deputy secretary of defense after McNamara departed in 1968, failing to obtain the Pentagon's top job. Photo courtesy of the LBJ Presidential Library.

LBJ's political fortunes plummeted. In the New Hampshire primary on March 12, Senator Eugene McCarthy came within striking distance of winning—leading Senator Robert Kennedy to announce his own candidacy on March 16. Nitze bailed on LBJ. He wrote the president that day saying he would not testify before the Senate Foreign Relations Committee. At Clifford's insistence, Nitze struck out the sentence in which he offered his resignation.

Johnson was understandably furious. He complained about Nitze to Senator Richard Russell in a phone call on March 22. "Refused to testify . . . said he didn't believe in the policy. Did not think we ought to be in Vietnam. Just wouldn't do it. Just insubordinate. Wrote me a letter." Senator Russell proposed that Johnson fire Nitze. "Well, I would," the president responded, "but Clifford said he just can't do it so quickly by himself."[30] In a subsequent meeting with Generals Earle Wheeler and Creighton Abrams, Johnson cited Nitze as one of the "civilians . . . cutting our guts out."[31] On March 31, LBJ announced new efforts to scale down the US commitment to Vietnam and withdrew as a candidate for reelection.

Arms Control: SALT, ABM, and NPT

With McNamara gone and Johnson a lame duck, Nitze—still in office—embraced the prospect of shaping strategic arms policies. Shortly after taking over from McNamara, Secretary of Defense Clifford had asked Nitze to sketch out US goals in future arms negotiations with the Soviets. Nitze gathered together Secretary of the Air Force Harold Brown, General Royal Allison, an assistant to the Joint Chiefs of Staff, assistant secretary of defense for ISA Paul Warnke, and Nitze's deputy on nuclear negotiations, Morton Halperin, a young Harvard professor who had studied with the renowned strategist Thomas Schelling.[32] On a separate occasion, Nitze discussed the role of ABM with Albert Wohlstetter, the University of Chicago professor and long-time consultant to the RAND Corporation.

When it came to strategic defenses, Nitze expressed qualified support. Area defense was impossible. Point defense could enhance "strategic stability" by reducing Soviet incentive to launch an attack. In other words, the ability to defend US Minuteman silos against the new "counterforce" SS-9s would neutralize their perceived first-strike advantage. Without a rationale for heavy missiles, the Soviets might be inclined to negotiate to limit or reduce their number. US spending on ABM could pay dividends if it led to fewer Soviet heavy missiles, which, in turn, would mean fewer US missiles to counter them. During these preparatory discussions for what became SALT, Nitze chose not to go after MIRVs directly.

Congressional attempts to cut funding for ABM only emboldened Nitze to support it. He saw two reasons to keep it. The first was that the United States would be better off building a robust system. The second was that it could serve as a bargaining chip in negotiations to get the Soviets to reduce their strategic offensive forces. By 1968, Washington had few other scraps to offer. An acute awareness of that fact led Nitze to take a dim view of whether to ban testing nuclear weapons underwater in the 1968 NPT. He believed it vital for the United States to understand undersea "nuclear effects." Given that, at a meeting of the Committee on Principals on May 14, 1968, Nitze asked "What kind of an area would the US want as a platform for its strategic nuclear delivery vehicles?" "Would we want it to be small, limited, and closer to cities?" The answer was probably no. Since the Soviet Union had a larger land mass and the United States had better access to the sea, the "sea was, therefore, a better place for the US to put nuclear weapons than for the Soviet Union."[33] Sympathetic to the need for a US position on this, Secretary Nitze said that more precise staff work was needed.

Nitze presumed that the Soviets would seize upon any loophole, no matter how small. "Under the Outer Space Treaty, the Soviets could orbit everything but the nuclear warhead," he warned at a meeting on June 3. "Under the [ACDA] proposal, the Soviets could deploy the weapon system on the seabed, to be armed with nuclear weapons at a time of their choosing—without (until the moment of arming) there being a violation of the treaty. They could aim for a first strike capability." Unlike the Department of Defense's support for the Limited Test Ban Treaty, which "was to avoid further contamination of the atmosphere," Nitze suggested that any potential restrictions on underwater would lock in Soviet advantages.[34] His bottom line was that the US side could not countenance anything in the NPT that restricted its freedom of action. "I believe it would be unwise to take a definite position on an arms control proposal banning weapons of mass destruction until we have a clearer determination of what kind of proposal, if any, is in the best interests of the United States," Nitze wrote ACDA director William Foster on June 7, 1968.[35]

On July 1, 1968, sixty-two countries signed the NPT. As self-declared nuclear powers, the United States, the United Kingdom, and the Soviet Union agreed not to help nonnuclear powers develop such arsenals. They also made a broad commitment to reducing their nuclear stockpiles. With momentum building for bilateral strategic arms negotiations, Nitze continued to press for a firmer articulation of US and allied objectives. "Deputy Secretary Nitze emphasized that we must understand all the facts on any positions before they are adopted," according to notes of a July 8 meeting. "For example, the proposal to freeze land-based ICBMs was, in fact, freezing the launch holes. Since the Soviet holes are larger than the US holes, they could exploit these to Soviet advantage." Even though "verification might be difficult, throw weight might be a better criterion for control than launchers," he said. "One must assume that in time the US would lose its technological advantage."[36]

On August 16, 1968, Walt Rostow submitted to President Johnson an initial SALT proposal (to which Nitze had assented) to "require cessation of the initiation of construction of any additional strategic offensive land-based missile launchers as of September 1, 1968." The Soviets would still be permitted to complete any launchers under construction as of that date. However, "Under no circumstances would either side be permitted to deploy more than 1,200 ICBM launchers."[37] The aspirational calculation was that the Soviets would accept the logic of the US side that setting limits on equal launchers enhanced strategic stability.

The problem was that the United States had no room to maneuver. It could not give up numbers or classes of weapons. It had already capped its Minuteman production. And, excepting Polaris, which was regarded as vital to maintaining a second-strike capability, the United States was not building new systems. That the prospective US negotiators had few cards to play proved to be a moot point. On August 20, 1968, Soviet troops invaded Czechoslovakia, making it exceedingly unlikely that bilateral arms negotiations between Washington and Moscow would commence that year.

In an August 22 meeting of the ExComm, Secretary of State Dean Rusk conceded that prospects were grim for the commencement of SALT that year. "[I]t was not the purpose of the Executive Committee meeting to consider that [the situation in Czechoslovakia made negotiations impossible]," but rather "to give the President the necessary material to go ahead with the talks if and when he desired." Considerable obstacles remained. The intelligence community had little insight into which Soviet antiaircraft systems could be upgraded to an ABM capability. "Mr. Foster asked whether the Soviets informing us that it was not an ABM would satisfy us," according to the record of the conversation. "[Deputy] Secretary Nitze said it might be useful for them to tell us this, and Secretary Brown said there might be some questions which could be answered which would give us increased confidence."[38]

Even if LBJ had prioritized talks after the Soviet invasion of Czechoslovakia, internal discussions such as those on August 22 hardly inspired confidence that his administration would have been prepared for them. For example, "Secretary Rusk asked whether we would be in favor of an agreement that banned all ABM's [sic] if the Soviets offered this. Secretary Clifford said not necessarily, since we had to worry about China. [Deputy] Secretary Nitze said it might be in our interest, but that was not obvious at this time."[39] More than five years after the resolution of the Cuban Missile Crisis, the US side still was not ready to articulate what it wanted to achieve from strategic arms negotiations with the Soviets—should they commence.

Meanwhile, Nitze's relationship with Clifford was rapidly deteriorating. The latter reversed his initial fervor for winning the war in Vietnam and sought a peace agreement. Tensions boiled over at a September 16 meeting in which Clifford recounted LBJ's plans to reach out to Kosygin on strategic arms negotiations if "Czech stays quiet for a week"—and to encourage the Soviets to press the North Vietnamese to reciprocate actions when LBJ halted the bombing. "Nitze at this pt. explodes!" according to George Elsey's notes. "It's asinine—it's 'pissing' away an advantage we have! It'll undo the N.Atlantic alliance if LBJ gets into bed with Kosygin." Elsey went on to record:

CMC [Secretary Clifford] expresses astonishment at Nitze's objections—
"You, Paul, wanted to get the Russians into [the] act."

"Yes," says Nitze, "but that was before Czechoslovakia & before NVN [arms] started to move!!!"

Elsey & Warnke argue that this won't work because timetable won't work; it'll take *too* long. We'll have an election before you can get the Russians in!

CMC grows irritated! "I'm for *anything* that will get the Pres. to stop the bombing!"

Nitze—"No, I'm not!! Not if it means doing things contrary to our national interest! Wrecking NATO by playing footsie with Kosygin wld do so!"

Nitze explodes again: "I feel passionately, not to jeopardize US boys, ever, any time, any place & there is *no* need now to play into Soviet hands & it would terribly . . . to do so!"[40]

On November 3, 1968, three days before the presidential election, Clifford expressed exasperation with Nitze's claim that the South Vietnamese had been promised to hold out for a better deal under Nixon. The meeting dissolved in frustration: the war in Vietnam had consumed all the energy and brought down Johnson's presidency. "(The longer CMC talks the madder [Clifford] gets at S.V.Nam—he's disgusted & ready to dump SVNam. 'Screw You' is all he says he'd tell them.)," according to Elsey's notes. He continued, "I do not believe we ought to be in V Nam," "I think our being there is a mistake," and Thieu's backtracking "demonstrates *to me* why I think it was a calamity." Nitze responded, "I thought it was a mistake in 65 & I said so, but that's irrelevant history. But we *are* there & we have had 29,000 men killed & we have a military success [*sic*] & now I don't want to throw it away by angry, ill-chosen reactions!"[41]

Nitze felt no outward remorse about the fracturing of the United States during eight years of the Democratic administrations in which he served. Three of his children participated in a protest that surrounded the Pentagon in 1967—during which Nitze was tasked with coming up with a defense of that very building—yet he did not dwell on the personal side of the United States' upheaval. "The student revolts of the sixties were a worldwide phenomenon comprising many subgroups with a wide range of asserted grievances," Nitze later recalled. "The words that excited many of the young of those days are now meaningless even to those who said them twenty years earlier. The vaguely Marxist authors whom they considered inspirational, such as Dr. Herbert Marcuse and Noam Chomsky, are no longer read."[42]

During his time as deputy secretary of defense, Nitze focused on Vietnam and arms control. He also oversaw over a million employees and represented the Pentagon in interagency efforts ranging from Africa to the Perkins Report on Foreign Aid, to negotiating fighter jet sales to Israel after the 1967 war, to environmental matters dealing with the continental shelf.

There was also sensitive intelligence work during an era when the executive branch operated basically without inhibition. Nitze collaborated smoothly and represented the Department of Defense on a par with director of the CIA Richard Helms in the "303 Committee," which oversaw covert actions. "I think you can emphasize that this is one of the less cumbersome, more effective, tight working groups in government with Rostow, Bohlen, Nitze, and Helms, men who have worked closely over the years and understand each other's problems. There is no friction and [instead] a sense of accomplishment," NSC staffer Jessup wrote Rostow in June 1968.[43] While it remains unclear precisely what they did, Nitze intimated later that he worked closely with Deputy Attorney General Warren Christopher to oversee computer databases used to profile and discredit radical leaders in the anti-war effort. While the details are murky, they appeared to be running a sort of domestic surveillance operation.

Contrary to Paul Nitze's assertion, college students still read the work of Noam Chomsky. Nitze was not famous enough to find himself in the crosshairs of the US counterculture in the 1960s. Yet he was the living embodiment of the architecture of the Cold War consensus that the Tet Offensive shattered in January 1968. Back in 1950 he had crafted NSC-68, which called for a global and militarized Cold War and stuck around through its implementation. He felt no remorse for Vietnam and its consequences—most notably a fractured United States. Nitze had been left out of the inner circle that decided to increase the United States' commitment to South Vietnam. Then, when he devised plans that he was sure would turn the tide, he failed to persuade.

Richard Nixon's November 5, 1968, victory did not allow Nitze to rest. As with the election of 1952, he considered his national security work above politics. He was also deeply frustrated by the trajectory of the Johnson administration—just as he had been by the end of the Truman administration. For Paul Nitze the highest tragedy was not Vietnam but rather that the United States had failed to preserve the strategic advantages that forced the Soviets to back down in the Cuban Missile Crisis. This allowed the Soviets to seize the opportunity of the United States' involvement in Vietnam to continue a buildup that he was convinced began even before October 1962.

The lesson from failure in 1963–68 was the same as from crises in 1961–63: US strength brought stability; US weakness brought instability. Individuals working in the field of national security should apply these lessons toward the execution of better policies. The United States had lost its preponderance of power and could restore it only through imaginative approaches to nuclear matters. Here Nitze relied on his vast knowledge of US nuclear history for the remainder of his career—a decade and a half in government, even after he turned sixty. With the possible exception of Henry Kissinger, when it came to nuclear weapons and US national security, Nitze was the closest to being in the middle of concentric circles of theorists, academics, and policy makers. And, while Kissinger's portfolio was about to expand exponentially beyond it, Nitze's narrowed exclusively to nuclear weapons.

CHAPTER 8

Negotiating from Weakness, 1969–1975

Paul Nitze spent Richard Nixon's administration pursuing a deal between the United States and the Soviet Union to limit the growth of strategic nuclear forces. But, as only the Department of Defense representative to the SALT, he was not in charge of US decision making. And his fundamental objectives differed from those who were.

National Security Advisor Henry Kissinger and President Nixon wanted a deal with the Soviets as part of their strategy of détente. The details of a potential nuclear arms accord with the Soviets did not matter to them. What did matter was obtaining a deal before the 1972 presidential campaign to help Nixon get reelected. Nitze saw things differently. He considered the objective in nuclear arms negotiations to be reversing Soviet gains in the strategic arms competition ever since the end of the Cuban Missile Crisis in October 1962. According to Nitze, the United States would be *worse off* if it accepted an interim deal with the Soviets that merely slowed the pace of the arms race while leading the American people and European allies to believe that that arms race was over. Indeed this was what ultimately happened, as the United States and Soviet Union signed an Interim Agreement in 1972 to go along with the permanent ABM Treaty.

By 1975, the Soviets had deployed SS-18s, which were heavy ICBMs that could knock out US Minuteman silos in a nuclear first strike. Whether or not Soviets leaders ever intended to launch a first strike, Nitze perceived the threat of the SS-18s to be that US leaders would eventually have to back down in a crisis. Confidence in that outcome would allow Soviet leaders to take risks in emerging strategic chokepoints such as the Middle East. Should a situation similar to the Cuban Missile Crisis arise, Soviet leaders would not back down.

Nixon Transition and Safeguard

Richard Nixon and Paul Nitze had maintained cordial relations since the 1940s. Still, when the Democrats went down in defeat in November 1968, Nitze "could think of no personal reason why [he] might be asked to stay on in some capacity."[1] He nevertheless wrote a paper laying out how the incoming administration should proceed on nuclear arms control. After Nixon's inauguration on January 20, 1969, Paul retreated to Causein Manor, an hour south of Washington. This was a farm his wife Phyllis had inherited. There the Nitzes enjoyed riding horses and raising pigs. But Paul was soon back in Washington, spending weekdays in his office at SAIS and staying at the Nitzes' home in Georgetown.

Other members of the Lyndon Johnson administration moved on. Nitze's most recent boss, Secretary of Defense Clark Clifford, and his top deputy, Paul Warnke, established a law firm, Clifford and Warnke. His previous boss, Robert McNamara, remained president of the World Bank for another decade. Sixty-two years old, Nitze had no interest in withdrawing from high policy debates. Instead, he renewed his professional association with yet another former boss, former secretary of state Dean Acheson, this time under the auspices of the Committee to Maintain a Prudent Defense Policy.

Sharing Nixon's priorities, Acheson and Nitze lobbied members of Congress over national security initiatives. These included appropriating funds for a new ABM system called Safeguard, which the administration planned to deploy in response to the emerging nuclear threat posed by China and the growing one posed by the Soviet Union. President Nixon rejected the "thin" approach of the Johnson administration—the Sentinel program of Spartan and Sprint nuclear-tipped interceptors totaling less than the sum of Soviet incoming missiles—while also opposing a more comprehensive, or "thick," defense against a full-blown Soviet attack.[2]

Safeguard was supposed to proceed in two phases. Phase One would protect only a pair of US missile sites. Phase Two would defend all US cities from potential attacks by the People's Republic of China, land-based attacks by Soviet forces, and accidental attacks from either country.[3] This was the ostensible purpose of Safeguard. However, the primary purpose of Safeguard was to provide US negotiators with leverage at the upcoming SALT that had been postponed following the Soviet invasion of Czechoslovakia in the summer of 1968.

Each of these rationales made sense to Nitze. Having rejected former secretary of defense Robert McNamara's concept of MAD, he advocated for missile defense. Using it as a bargaining chip in negotiations was also a fine idea. And Nitze felt that some critics of missile defense were distracted by irrelevant influences. "The more I looked into it, the more I believed that the basis of the anti-ABM campaign was to be found in the country's disenchantment with the Vietnam War," he later recounted, "in the widespread alienation from the government of former supporters of the nuclear defense program, and in the desire of many to wish away the problems of national security."[4]

Nitze recruited as interns three graduate students of the University of Chicago professor of political science Albert Wohlstetter: Peter Wilson, Paul Wolfowitz, and Richard Perle. He also coordinated efforts with the Office of Strategic Services veteran William Casey, a New York City investment banker and future director of the CIA under President Ronald Reagan. For his part, Acheson rallied fellow "wise men" from the Truman administration, among them Robert Lovett, to play up the bipartisan consensus of that era and exhort the Democratic Party to return to its first principles on foreign policy. Such were two themes of his Pulitzer-Prize-winning 1969 memoir, *Present at the Creation*.[5]

These efforts succeeded. After Safeguard passed the US Senate by one vote in August 1969, his protégés spread out across Washington, DC: Wilson joined RAND, Wolfowitz headed to ACDA, and Perle went to work for Senator Henry "Scoop" Jackson, who was one of Nitze's perennial defenders on the Hill, and whose top foreign policy aide—Dorothy Fosdick—had once worked for him on the Policy Planning Staff.

For his efforts on behalf of Safeguard, Nitze earned the gratitude of Richard Nixon. The president regarded him as knowledgeable, challenging, and—perhaps most importantly—able to deliver congressional support to Richard Nixon. On the advice of Secretary of Defense Melvin Laird, he offered Nitze the job of the secretary of defense's representative on the US delegation to the upcoming SALT in Helsinki. However, that was not all. "Paul," he purportedly told Nitze, "I very much want you to take this job. I have no confidence in [Secretary of State William] Rogers nor do I have complete confidence in [chief negotiator] Gerry Smith. I don't think they understand the arms control problem. So I want you to report anything you disapprove of directly to me."[6] Nitze accepted the job offer but rebuffed the invitation to be the president's "inside man" on the delegation.

SALT I

Nitze disapproved of many things during the SALT negotiations. He opposed the president's fundamental approach to pursue an "interim agreement." The problem with an interim agreement was that the Nixon administration would not be able to obtain from Congress sufficient spending on strategic forces to preserve whatever leverage (e.g., Safeguard) had led the Soviets to agree to it. Soviet leaders, able to read US politics clearly, had no problem stonewalling. They could hold the administration politically hostage until it conceded on outstanding points of contention. Nitze was certain only a comprehensive and permanent deal could prevent that from happening. Moreover, such a deal had to reduce Soviet advantages and preserve US advantages.

Unfortunately for Nitze, he was not the man of action on SALT. Not even the ostensible lead US negotiator was in charge. Shuttling between the White House and meetings with Soviet counterparts, National Security Advisor Henry Kissinger worked out the critical portions of what became the Interim Agreement, casting aside what turned out to be legitimate concerns on the part of Nitze, Smith, and legal and technical experts in ACDA.[7]

In preparation for the initial rounds of SALT, Nitze worked in a windowless office in the Pentagon, the building in which he so recently served in a chief operating role. He surrounded himself with talented younger colleagues such as James Woolsey, T. K. Jones, and James Wade. He was not constrained by any allegiance to the office of the secretary of defense. Nor did demotion in rank diminish his forcefulness. "Nitze was a principal in a way that the other agency representatives were not," according to one NSC official from the time. "He did not regard his function as simply to faithfully reflect whatever the OSD bureaucracy was saying that week."[8]

Nitze took the initiative to establish an essential US position on SALT. He had already formulated the basic options in his paper of November 6, 1968—the one he wrote a day after the election. He grouped these options within three categories which he presented to the NSC one year later: "1) those options which provide for no MIRV ban and no reductions (Options I, II, III, III–A); 2) those options which include a MIRV ban (Options IV, V, V–A and VI); and 3) the option which provides for mutual reductions of fixed land-based missiles, and thus reduces the significance of MIRVs as a counterforce threat (Opinion VII)."[9] Nitze sought, with his plan, to prevent the US side from getting bogged down while establishing its position.

Nitze misread the power dynamics of the Nixon administration. Unlike meetings of the Acheson group during the Berlin Crisis in 1961, at which Kissinger was junior to Nitze, the positions were now reversed. Kissinger had not yet become a household name.[10] Nor had he fully implemented the NSC system in which he chaired every interagency committee.[11] But he was on the ascent. Kissinger flattered Nixon and led him to believe that the president was responsible for establishing the fundamentals of US foreign policy. Neither man shared Nitze's singular focus on obtaining a deal based on its merits—at least, according to Nitze.

Hovering over the early stages of SALT was the US development of MIRVs. MIRVs held the immediate promise of the United States holding "at risk" Soviet targets by adding two more warheads each to the roughly one thousand Minuteman III missiles. Yet the Soviets were bound to catch up. That inevitability was apparent to Nitze in the NSC meeting of November 10, 1969. The fundamental problem for the United States—looking ten or twenty years down over the horizon—was that Soviet leaders could order bigger missiles on which to load their MIRVs and more of them. Unlike US leaders, Soviet ones faced no domestic political pushback for choosing guns over butter. They could also deploy missiles wherever they wanted inside the Soviet homeland.[12]

Nitze reasoned that, in the upcoming SALT negotiations, it would be in the Soviet self-interest to pursue either a MIRV ban or a moratorium on further testing. They might also go for a freeze on ABM systems. While the United States had just authorized money for Safeguard, it had not yet built anything near the equivalent of the Soviet Galosh system that surrounded Moscow. And, again, for domestic political reasons, it was implausible that the United States would ever construct a nuclear-tipped missile defense system around New York City or Washington, DC.

Nitze attempted to overwhelm Nixon and his advisers with his command of nuclear "theology." During the 1968 election campaign, Nixon lambasted the Johnson administration for allowing the Soviets to gain the upper hand in the nuclear arms race. Even though Nitze disagreed with McNamara's decision to set arbitrary limits on US forces, he wanted to convey McNamara's intent. "[W]hen we talked of freezing the Minuteman force at 1000 and subs at 400, we had planned to MIRV that force," Nitze told Nixon. "This would give us an extra capability. The submarines are in for conversion, and Minuteman III [each one slated to hold three MIRVs] is about ready."[13] Here, and in all subsequent strategic arms negotiations, the riddle for the US side was how to distinguish between capabilities—qualitative or quantitative—that were vital to US national security and those capabilities that Washington could trade away in exchange for reductions in the most destabilizing Soviet systems: their very large land-based ICBMs.

"Since 1966, our effort has been based on the assumption that Minuteman III and the Poseidon would balance their SS-11s and SS-13s," Nitze said at the

November 10 meeting. "The Soviets have much greater throw weight." Giving up MIRV meant "they may have as much as a 3 to 1 advantage in throw weight." The United States could build ABMs more extensive than the Soviet Galosh system, which was still rudimentary. "But if [the Soviets] go further, or if they expand their radar, then that would be a major threat to us."[14]

A testing moratorium was not in the US interest, according to Nitze. Both ABM systems and MIRVs required testing to understand "nuclear effects" in order to predict how multiple nuclear explosions in close proximity might affect interceptors or reentry vehicles. Yet, a potential ban on MIRV deployment came down to two considerations: "(1) We must have a high assurance that ABMs and SAMs won't expand. But how can we get this assurance. (2) If we cannot get clear on how to control the radar networks, then what assurance do we have of launchers?" When President Nixon asked Gerard Smith, the lead negotiator, whether "we have to discuss MIRV or there is no game?" Smith responded, "I think this is about 70% of the issue." Nitze added, "It doesn't have to be so." In front of the president, he also contradicted Smith on whether to inform the North Atlantic Council of US intentions.

Nitze regarded himself as the nexus between defense matters and diplomacy. Yet he needed direct access to the president. He did not play up to Nixon as Kissinger did. The three men shared a cynicism toward Soviet leaders and skepticism toward the US intelligence community. Moreover, as illuminated by John Maurer, Nixon and Kissinger privately regarded their own particular approach to arms controls as favorable to US advantages in the strategic arms competition.[15] Nitze did not believe that to be the case. Simply put, he regarded himself as the more knowledgeable about how nuclear weapons shaped international politics.

In the aftermath of the Cuban Missile Crisis, the Soviets constructed the SS-9. This was more devastating than anything in the US arsenal. It had a length of some thirty-two meters with a launch weight of some 180 tons. This compared with the Minuteman III's length of some eighteen meters and launch weight of some seventy-eight tons. Its increased size meant that the SS-9 could launch a warhead (or warheads) larger than would be necessary to destroy a US city.

Did the Soviets intend to use the SS-9 in a "counterforce" strike to preemptively take out the US Minuteman fleet as they sat in their silos? What were the Soviets seeking to achieve in their buildup? At what point would they stop? Answers to these questions were fiendishly tricky to ascertain. "I recall that as we were preparing our negotiating position in 1969, an intelligence estimate approved by the Joint Chiefs came across my desk setting forth the judgment that once the Soviets attained parity they would cease the buildup of their forces, seeing no useful purpose in going further," Nitze later recounted.[16] He called the head of the Defense Intelligence Agency, Major General Daniel Graham, to ask on what evidence this estimate had been based. "It turned out that they had no factual evidence whatever; the estimate merely reflected their own consensus based on guesswork and hope."[17]

The methodology came down to "mirror imaging"—the presumption that Soviet leaders held the same perspectives about war and peace as their US counterparts. Nitze "concluded from this experience [speaking with Daniel Graham] that in the absence of hard information to the contrary, the intelligence community was prone to assume that the Soviets would look at matters [as] Americans would." Nitze rejected that assumption. The Soviets, as evidenced by their ability to withstand unbelievable losses in World War II and their construction of an extensive shelter system in Moscow—which Nitze had seen with his own eyes in the summer of 1955—were prepared to fight and survive a nuclear war. They would not settle with "parity" after erasing the US margin of nuclear superiority in the aftermath of the Cuban Missile Crisis. Neither on this occasion nor on many others did Nitze consider the prospect that by seeking strategic superiority the Soviets *were*, in fact, acting the same way as their US counterparts.

Nitze persuaded the leadership of his old office, the Office of the Secretary of Defense's ISA, to launch a "Red Team" exercise to try to get into the mindsets of the opposing Soviet delegation. He engineered the appointment of his friend Charles Burton Marshall, now a SAIS professor, as head of the team. Nitze expected that the Soviets would approach the negotiations "as being merely one more arena in their ongoing confrontation with the United States." The Red Team predicted that, rather than a means to establish genuine détente, the Soviets would consider arms control negotiations as essentially another venue for waging the Cold War. Here, again, Nitze did not consider that the US side might be doing the same thing.

Soviet negotiators possessed an inherent advantage in that they could stonewall at the negotiating table and then blame the intransigence of the West when the talks produced no results. Nitze felt the *New York Times*, *Washington Post*, and *Time* would amplify such a narrative, much as they had done in covering Vietnam. He had witnessed this firsthand during his eight years at the Pentagon under Kennedy and Johnson. So, with very modest expectations, Nitze prepared to depart for Helsinki. He expected a zero-sum game in which the Soviets sought "to obtain the best results possible for the USSR and the worst results possible for the United States."[18]

Nitze knew what the United States *ought* to be seeking: a nuclear arms agreement to be implemented in two phases—limitations and reductions.

These could be negotiated simultaneously. His "comprehensive plan" would restrict the ICBM arsenals of each side to five hundred launchers with a maximum volume of fifty cubic meters. There would be an overall cap of 1,300 across the other legs of the (air-, land-, and sea-based) nuclear triad. Nitze calculated that such figures would reduce overall Soviet throw weight by a factor of one-seventh. This would create a more stable relationship between Washington and Moscow. To achieve this objective, however, the US side needed to offer the Soviets incentives to reduce their burgeoning lead in "heavy missiles." Possibilities could include US flexibility to negotiate restrictions on Safeguard, which Nitze had helped the administration get through the Senate for this express purpose; caps on the number of Minuteman III missiles that were being deployed; and potential restrictions on MIRVs, where the United States held a fleeting technological advantage.[19]

Negotiating both phases at once meant for Nitze that the Nixon administration could prevent the evaporation of US political will while maintaining support for the systems that gave the United States leverage. For instance, an agreement to restrict Safeguard might entice the Soviets to *limit* their production of SS-9s. However, if Congress subsequently cut the funds for the rest of Safeguard following the first phase, the Soviets would have no incentive to *reduce* SS-9s as part of a second phase. "The President should be aware, that if the agreement expires under circumstances where continuation on the same terms would be disadvantageous to us, we may not then be able to negotiate an adequately improved agreement," Nitze purportedly told Deputy Secretary of Defense David Packard. "Failure to negotiate a new agreement after expiration of the first could result in an arms race substantially more serious than the present one."[20]

When the SALT negotiations began in Helsinki on November 17, 1969, Nitze was gloomy. The international press corps that had camped out in the city expected a breakthrough. Yet there were no clear instructions from the White House, nor was there even a consensus position within the Nixon administration. The US delegation professed agreement with Soviet counterparts: there was to be no "linkage" between an arms control deal and Vietnam (or the Middle East). Yet—as Nitze and others would learn from Richard Nixon's memoir—that was precisely what the president had in mind. And, in his back-channel negotiations with Soviet ambassador Anatoly Dobrynin, National Security Advisor Henry Kissinger was pursuing that objective.

Moreover, members of the Senate Foreign Relations Committee distrusted Nixon. While Democrats wanted to curb the nuclear arms race, they did not want to give the president credit for doing so. "In short, there was a general pressure on us to be flexible," Nitze later recounted. "As a result, we never did

FIGURE 8.1. (L–R) Delegates Harold Brown, Paul Nitze, and Royal Allison, Helsinki, November 15, 1969. Nitze represented the Department of Defense at the Strategic Arms Limitations Talks. He had low expectations. Photo by Bettmann/Getty Images.

have a solid US position to put forward, one that [had] the full support of Congress as well as of the administration."[21] The Soviets, who were keen observers of US politics, "tailored their negotiating tactics accordingly."[22] As a result the United States was not negotiating from a position of strength.

Nitze warned that the US side was falling into a trap. "[T]he Soviets are laying the foundation for a plausible agreement to curb the arms race in a manner inconsistent with approved US positions, the logic of which, however, will be difficult to resist," as NSC staffer Helmut Sonnenfeldt summarized Nitze's initial assessment. "The main points will be a zero level of ABMs, a ban on MIRVs, and [a] simple flight test ban, with third country threats met by politico-strategic consultations. They may also have in mind a halt to further construction of offensive launchers, if the above conditions are met." "This position may be difficult, [Nitze] feels, unless we lay foundation for limiting and reducing offensive launchers, while permitting MIRVs and nationwide ABMs, or by guiding a MIRV test ban in the direction of the [o]ption that provides for limit on number of SS-9 and throw-weight. If, however, we want to move toward a MIRV ban, then there may be advantages in raising moratorium now rather than postponing."[23] This depiction underscores the extent to which Nitze's cynicism could get the better of him. The fact that the Soviets aspired to seek a ban on MIRVs meant—to him—that the United States ought to oppose a MIRV ban.

As the Verification Panel reconvened following the first round of SALT, Nitze associated himself with a group believing "that reductions are the most dramatic, yet serious, proposal we could make other than proposing a MIRV ban and that reducing offensive missile potential on both sides would be advantageous for the United States because otherwise, the Soviets will build up an enormous advantage over us in offensive missile payload."[24] This distinction between limitation and reduction lost sight of the main thing that interested President Nixon—obtaining a deal.

On March 25, 1970, the president convened a meeting of the US delegation and Kissinger. Nixon pondered whether the Soviets might one day agree to on-site inspections to verify that they were adhering to a test ban that went beyond the Limited Test Ban Treaty of 1963 and set limits on testing yields. To no one's surprise, Nitze expressed doubt. On MIRVs, Nixon stated: "I want to hear Paul Nitze's argument." Nitze reiterated the president's criteria for "sufficiency," as he had articulated the previous fall, meaning a second-strike capability, no temptation for a Soviet first-strike, and no "great disparity in damage capability."[25] "The United States is the first nation in the world in strength," Nixon responded. "In terms of diplomacy, I would not like to see the President of the United States in a situation with a significant Soviet advantage. I don't want them 2–1 over us, they with ABM and we not, etc., etc.," the president went on to say. "We can't let the world know we are #2."[26]

All the men in the room wanted the United States to be number one. Nitze saw the means toward that end as a robust, comprehensive arms deal crafted entirely on its own terms. He, however, did not have to deal with any other foreign policy problem, and he did not have to run for reelection. For Nixon and Kissinger, SALT was linked to their efforts to extricate US forces from Vietnam and restore US prestige on the world stage. Their reasoning accorded with Charles Burton Marshall's Red Team's analysis of Soviet leaders' intentions toward SALT: waging the Cold War more effectively.

"We can't let the world know we are #2," Nitze agreed with the president. "To get assurance of destruction, we need MIRV." MIRVs were necessary for the same logic that Nitze had urged the pursuit of the hydrogen bomb back in late 1949: "[The Soviets] will go to MIRV." After which US Minuteman silos and B-52 bomber bases would be vulnerable to a Soviet first strike. US strategic forces would have to be reconfigured to emphasize the sea-based leg of the triad, something that could not be achieved until 1978, after Nixon left office. Only *reductions* could achieve the criteria that Nixon had laid out. "I am not at all sure it is negotiable," Nitze told the president and his advisers. In short, "There is certainly no panacea."[27]

Nitze was backtracking his stance of the previous year, when he advocated for banning MIRVs. "Two considerations predominated in my changed thinking," he later recounted—without reflecting on how Soviet aspirations for a MIRV ban might have shaped this change in thinking—"first, our greater reliance on MIRV technology; and second, my waning confidence that on-site inspection would solve the problem of monitoring a MIRV ban."[28] On the latter, Nitze was persuaded by a conversation with his Soviet counterpart, who explained that one side could easily switch out MIRVs for individual warheads just before the arrival of inspectors.

The Problem of Fixed Land-Based Missiles with MIRVs

Fixed land-based MIRVs complicated the nuclear arms race. The United States could leverage its industrial base and superior miniaturization technology to produce MIRVs to place on its fleet of Minutemen III missiles. Yet the Soviets would inevitably catch up. Whether their own MIRVs proved to be more accurate was a second-order problem. Fixed land-based MIRVs on either side were strategically too important not to launch upon warning of an imminent attack from the opposing side. Such a warning could turn out to be a false alarm. Yet the missiles would already be in the air. With the early indications of an attack, US or Soviet leadership would have no choice but to "use them or lose them."

In a 1969 article, "To Cap the Volcano," former national security adviser McGeorge Bundy wrote: "In light of the certain prospect of retaliation, there has been literally no chance at all that any sane political authority, in either the United States or the Soviet Union, would consciously choose to start a nuclear war."[29] Bundy's prospect was "true for the past, the present and the foreseeable future." Yet he and Nitze had both participated in meetings in 1961 where President Kennedy and his advisers discussed nuclear options over Berlin. In 1950, Nitze weighed in the prospect of atomic use in Korea. There had been at least some chance that the US president would have gone in that direction—especially had Khrushchev not backed down over Berlin and Cuba. And even if there was no chance, it did not hold that the situation remained constant in a world where MIRVs made fixed land-based missile silos exponentially more valuable. In the scenario of "use them or lose them," the US president or Soviet premier would be operating under the assumption that the other side had already started a nuclear war, and he would be merely retaliating.

There was also the prospect of a "non-sane" Soviet political authority who would take out US land-based forces to preempt what he anticipated to be an impending attack. Such a "counterforce" strike would spare US cities. Would the US president retaliate against Soviet cities, knowing that this action would precipitate a Soviet strike on US cities? Such was Nitze's premise as he started to flesh out as a scenario for US defeat in a nuclear war. He was certain that, short of starting an actual war, the Soviets—influenced by the proliferation of MIRVs—might be emboldened to take risks everywhere.

When it came to SALT, Kissinger kept the US delegation—including its head Gerard Smith—as well as Secretary of State William Rogers, in the dark. Instead, he negotiated via a back channel with the Soviet ambassador to the United States, Anatoly Dobrynin. Kissinger's exploits notwithstanding, the SALT delegation produced the "Vienna Option" of 1970, which separated weapons that could hit the Soviets—medium-range and intermediate-range ballistic missiles, and forward-based systems, which included US fighter bombers in Europe—from the counting formulas for strategic arms. Under terms worked out by the delegation, SALT consisted *only* of land-based missiles, submarine-based missiles, and bombers that the Americans and Soviets had targeted at each other and with a range greater than the closest distance between the Soviet Union and the continental United States. The "Vienna Option" grouped US and allied missiles that could strike the Soviet Union with Soviet missiles that could not reach farther than US allies. "Non-strategic" systems could not reach the American homeland. This was a critical distinction that ultimately redounded to the US advantage.

The Problem of Missile Defense

Following the lackluster first round of SALT, Nitze helped craft a plan to introduce a draft ABM agreement in early 1970. With Congress on the hunt to eliminate Safeguard, Nitze urged the Nixon administration to play the ABM card as quickly as possible. Not only were the Soviets expanding the Galosh system around Moscow, they were constructing another one (Talinn) to protect against missiles breaching their perimeter. Nitze pressed the administration to propose either a ban on ABM altogether or limit them to two sites: one to protect the "national capital region" and a faraway one to protect a missile field—in the US case, one of the Minuteman fields in North Dakota, South Dakota, Wyoming, Montana, or Missouri.

Critics of détente played up the fact that the Soviets had installed an ABM defense system around Moscow. Yet they seldom acknowledged that it comprised nuclear-tipped interceptors that would obliterate the outskirts of the city and fail to stop all incoming missiles. There was virtually no chance that

Congress would ever approve such a system around a US city—or that sub-urban residents would allow nuclear-tipped anti-missile batteries in their backyards.[30] In other words, placing restrictions on ABM would prevent the Soviets from building something for which a US counterpart was politically impossible.

Integrating ABM restrictions into the SALT negotiations was a challeng-ing task, however. At a June 24, 1970, meeting of the Verification Panel, Dep-uty Secretary of Defense David Packard argued that "NCA [national capital region option] is not a very useful approach for us." Gerard Smith agreed: "Raising the Zero ABM will confuse negotiations."[31] In subsequent meetings in Washington and rounds with the Soviets alternating between Helsinki and Vienna, Nixon's advisers and negotiators debated whether to pursue a limited or outright ban on ABM defense. From Nitze's perspective, the Soviets would never dismantle the elaborate system they had constructed around Moscow. As he had seen firsthand in the summer of 1955, the city also had a compli-cated civil defense system designed to shelter or evacuate millions of its citi-zens. Galosh was the first line of defense in limiting damage from a nuclear attack. Demanding that the Soviets give it up was not feasible.

Others recognized the vital importance of Galosh to Soviet security. The Soviets needed a defense against China, as Gerard Smith said to President Nixon in an NSC meeting on June 30, 1971. "I think there is another reason the Soviets want the Moscow System," Nitze interjected. "The Soviet High Command, which meets in Moscow, is the main thing to be protected." This was a long-standing assumption for which there was no solid evidence to sup-port or disprove it. However, Nitze felt there was no solid evidence to rule out that the Soviets wanted to protect the entire country from nuclear attack. "The Soviets will continue to have a light defense of Moscow while continu-ing to vigorously pursue R&D for thick defense [of the rest of the country] which they would also like to have." Nitze concurred with Nixon's assess-ment that Soviet leaders held an "emotional attachment" to the defense of Moscow—one that Nixon did not apparently hold for Washington, DC. While the Soviet position in the SALT negotiations was to limit ABM inter-ceptors to one hundred, Nitze was convinced they were bluffing.[32]

Nitze spent the next few months crafting the basis for an ABM agreement. The peculiarities of the English and Russian languages made this about more than just a matter of numbers. "Nitze feels good progress is being made on developing common language, on well-defined differences, on the definitions and conditions that go into an ABM agreement," Assistant Secretary of De-fense Gardiner Tucker wrote Deputy Secretary of Defense Packard after speak-ing with Nitze on September 11, 1971.

Nitze was more upbeat about ABM than the rest of SALT since he believed there had been a rapid deterioration in the overall strategic balance since 1969. Anticipating that the Department of Defense was about to launch a campaign against Kissinger's proposed limits on strategic forces, Wayne Smith of the NSC staff wrote Kissinger on October 6, 1971, pointing to "recent remarks by Paul Nitze to the effect that the question of survivability of strategic forces under a SALT agreement had changed radically since last March." Smith warned Kissinger—who could not have been pleased—that "we need to look again at our entire proposal in light of the numerical growth of Soviet forces and of the developments . . . disclosed by recent photography."[33]

The Imperfections of SALT I

Gerard Smith, not Nitze, headed the US SALT delegation. Unfortunately for him, Kissinger continually undermined his authority. President Nixon had instructed the national security adviser to emerge with a deal before the November 1972 election. Whatever insight Nixon may have gleaned from Nitze's knowledge about nuclear weapons during the first year and a half of his administration was overshadowed by that political objective. In a meeting with Smith and Deputy National Security Advisor Alexander Haig on March 21, 1972 (at which Kissinger was not present), Nixon suggested that Nitze's role should be to generate Democratic support when it came time to secure the Senate's advice and consent for the Interim Agreement. SALT I was not a treaty requiring the approval of two-thirds of the Senate; the barrier to success was lower. The ABM Treaty, in contrast, required approval by two-thirds of a Senate, in which Democrats held a ten-seat majority.

More important than obtaining an agreement or even holding the upcoming summit—which Nixon professed his willingness to cancel—was to ratchet up pressure against the North Vietnamese in retaliation for the Easter Offensive and force them to accept a deal at negotiations in Paris. Nixon needed this to occur in advance of the November presidential election. Kissinger kept the US SALT delegation sequestered in Helsinki in the leadup to Nixon's signing of SALT I and the ABM Treaty in Moscow on May 26, 1972. He and Nixon arrived in Moscow before the final agreement on the Interim Agreement's terms. At the last minute, Kissinger finally relented and told Smith to come to the signing ceremony and bring Nitze along.[34]

Nitze's return to Moscow was inglorious. Detained at the airport, initially blocked from getting into the US embassy, he announced himself to a marine as the former secretary of the navy and was placed in a headlock. Nitze arrived at the signing ceremony for SALT just after Nixon and Kissinger had signed the agreements and departed. Nitze regarded the ABM Treaty as incrementally positive. On the other hand, SALT I encapsulated his concerns from the start: an interim deal concocted to meet a political timetable would not achieve the objectives of arresting the Soviet buildup and restoring US strength.

Upon their return from Moscow, Nixon and Kissinger plotted a strategy for shepherding both SALT I and the ABM Treaty through the Senate. The president considered Nitze one of the rare few who could advocate for the administration's policies in front of skeptics such as Democratic senators, academic elites, and the editorial board of the *New York Times*. On June 14, 1972, Nixon asked Kissinger whether Nitze was really on board.[35] Grudgingly, Nitze agreed to testify before the Senate. In a June 17 meeting of the Verification Panel, he expressed doubts about how the administration presented the Interim Agreement (SALT I) to Congress. Nitze thought it should have been linked to a request for commitments to US strategic modernization. He also bridled at the suggestion that Soviet diesel submarines were not threatening the American homeland, "What do you mean they can't reach us!" he exclaimed. "These 'G' class subs have been on station against the continental US and now they plan to use them against our allies." He noted that they had also been "on station against us" during the Cuban Missile Crisis and afterward. When he was secretary of the navy, they had been "a matter of great concern to us." "Sir, that was a long time ago," CIA analyst Bruce Clarke responded. "They have been carried for at least the last five years as only a peripheral threat."[36]

Nitze would not let go of the Cuban Missile Crisis. The danger of SALT— as Nitze had stated at the outset—was that Congress and the US public would consider the strategic arms competition to have ended. He feared that Congress would not appropriate the funds necessary for systems that provided leverage to constrain the Soviet arsenal, which would continue to grow. Only through a reduction in Soviet forces could the two sides reach a point of strategic stability that would actually lessen the chances of nuclear war. That remained his key takeaway from the Cuban Missile Crisis. Chastened by the real prospect of nuclear war, the American people had mistakenly accepted the premise of MAD and let Secretary of Defense Robert McNamara impose an arbitrary limit of one thousand Minutemen.

Moreover, Kissinger's SALT interventions meant that the United States wound up taking shortcuts. The national security adviser was bound to give up something in the final hours by arriving in Moscow for the summit before the deal was settled. It was only a matter of time before Senator Henry "Scoop" Jackson and others demanded to know what Kissinger had conceded.

Ultimately, SALT I was an imperfect agreement that yielded modest results. Its intention was to slow down the arms race, which did not happen. Even with comparative and absolute advantages in MIRV technologies, US negotiators declined to leverage this strength to take off the table the weapons that posed the greatest threat to peace. Adherents to MAD claimed that ABMs were destabilizing. Yet MIRVs were far more destabilizing than ABM systems. And there was no way that the United States would construct a perimeter of nuclear-tipped interceptors to shoot down all Soviet missiles.

If the agreement was imperfect, Kissinger does not deserve all the blame. Never before had leaders from the United States and the Soviet Union (or any other country) signed a pact limiting offensive nuclear weapons. The president had tasked him to obtain one before the election. And he did, even if it was one that failed to stop the main strategic threat to US land-based forces: the Soviet SS-9, which was far larger than anything in the US arsenal (and would evolve into the even-more-menacing SS-18 "Satan").

Nitze presumed that the Soviets intended for this line of heavy missiles to provide, potentially, a "first strike" capability to destroy US Minuteman silos. No other justification was plausible. The SS-9 was too big to be used merely against US cities. Fixed land-based missiles could not be part of a secure secondary strike reserve force. They only made sense to be used first; or, to deter the US side from launching a first strike against them. The US side could make marginal adjustments, such as improved accuracy of the Minuteman III and its reentry vehicles. As a signatory to the NPT, the United States had pledged only to modernize—not increase—its strategic arsenal and to pursue negotiations to reduce overall stockpiles.

The "modernized" mainstay of US land-based forces—the "Missile Experimental," or MX—consisted of miniaturized warheads and a sleeker delivery vehicle. Yet neither the Nixon administration nor its successor could muster the political will to fund it. As subsequent presidents would find, a combustible mix of technical and political considerations stymied policy makers' attempts to base such an inviting target in the US heartland.

SALT II

The US Senate ratified the permanent ABM Treaty on August 3, 1972. The following month, it voted to approve the Interim Agreement (SALT I). Authorization of that five-year accord came with an amendment sponsored by Senator Henry "Scoop" Jackson (whose staff included Nitze's former intern, Richard

Perle) requiring that any future agreement "would not limit the United States to levels of intercontinental strategic forces inferior to the limits provided for the Soviet Union."[37] The Jackson Amendment hovered over strategic arms control for the remainder of the Cold War.

That fall, with Nixon headed toward a smashing victory over Senator George McGovern, his administration planned for the next phase of negotiations. SALT II meant not only to slow the arms race but to *reduce* arsenals. Unlike SALT I, it was intended to be a permanent treaty of indefinite duration. An initial round of SALT II took place in Moscow, yet negotiators bided their time, awaiting the outcome of the presidential election.

In a Verification Panel meeting on October 31, 1972, Nitze laid out what he considered the priorities to be after the November 7 election. To get real reductions, US negotiators should consider equal aggregates of forces. They needed to insist on a definition of "strategic forces" that included Soviet Backfire bombers and excluded US forward-based systems. The main objective should be curbing "throw-weight," or the gross sum of payloads that the Soviet missile fleet could launch into space. "Equal aggregates" were insufficient without equal limits on missile throw-weight, Nitze insisted, as the latter was not comparable to bomber payloads.[38]

Limiting Soviet throw weight offered a way to reduce Soviet heavy missiles armed with MIRVs. This became Nitze's obsession. Although he had previously told Nixon there was "no panacea," restrictions on throw weight solved the problem of MIRV counting (which was impossible through "National Technical Means"—since overhead surveillance cannot discern the number of reentry vehicles atop a ballistic missile). Even with on-site inspections, which the Soviets had always ruled out, technicians could apparently switch the number of reentry vehicles on a missile in only six hours—as Nitze was certain—making it easy to cheat. Throw weight was measurable, and its sum was countable.

Nitze's pessimism about concluding sequential agreements proved justified. Congress provided no real leverage for US negotiators in 1973. Critics of détente pounced on the fact that the Soviets held a numerical advantage in an arms race that was set to continue. Moreover, arms accords had not curtailed Soviet interventions in the Third World.

Following Nixon's landslide reelection, the president cleaned house. Gerard Smith departed the ACDA, and a purge of that body ensued.[39] Suspicions about General Royal Allison's "firmness" apparently led the Joint Chiefs of Staff to replace him with General Edward Rowny, a hard-liner. Within the Pentagon, the departure of Melvin Laird—whom Nixon and Kissinger had long distrusted—preceded those of Johnny Foster and Gardiner Tucker, two figures respected, who remained as the Department of Defense representative to

SALT II under the new secretary of defense, Elliot Richardson. Secretary of State Henry Kissinger retained the title of national security adviser.

Nitze was skeptical about SALT II from the start. As he saw it, the principal US goal should be to get the Soviets to accept the concept of "essential equivalence," which the Jackson Amendment had codified.[40] That would be difficult. "If the problem is a domestic one, we can demonstrate that we have made a serious effort to negotiate a MIRV ban," Nitze stated at a meeting of the Verification Panel on August 13, 1973—even though such a deal was unlikely to materialize. "We need to make a real try to reduce throw weight or we have to improve the survivability of our own forces." Yet neither of those things seemed likely to happen either. Kissinger asked, "What would we want to get strategic stability?" Nitze responded, "We would want a provisional MIRV ban, but that's not negotiable. I don't see the types of measures that would be negotiable which would reduce our problem of survivability." The United States should consider building mobile land missiles, which could theoretically survive a Soviet first strike. Yet the administration could not count on Congress to nurture programs that would resolve US vulnerabilities. That meant the Soviets had no incentive to trade away something they knew threatened to exploit US vulnerabilities. "We have one concrete problem," professed an exasperated Kissinger at one point. "The negotiation opens in September and our negotiator needs instructions."[41]

On October 6, 1973, Egyptian and Syrian forces launched a surprise attack against Israel during the high holiday of Yom Kippur. Initially caught flat-footed, the Israel Defense Force repelled the attack—despite the Nixon administration's wavering on its commitment to resupply Israel.[42] In a moment that has attracted considerable attention among scholars of the role of nuclear weapons in international affairs, Kissinger ordered the defense readiness condition (DEFCON) level lowered (i.e., closer to nuclear war) to signal US resolve in light of Brezhnev's threat to intervene.[43] Nitze played no role in this oft-cited example of successful nuclear signaling, and did not speculate about this moment either then or in later years. It likely would not have mattered to him. His main takeaway was that the Soviets had greenlighted the attack on Israel—just as they must have done with Korea in 1950. In 1973, it revealed to Nitze Moscow's lack of commitment to détente.[44]

Watergate and US Diplomacy

Meanwhile, President Nixon was busy trying to deflect revelations about the 1972 break-in at the Democratic National Headquarters at the Watergate complex in Washington. Nitze and State Department representative Alexis Johnson, following a blunt conversation in November 1973 with Soviet negotiator Vladimir Semonov, concluded that the Soviets would stonewall on SALT II so long as the Watergate scandal weighed on the president.[45] Nitze returned home and wrote a paper he distributed to the new team working on arms control. "As they say in the journalism trade," he later characterized it, "Henry [Kissinger] 'spiked' my paper."[46] Nitze confided in the newly appointed secretary of defense, James Schlesinger, that he was about to resign.

However, Nitze stayed on. He exhorted the Verification Panel in November and December to focus on reducing Soviet throw weight, scoffing at any proposal that did not do so. "In addition to the advantage in number of missiles MIRVed," another interim agreement with the Soviets "would also give them a substantial advantage in throw-weight," he wrote on November 23.[47] Nor should counting be limited solely to the throw weight of MIRV missiles. "We're only talking about MIRVed throw-weight. They would sacrifice some excess throw-weight," Nitze chided the group on December 28. Soviet single warheads—which had much higher yields than US equivalents—contributed to the importance of using throw weight as the metric. "Trying to get throw-weight equality is more important than MIRVed throw-weight."[48]

There was one other consideration. In a substantive session on January 30, 1974, Nitze seized on the other problem with MIRV negotiations: the United States had in development the Undersea Long-Range Missile System (ULMS) and its planned follow-on system, ULMS II. This would evolve into the Trident II SLBM, a highly secure counterforce weapon. There was no way that Congress would support the SLBM program, which was considerably more expensive than land-based missile launchers, if it were equipped only with a missile carrying only a single reentry vehicle (RV). Nitze stated in his consistently logical approach: "We need 3.5 million pounds of throw-weight for our SLBM program. We want 1.3 million for ICBMs. That's an aggregate of 4.8." To which Kissinger responded: "We can't sell [to Congress] 1.3 land-based and 3.5 SLBMs."[49]

Almost twenty years after their initial encounter in the Council on Foreign Relations study group, Nitze and Kissinger were still arguing over the details of what the Soviets would or would not accept—and what Congress would or would not accept. At issue here were the fine details of a nuclear agreement the basic premise of which most Americans thought was a good thing. Few congressmen understand, or cared, about "MIRVd throw-weight" versus "aggregate throw-weight." The headline issue for critics of détente was that SALT I had failed to stop the nuclear arms race and that Soviet risk-taking abroad had only increased.

Nitze attempted to extricate himself from SALT. In January 1974, amid the haggling between him and Kissinger, Secretary of Defense James Schlesinger offered Nitze the position of assistant secretary of defense for ISA, the job that he had once held and been offered on two other occasions. Yet Senator Barry Goldwater apparently blamed him for Lyndon Johnson's notorious 1964 Daisy Ad, in which a young girl plucking flowers was interrupted by a nuclear blast. At Goldwater's request, the White House rescinded the nomination.

On April 23, 1974, Kissinger joked to Schlesinger and Deputy National Security Advisor Brent Scowcroft that "Brezhnev's obsession on warheads was like Nitze's on throw-weight."[50] This comparison was not without merit. A few minutes later, in a meeting of the Verification Committee, Nitze continued to point out flaws in the US positions on SALT II. The conversation went nowhere. "Reductions coupled with MIRV restrictions would be useful, but reductions as a substitute for MIRV restrictions would be useless," Kissinger stated. "I'm not sure," Nitze responded. "It depends whether you look just at the survivability of Minuteman or at the whole strategic situation. It helps the latter." The two men continued a fruitless dialog:

SECRETARY KISSINGER: Why?
MR. NITZE: It reduces their throw-weight and targets. We come out better on the difference between a first and second strike.
SECRETARY KISSINGER: They won't reduce land-based missiles.
MR. NITZE: I admit there is a question of negotiability.[51]

"It's hard to foresee what we might want in five or ten years," Nitze said later on in the Verification Meeting, which would be his last. "We might not want a defense of Washington in the next five years, but we might in the future."[52] On May 28, 1974, Nitze submitted his letter of resignation. Failing to elicit a response, he wrote again on June 14, unilaterally terminating his appointment. He also released a public statement citing the ongoing Watergate scandal: "Until the Office of the Presidency has been restored to its principal function of upholding the Constitution and taking care of the fair execution of the laws, and thus be able to function effectively at home and abroad, I see no real prospect for reversing certain unfortunate trends in the evolving situation."[53]

The explanation in Nitze's letter was not altogether true. He had worked for the Nixon administration long after the Watergate scandal broke and had no problem accepting Secretary of Defense James Schlesinger's offer to become assistant secretary of defense for ISA prior to Goldwater's nixing it. His frustration mounted when the US side did not take his advice on SALT II. The ABM Treaty was worthwhile, yet it was also premised on the search for a permanent agreement to follow. There could be no permanent agreement that

Congress could ratify under the terms of the Jackson Amendment so long as the Nixon administration disregarded Nitze's concerns. At the same time, Congress was not willing to sign off on the funding needed to give US negotiators leverage in the negotiations.

Still, Nitze's point about the damage of Watergate was valid. Nixon complained that his critics were weakening the executive branch and, by extension, US SALT negotiators in Geneva. The president, however, bore responsibility for those circumstances through his actions. Nitze surmised that the Soviets were taking advantage of Kissinger, in the summer of 1974, by accepting his proposal to reorient SALT II as a ten-year agreement rather than a treaty of unlimited duration. During those years, Moscow could continue its buildup while Washington slashed military budgets. He was probably correct in that assessment.

Weakness

Upon his inauguration on August 1974, President Gerald Ford said that the United States' "long national nightmare is over."[54] That did not change Paul Nitze's sense of how the Soviets perceived the United States. "With our three-hundred-million-dollar budget ceiling, our chronic balance of payments problems, and the approaching onset of double-digit inflation adding further to our economic woes, they had to see some prospect of our not adding to our strategic programs sufficient additional real resources to change the relative trends."[55] Here—as opposed to the debate over strategic parity—Nitze presumed that Soviet leaders thought the same way that US leaders would in their place.

After meeting with Soviet general secretary, Leonid Brezhnev, in Vladivostok in November 1974, Ford and Kissinger came away with a draft formula placing equal ceilings on the aggregate mix of ballistic missiles and long-range bombers, as well as an agreement to exclude forward-based systems from a potential SALT II. Outside of government, Nitze did not share the optimistic tenor following Vladivostok. Those agreements placed no restrictions on Soviet throw weight, his favorite metric.

Nevertheless, Nitze afforded Kissinger the benefit of his opinion at lunch with him alone in January 1975. From Kissinger's perspective, the Vladivostok formula was the best that the administration could have expected. He shared with Nitze an account of a recent meeting with Soviet ambassador Anatoly Dobrynin, who had told him that leaders in the Kremlin did not regard the Ford administration as reliable. Now the problem was no longer Watergate but rather the Church Committee in the Senate and the Pike Committee in the House of Representatives. Both were holding extensive hearings looking into the executive branch—the White House and the CIA. "Any government that can't protect its intelligence and security agencies is not to be taken seriously," Dobrynin told Kissinger.

Nitze and Kissinger believed that a weakened presidency was bad for the United States. While Nitze did not find himself under fire during the Church and Pike hearings, he, by his later admission, participated in surveillance and subterfuge against US citizens in the anti-war movement during his time as deputy secretary of defense. Nitze's allegiance to Nixon personally was limited. What got to him was the glee with which members of his own Democratic Party continued to go after the institution of the presidency even after President Lyndon Johnson declined to run again in 1968 and Richard Nixon stepped down in 1974. Supporters of 1972 Democratic presidential nominee George McGovern felt vindicated when Nixon resigned in advance of impeachment. Still, from Nitze's perspective, to revive the call "Come Home, America" was to betray the party's noble tradition of applying US power toward noble ends. And to destroy the power of the US presidency was to neuter the country's ability to compete with the Soviet Union.

"During the late 1940s and early 1950s, it had been a Democratic administration that had led the way toward the economic and political recovery of those great areas of the Eurasian landmass which had either been devastated by World War II or had to face the difficult transition from colonialism to independence," Nitze later wrote. In leading such efforts, the Democratic Party had called for solid defense and alliances to oppose aggression. "But by the mid-1970s, this consensus had largely broken down under the divisive effects of Vietnam and the unsettling political atmosphere generated by the Watergate affair."[56] Nitze remained a Democrat, yet he regarded Harry Truman—not George McGovern—as the embodiment of first principles. Beyond a consistent preference for raising taxes—to support defense spending—he did not have much to say about domestic politics. His creed of bringing harmony from the "tension between opposites" mattered more than political partisanship. No other national security figure of his stature served in government during the entirety of the Kennedy and Johnson administrations and the entirety of the Nixon administration.

Accepting former New York governor Averell Harriman's invitation to participate in a foreign policy study group for the Democratic Advisory Council shortly after his resignation from the SALT II delegation in 1974, Nitze was dismayed by his younger colleagues, whose views were forged by watching the disintegration of the US polity over Vietnam. Not surprisingly, given every one of his previous stances since World War II, Nitze emphasized to younger (and some older) colleagues the necessity of increasing the defense budget. He allowed that second-generation national security practitioners recognized nuclear proliferation to be a serious problem. But such proliferation, he insisted, was really the consequence of a growing strategic imbalance that favored the Soviet Union.[57] Others spoke about human rights and the importance of the Helsinki Accords which President Gerald Ford, General Secretary Leonid Brezhnev, and the heads of thirty-three other nations signed in 1975. To Nitze, the US promotion of human rights was hypocritical and pointless.

From outside the government, during the Ford administration, Nitze involved himself in waging a personal Cold War against Kissinger (even though they took time out to lunch together). Chief of Naval Operations Elmo Zumwalt, who had worked for Nitze when the latter was assistant secretary of defense ISA and the secretary of the navy, took up the mantle of opposing Kissinger on arms control and pretty much everything else. This intra-agency spat was picked up in the press and made its way into international negotiations, including Kissinger's July 15, 1974, meeting with the People's Republic of China ambassador, Huang Chen. When Chen mentioned reading press reports about Zumwalt's criticism, Kissinger responded. "When I read them I get scared myself! We don't have the practice in our country of sending our military leaders off to the provinces."[58] Nor was there any way to stop Paul Nitze, who spent the rest of the decade as a thorn in the side of incumbent national security teams.

The Soviet deployment of the SS-18 missile in 1975 reinforced every one of Nitze's critiques about US nuclear strategy over the previous decade. Ten MIRVs on fixed land-based missiles created a scenario of "use them or lose them" that invited a first strike in a crisis such as the one that Washington and Moscow had experienced with Berlin and Cuba. Worse, the Soviets were building them without limits, while the US side had arbitrarily capped its own production of its Minuteman forces. Paul Nitze saw the ABM Treaty as incrementally positive, yet otherwise saw arms control agreements with the Soviets as unhelpful.

"Neither side need acquire more than a second-strike capability and, if either does, the other need not respond since its security is not threatened," as the eminent political scientist Robert Jervis once put it.[59] "Need not" did not capture what both sides in the Cold War actually did. There was simply no way that US policy makers could say that Soviet SS-18 did not threaten US security. The United States was pursuing a new generation of SLBMs—the Trident I—yet the destabilizing effects of heavy land-based ICBMs outweighed the advantages of a secure second-strike capability.

During the initial rounds of SALT, the US delegation had the opportunity to leverage its short-term advantage on MIRV deployment yet failed to do so. "I would say in retrospect," Kissinger stated in a background briefing in December 1974, "that I wish I had thought through the implications of a MIRVed world more thoughtfully in 1969 and 1970 than I did."[60]

During those earlier years, Nitze initially supported a MIRV ban but then reversed course for three main reasons: first, he and Kissinger simply did not want to give them up. The second was that the US side thought the Soviets would not negotiate over them. The third was that he became entranced by the technicalities of verification.

Nitze, Kissinger, and Nixon shared a desire to regain strategic superiority. All three men concurred that the United States had prevailed in the Cuban Missile Crisis—at least, in the short term—because of overwhelming US strength. All three agreed that they could not muster enough political support to build up the number of US missiles. Their views differed over what exactly regaining strategic superiority would look like. Nixon and Kissinger made a virtue out of necessity by attempting to play up US technological advantages. Yet they did not share Nitze's sense that an arms control accord needed to be crafted on its terms, independently from the other Cold War political flashpoints. The circularity of Nitze's approach was that he regarded overwhelming US strength as a prerequisite for achieving a strategic arms accord, which itself was meant to restore US preponderance. None of the principals—Nixon, Kissinger, or Nitze—realized that the Soviets did not regard the SS-18 to be an element destabilizing US national security.

Political expediency, which had influenced Nixon's and Kissinger's approach to SALT, had negative consequences when it came to constraining the nuclear arms race. They had wanted a deal in advance of the 1972 presidential election in order to hit a political trifecta—China, Vietnam, and SALT—and succeeded.[61] This trifecta came at a price. The Jackson Amendment stated that the Senate could never again sign off on a deal unless there was strict equality in numbers. Kissinger attempted to sell any disparity in numbers by reiterating that the United States had advanced technology and held a MIRV advantage. Both sides were led to invent categories of nuclear weapons, coming up with creative definitions of what constituted a nuclear warhead.

Nitze could do such things. In the spring of 1974, Director of the Office of Net Assessment Andrew Marshall, who had served on Kissinger's NSC staff, tasked the Historical Office of the Secretary of Defense with preparing a comprehensive analysis of the strategic arms competition. The substance of the resulting study contained little beyond what Paul Nitze knew—or presumed to know—having participated in nearly all of the nuclear debates since the inception of the atomic era. "Both at the beginning and the end of the [1970s]," as his biographer Nicholas Thompson correctly states, "he knew more about nuclear weapons than almost any other man alive."[62] That did not mean his policy prescriptions were the right ones or that he was in a position to implement them. It meant he could offer the most authoritative and withering criticism of those who believed they had the right answers and were in places to put their ideas into motion.

CHAPTER 9

The Nitze Scenario

Sixty-nine years old in 1976, Paul Nitze aspired to return to a high government position. under the next Democratic president. Instead, that summer, he antagonized the Democratic nominee, former governor Jimmy Carter, in a meeting with his top advisers. Shut out of the Carter administration, Nitze managed to remain as relevant as he had been during the Dwight Eisenhower administration. He maintained active security clearances to keep abreast of intelligence and military matters, drawing upon his expertise on nuclear policies to mount never-ending attacks on the president. Part of Nitze's motivation was spite. Yet, under Carter's presidency, the Soviets seemed to him to be gaining strength and using their perceived power to take risks and gain geopolitical influence.

Meanwhile, Carter and his aides embraced strategic arms control policies that Nitze regarded as counter-effective. The president acknowledged there were significant problems with the US nuclear deterrent. The difference between Carter and Nitze came down to whether SALT II would buy time to enact a more ambitious agenda to reduce destabilizing Soviet systems finally— or whether it would make that impossible. Carter and his team believed that SALT II would pave the way for Congress to sign off on strategic modernization. Nitze thought the opposite: a modest deal that failed to address the main problem would only lead to less support for strategic modernization and to worse bargains. From his perspective, the Soviet invasion of Afghanistan in

December 1979 exemplified everything he had been saying about the erosion of US strength and its consequences for Soviet risk-taking. That invasion, which accelerated the collapse of détente, encapsulated the dangers laid out in the "Nitze Scenario."

"Strategic Stability" and the 1976 Presidential Election

In the Nitze Scenario, the Soviets could launch a "counterforce" first strike that limited US civilian losses while simultaneously sending a message to the US president: surrender or die. The US president could then call on second-strike forces at sea or in the air to retaliate against Soviet cities—which would by then have been evacuated or sheltered—after which the Soviets would still have sufficient forces to take out US cities. Or, the president could surrender, avert a partial genocide of Soviet civilians, and save one hundred million US lives. The chances of that second response happening were extraordinarily slim—but not impossible. Its *plausibility*, however, emboldened Soviet risk-taking in all contested areas of the Cold War. Nitze felt sure the Soviets *knew* they could press their advantage because any US president would fear that a crisis like that in Cuba would result in a reversed outcome. At some point, the United States would have to back down, as the Soviets had done in October 1962. From 1975 onward, Nitze worried over the psychological consequences of the Soviets building enough SS-18 missiles to take out the entire US Minuteman fleet.

Perceptions had consequences. For Nitze, few perceptions were as dangerous as the presupposition that Soviet leaders thought about nuclear war in the same way as US leaders. "Americans have thought throughout the last 30 years in terms of deterring nuclear war, with the debate centering on how much effort is necessary to maintain deterrence, to keep nuclear war unthinkable," he wrote in the January 1976 edition of *Foreign Affairs*. Yet the Soviets did not regard nuclear war as unthinkable. They had "meticulously planned civil defense"—which Nitze had seen firsthand during his trip in 1955—demonstrating their preparedness for waging such a war. Soviet capabilities now enabled them to take out the US land-based ICBMs while limiting damage from retaliatory strikes from the sea- and air-based legs of the US nuclear triad.

Strategic stability remained achievable. As Nitze laid out in his *Foreign Affairs* article, that concept meant "minimizing both the possibility of nuclear war and the likelihood that nuclear arms might be used by either side as a means of decisive pressure in key areas of the world."[1] It was not just the prospect of a nuclear war that resulted from strategic instability: confidence in the superiority of one's side emboldened leaders to become aggressive in areas of the world where there was not necessarily confrontation between the military forces of East and West. Those actions could increase the likelihood of war, drawing more people into the communist orbit.

Nitze described how the United States retained nuclear superiority until 1954 and regained it—through improvements in missile technology—between 1956 and 1962. He touched on his association with former secretary of defense Robert McNamara in the early 1960s. "In essence, the United States opted at that point to stress technological improvement rather than expanded force levels."[2] The US side pursued "crisis stability"—"where neither side could gain from a first strike"—and "mutual assured destruction," meaning that "each side would have a fully adequate second-strike capability to deter the other." The objective was "to downgrade nuclear weapons as an element in US–Soviet competition and to prepare the way for systematic reductions in nuclear arms." As the US side "adjusted its posture," it gave clear signals to the Soviets to reciprocate "and stop there." "Unfortunately, however, the Soviet Union chose to pursue a course that was ambiguous: it could be interpreted as being aimed at overtaking the United States but then stopping at parity; it could, however, be interpreted as being aimed at establishing superiority in numbers of launchers and in throw-weight and perhaps ultimately, a nuclear-war winning capability on the Soviet side."[3]

SALT I and the prospective SALT II agreement failed to arrest the Soviet buildup. Nitze included two charts of Soviet–US throw-weight ratios—compiled by his former assistant T. K. Jones—that predicted immense Soviet superiority within the next decade. "In sum, the trends in relative military strength are such that, unless we move promptly to reverse them, the United States is moving toward a posture of minimum deterrence in which we would be conceding to the Soviet Union the potential for a military and political victory if deterrence failed."[4] To solve the problem of Minuteman vulnerability he proposed a "proliferation of low-cost shelters for what is called a multiple launch-point system," based on "a large number of shelter installations so that the smaller number of actual missile launchers could be readily moved and deployed among these installations on a random pattern deliberately varied at adequate intervals of time."[5]

Whether or not Nitze grasped the sheer cost of such a plan is unclear. What is undoubtedly clear is that he believed Americans could afford to pay more to defend the American way of life, which he was sure that Soviet gains endangered. Nitze may or may not have realized he was conflating "strategic stability" with "US strategic stability." For him the world was inevitably more stable when the United States maintained nuclear and conventional superiority, even though he doubted that US leaders would actually launch a first strike against the Soviets; they very likely would not even launch a second strike. For him, the Soviets would not be so constrained.

Nitze hoped his *Foreign Affairs* article would resonate with the field of Democratic candidates gearing up to challenge President Gerald Ford in the November election. Notwithstanding his time in the Nixon administration, Nitze remained a Democrat, and he initially favored Washington Senator Henry "Scoop" Jackson in the 1976 presidential primary.[6] However, when Jackson's candidacy fizzled, Nitze did not know who to support. His children recommended Jimmy Carter.[7]

The former governor of Georgia, Carter, concentrated his efforts on the early Iowa caucuses. A former naval lieutenant on a nuclear-powered submarine, he took a keen interest in defense matters. Democrats had a thin roster of national security professionals; fallout from the US involvement in the Vietnam War had decimated their ranks. Carter's closest foreign policy adviser, Zbigniew Brzezinski, had been a relatively junior member of the Policy Planning Staff during the Johnson administration. There he got to know Carter through their work on the Trilateral Commission, which the banker and family scion David Rockefeller sponsored to increase cooperation between the United States, Western Europe, and Japan. Nitze had vastly more experience than Brzezinski. He sent Carter his writings and met with him in Washington. Carter impressed Nitze: "He had read the speeches and the articles that I'd sent him and really understood them."[8]

The circumstances of the 1976 matchup were peculiar. Ford ran as the incumbent, having been elected neither vice president nor president. He nearly lost in the Republican primary to the former governor of California, Ronald Reagan. In the general election, Carter reiterated several of Reagan's criticisms of Ford's foreign policy while assailing him as weak on human rights. Ford's advisers saw the former Georgia governor as lacking conviction. "There is the Carter, who has Paul Warnke as a national security advisor and will cut $7 billion from the defense budget and there is the Carter, who has Paul Nitze as his advisor and will add $30 billion to the defense budget," according to a publication that came across the desk of White House Chief of Staff Richard Cheney.[9]

On July 26, Nitze was the senior member of a delegation of advisers on foreign and defense policy that met with Carter at his mother's home in Plains, Georgia. On the bus ride from the airport to Plains, Nitze perused a recent study cowritten by Harold Brown, who was also on the bus. Nitze grew irritated with Brown, the physicist and former president of Caltech with whom Nitze had served on the SALT I delegation (and, before that, had been secretary of the air force while Nitze was deputy secretary of defense). He pressed him on the details. "I went through it with him . . . and pointed out some things in it that were totally incorrect. I said, Harold, I can't understand this." Brown claimed that he had not written the portions with which Nitze took umbrage. Nitze responded: "yes, Harold, but you signed the god-dam thing. It's got your signature on it."[10]

The subsequent meeting in Plains did not go well for Nitze. While he knew almost everyone in attendance, relationships with some had frayed. According to Cyrus Vance, the lawyer whom the Kennedys had preferred over Nitze for the position of deputy secretary of defense in 1963, "all of the advisors present at the meeting agreed that there was rough equivalence between US and Soviet strategic forces at present . . . [and] there was disagreement among the group as to where present trends in strategic deployment programs were leading, and what the United States should do about these trends."[11] Brown spoke next, followed by four others, including Paul Warnke, who had succeeded Nitze as assistant secretary of defense for ISA and worked under him when Nitze was later deputy secretary of defense. As the report for Cheney intimated, he saw things differently from Nitze.

Warnke delivered a sanguine account of the Cold War nuclear balance. He "stressed that the present situation is not too bad from the United States' perspective." The overriding objective was to "avoid a deterioration in the present strategic balance," and the best means to that end was to obtain a permanent SALT agreement (i.e., SALT II); this was preferable to "responding to Soviet strategic programs with step-ups in US strategic programs." If elected, Carter would have little time to achieve results. Without further agreements, domestic and allied political pressures would probably force the United States to respond with "step-ups," even though "they would not mean anything in military terms."[12] Although he did not phrase it in such evocative terms, Warnke was recapitulating the gist of his own *Foreign Policy* article, "Apes on a Treadmill," in which he called for a halt to the nuclear arms race and characterized the United States and the Soviet Union as primates.[13] Dissatisfaction with that article inspired Paul Nitze to write his January 1976 *Foreign Affairs* article on strategic stability.

Nitze responded negatively to Warnke's briefing in Plains. When it came his turn, he noted "disagreement with much of what had been said so far." Nitze "emphasized that he was more pessimistic than most of the other people in the room, that he thought that the existing trends were extremely negative," and "that if the trends were not reversed quickly, that within ten years the ratios of US and USS.R. [sic] strategic capabilities that would survive a counterforce exchange would be most unfavorable from the US perspective." Citing a recent study, he pointed to calculations that, by the mid-1980s, US forces retaliating against a Soviet first strike would "be able to kill only 4.5 percent of the Soviet population"—hardly a statistic that would ever deter the Kremlin from striking first.[14]

"Soviet forces surviving a US counterforce attack, under present plans, would be able to destroy a much larger proportion of the US population," Nitze said. The salient point was that "the assumptions underlying statements made by the majority of the group were not supportable by the data—that, in fact, the data showed that in the future the Soviet Union would be able to survive a nuclear exchange but that the United States would not; and that, in [Nitze's] view, if such a situation were to develop, it would have major impact on the two nations' respective behavior."[15]

Nitze did not elaborate on all of the implications of accepting a Soviet first-strike capability. Instead, Vance, Brown, and other group members interjected that his calculations portrayed a worst-case scenario and that Nitze had based his predictions on questionable assumptions about Soviet civil defense and US targeting policies. James Woolsey, who had served under Nitze on the SALT delegation, came to his defense. He and Nitze were outnumbered. Responding to Carter's questions about Soviet and US attitudes toward limited nuclear war, the other participants responded that the United States had always considered the likelihood that it would be the first to use nuclear weapons in defense of allies in Europe and Asia. It was unclear what the Soviet position was. Nitze had no reason to reject this analysis. But he thought the conversation had strayed from the heart of the matter, with Vance and Brown more interested in flattering Carter than establishing sound policy prescriptions.

The dynamics with the future president resembled those of meetings Nitze had sat through in the Oval Office. At first, Nitze forcefully stated his conclusions. For the rest of the session, which covered SALT II and overall force structure, Nitze bit his tongue. Only twice more did he speak. First, during the discussion of NATO capabilities in a conventional war to say that he "took a more pessimistic view of the situation than did the other members of the group." Then in a discussion of limiting the transfer of arms to governments in so-called third world countries, to say that he was "generally . . . less hostile to such arms sales than other members of the group."

Realizing that the discussion had gone against him, Nitze was surprised when Carter asked him to follow up with a report laying out fundamental arms control objectives.[16] By September, he had prepared a paper incorporating his concerns about SALT II. In it he urged Carter to seek—should he prevail in November—a treaty of unlimited duration in which neither side could launch a first strike. Additional strategic offensive arms reductions could be deferred to follow-on SALT III negotiations. Nitze delivered these recommendations to the home of one of Carter's campaign assistants, Anthony Lake (who would go on to lead the Policy Planning Staff under Carter and serve as national security adviser to President William Clinton). Carter never received it.[17]

In preparation for one of Carter's debates with Gerald Ford, where the former governor would go after the sitting president for pursuing an amoral foreign policy that was weak on human rights, a member of the former governor's campaign reached out to Admiral Elmo Zumwalt for his advice. Associating himself "with the views of Paul Nitze," according to campaign staffer Nick Macneil, who was reporting to another one, Richard Holbrooke, Zumwalt asserted: "When Carter takes office and has full access to the facts he will see that he faces Soviet superiority in both nuclear and conventional weapons."[18]

Team B and the Carter Transition

When Secretary of the Air Force Thomas Reed called on outside experts to revisit the 1974 Joint Strategic Bomber Study, he chose Nitze. Along with the other two members, they recommended in October 1976 that the United States pursue the B-1 bomber, which could allegedly penetrate Soviet defenses.[19] Nitze considered his expertise on nuclear matters viable because of his access to classified material. His message to the Carter campaign was: I know the whole story, based on classified material I cannot describe; if and when you see it, you will agree with me.

What became known as the "Team B" exercise, in which Nitze also participated, was more consequential than the bomber study. In 1976, the CIA director George H. W. Bush authorized an alternative national intelligence estimate by which outside experts (Team B) examined the same raw intelligence as a Team A consisting of analysts serving in the CIA and other components of the government. Team B was to independently take on Soviet intentions and capabilities. Going over the same sets of evidence, Team B—which included Nitze's protégé, Paul Wolfowitz—demolished Team A. Harvard University professor of history Richard Pipes wrote the final report, which painted a dire portrait of a decade of neglect and faulty analytic assumptions on the part of the US intelligence community.[20] It was leaked to the press shortly after Carter defeated Ford in November 1976.

Unlike previous studies in which Nitze had participated, Team B was focused on the present—not five to ten years into the future. Its purpose was not to throw the election one way or another but rather to pressure whoever became president in January 1977 to take a harder line concerning the Soviet Union. Subsequently, the vanguard in that effort became the Committee on the Present Danger (CPD), a bipartisan group of national security veterans that took its name from a group that Harvard president James Conant had established in 1950 to support the policy recommendations of NSC-68 (namely, support for increased defense spending).

Nitze ramped up his involvement with the CPD even as he held out hope for joining the administration at the start. He was not completely out of the running. A January 1977 Carter transition memorandum included Nitze as one of ten possibilities for top jobs on the national security team—the others were James Schlesinger, George Ball, Cyrus Vance, Zbigniew Brzezinski, Harold Brown, Anthony Lake, Ted Sorenson, Richard Holbrooke, and Paul Warnke.[21] Nitze and Ball became the only ones not nominated or appointed to a high-level position. In later years, Harold Brown recalled that he had broached with Carter the idea of making Nitze undersecretary of defense for policy—a newly created position between assistant secretary of defense for ISA and the secretary of defense—but that Carter nixed it citing the July 1976 meeting in Plains that had gone so badly.[22]

Nitze's retaliation was swift. He bitterly attacked his onetime friend, Paul Warnke, whom Carter had nominated as head of the ACDA and the chief negotiator on SALT II. Nitze spoke neutrally about Warnke's qualifications in an uneventful first session. According to Nitze's biographer, Nicholas Thompson, Warnke's testimony a few days later greatly agitated Nitze; as did murmurings about what Warnke and allies thought of his own.[23] When he returned to Capitol Hill for a second testimony, Nitze tore into Warnke, his former subordinate and friend.

The personal drama coincided with a substantive debate over how to restrain the nuclear arms race. Warnke advocated for pursuing agreements wherein both sides agreed to curb their buildups. However, Nitze insisted that the United States must first restore its strength. Here and elsewhere, Nitze hammered home the themes that past arms control agreements had failed and that the only prospect for future success was to reduce Soviet throw weight. However, his substantive points received less attention than a moment of crosstalk in which Nitze responded to a senator's question, implying that he considered himself a "better American" than Warnke.[24] "At one time or another, [Warnke] had opposed almost every effort to modernize or improve US strategic systems, including the construction of the B-1 bomber, the MIRVing of the Minuteman III force, conversion of the Polaris submarines to Poseidon, and construction of the Trident force," he reasoned in his memoir. "Had Warnke's advice in these matters been followed, our strategic forces would have rapidly grown obsolete."[25] In the same memoir, he attributed the "better American" line to a misunderstanding of what he heard. Yet he remained convinced of the severity of his charges. "Well, frankly, I think Warnke was a complete horse's ass with zero character and no sense," he said privately.[26]

President Carter took notice of Nitze's attack and defended his man in a March 9 press conference. On March 16, Nitze wrote Carter to say that the president had mischaracterized his reservations about Warnke. More critical than mollifying any hurt feelings, Nitze felt, was dispelling Carter's illusions about the state of the strategic balance. "It is possible that you may actually believe that a mutually agreed reduction in the number of strategic launchers below 2,400 and/or MIRVed launchers below 1,320 will, in fact, 'reduce the threat of nuclear destruction of the world,'" Nitze wrote Carter. However, the reverse was true. The threat of nuclear destruction would *increase* "unless such a reduction in numbers of launchers is coupled with other provisions which will both substantially reduce Soviet ICBM throw-weight and effectively lower the ratio of Soviet missile throw-weight advantage over the US toward parity." Not only did US national security depend on reductions in overall Soviet throw weight, those cuts needed to be substantial. So long as the Soviets possessed the upper hand in throw weight, Nitze was convinced, they had a massive advantage in MIRVs that could take out the entirety of the US ground-based nuclear arsenal.

Nitze urged Carter to jettison his campaign pledge to cut the defense budget. Stagnant growth in US defense spending and the lack of upgrades in the nation's strategic capabilities virtually guaranteed that the Soviets would defer actually reducing the systems they had been building ever since the early 1960s. "It is not conceivable that such radical reductions toward parity are negotiable under current circumstances or those foreseeable in the intermediate range future," Nitze insisted (while also conveying the point that it was now up to the United States to rearm itself "toward parity"). Instead, the United States needed to ratchet up efforts, starting with the deployment of something Nitze had described in his *Foreign Affairs* piece in January 1976: semi-mobile US ICBM systems with multiple launch and aim points. "I, and I am sure many others would be much relieved if your advisors were prepared to suggest some practicable alternate approach which would meet the objectives of strategic stability and rough equivalence more promptly, at less cost," Nitze summed up. "We have been [thus far] unable to find one."[27]

Carter read Nitze's letter and declined to respond.[28] He may not have ruminated on Nitze's critiques at the moment, yet, later on, he did recalibrate his overall approach to the Soviets. Throughout his first year in office the former governor and naval lieutenant was concentrated on a systematic review of US strategic systems with a determination to keep his promise to decrease defense spending. On June 30, 1977, he canceled the B-1 bomber, the supersonic plane that was designed to succeed the B-52 as the air-based leg of the nuclear triad. (The president's more affordable alternative—and one that proved to be far more effective—was to develop air-launched cruise missiles [ALCMs] to be placed inside refurbished B-52s.) It is important to note that Carter embraced strategic modernization so long as it did not imperil his campaign promises. On July 8, Secretary of Defense Harold Brown wrote Carter that the United States had terminated the line of production for the Minuteman III, which constituted the land-based leg—ensuring that Washington could not build beyond its self-imposed one thousand limit. In his justification, Brown noted, "Even Paul Nitze's 'Committee on the Present Danger' looks ahead to other strategic options, suggesting that the M-X 'may well be the next important issue' in strategic arms planning."[29]

It might have made more sense to withhold these decisions, using them as bargaining chips in the negotiations. The Soviets had rejected both the grand and modest packages that Secretary of State Cyrus Vance had offered them during his visit that March. Unilaterally canceling B-1 did not bring them around. In justifying that decision, President Carter cited the work on cruise missiles, MX, the Trident SLBM, and the ultra-secret stealth bomber program that became the B-2 bomber: these were all systems that he regarded as vital— meaning that he would never put them on the table to trade. By the summer of its first year in office, the Carter administration was no closer to a SALT agreement. And the president's failure to respond to Nitze's letter was a slight that he would not forget.

SALT II Signing and Ratification

Nitze refused to be ignored. He was convinced that his diagnosis of the problem was accurate. Only his prescription could solve it. Moreover, his takeaway from the first six of the Eisenhower years—when he had blasted the administration's spending priorities and nuclear strategy—was that he was not powerless to bring about a shift in high policy. Nitze generated fear inside the White House that he would attack it in op-eds in the top daily newspapers and quarterly editions of *Foreign Affairs*. Republicans would then cite Nitze's criticism of Carter as evidence that the president was choosing the softer line and abandoning the first principles of Truman Democrats.

On August 4, 1977, President Carter hosted Nitze and other SALT II critics.[30] The meeting went similarly to the unfortunate one earlier in Plains, Georgia. "Met with the Committee on the Present Danger, Paul Nitze, Gene Rostow, and others," the president wrote in his diary afterward. "It was an unpleasant meeting where they insinuated that we were on the verge of catastrophe, inferior to the Soviets, and I and the previous president had betrayed the nation's interest." Carter told them he welcomed "constructive advice, balancing all factors with at least the possibility that the Soviets did want a permanent peace and not suicidal nuclear war." However, the president was not confident these individuals would help.[31]

Needless to say, Carter's depiction of this meeting would have displeased Nitze. Neither he nor other CPD members accepted the framework of "permanent peace" versus "suicidal nuclear war." Nuclear war was not suicidal if Soviet cities could be spared following a preemptive attack on the US land-based deterrent—that was the apparent danger of the SS-18. Permanent peace was unattainable so long as Soviet leaders believed that they could continue to pursue gains in the third world, confident that a US president would eventually back down in a nuclear crisis.

Following up later that month, Secretary of Defense Brown and National Security Advisor Brzezinski met with Nitze and Admiral Zumwalt. The four men argued over scenarios that would have confounded the American people. "Paul feels that 100 million Soviet and 70 million US casualties is a distinctly different situation than 70 million Soviet and 100 million US casualties, and that our actions in the face of such estimates would clearly be different in one case than the other," Brown wrote Carter. "I disagree, not only because of the difficulty in distinguishing between one catastrophe in that range and another, but also because of the immense uncertainties in such estimates in the first place." An even more obscure and grim discussion followed. "Paul is interested in the relative US and Soviet positions in terms of surviving nuclear forces after a protracted series of exchanges aimed primarily at the opposing nuclear forces," Brown went on to write the president. "He feels that if the Soviets should end up with any significant advantage over us in these terms, they could prevent our recovery and coerce us at will for many years. We have agreed to make and compare analyses of that case."[32]

Although Nitze opposed the Carter administration on SALT II, his views on the scenarios of nuclear warfighting received considerable attention inside it. As with John Foster Dulles, in the mid-1950s, Nitze made life miserable for an incumbent yet remained indispensable on matters of national security. He possessed intimate knowledge about a theoretical subject impossible for others to master: nuclear weapons and the calculus of decisions leading up to a nuclear war between two nuclear powers. Among the surviving ExComm members from the Cuban Missile Crisis, nearly all were either Kennedy loyalists or politically toxic after Vietnam—or both. And, as he had in the 1950s, Nitze retained active security clearances, now to support his contract work for the

CIA and Department of Defense. He stayed up to speed and was impossible to ignore.

Moreover, Brown, Brzezinski, and Carter took an intense interest in the macabre details of waging nuclear war, the extent of which probably exceeded that of Nitze himself. His focus was more on how to prevent a further decline in the US–Soviet strategic balance in the years following the resolution of the Cuban Missile Crisis—not nuclear targeting or the logistics of an actual "nuclear exchange." In or around September 1977, Brzezinski wrote Carter following up on questions the president had posed to Secretary of Defense Brown about limited nuclear war and the survivability of US command and control systems under nuclear attack.[33] Brzezinski recommended that President Carter visit Strategic Air Command Headquarters in Omaha for briefings on limited nuclear options. Over the next two years, Carter and Brzezinski, working in concert with the latter's military assistant, William Odom, devoted considerable attention to such matters.[34]

Surprisingly, Nitze did not know that the Carter administration was devoting so much time to coming up with limited nuclear options. Had he known, he probably would have disapproved. He viewed the Soviet fleet of SS-18 missiles—rather than vulnerabilities in US nuclear employment doctrine and connectivity—as the heart of the matter. However, the critical point here is that the Nitze Scenario spurred the Carter administration to take these initiatives. The purpose of coming up with limited nuclear options was to avert the moment in the scenario where the president had to decide whether to launch a nuclear strike against Soviet cities, knowing that this would cause immediate retaliation against US cities.

Carter and Brzezinski figured that SALT II could serve as a bridge to SALT III, hopefully including reductions in Soviet heavy missiles. Yet Nitze fundamentally rejected that prospect. SALT I confirmed to him that an interim agreement would provide Americans a false sense of security, leading to strategic apathy; meanwhile, the Soviets continued to build. And Moscow would continue to probe in areas such as the oil-rich Middle East, looking for resistance and confidence in the knowledge that the United States would eventually back down in a crisis.

SALT II was hardly the abomination that Nitze alleged. US crafters of it attempted to redress the deficiencies of SALT I. Its basic counting formula for SALT II took seriously Senator Jackson's criticism that SALT I afforded the Soviets higher numbers of ICBMs. And the concepts of "equal aggregates" and "freedom to mix" grew out of the 1975 understanding between President Ford and Premier Brezhnev at the Vladivostok Summit. Sticking points remained.

There were intense debates about such obscure matters as whether to count the Soviet Backfire as an intercontinental bomber and permit mobile ICBMs.

The Carter administration probably erred in trying to supplant the 1974 Vladivostok formula of 2,360 ballistic missiles for the Soviet Union and 1,710 for the United States. They attempted to allay critics' concerns by pursuing a permanent treaty. In a November 4, 1977, memorandum to Carter, Brzezinski rebutted the critique against SALT II. "Mobile ICBMs should be permitted since there is little chance of saving Minuteman," Brzezinski noted. "Nitze, in particular, is adamant on this issue." "The ban on mobile ICBMs is only for the period of the Protocol and will have no impact on the US M-X mobile ICBM development program. In the interim, we have halted the Soviet mobile ICBM program," Brzezinski claimed. "Permitting deployment of mobile ICBMs would open a new avenue in the strategic arms race and cause serious arms control verification problems," he said. "We have essentially deferred that important decision." "Permitting" was hardly the appropriate word here. As Nitze reminded the Carter administration at every available opportunity, the Soviets were moving ahead with deploying mobile ICBMs.[35]

Given concerns about strategic and crisis stability, Carter sought to reach a SALT II accord with the Soviets. This topped his foreign policy agenda throughout 1978. Paul Nitze remained its most high-profile nemesis. As Brzezinski and his military assistant Odom pursued efforts to resolve the deficiencies of following through on National Security Decision Memorandum 242, "Policy for Planning the Employment of Nuclear Weapons," the January 1974 strategy directive that emphasized counterforce. They self-consciously grappled with "Paul Nitze's scenario, where we lose our ICBM force to a Soviet first strike and then would not want to retaliate because the Soviets could then attack our cities."[36] That is to say: his criticism haunted the administration on policy, not just political, grounds. The difference was that Brzezinski and Odom chose to focus on upgrading "strategic connectivity" in the event of a nuclear war, as opposed to pursuing capabilities that could be traded away at the negotiating table in Geneva to reach the type of accord that Nitze might endorse.

Strategic Stability Revisited

On March 24, 1978, Nitze responded to a letter from a Korean scholar who had written him about his January 1976 *Foreign Affairs* article on strategic stability. The vulnerability of US Minuteman fields was worth considering alongside the outbreak of World War I, Nitze wrote. "In 1914, each of the major powers in Europe depended upon the speed of their mobilization for relative advantage in the event of war. As a result, when the Austrians began to mobilize, the Russians felt they also had to mobilize. That, in turn, caused the Germans to mobilize, which caused the French to mobilize. A set of forces was thus created which made it almost impossible for statesmen to avoid the outbreak of World War I." He applied the same (overly simplistic) model to the fundamental problem of the nuclear era. "In the strategic nuclear field, a situation in which the nuclear forces of one side are vulnerable to destruction by an initial strike by less than all of the nuclear forces of the other side is inherently unstable in a comparable manner."[37] Such was the situation in 1978: US nuclear forces remained vulnerable to destruction by an initial strike by less than all of the nuclear forces of the Soviet Union. Just as the mutual dependence on speedy mobilization made 1914 fundamentally unstable; so would Soviet first-strike capability *increase* the likelihood of a crisis turning into war.

At the Yale Political Union that fall, Nitze elaborated on instability in an era of détente. On September 19, 1978, he joined *Firing Line* host William F. Buckley to debate Senator George McGovern and retired admiral Eugene Larocque on whether SALT II advanced US interests. Nitze estimated the amount of money that the United States spent on strategic systems at around $10 billion and declared that this was a small price to pay for ensuring the safety of the nation in light of the continued buildup of the Soviet Union, which had introduced four new missiles since the signing of SALT I in 1972, and whose own military budget was expanding at a rate of between 4 and 5 percent a year.[38]

"At the time of the Cuban Missile Crisis, I know of no one who did not believe that the US had strategic superiority over the USSR," Nitze said.[39] He saw it as "highly unlikely that one will achieve through these negotiations a SALT Two agreement which will be in the strategic interest of the United States."[40] This was because the Carter administration was negotiating from a position of weakness. And, by telegraphing its unwillingness to devote resources to rebuilding its strength—by canceling the B-1 bomber and promising to cut defense spending even further—it gave the Soviets no incentive to make concessions on anything, least of all their first-strike capability. "How does one reduce the likelihood of nuclear war?" That was ever the most pertinent question to Nitze. US strength would prevent crises that could devolve into a nuclear exchange.

This fundamental point was more significant than a set of particular numbers: Nitze blamed the dismal state of the Cold War on the long-term loss of US strategic superiority. In his view, so much of the trauma of the previous decade and a half—the fiasco in Vietnam and the inability of successive US administrations to reach lasting stability with the Soviets through détente—stemmed from the same cause. Under the Nixon administration, Kissinger's opening to China and his shuttle diplomacy in the Middle East may have produced short-term political advantages; they had not changed for the better the overall Cold War situation.

Everything boiled down to the Nitze Scenario—to which Brzezinski and Odom referred privately. Were the Soviets to take out US land-based missiles, Washington would retain a secure second-strike force to retaliate against Soviet cities. Nitze acknowledged this before the audience at Yale. Yet if the Soviets had purposely struck first and avoided US cities, the consequence of a US president's attacking Soviet cities—an act of "genocide" in itself—would be immediate retaliation against every US city. Soviet leaders *knew* that a US president would not take such action. That meant they *also* knew that a US president would eventually back down.

"The problem of Minuteman vulnerability is unpleasantly real," former national security adviser McGeorge Bundy wrote Brzezinski on September 19, 1978, the same day as Nitze's Yale debate. "The Nitze scenarios [of a Soviet first strike] are highly implausible, but the increasing exposure of the Minuteman system is simply not what was aimed at when it was built. It is not about to become worthless, but in less than five years it will no longer be the secure second-strike system it was designed to be."[41] By Nitze's view of things, five years was nothing. Even this optimistic estimate would render it useless almost immediately. The Soviets could quickly draw out SALT II for another five years, confident that the Carter administration was committed to cutting defense spending and making glacial progress on the complicated matter of MX basing.

His public criticism notwithstanding, members of the administration hoped that Nitze could still be coaxed aboard. On November 20, 1978, Director of Central Intelligence Stansfield Turner gathered outside experts to discuss matters of arms control verification. He included Nitze. "[I]n order that we may be unfettered by problems of security," Turner wrote Nitze, "all the guests invited for the occasion will have SI (code-word) clearances. Nevertheless, I trust that our discussion will not become entangled in the pros and cons of a SALT II agreement but rather will rove widely over the subject of arms control verification, emphasizing the conceptual, even philosophical, aspects of the problems of verification." Nitze also met with Turner on December 7 to discuss the distinction between "violation" and "non-compliance."[42] As he had done during the Eisenhower years and at the tail end of Nixon–Ford, when Kissinger provided him special intelligence briefings, Nitze participated in closed-door, classified debates over national security—even as he pilloried the administration outside of those settings.

Turner did not change Nitze's mind on SALT II. Two days before, on December 5, 1978, at the Chicago Council on Foreign Relations, Nitze laid out his objections to the deal, which Secretary of State Vance had recently declared would be ready to sign before the end of 1979. As Nitze reminded the audience, the potential treaty was far less ambitious than the agreement of unlimited duration that US and Soviet negotiators had pursued after the 1972 Interim Agreement (SALT I), only to abandon it in 1974. SALT II was designed to last only until 1985, a "time when the strategic relationship between two sides is likely to be least favorable to the United States."[43] Another concession from the original objectives for SALT II—which Nitze knew plenty about because he served on the delegation—was equality: while the numbers of launchers were the same, the Soviets would be permitted to have three hundred very large ICBMs of the latest type; the United States, again, was not expecting to deploy MX before 1985. The timing of MX deployment would also make it impossible to have more than 550 of the 820 MIRVed ICBM launchers permitted under the treaty—so the breakdown was effectively 820 to 550.

The implications for "crisis stability" were worrying. During the previous fifteen years "it would not have profited either side to attack first. It would have required more ICBMs by the attacking side than it could have destroyed." However, that situation was set to change as the 1980s approached. "By that time, the Soviet Union may be in a position to destroy 90 percent of our ICBMs with an expenditure of only a third of its MIRVed ICBMs. Even if one assumes the survival of most of our bombers on alert and our submarines at-sea, the residue at our command would be strategically out-matched by the Soviet Union's retained war-making capability."[44] A final casualty of SALT, according to Nitze in his Chicago Council speech, was the ambition to achieve "true reductions" of the most destabilizing forces. As with the Interim Agreement, SALT II was intended to limit numerical growth—not reduce existing weapons.

Despite his public invectives against the Carter administration, its senior officials did not shun Nitze. On June 5, 1979, a little less than two weeks before President Carter and General Secretary Brezhnev were scheduled to sign SALT II, Nitze met with Secretary of State Vance and recounted the litany of US strategic deficiencies and negative trends over the previous decade. "Secretary Vance said that nevertheless was it not true that there were useful provisions in the treaty?" according to Nitze's notes. "Wasn't the limitation of 10 RVs per SS-18 launcher a useful limit?" Nitze thought it was not. Treaty or no treaty, the Soviets probably would not load that many RVs onto their giant SS-18 "Satan" missiles before the expiration of the agreement on December 31, 1985. The salient point was that SS-18s had a launch weight of over two hundred tons and a length of some thirty-three meters, while the Minuteman IIIs had a launch weight of some seventy-eight tons and a length of some eighteen meters. The SALT II treaty failed to bring about meaningful reductions. The public perception that it would slow the arms race redounded to the Soviets, from Nitze's perspective, because it meant that Congress would not fund the necessary strategic modernization.

"I could understand why the Executive Branch had closed ranks in a coordinated and full-scale effort to support ratification of the treaty," Nitze told Vance. "If they had not done so, the outside critics would have commented on their tactical ineptness in not having done so. But, to be frank, it was my view that most of the things that the President was saying about SALT II were simply untrue and that much of what Harold Brown was saying was misleading."[45] At the end of their meeting, Vance told Nitze that he "was one of the few opponents of the treaty who understood the treaty and what it was about."[46] Such words from Vance hardly constituted a full-throated defense of the agreement.

"The Executive Branch has now done an Alice in Wonderland on us," Nitze wrote in a memorandum to himself on June 11. "The word 'verify' no longer means what it used to mean. The CIA can no longer be asked any question about 'verification.' What they do is not now verification; it is now covered by a different word—the word 'monitor.'" Even apart from the linguistics of "verification" versus "monitoring," Nitze again seized on the critical deficiency in the treaty. It did not limit such a thing as Soviet throw weight.[47]

In a July 20, 1979, speech to the Commonwealth Club of California, Nitze came out forcefully against the Senate's ratification of SALT II.[48] He warned that NATO's conventional forces could last only a few weeks against a Soviet assault on Western Europe and that "essential equivalence" was a sham. Under a SALT II regime, Soviets would be able to destroy 90 percent of US ICBMS with only a fraction of their forces, while the United States' remaining forces following counterforce attack would be useless. By 1985, when SALT II was set to expire, the United States would find itself outmatched.

Nitze singled out potential swing votes in the Senate. In a September 24, 1979, letter to Senator Frank Church, Nitze criticized the recent testimony of Secretary of Defense Harold Brown, who reiterated confidence in the "essential equivalence" of both sides in the grizzly event of an all-out nuclear war—meaning neither side had any incentive to strike first. Nitze retorted, "As a result of [a Soviet initial attack] we could expect to lose approximately 90 percent of our ICBMs, 35 percent of our SLBMs, 50 percent of our bombers, and a higher percentage of our tankers." Nitze argued: "Our C^3+I [command, control, communications, and intelligence] capabilities would be severely degraded." In achieving that outcome, the Soviets "would have used up about 35 percent of its ICBM RVs, less than 20 percent of its SLBMs, and none of its bombers."[49] In addition to Senator Church, Nitze sent the letter to Republican Senator Jacob Javits, noting that he had gone over it with Admiral

Elmo Zumwalt and General Edward Rowny, who had assured him that "it is consistent with the insights they have gained as a result of reviewing SIOP/ RISOP [Red Integrated Strategic Offensive Plan] and SAGA [Studies, Analysis, and Gaming Agency] calculations over a number of years." It was impossible to rebut this last point. Members of Congress were not allowed to see the ultra-secret SIOP and the Red Team version of it—the RISOP. They had to take Nitze's word for it and, even though he had not seen the most recent SIOP and RISOP, his word carried significant weight.

In sum, Nitze was a formidable political force regarding the fate of SALT II in the Senate. No one could prove or disprove his ideas about what would or would not happen in the early hours and days of a nuclear war. He spoke with commanding authority and deployed arguments supported by evidence focused on worst-case scenarios. The targets of his criticisms responded—as Brown and Vance had in the summer of 1976—that the situation was not quite bad. However, as they acknowledged in Presidential Directive 18, there were significant problems with the US deterrent.

20th Century Fox, NSC-68, and the 1980 Election

Amid his contestations with the Carter administration, Nitze made a brief re-entry into the world of private sector dealmaking. Flush with cash from the release of the movie *Star Wars* on May 25, 1977, 20th Century Fox acquired the Aspen Skiing Company, of which Nitze was a significant shareholder. *Star Wars* may not have been his choice of entertainment, but a certain Ronald Reagan enjoyed it. Former governor of California and member of the CPD, the erstwhile screen star had very nearly defeated Gerald Ford in the 1976 Republican primary and was planning to run again in 1980. He frequently cited Nitze in his radio addresses. Considering Reagan an attractive candidate, Nitze lent him credibility. He seemed to embody the US Cold War first principles of Harry Truman, for whom Reagan had voted.

Declassified only in 1975, NSC-68, "United States Objectives and Programs for National Security," which Nitze had drafted in 1950, soon became a centerpiece of former governor Reagan's outreach to Truman Democrats. In a radio address on May 4, 1977, Reagan quoted passages from it, including: "no nation ever saved its freedom by disarming itself in the hope of placating an enemy."[50] Twenty-seven years after Truman signed off on a basic Cold War strategy, Reagan cited the efforts of Nitze, former secretary of state Dean

Rusk, former deputy secretary of defense David Packard, and others, who, through the reconstituted CPD, warned of a "Soviet drive for dominance based upon an unprecedented [military] buildup." The summation of the CPD's message was that "if the present drift continues, the US could find itself isolated in a hostile world with a succession of bitter choices between war & surrender."[51] In other radio addresses, Reagan cited former undersecretary of state Eugene Rostow's opinion—which Nitze shared—that during the Cuban Missile Crisis the Soviets backed down because the United States so vastly outmatched them in overall numbers of nuclear weapons.

When the Soviets invaded Afghanistan in December 1979, the Carter administration withdrew from Senate consideration SALT II. Nitze felt temporarily victorious since it was clear that SALT II was off the table for the foreseeable future—even though the United States still adhered to the unratified treaty until it would have expired anyway. Nevertheless, Nitze was unwilling to retire from the practice of national security.

Nitze went all-in against Jimmy Carter ahead of the 1980 presidential election. He would later describe this period with little self-awareness or self-reflection. He had somehow convinced himself that his "political involvement" in 1980 was considerably less than in 1976—but that was delusional. This came after he convinced himself that he had not told Senators to vote against ratification of SALT II—that he had merely wanted them to understand what the treaty meant—while he, in actuality, railed against SALT II publicly both in print and person.

"I believe we already know enough about the strategic nuclear situation and the Soviets to see that we have no real choice but to commit a major portion of our GNP [gross national product] to rearmament and improvement of ICBM survivability," Nitze wrote novelist Douglas Terman on February 20, 1980. In the wake of the Soviet invasion of Afghanistan, Carter asked Congress to raise the defense budget. From Nitze's perspective, this was precisely what he had advocated back in the summer of 1976 and again in early 1977.

As he had done in the 1950s, Nitze blended academic writings, government commissions that included classified information, and partisan politics— though he was loath to acknowledge the last. He was not a political person— even though he made sure people knew that he remained a registered Democrat. He supported Reagan, and the former governor supported him.[52] In his speech on August 18, 1980, Reagan, criticizing Carter's national security policies, quoted Nitze as saying, "The Kremlin leaders do not want the war; they want the world," "For that reason, they have put much of their military effort into strategic nuclear programs," Reagan went on to say. "Here the balance has been moving against us and will continue to do so if we follow the course set by this administration."[53] On November 4, 1980, Reagan defeated Carter in a landslide.

Out of government, Nitze's impact on US national security matched or exceeded that of previous phases when in government. President Carter and his advisers wanted to sign SALT II because they figured it would slow down the nuclear arms race. Nitze and his associates at the CPD predicted the opposite. Members of the Carter administration had hardly rejected Nitze. They listened to his concerns and attempted to win his support. In this, they failed.

A distinguished academic with expertise in nuclear weaponry, Robert Jervis, did not believe as Nitze did. In a June 1980 article titled, "Why Nuclear Superiority Doesn't Matter," he wrote, "The healthy fear of devastation, which cannot be exorcised short of the attainment of a first-strike capability, makes deterrence relatively easy." He continued, "The military advantages of striking first can only be translated into political gains if the war remains counterforce and the state with the most missiles left after a series of exchanges prevails without losing its population centers." Jervis noted that Nitze himself had overlooked that point in his January 1976 *Foreign Affairs* article, "Assuring Strategic Stability in an Era of Détente."[54]

Nitze felt that the Jervis argument was premised on the Soviets regarding nuclear war—both launching and enduring it—in the same way that Americans did. To them, perception of an imminent first-strike capability meant that they could blackmail US leaders and take tremendous risks. Invading Afghanistan in December 1979—Moscow's first deployment of military forces outside the Warsaw Pact since World War II—was just such a risk.

Four decades later, the most compelling explanation for that aggression was that Brezhnev feared the rise of a US-friendly regime on Soviet borders and regarded NATO's December 1979 Dual Track decision to deploy intermediate-range nuclear forces in Western Europe as evidence that détente was dead. This interpretation says that the Soviets acted out of a sense of desperation. By Nitze's logic, were Brezhnev to have considered Afghanistan in the summer of 1961 and fall of 1962 (as Nikita Khrushchev had pondered Berlin and Cuba), he would not have dared to invade. That assertion is, of course, impossible to prove or disprove.

The United States *did not* possess preponderant power in 1979. The strategic balance by the 1970s was at best "essential equivalence" in which Soviets held advantages neutralized by US advantages. And as to the "worst-case scenario" about which Nitze warned: the SS-18s indeed provided the Soviets a first-strike capability that they could leverage in geopolitical crises. While US economic capacity continued to surpass that of the communist world, stag-flation and oil shocks sapped the confidence of its citizens. By the end of the 1970s, few Americans believed the United States was winning the Cold War—Paul Nitze least of all. He was about to embark on a final government assignment in which he could play a critical role in crafting and negotiating the Cold War's most ambitious nuclear arms agreements. Doing so, he would fret about Moscow's nuclear superiority right up until the Soviet Union's collapse.

CHAPTER 10

A Walk in the Woods, 1981–1984

Paul Nitze found himself once again at the center of the US debate about nuclear weapons in the first half of the 1980s. On one side of that debate were proponents of a unilateral US freeze on nuclear weapons. Hoping that the Soviets would reciprocate, they advocated a freeze even though Moscow had deployed massive SS-18 "heavy missiles" and SS-20s that could hit all European capitals, while the United States and its allies had fielded no equivalent systems. On the other side were core supporters of President Ronald Reagan's promises to rebuild strength through a strategic modernization that aspired to match and surpass the Soviets in every category. More nuanced gradations of these positions existed on both sides. Divisions tended to align with partisan politics, yet not always. Nitze held the middle ground in these debates.

From the fall of 1981 to the end of 1983, Nitze headed the US delegation to the INF negotiations in Geneva. Outside that city in the summer of 1982, he went on a "walk in the woods" with his Soviet counterpart, Yuli Kvitsinsky. There Nitze broached the prospect of a deal that would limit US and allied deployment of land-based cruise missiles (and obviate the need for the Pershing II intermediate-range ballistic missiles), in exchange for sharp reductions in Soviet SS-20s. Nitze had exceeded his authority. Even without an especially close relationship with President Reagan, however, he kept his job.

Mission Capabilities Study

Nitze had supported Ronald Reagan in the 1980 presidential election but did not receive an appointment to a high position on the new team at the start of the Reagan administration. He nonetheless went to work at its behest. Director of Central Intelligence William Casey tasked Nitze with writing an outside analysis of the crisis in communist Poland, where rampant inflation, as well as strikes led by Solidarity, ground the economy to a halt. Speculation was mounting that the Soviet Union would intervene militarily, as it had done in Hungary in 1956 and Czechoslovakia in 1968. Nitze's assignment was to evaluate the likelihood of that happening.

Casey then asked Nitze for a comprehensive analysis of US and Soviet capabilities. This project generated controversy within the interagency bureaucracy. Since it was a "net assessment" that compared Soviet and US force structures (as opposed to an analysis of just the Soviet side), Pentagon officials insisted that the Defense Intelligence Agency should take the lead. The CIA countered that its analysts had the most accurate and up-to-date information about the Soviet Union. Through the System Planning Corporation, which had sponsored Nitze's work on Team B and other projects, the CIA insisted Nitze be in charge of leading the study, which integrated analysis from the Defense Intelligence Agency, the Office of Naval Intelligence, and the RAND Corporation. Nitze's conclusion cut through the bureaucratic squabbling: the Soviets possessed strategic superiority.

Nitze's determination that the Soviets were ahead did not mean he embraced President Reagan's domestic priorities or devotion to conservative shibboleths. In a June 2, 1981, episode of William F. Buckley's Firing Line, Nitze dismissed supply-side economics, calling it "extremely dangerous" to cut taxes while pursuing a much-needed increase in defense spending. He also did not regard the proposed Reagan defense buildup as sufficient to redress the problem of Soviet strategic superiority "either in the conventional or in the strategic nuclear sphere."[1]

Nitze reflected on "whether it was better to be red than dead." This question was central to the US modern conservative movement of which Buckley and President Reagan were iconic figures. Nitze was "inclined to think it is better to be red than dead if that is the question." Yet it was *not* the fundamental question that had animated US policy makers' response to communism. Nitze told Buckley's audience: "What we've tried to do over the entire period from 1946 to the present is to so conduct affairs that that would not be the question." And the best way to do that—whether in the late 1940s or early 1980s—was "to be sure that we had such forces that it would not profit the

Soviet Union to undertake a course of action likely to lead to a nuclear war."[2] In other words, the purpose of US and allied strength was to disincentivize Soviet aggression—not accept the inevitability of an apocalyptic showdown.

"Now, the situation has not improved in that regard," by Nitze's estimate.

It has gotten worse in the last 10 years. It has gotten materially worse. Today it is conceivable that the Russians could gain in initiating a nuclear war in a crisis. I'm not saying I want a nuclear war, but it is today I think conceivable that they could; it could be ever more so unless we cure some of these deficiencies. But at a minimum, I think the situation is one where the Soviets may not feel deterred about, for instance, invading Poland, renewing a blockade of Berlin, bringing pressure upon Europe and even more likely, taking positions in the Persian Gulf which go beyond what they've done to date and a position where Europe and Japan are no longer in a position to resist effectively and where we're faced with really very grave difficulties.[3]

Nitze's ongoing work for the CIA must indeed have reaffirmed his prior assumptions. He did not mention that he had access to classified intelligence on the situation in Poland as well as Soviet nuclear capabilities. His bottom line was that the United States needed to restore its strength to prevent the Soviets from invading Poland or instigating another Berlin crisis, spreading its influence in the Middle East, thus neutralizing the abilities of the Europeans and Japanese to resist the Kremlin's diktats.

Nitze, as so often, painted a grim picture. The trends of the previous quarter century had gone against the United States and its allies. Between 1956 and 1962, the United States cut spending on intercontinental nuclear capability by one-third "to what it has been during the last six years, so we've gone down by a factor of 66/23 in the amount of effort we've been putting into our defense program."[4] During the same period, the Soviets had been increasing their effort by 5–6 percent annually. The result was that they had spent three times as much per annum on strategic armaments.

In his *Firing Line* appearance and elsewhere, Nitze acknowledged that he had supported President Kennedy's cuts to ICBM spending. These were partly to provide for a conventional buildup that Nitze supported. Both types of weapons were now necessary—not because Nitze was a warmonger or even a hawk, but because of what he perceived to be a relentless Soviet buildup. He dismissed the notion of an "arms race" in the 1960s and 1970s; only one side—Moscow— was racing. Regarding the "arms race" and the calls for a mutual commitment to a nuclear freeze, Nitze stated: "I'd love to reverse it and I'd love to get it down to zero." However, it was incumbent upon the Soviets to take the first step.

"First strike" had become a term commonly associated with Nitze's fears of the consequences of a Soviet margin of superiority. Yet, he preferred the term "preemptive strike" in his renderings of the Nitze Scenario. "I don't think they want a first strike," he explained to Buckley, "but I think the problem is that they will feel that, if necessary, and if they feel that there's some danger that we might escalate rather than surrender in the Middle East or do this, that or the other—surrender in Europe—that we might engage in such a strike, then they will preempt and it was really a preemptive strike that seemed to me to be more appropriate wording than first strike." Indeed, the United States retained two other legs of the triad—bombers and submarines—that were in better shape than its land-based missiles. It all boiled down to the fundamental question: "how unequal are you prepared to have the situation and still feel comfortable with it?"[5]

His solution to these problems remained: rebuild US strength. The Soviets would have no incentive to launch a preemptive strike somewhere in, say, the Middle East if the United States possessed sufficient conventional power to come to the defense of its allies. Nor would they have the incentive to launch a preemptive strike against US land-based missiles if they knew that the land-based leg of the nuclear triad was "hardened" and survivable against a Soviet attack.

Command and Control

Around the time he appeared on *Firing Line*, Nitze gave a follow-up interview with official air force historians in which he summed up deterrence in the nuclear era.

> In first place, I think it is correct to say our fundamental objective is deterrence. We don't want a nuclear war. Then the question is: How do you assure deterrence? You are not going to get assurance unless you have the capability to deal with the situation in the event deterrence fails. So when you look at the second level, your objectives have to be related to the assumption that deterrence might fail, and that you can deal with the situation where deterrence has failed. There is a preliminary point to that even. That is, it makes a difference, if deterrence fails, what the mode is in which deterrence fails. If deterrence failed because of the fact that there is a significant advantage to be gained from striking first, that both makes it more likely that deterrence will fail and also makes it more likely that you will be behind the eight ball if deterrence does fail. Therefore, there is the

strongest possible motive for trying to see to it that the disposition and posture of our forces is such that the enemy cannot gain by striking first in a crisis or by striking first out of the blue. Now that is tough to do. It can be done, but we haven't in the past addressed ourselves to it with the priority that I think is merited. That is an important objective and one that we certainly ought to work on.

US leaders needed to feel strong enough to take the initiative in a crisis without fearing that the other side would launch a preemptive strike. If leaders were so worried, they would self-deter rather than deter the adversary.

"The second objective is to be sure that there isn't any doubt that we would have continuing command and control for some extended time period, not just for the moment that it is necessary to retaliate but for an extended period of time," Nitze went on to say.

> Because, if you don't have that, then the Soviets might look at the situation and say, "It's a little uncertain as to how things will come out in the initial exchange, but one thing is clear, after the initial exchange, we will have suffered all the damage that we are going to suffer because the US side isn't going to have any way in which it can manage and control its forces in any intelligent way. So we can go about reconstituting forces, recovering, and they are not going to be able to because we are going to be the only one who can still conduct war in an intelligent way. We are bound to win the war. It is just a question of how much damage we sustain in the initial attack." It is terribly important to be able to assure endurance of our command and control, survivability, and "reconstitutability" so you have an enduring capability for command and control.[6]

Command and control was not some problem in the abstract. On March 30, 1981, an assassination attempt against President Ronald Reagan demonstrated a significant problem in Washington's ability to convey to the Soviets that it had clear command and control in the event of a decapitation attack. Chaos erupted in the White House Situation Room as Vice President George H. W. Bush was flying back to Washington. That experience was encapsulated by Secretary of State Alexander Haig's appearance in the White House Briefing Room and ill-chosen line, "I am in control here."

The full extent of the chaos in the White House Situation Room was unknown to Paul Nitze or the US public. Nor did they know that Reagan sent a Hotline message as he was convalescing in George Washington University Hospital. "I wish to make clear to you the seriousness with which the United States would view such an action [i.e., a Soviet invasion of Poland], to which we would be compelled to respond," Reagan wrote Brezhnev on April 3. "I take this step not to threaten the Soviet Union but to ensure that there is no possibility of your misunderstanding our position or our intentions."[7]

Not that the United States and the Soviet Union were anywhere close to war in 1981. Several rounds of destabilizing crises—or externalities, such as the assassination attempt against the president—could rapidly change the trajectory of the Cold War. Soviet leaders might be emboldened to take aggressive action, secure in their knowledge of US weakness and vulnerability; as well as in their conviction that, far down the line, no US president would actually press the button. The Soviet economy was probably weaker than Moscow, or even CIA analysts, let on. Yet it was not too weak to sustain a war. "Look at what they did during World War II when the Germans had occupied most of their industrially productive cities during 1941–42, up to the battle of Stalingrad," Nitze told air force historians in 1981. "They still sustained a tremendous war economy. They moved all those factories out to Siberia. . . . So there is an *enormous* amount that people can do in wartime."[8]

Theater Nuclear Forces/INF

What Western European leaders *did* care about was countering the Soviet threat of SS-20s, a concern that preceded the Reagan administration. In a speech at the International Institute for Strategic Studies in London in October 1977, the Federal Republic of Germany Chancellor Helmut Schmidt declared that SALT negotiations between the United States and Soviet Union had reduced the credibility of the US pledge to use nuclear weapons in defense of NATO allies. Schmidt called for redressing the nuclear balance within the European theater. Initial Soviet deployments of SS-20s the previous year, he warned, required a commensurate response. Two years later, on December 12, 1979, NATO announced its "dual track" decision. West Germany planned to accept US Pershing II ballistic missiles and ground-launched cruise missiles, while other NATO allies would accept cruise missiles on their territories. Deployment was scheduled for no later than 1983. Meanwhile, the United States and its allies would seek to negotiate with the Soviets to reduce its deployment of SS-20s and older SS-4 and SS-5 missiles, which were similarly threatening to the Europeans.

In early 1981, ACDA director Eugene Rostow recommended that President Reagan appoint Nitze to lead the US delegation to the theater nuclear forces talks in Geneva. Secretary of State Alexander Haig, competing with Rostow for authority over arms control, expressed reservations, but National Security

Advisor Richard Allen persuaded Reagan to stick with Nitze.[9] Theater nuclear forces had not previously caught Nitze's attention. "Paul, you really should think seriously about accepting this offer," ACDA general counsel Tom Graham told Nitze at his summer home on Mount Desert Island, Maine. "It is the only game in town right now because the strategic negotiations haven't begun again."[10]

Nitze may have aspired to lead the US delegation to the Strategic Arms Reduction Talks (which replaced SALT II), yet that position went to retired general Edward Rowny. Seventy-four years old, Nitze joined an administration in which one of his former interns, Paul Wolfowitz, held the position of director of the Policy Planning Staff; and another, Richard Perle, was the assistant secretary of defense for international security policy.

As negotiator-designate, Nitze flew to Europe to consult with European leaders. There he encountered objections to the terms "theater nuclear forces" and "Euromissiles," both suggesting that a nuclear war could somehow be limited to Europe. Returning to Washington, Nitze succeeded in changing the name to the negotiations on INF. Changing the terms of the debate—to an entire class of missiles—also allowed Reagan to make good on his promise to Japanese prime minister Yasuhiro Nakasone to prevent the Soviets from moving the SS-20s east of the Ural Mountains to comply with an agreement strictly limited to Europe.[11]

In their September 23, 1981, meeting in New York City, Secretary of State Haig and Soviet foreign minister Andrei Gromyko agreed that Nitze and Yuli Kvitsinsky would lead delegations in the INF talks.[12] On October 13, 1981, Reagan led an NSC meeting in which Secretary of Defense Caspar Weinberger advocated for a "zero option" on INF.[13] In his words: "The Soviets will certainly reject an American 'zero option' proposal." "But whether they reject it or they accept it, they would be set back on their heels. We would be left in good shape and would be shown as the White Hats." "On the 'zero option,'" ACDA acting director Norman C. Terrell responded, "we believe it requires further study, and that it should be considered principally in terms of its impact on our deployment schedule in 1983."[14]

This was a tepid response by Terrell, who had no real clout in the Reagan administration. In the absence of Rostow and Nitze, no one in the meeting had the sufficient background knowledge and willingness to cross Weinberger, who was regarded as especially close with the president. On November 18, 1981, President Reagan delivered a speech to National Press Club members, proposing: "The United States is prepared to cancel its deployment of Pershing II and ground-launch cruise missiles if the Soviets will dismantle their SS-20, SS-4, and SS-5 missiles."[15] Two days later, the president announced that Nitze would serve as head of the United States delegation to the INF negotiations set to begin in Geneva on November 30, 1981.

Nitze did not put much stock in a zero option, but he did regard it as a good opening position. Calling for something that the Soviets might declare a nonstarter was precisely what he had wanted to do to achieve reductions in overall Soviet throw weight during the early rounds of SALT back in 1969–70. Now, in meetings with Soviet officials in the fall of 1981 and spring of 1982, he expressed support for the president's proposal.

On November 18, 1981, Nitze attended a luncheon hosted by Soviet ambassador Anatoly Dobrynin. He told Dobrynin privately that he "hoped for an agreement by next February." That was because "the logic of our case was clear." And, he understood "Mr. Kvitsinskiy to be a competent and intelligent man" who would acknowledge the logic of the US case and help expedite an early agreement.[16] Dobrynin disagreed. "He said he had listened to the President's speech [on November 18] and could not believe that he was serious," according to Nitze's notes. "There was no possibility that the Soviet Union would agree to what [President Reagan] was proposing." Nitze responded that he had read General Secretary Leonid Brezhnev's interview with the German magazine *Der Spiegel* and similarly concluded: "there was no possibility that the US would agree with [Brezhnev's] proposals." Distance between the two sides, he felt, only accentuated the need for good-faith negotiations. Turning to substance, Nitze stated that the US side intended for "'intermediate-range' to cover the entire range intermediate between that of battlefield weapons and intercontinental-strategic weapons."[17] Limiting nuclear weapons "by range class rather than location" was the top priority.

Cordial though never close, the two men reflected on their long careers in Washington (Dobrynin had served as ambassador to the United States since the start of 1962). Nitze surmised that disputes between Washington and Moscow "had little to do with direct conflicts of interest between the USSR and the US as such." Instead, the problem was "conflicts of interest with respect to geopolitical situations between our two countries, particularly in Europe, the Middle East, Africa, South and Southeast Asia, and the Far East." On the relationship between INF and strategic arms negotiations, Nitze said, "it was possible to have a useful agreement on INF without necessarily simultaneously having an agreement on SALT [or START]." Dobrynin pressed Nitze on his opposition to the US Senate's ratification of SALT II, to which Nitze repeated his strained justification that he had not urged senators to vote against it but instead had attempted to make them aware of the substance of the agreement. While it was now outside his immediate jurisdiction, Nitze proposed "a limitation on the number of reentry vehicles with a further limitation on the power of individual reentry vehicles to prevent rabbits from being equated from elephants."[18] In other words, he maintained that the central objective of a strategic arms treaty should be to reduce Soviet aggregate throw weight.

Nitze reiterated his conviction that agreements should be bold and comprehensive. He was "inherently a 'big' agreement man." Reducing the risk of nuclear war could not be achieved through instruments that were merely "cosmetic" and intended to ease public fears; such treaties produced nothing of substance. Instead, the two sides had to address the fundamental causes of strategic instability—"to do so might be more expensive, but that it would be worth the cost." Dobrynin and Nitze "agreed that both sides have gone to MIRVed weapons primarily because they are more cost-effective per unit of destructiveness than single RV weapons."[19] They also agreed that stabilizing the superpower arms race to minimize the chances of nuclear war was worth spending more money.

"I had been engaged in the subject of US/USSR relations perhaps as long as anyone who was still around," Nitze said. He recounted his running into William Bullitt on the subway in New York City in 1933, after which he invited Bullitt to dine with him and his roommate Sidney Spivak, an aide to President Franklin Roosevelt. That dinner led Spivak to introduce Bullitt to Roosevelt, who was persuaded to establish relations with the Soviet Union (and appoint Bullitt as ambassador).[20]

Dobrynin could have thought Nitze was intending now to set up a back channel for INF negotiations. After all, during the SALT negotiations a decade earlier, Dobrynin had served as one-half of such a back channel along with National Security Advisor Henry Kissinger. That did not happen in this case with Paul Nitze. As with SALT, negotiations did not occur in a geopolitical vacuum. After the Polish government declared martial law in December 1981—a decision that the Reagan administration presumed was greenlit by the Kremlin—Secretary of State Alexander Haig instructed Nitze "to inform the Soviets in private [that] their conduct vis-à-vis Poland could affect the course of [the INF] negotiations." Unlike Richard Nixon with SALT, President Reagan did not doubt the ultimate objective. "Met with Paul Nitze & Eugene Rostow who are here for a few days before going back to the arms reduction talks in Geneva," he wrote in his diary on January 7, 1982. "I told them even 1 nuclear missile in Europe was too many and that if anyone walked away from the table it would have to be the Soviets."[21]

Independent British and French nuclear forces complicated the INF negotiations. Along with precluding the deployment of any US INF forces in Europe, the Soviets set a ceiling of three hundred medium-range missiles and nuclear-capable aircraft on either side and counted British and French independent forces toward Washington's sum.[22] Soviet foreign minister Andrei Gromyko insisted on this last stipulation. Tasked with holding the line to exclude other countries, Nitze put forward a draft treaty that limited a potential INF agreement to US and Soviet forces. The Soviet delegation responded by grouping together aircraft with missiles and insisting on "compensation" for British and French forces.[23] Consequently, the INF negotiations produced little results in 1982.

Meanwhile, the nuclear arms race generated considerable angst. The Spring 1982 edition of Foreign Affairs featured an article cowritten by George Kennan, McGeorge Bundy, Robert McNamara, and Gerard Smith, in which the four men (each of whom had worked at administrative levels higher than Nitze but had been out of government for some time) came out in support of the United States renouncing "first-use" of nuclear weapons. They chronicled their participation in nuclear debates going back to the end of World War II and offered self-reflection and even some contrition. "On this issue [of nuclear first use], if you haven't changed your mind, you haven't been using your mind," Bundy told a reporter for the New York Times.[24]

Nitze's mind remained firm. Yet, at the same time, he recognized the context of the article: a growing nuclear freeze movement in the United States. Playing on this legitimately grassroots effort, the Soviets attempted to seize the role of champions of peace. At a special UN session on disarmament in June 1982, Foreign Minister Andrei Gromyko announced that the Soviets were renouncing the first use of nuclear weapons. This pledge was of little military consequence, given the disproportionately large Soviet conventional army and its ability to mobilize rapidly and reinforce its positions in Eastern Europe. Danger lurked in the prospect that the US Congress would accommodate the Russians by responding to public anxieties about nuclear war: they might defund planned US systems that gave US negotiators leverage in Geneva. From Nitze's perspective, this was precisely the set of circumstances that prevented SALT from stabilizing the nuclear arms race back in the 1970s.

Soviet negotiators did not have to worry about public opinion. Nor did they have to worry about allies given that the Warsaw Pact—unlike NATO—did not consist of democracies. On the other hand, Soviet negotiators and Kremlin leaders had many years of experience as astute observers of Western politics. They had no problem waiting for some government or coalition to fail. Short of that, the KGB did sponsor a campaign to infiltrate the indigenous peace movements in Western Europe that coalesced around stopping INF deployment; these movements did not have sufficient resources to protect against such interventions.[25] In the United States, there was no need for the Soviets to meddle. On June 12, 1982, rock stars Bruce Springsteen, Joan Baez, and others performed at a rally in Central Park to support a nuclear freeze.

The New York City Police Department estimated that the concert drew five hundred thousand people.[26]

From Nitze's perspective, the rush to a quick "first stage" agreement would reduce and weaken the US leverage to get a more comprehensive deal later. US allies might lose the political will to carry through the INF deployment. While Reagan did not face voters until 1984, in parliamentarian systems in Western Europe, leaders could face votes of "no confidence" at any time. While the Falklands War buoyed Prime Minister Margaret Thatcher's political standing in the late spring of 1982, she had not been so popular when Nitze led the US delegation's early rounds of INF negotiations. In West Germany, Helmut Schmidt faced tremendous pressure from his party, the SPD, which would eventually oust him as chancellor.

Walk in the Woods (Summer 1982)

With INF deployments scheduled to commence by the end of 1983, Nitze anticipated the prospect that the barrage of Soviet propaganda would sap US and allied political will to counter the Soviet SS-20s. Back when Jupiter missiles in Turkey complicated the Cuban Missile Crisis, he feared (unjustifiability, as it turned out) nothing less than the collapse of NATO. Now, with a combination of accumulated knowledge about nuclear policies, confidence in his judgments, impatience with bureaucracy, and a willingness to exceed his instructions, Nitze set out to make a deal with his Soviet counterpart. "We did not see how we were going to achieve agreement involving substantial movement on the Soviet side unless we were prepared for substantial movement on our side," he later recounted. After all, the president had given him authority to "explore with my opposite number any possibility of significant movement on issues of interest to us."[27]

Nitze seized the initiative. Setting up a private meeting with Soviet negotiator Kvitsinsky, he prepared four papers filled with "logic chains" explaining why the US and Soviet sides each needed to make concessions to enhance their security. Finally, a potential compromise package emerged. The Soviets would reduce Soviet SS-20s while NATO would deploy only cruise missiles. Pershing IIs could be scrapped and replaced with a limited number of conversions from existing P1a to P1b. This was certainly not what the president had in mind when he told Nitze and Rostow that even one Soviet SS-20 was too many.

On July 17, Nitze met up with Kvitsinsky a brief distance from Geneva, and the two men walked in the woods. After discussing their need to make progress, Nitze took out paper A, which laid out the reasoning for "a package solution containing all the necessary and sufficient elements of an agreement."[28] Then, sitting atop a pile of felled trees on the side of the road, Nitze showed Kvitsinsky the three additional papers. Paper B laid out six presumptions, starting with the assumption that the Soviets would not accept "zero/zero," and the United States would consider the inclusion or compensation for British and French forces. Paper C laid out possible concessions to previously stated Soviet concerns. Finally, paper D stated fifteen elements of a possible compromise. Kvitsinsky apparently read the papers carefully and offered his comments before his driver reappeared.[29]

The following day, July 18, a Sunday, Nitze called Eugene Rostow in Washington to tell him about the encounter. He briefed the US delegation on Monday and flew to Washington on Tuesday. In a meeting on July 27 with National Security Advisor William Clark and the NSC's senior director for arms control Richard Boverie, Nitze described his conversation with Kvitsinsky. He went through the papers he had shown the Soviet negotiator—none of which he had cleared with the White House or State Department—and went through potential next steps.[30]

"The Rostow/Nitze approach has uncertainties, but could form a basis for early movement if there was a political judgment to discard the currently existing President guidance and push for an early agreement," Boverie wrote Clark on July 29, 1982. While the ideas were intriguing, there were "potentially very severe bureaucratic and substantive problems," Boverie went on to say. "Mr. Nitze has strayed way off the reservation—he has gone far beyond his instructions," and his actions could potentially set a precedent for others to take end runs around established policies. "Moreover, Mr. Nitze may have undercut the future of the Administration's 'zero option' with the Soviets by dealing informally with the Soviets on a 'non-zero' approach." Proponents of the zero option within the administration, as well as US allies, could accuse the Reagan administration of double-dealing—much to the delight of a hostile press corps. "I have the greatest admiration and respect for Mr. Nitze," Boverie said, "and I would hate to see him thrown into a potential meat-grinder; however, the President's interests clearly and unequivocally come first."[31] In other words, Nitze's proposal should be dismissed.

Even though proponents of the zero option were furious at Nitze for attempting to broker a deal—the ostensible purpose of a lead negotiator—the Reagan administration took the prospect of at least an interim agreement on INF systems seriously. At the very least, Nitze faced no disciplinary action. And, in advance of a September 13, 1982, NSC meeting, Under Secretary of State for Political Affairs Lawrence Eagleburger wrote Secretary of State George Shultz that something had to give on the US side.[32]

Even Reagan's closest advisers saw support for the zero option as challenging to sustain. "Our arms control negotiators in START and INF see the Soviet delegations as stonewalling with Moscow likely, at sometime soon in INF, to put out an unacceptable but publicly appealing offer and then launch a propaganda barrage to blame American inflexibility for the failure of the negotiations," Director of Central Intelligence William Casey wrote President Reagan on November 22, 1982. "Nitze speculates that the new Soviet proposal would likely call for 200 intermediate range missiles on each side, including UK and French systems, and 100 bombers. The Soviets now have 200 SS-20s west of the crest of the Urals, thus they could dismantle their obsolete SS-4s and 5s and not have to destroy a single SS-20. Obsolete badgers and blinders could be moved or destroyed, and excess Backfires could be moved east of the Urals. We should be prepared for a leak or other announcement of this proposal."[33]

Having failed to secure a deal in his walk in the woods with Kvitsinsky, Nitze feared what he regarded as the collapse of US and allied will. In interviews with his memoir coauthors Steve Reardon and Ann Smith, Nitze expressed concern that Soviet leader Leonid Brezhnev intended to place nuclear weapons in Cuba without a deal on INF—in other words, to repeat the circumstances that triggered the Cuban Missile Crisis. Not only were the Soviets on the "political offensive," as he put it in December 1982, but a potential crisis with Moscow at any point in the coming decade would force Washington to back down. Nothing about the Reagan arms buildup would alter the fundamental premises of the Nitze Scenario. "Demonstrably so—that's right," was Nitze's response to the question of whether the United States was in an inferior position concerning the Soviet Union.[34] Especially aggravating to him were McGeorge Bundy and Robert McNamara, who disavowed the primary role that US strength had played in bringing the Cuban Missile Crisis to a successful conclusion. Their ulterior motive, he presumed, was to cast aspersions on the Reagan administration's efforts to restore the United States' strength.[35]

In NSC meetings throughout the summer and fall of 1982, Nitze played the good soldier. His immediate boss, ACDA director Eugene Rostow, apparently did not. Claiming that Rostow weighed in on topics outside his purview, National Security Advisor William Clark fired him.[36] Subsequently, a January 16, 1983, *New York Times* article released details of Nitze and Kvitsinsky's walk in the woods the previous summer and cited it as one reason behind Rostow's dismissal. "There is considerable speculation about Mr. Nitze's future," the article said. "Some Rostow aides predicted that Mr. Nitze would resign in a few months if there is no accord."[37] State Department officials, however, "described him as a veteran who believes strongly in the importance of an agreement and is willing to stick with his instructions, perhaps in the expectation that with

FIGURE 10.1.   President Reagan and Intermediate-Range Nuclear Forces chief negotiator Nitze, May 12, 1983. President Reagan respected Nitze and did not fire him after the "walk in the woods" episode. Photo by Bettmann/Getty Images.

Mr. Shultz in charge of arms control affairs, the Reagan Administration will authorize a compromise by the summer."[38] In sum, Nitze paid no price for his role in crafting the walk in the woods proposal in the summer of 1982.

The Strategic Defense Initiative

President Reagan regarded Nitze as a link to President Harry Truman, whom he had supported. He would never fire Nitze. "Met with Nitze and Rowny who are headed back to Geneva for the arms negotiations," the president wrote in his diary on January 21, 1983. "The Soviets are pulling out all the propaganda stops trying to turn off the allies. I think I can top them."[39] That same month, Reagan had announced the "President's Commission on Strategic Forces," comprising a bipartisan group of former secretaries of defense along with technical experts led by retired air force general and national security adviser Brent Scowcroft. "An almost 2 hr. lunch with Joint Chiefs of staff. Most of time spent on MX & the commission etc.," Reagan wrote in his diary on February 11, 1983. "Out of it came a super idea. So far the only policy worldwide on nuclear weapons is to have a deterrent. What if we tell the world we want to protect our people not avenge them; that we [a]re going to embark on a program of research to come up with a defensive weapon that could make nuclear weapons obsolete? I would call upon the scientific community to volunteer in bringing such a thing about."[40]

"We can't afford to believe that we will never be threatened," Reagan stated in a nationally televised address on March 23, 1983. "There have been two world wars in my lifetime. We didn't start them and, indeed, did everything we could to avoid being drawn into them. But we were ill-prepared for both. Had we been better prepared, peace might have been preserved."[41] Preparedness, which had been a hallmark of Nitze's career going back to the Strategic Bombing Survey, was central to Reagan's message that evening. The president closed by stating that strategic modernization was not enough to reduce the prospects of nuclear war. "What if free people could live secure in the knowledge that their security did not rest upon the threat of instant US retaliation to deter a Soviet attack, that we could intercept and destroy strategic ballistic missiles before they reached our own soil or that of our allies?" the president asked. He signed off by challenging the scientific community to devise a way to defend US lives rather than, as he said, avenge them.[42]

The Strategic Defense Initiative (SDI)—or "Star Wars," as it was colloquially known—surprised Nitze and nearly everyone else in the Reagan administration. It needed to be made clear how the president expected to integrate his proposal into the ongoing negotiations in Geneva. It could have been clearer what exactly SDI was. The president was now contemplating the prospect of doing the thing that had landed Nitze in hot water—pursuing a deal short of zero INF. "I'm of the mind we should tell Nitze to offer an interim missile reduction plan to the Soviets while still claiming zero is our ultimate goal," he wrote in his diary after an NSC meeting on March 18. Two weeks later, Reagan proposed an interim Intermediate-Range Nuclear Force Reduction Agreement. "To this end," the president announced at the White House, "Paul Nitze has informed his Soviet counterpart that we are prepared to negotiate an interim agreement in which the United States would substantially reduce its planned deployment of Pershing II and ground-launched cruise missiles, provided the Soviet Union reduce the number of its warheads on longer range INF missiles to an equal level on a global basis."[43] In other words, Nitze's longtime approach—if not necessarily in all its precise details—had now become the US negotiating position.

Reagan was acknowledging reality. His modulation on INF came just before the Scowcroft Commission's April report recommending a compromise: a portion of the MX missiles could be deployed in fortified—or "hardened"—Minuteman silos, while the United States would pursue research on a single-warhead rocket on a mobile launcher.[44] This portable system, now called

Midgetman, was the type of system Nitze had called for in his January 1976 *Foreign Affairs* article.[45] President Reagan immediately accepted the Scowcroft Commission's recommendations. The president rechristened the MX missile, which was set to be deployed in 1985, "the Peacekeeper" and authorized research and development for the Midgetman.

On May 11, 1983, Nitze sat for an interview with Gregg Herken, who was writing a book on US Cold War nuclear policy. Nitze praised the Midgetman and expressed his long-standing support for a small ICBM with a single RV to solve the problem of strategic instability. He contended that switching from large land-based MIRVed ICBMs to small, mobile non-MIRVed ICBMs would eliminate the issue of "use them or lose them"—in other words, the pressure to launch one missile with numerous warheads upon warning of an impending attack against it. In addition, the size of such a missile fleet would also ensure that bad actors such as Libyan strongman Mu'ammar Gaddafi "wouldn't be a threat." Nitze told Herken that he had explained all this previously to Jimmy Carter, who had refused to take his advice.[46]

The Soviets were unlikely to accept such a fundamental shift. However, that would not be sufficient grounds to reject such a proposal. The steeper obstacle was that the Midgetman cost more money than MX, and Congress had been reluctant to fund that for nearly a decade. The logic of the new weapon, according to Nitze, "rests upon the wholly solid premise that the avoidance of nuclear war is much more important than increasing welfare payments."[47] The tradeoff—for both Democrats and Republicans—was between long-term security and short-term political gain. Nitze concluded US leaders were just unwilling to ask Americans to pay what they could afford to bolster defenses to deter nuclear war.

Midgetman never sparked Reagan's imagination. The SDI did. NSSD 6-83, which the president signed on April 18, called for a "Future Security Strategy" and "Defense Technology Plan." Throughout 1983, however, the top priority remained to shepherd the INF deployment slated for that fall. "Met with Dr. Nitze who leaves Sat. for Geneva to resume the Nuc. Reduction talks we call I.N.F.," Reagan wrote in his diary after he signed NSSD 6-83. "Like me he believes the Soviets wont [*sic*] move until & unless we display our Intermediate missiles in Europe."[48]

Nitze was not so sure of that. He hoped to broker a last-minute INF deal in Geneva prior to NATO's deployment. Over dinner on October 26, 1983, Kvitsinsky told Nitze that Soviet general secretary Yuri Andropov (who had taken over when Leonid Brezhnev died on November 12, 1982) remained prepared to reduce SS-20 deployments so long as the US side consider "equal reductions."[49] What transpired next made Nitze lose all respect for his Soviet counterpart. The Soviets leaked word that Nitze had put forward another proposal limiting US and allied deployments. US officials presumed the intention was to sow discord among the Western allies and damage Nitze's standing within the Reagan administration. Secretary of State George Shultz stood by Paul Nitze.

On November 22, the West German Bundestag approved the Pershing II deployments. The next day, Soviet negotiators walked out of the INF negotiations. "The United States profoundly regrets the unilateral decision of the Soviet Union to suspend the INF negotiations," Nitze announced in a prepared statement. However, it was unreasonable for them to point blame at the United States and its NATO allies, which had decided in 1979 to pursue deployment and negotiations at a time when the Soviets had deployed 140 SS-20s, a figure that had reached 360 by November 1983. "The schedule for US deployments has never been a secret," Nitze stated. "Nor has the reason for them."[50]

Soviet Walkout (December 1983 to December 1984)

Nitze returned to Washington. Even though there was no longer a delegation for him to lead, ACDA still employed him. And he saw no reason to quit. "No one can ever relax in this business," he told Robin MacNeil in a December 8 appearance on the PBS *Newshour*.[51] "Met with Paul Nitze," President Reagan wrote in his diary on January 17, 1984. "He too believes we must not yield to Soviet pressure to make a new offer to get the Soviets to resume the I.N.F. talks. That would be rewarding them for walking out."[52] "Yielding" was not the word anyone in the Reagan administration wanted to use, so Nitze, Shultz, and others spent the year trying to mold a new framework of negotiations by which the United States and Soviets could resume talks on INF and START. This period tested Reagan's commitment to arms reductions: deployment of the Pershing IIs and ground-launched cruise missiles bestowed strength on the United States and its allies. Would they now "trade" them for the SS-20s? Moreover, it was not at all clear that the Europeans would agree to the SS-20s stationed west of the Urals and might balk at risking an agreement for a global ban. The Japanese had to be taken into account. And, never before in the Cold War had the two sides agreed to eliminate an entire class of nuclear missiles.

"An initiative should make no substantive concessions to the Soviet side," Nitze wrote Reagan on March 23, 1984. The United States should indicate a willingness to bargain, yet "the reactions in Europe, the Congress and US public opinion would all be negative if there were any indication that we were rewarding the Soviets for having broken off the negotiations." The Soviets "would look upon it as weakness on our part."[53] Nitze recollected from his SALT experience that it was especially risky to conduct arms control negotiations during a presidential election year—the Soviets would seize the opportunity to pin down the incumbent. Unlike in 1972, "the initiative [in 1984] should be in the form of spelling out in more specific terms past policy formulated in such a way that it could be advanced unilaterally." One option would be to halt deployments at the end of 1985—at 236 warheads—if the Soviets agreed to reduce their long-range intermediate nuclear force missiles in Europe to match that figure and make "collateral reductions in Asia."[54]

Nitze's ideas gained traction. In preparation for a March 27, 1984, meeting of the National Security Planning Group (NSPG), National Security Advisor Robert "Bud" McFarlane proposed to President Reagan that he send Ed Rowny and Paul Nitze to engage in private talks with the Soviets.[55] "It is not impossible to get an agreement, but 90% chance you won't," Nitze stated at the NSPG meeting that day. "It is wholly unlikely that Moscow will negotiate seriously in an election year." Reagan floated McFarlane's suggestion of offering up Rowny and Nitze, though did not express much urgency. "I think the Senior Arms Control Policy Group should accelerate their work and present me with options for new START/INF positions within a few weeks," the president stated.[56]

That summer, the Soviets proposed negotiations aimed to prevent the "militarization of space." US officials regarded this phrase as targeting the SDI. Secretary of State Shultz devised a plan to broaden the scope. "Our approach is to include the subject matter of START and INF . . . whereas the Soviets are claiming that our desire to talk about ballistic missiles means that we are imposing preconditions to any negotiation on what they call the 'militarization of outer space,'" according to Deputy Secretary of State Kenneth Dam. "This is a rather delicate war of words, because we are saying that we have accepted the Soviet proposal to talk about the militarization of outer space and that all we want to do is to talk about the whole picture, which includes ballistic missiles passing through space, and in any event the overall subject matter cannot be limited simply to weapons originating in space or used against space objects."[57] This meant the Shultz plan was to turn negotiations on the "militarization of space" into negotiations on ballistic missiles, which traveled through outer space.

Nitze agreed with this approach. On July 17, 1984, he sent McFarlane a memorandum concurring that the Soviet objective was to block the SDI and recommending that the Reagan administration respond by recasting the initiative as a comprehensive set of negotiations that would include START and

INF. "I also proposed that the United States should examine the relationship between offensive and defensive system and the linkage we might draw between them once the Vienna talks were under way," he later recounted.[58]

The following month, Deputy Secretary of State Dam sent Secretary Shultz a paper written by his arms control adviser, James Timbie, on the history of strategic nuclear arms control. Timbie stressed the importance of "leader-to-leader" exchanges in achieving any potential deals with the Soviets. "Delegations in the field have a role to play, especially in working out the language of formal Treaties," said Timbie. "Delegations, however, are extensions of bureaucracies, and the US and Soviet bureaucracies are incapable of significant arms reductions agreements," he said. "The basic elements of all significant arms control agreements have without exception been worked out in direct exchanges between the leadership of the United States and the Soviet Union."[59] Leaders had to make choices, in other words.

Nitze had participated in each of the negotiations that Timbie cited. But, given the upcoming election in November, he cautioned against the temptation to strike a quick deal for short-term political advantage. "I'm a skeptic on interim agreements," Nitze declared at an NSPG meeting on September 18, 1984. "They are all poison. If you want a useful agreement, don't go down the interim agreement path."[60] Such was the lesson of SALT I, where Kissinger had sidelined the delegation and jettisoned legitimate US concerns to obtain an agreement before the 1972 presidential election.

The role of domestic politics in arms control could not simply be wished away. The publication of Strobe Talbott's book, *Deadly Gambits* in September 1984, inserted both that topic and Nitze himself into the presidential campaign.[61] In Talbott's depiction of INF and START, the Reagan administration had put forward positions that it knew the Soviets would never accept. According to Talbott, the purpose of that cynical approach was to obtain congressional support for strategic modernization and INF deployment. He thought the administration never actually wanted a deal.[62] In this account Nitze was a constant presence, as he had been in Talbott's previous book, *Endgame*, which chronicled Nitze's attacks on SALT II.

Nitze thought that neither Talbott, nor his employer *Time*, wanted to modify the Reagan administration's efforts to seek a genuine deal; rather, they wanted "to get Reagan out."[63] To Reagan's critics in Congress—among them Senator Paul Tsongas, who complained about Reagan's rhetoric—Nitze suggested that they pose the question to their constituents: "Well, the only thought that crosses my mind is that you might suggest to them first that they ask themselves whether a proposition is true or false. Is [the USSR] an evil empire and do they lie?"[64] Nitze believed the answer was yes on both counts.

Senator Tsongas, an avowed liberal, believed Reagan's rhetoric was dangerous. McGeorge Bundy and Robert McNamara, who remained Democrats, considered his nuclear weapons politics also dangerous. A grassroots nuclear freeze movement galvanized activists on the left, and some evangelical Christian circles on the right, to apply pressure on elected officials to stop the rearmament of US forces during the early 1980s. Within the Reagan administration, however, long-standing associates of the president such as Secretary of Defense Caspar Weinberger encouraged him to get tough on the Soviets. Achieving a deal with them did not matter because the Soviets could cheat anyway. In Congress and conservative intellectual circles, various of the president's champions lamented that he was not sticking to his guns regarding the Soviets. Very importantly, as November 1984 approached, the Reagan administration had not realized its strategic modernization aspirations, as it had put forth in a National Security Study Directive (NSDD-12) back in 1981.

Throughout 1981–84, Nitze pursued the middle way in the nuclear debate. He *wanted* a deal on INF to preserve the Western alliance. The nuclear freeze movement did not lead him to question his assumptions about the utility of modernizing US forces; he was concerned that political headwinds would stop the strategic modernization program that the Reagan administration launched in 1981 as well as the US commitment to NATO that President Carter had approved in the dual-track decision of 1979. Nitze may have been skeptical that the Soviets would ever agree to US proposals such as cutting aggregate throw weight. However, he pursued them in earnest.

The walk in the woods did not prove a threat to Nitze's job. While the president and he were not personally close, Reagan did not want to lose this direct link to Harry Truman—a Democrat (as Reagan had been through the 1940s) who stood by Cold War first principles and never apologized for the United States. And Nitze neither flattered the president nor bad-mouthed him behind his back.

The bond Nitze developed with George Shultz, who was confirmed as secretary of state during the initial fallout from the walk in the woods, sustained the next phase of Nitze's enduring career. In December 1984, President Reagan appointed Nitze as special assistant to the president and secretary of state for arms control. Shultz's intervention meant he would set up shop on the seventh floor of the State Department—not at the Old Executive Office Building. At age seventy-seven, he was about to begin his most important assignment.

CHAPTER 11

The Strategic Concept

The second Ronald Reagan administration was the most significant period of Nitze's government service since his time in the Truman administration. While he authored no strategy statement equivalent to NSC-68, he did report directly to Secretary of State George Shultz and used that proximity to a "man of action" to press for a grand package on offensive and defensive arms. His ideas and actions were vital in turning President Ronald Reagan's dream of a nuclear-free world into a concrete plan of action.

Nitze's personality and professional traits served to his advantage. As with the walk in the woods episode in 1982, he seized the initiative to set forth policy. Nitze persevered in the chaotic scenes of the second Reagan administration—where the president nearly faced impeachment over the Iran-Contra scandal. NSC staffers and subordinates of Secretary of Defense Caspar Weinberger—including Nitze's one-time protégé, Richard Perle—now regarded Nitze with skepticism; they thought he was out to trade away the SDI for an arms agreement. Nitze was indeed seeking a deal, yet his objective was to connect Reagan's romantic vision of a world without nuclear weapons to a more achievable—no less ambitious—transition from strategic offenses to strategic defenses. This helped usher in the remarkable advances in nuclear arms control that occurred from 1985 to 1988: the heady days of Reagan's interactions with the new Soviet leader, Mikhail Gorbachev. Even then, Nitze, who found Gorbachev underwhelming, was disappointed.

Preparing for Geneva (Again)

On October 12, 1984, less than a month before a presidential election in which Reagan was expected to prevail, Deputy Secretary of State Kenneth Dam met with Paul Nitze to discuss potential objectives for arms control in a second Reagan administration. Dam found Nitze "in an exceedingly pessimistic mood"; he believed "that the odds were against reaching any arms control agreement that would be in the national security interests of the United States."[1] "[I]t was desirable to engage the Soviets on grand principles," Dam quoted Nitze, "not so much because he thought there was any chance of agreement, but because he thought it was necessary from the standpoint of public opinion in the United States and of relations with the Allies to be engaged with the Soviets in arms control discussions."[2] Nitze liked the idea of negotiating on a twenty-year perspective. It was necessary to be open to "pragmatic and practical arrangements that might be possible." However, it was essential to avoid interim agreements and moratoria, which had tended to benefit the Soviets, not the Americans. As he often did, Nitze pointed to the 1972 SALT I agreement, which may have given the appearance to Americans and allies of slowing the nuclear arms race but had not stopped the Soviets' relentless buildup.

Here and elsewhere, the problem remained constant: "it was unquestionably a fact the Soviets had nuclear superiority over the United States," Nitze told Dam, pointing to his work for CIA director William Casey in early 1981. The Reagan buildup during the first administration notwithstanding, Nitze told Dam, "nothing had fundamentally changed."[3]

Meanwhile, acting upon the Soviets' proposal for anti-satellite negotiations earlier that summer, President Reagan signed National Security Decision Directive (NSDD) 148 on October 26, instructing his team to begin exploring approaches to commence talks on "the more general topic of militarization of space, and to resuming negotiations on the reduction of offensive nuclear arsenals." Clearly, Reagan's national security team anticipated that the Soviets might reach out after the election.

A few weeks before that November election, National Security Advisor Robert "Bud" McFarlane advocated for bringing Nitze into the White House. "Mr. President, I thought you would find this interesting," he wrote at the top of a memorandum written by NSC staffer Jack Matlock. "It reinforces the value of bringing Paul Nitze into the White House."[4]

Following Reagan's triumphant victory over Walter Mondale on November 6, 1984, the president received a letter from Konstantin Chernenko calling for the resumption of nuclear arms negotiations to "remove the threat of war and radically improve the international situation."[5] This stated objective surely would not have impressed Nitze, who harbored serious doubts about Soviet leaders—especially Chernenko, the most pathetic of all of them. Nevertheless, four more years of Reagan drew the Soviets back to the negotiating table. Here was the scenario that Richard Nixon and Henry Kissinger had forfeited by rushing to obtain an interim agreement before November 1972, when then-president Nixon won his own smashing reelection.

Secretary of State Shultz prepared to meet Soviet foreign minister Andrei Gromyko in early 1985 to relaunch negotiations. Meanwhile, Bud McFarlane advocated for bringing over to the NSC a point person for arms control with sufficient gravitas "to coerce the system into more timely products" and educate President Reagan on the intricacies of nuclear matters.[6] Paul Nitze was that person. According to Shultz, recalling a conversation with McFarlane the day before the election, only he could fit the bill. The secretary requested that Nitze serve as his adviser in the forthcoming talks with Gromyko in Geneva.

On November 16, President Reagan wrote Soviet leader Chernenko proposing that each side "designate a representative who is thoroughly familiar with the strategic thinking of his highest political authority and who would meet with his counterpart with a mandate to develop specific proposals for submission to us for consideration."[7] "It was determined that Paul Nitze should be our man and that the chain of command should run from Nitze to me to President Reagan," Secretary of State Shultz later recounted. "Interagency committees would meet, and NSC members would fight for their views, but ultimately the decisions would be made through the Nitze–Shultz–Reagan lineup."[8]

"I believe we gained Cap [Weinberger] and Bill [Casey's] approval for Paul Nitze to accompany George to the January sessions to be able to handle the technical issues and stay in place should George and Gromyko have to turn to other duties," McFarlane wrote Reagan in Santa Barbara on November 18, 1984.[9] This meant Nitze would be the lead arms negotiator supporting the secretary of state. The "Nitze–Shultz–Reagan lineup" did not appear on the organization chart for the NSC at that time. Yet it would prove vital to establishing the most ambitious nuclear arms proposals since the Acheson–Lilienthal and Baruch Plans of 1946.

Nitze's suggestion of "forgoing some aspects of SDI" gave certain of Reagan's advisers—particularly Secretary of Defense Caspar Weinberger—reason to view him with suspicion. Nitze acknowledged that obtaining a treaty of indefinite duration on nuclear arms might require scaling back ambitions to create a shield in outer space to protect against Soviet nuclear missiles. But, to arms control skeptics within the administration and the lobbying group High Frontier outside it, the Nitze approach repeated the mistake they thought Nixon and Kissinger had made in 1972: to give up the US ability to build a national defense while allowing the Soviets to cheat on their commitments to both SALT I and the ABM Treaty.

Yet, George Shultz—not Caspar Weinberger—had emerged as Reagan's indispensable adviser by the start of the second administration. Nitze had sufficiently impressed Shultz that the secretary wanted him to be nearby, and his survival after the walk in the woods episode had demonstrated Reagan's support of him. This did not mean that battles between Shultz and Weinberger were over: it meant, rather, that Shultz had a forceful ally who could draw upon forty years of experience to rebut the assertions of Weinberger and others. Shultz intervened to ensure that Nitze's office was on the top floor of the State Department. As a result, Nitze received the title special assistant to the president and secretary of state for arms control matters. He no longer worked for ACDA director Kenneth Adelman, who did not share Shultz's enthusiasm for reaching agreements with the Soviets. As Shultz's top lieutenant for nuclear arms control matters, Nitze attended meetings of the NSPG, the most critical standing deliberative body of the Reagan presidency.

In December 1984, the State Department's in-house nuclear physicist, James Timbie, assisted Nitze in drafting a "central concept" for Shultz that he could convey to Gromyko in Geneva. Rather than rely on a formal interagency process, Nitze crafted the US position by drafting a memorandum that the secretary of state would send to the president. The central concept needed to be simple. "We need a clear central concept to guide our planning for the Geneva meetings and subsequent negotiations—and our program for handling Congress, Allies and publics." Nitze stated four propositions: (1) the US objective over the next decade was a radical reduction in nuclear weapons; (2) that period should begin a transition from offensive nuclear weapons to nonnuclear defensive forces; (3) the transition should set as the long-term objective the eventual elimination of nuclear weapons; (4) a world without nuclear weapons was in the interest of the United States, Soviet Union, and all other nations.[10]

In submitting this "strategic concept" to Reagan, Shultz included a separate paper Nitze also authored. "The United States has no territorial ambitions," Nitze contended. "It is inconceivable that the US would initiate military action against the USSR or the Warsaw Pact unless it or its allies were to be directly attacked." While US leaders could hope that "the USSR comparably has no intention of initiating an attack on the US or its allies," they needed to assure the American people and the country's allies "of a high-quality deterrent to an attack by anyone on our vital security interest." Our leaders could assume that their Soviet counterparts also sought at the very least a high-quality deterrent. The Soviet Union previously emphasized "massive expansion and modernization of its own nuclear forces, both offensive and defensive,"

Nitze said. As a result, he could envision a regional crisis leading to the high risk of war between the United States and the Soviet Union, in which leaders on each side felt compelled to take drastic action to deny victory to the other side. "Under today's conditions and those of the foreseeable future, both sides have certain incentives to act quickly and decisively with their military power, both nuclear and conventional," Nitze concluded. "This creates an unstable situation which could make crises more difficult to manage and, if conflict breaks out, makes rapid, perhaps immediate, escalation to high levels of destruction more likely."[11]

The aims of US policy makers back in the 1960s had been that both sides would agree on a rough equality of offensive forces, and that those forces should be limited with defensive systems. By December 1985, however, "both sides have substantially greater offensive nuclear capabilities than we had in 1972." Moreover, the Soviets had violated the ABM Treaty by deploying early warning radars and ABMs that could be used in mobile formats. In the short term, Nitze advocated for negotiating a follow-on treaty on strategic offensive arms (START) to accompany the ABM Treaty—even if that meant limiting SDI research. In the long term, Nitze advocated for "bolder and more radical objectives." Both sides now apparently "agreed that[,] with respect to nuclear weapons as a whole, the objective should be their total elimination . . . worldwide and agreed to by all nations."[12] Achieving that objective required a period of transition, going from reliance on offensive arms to one on defensive capabilities. New technologies were essential; the ingenuity of the American people would produce them.

Democrats and other proponents of MAD were attacking SDI as destabilizing. Nitze responded: "The approach outlined above positions the Secretary to defuse SDI as an issue by linking it to our concerns regarding Soviet defensive programs and compliance with the ABM Treaty and the absence of a comprehensive agreement limiting offensive arms." While it was "unlikely the Soviets will be ready to comply with the ABM agreement in this manner," their reluctance could be "useful in defusing SDI with publics, Allies, and Congress, as well as refocusing their attention on our concerns about Soviet compliance with the ABM agreement."[13]

Paul Nitze aimed to redefine the terms of the debate over nuclear weapons and arms control. He exhorted the US side to lead the "transition to a defense-dominant relationship."[14] This would accord with Reagan's grandest aspiration: to achieve a world without nuclear weapons. By Reagan's formulation, SDI was an insurance policy for *both* Washington and Moscow. The president wanted to abolish nuclear weapons and protect the United States against a rogue actor such as Libyan strongman Mu'ammar Gaddhafi. This integration of strategic defenses and strategic offensive arms ran counter to MAD. It was more than just a "fact of life" to presidents who had to ponder the terrible prospect of ordering the launch of nuclear missiles to avenge the deaths of tens of millions of Americans. MAD was meant to assure that no Soviet leader would ever put the US president in that position. Yet neither Reagan nor Jimmy Carter (nor their predecessors) approached the Cold War with such confidence.

"[T]hink more about the theme of elimination of nuclear weapons," Shultz instructed the large and contentious team that accompanied him to Geneva in January 1985. "Everyone thinks it is rhetoric, but rhetoric said often enough by important people tends to wind up with an operational character to it."[15] In the case of Ronald Reagan and nuclear weapons, his rhetoric and deep conviction about eliminating nuclear weapons based upon a defense against incoming missiles could not be operationalized without critical advisers who could grasp the issues and advocate forcefully for their positions. They had to persevere in a fractious environment with a president who preferred not to intervene in settling personality conflicts. An exhausted McFarlane had nearly resigned at the end of 1984 and finally left the White House in late 1985. George Shultz's approach was to throw temper tantrums and threaten to resign, but then accept the president's entreaties to stay on.

Paul Nitze, who was seventy-seven years old, did what he had done for nearly forty years. He pressed the boundaries of what was bureaucratically acceptable yet managed to retain the ears of the top individuals in power. His role in crafting US positions on the eve of the resumption of strategic arms talks stood high among his policy achievements. And it is worth contrasting this work with fellow cold warriors George Kennan, Robert McNamara, and McGeorge Bundy, who published op-eds in *Foreign Affairs* and elsewhere, criticizing SDI as fundamentally destabilizing. Now, the Soviets were returning to the table. Nitze—once skeptical of SDI—now saw it as vital to establishing a strategy to bring about long-term reductions in nuclear arsenals. The predictions of outsiders were mistaken, and their policy prescriptions became irrelevant.

Meanwhile, in London in December 1984, Prime Minister Margaret Thatcher met with a young Soviet member of the Politburo named Mikhail Gorbachev. "I like Mr. Gorbachev . . . we can do business together," she famously declared, conveying that message to Reagan when she next saw him in person.[16] Gorbachev would ascend to power in the Kremlin in March 1985 and launch radical political and economic reforms. Yet, the resumption of nuclear arms negotiations preceded the commencement of perestroika—as his reforms would become known. The United States' phased approach for reducing and eliminating nuclear weapons came first.

On January 5, 1985, the White House instructed US embassies in NATO countries to brief allies in advance of Shultz's meeting with Gromyko. The telegram laid out a four-sentence "strategic concept" for how SDI would fit into the president's objectives for arms control during his second administration. A slight variation of Nitze's proposal from December, it stated:

> During the next ten years, the US objective is a radical reduction in the power of existing and planned offensive nuclear arms, as well as the stabilization of the relationship between offensive and defensive nuclear arms, whether in earth or space. We are even now looking forward to a period of transition to a more stable world with greatly reduced levels of nuclear arms and an enhanced ability to deter war based upon the increasing contribution of non-nuclear defenses against offensive nuclear arms. This period of transition could lead to the eventual elimination of all nuclear arms, both offensive and defensive. A world free of nuclear arms is an ultimate objective to which we, the Soviet Union, and all other nations can agree.[17]

This was the most ambitious proposal since 1946 when the Acheson–Lilienthal Report and consequent Baruch Plan called for the transfer of atomic weapons to the custody of the UN.

Two days later, in the first session in Geneva, Shultz presented this proposition to Gromyko. Paul Nitze's ambitious long-term policy proposal had become the official position of the United States. Although Gromyko griped about Nitze's presence at the meeting, he expressed moderate interest in the proposal. With the shared objective of zero nuclear weapons, Shultz and Gromyko agreed that the two sides would launch "umbrella" Nuclear and Space Arms Talks (NST) in Geneva that coming March. NST consisted of three negotiations—START, INF, and Defense and Space Talks (DST)—with an overall head of the delegation of each side. Nitze found himself in consideration to lead the US delegation. He quickly declined on account of his ailing wife, Phyllis, who was receiving treatments for emphysema. Although they selected Max Kampelman, another seasoned Democrat already serving in the administration, Reagan and Shultz still intended for Nitze to be the conduit between the Geneva delegation and Washington.

The Monday Package

On January 24, 1985, President Reagan signed NSDD 160, "Preparing for Negotiations with the Soviet Union," appointing the formal leaders of the delegations and specifying the roles of Nitze and Edward Rowny. Rowny and Nitze retained seats at the table in meetings of the NSC, NSPG, and Senior Arms Control Group and kept their direct access to the president and secretary of state.[18] Rowny, who was Nitze's sometime rival, had known Reagan longer; yet he did not command the respect of the indispensable figure in Reagan's administration: George Shultz.

Nothing was easy about crafting policies that could survive interagency battles and congressional scrutiny in Washington, let alone negotiations with the Soviets. Following a February 27, 1985, meeting with arms control negotiators, Deputy Secretary of State Kenneth Dam acknowledged the apparent inconsistency between strategic defenses and the aspirations for deep reductions—especially to a public used to hearing that MAD kept the peace. "The fact of the matter is that SDI and deep reductions are both articles of faith with the President, and the question of how they are presented in a consistent way is being left to an interagency process which is simply unable to confront basic questions of this nature." Dam went on: "Fortunately Paul Nitze is with us," and it was Nitze's aspiration to "move on both fronts simultaneously."[19]

Nitze's approach followed a familiar pattern: he gathered around him experts, absorbed their knowledge, and constructed his own theory of the case. The existing "paper flow" of the State Department and NSC meant nothing to him. He advocated forcefully for his positions in small meetings and made sure that the president received his input. He educated himself about SDI by consulting with top scientists at the national laboratories—some of whom he had known for decades. He also sought the advice of Franklin Miller, a career civil servant in the Office of the Secretary of Defense, whose knowledge of strategic doctrine and targeting was as sophisticated as that of the State Department's James Timbie, who specialized in matters of nuclear arms control.

Miller's participation would not have been possible under routine bureaucratic protocol—he worked for Secretary of Defense Caspar Weinberger, a rival of George Shultz. It helped Nitze to formulate the critical elements required for strategic defenses to work. In a February 1985 speech to the Philadelphia World Affairs Council, Nitze described the strategic concept—which the president had not actually announced publicly—and elaborated upon what three potential phases might look like. He also enumerated what became known as the "Nitze Criteria" for strategic defenses: effectiveness, survivability, and "cost-effectiveness at the margins"—meaning it had to cost the Soviets more resources to build new offensive systems than it did for the United States to deploy defense systems.[20] The speech drew scorn from fervent SDI supporters, who regarded the threat posed by Soviet missiles as its sufficient justification. "The Nitze criteria were put in to kill—not to enhance—the prospects for SDI," claimed Daniel Graham, a retired general who had led the High Frontier organization that advocated for ballistic missile defense. General William F. Burns, who had served on Nitze's delegation during the INF talks, rebutted that charge—it "was a formula for killing an early, imprudent deployment of SDI when we didn't know what we were deploying or whether it would work."[21]

Outside criticism had little impact at that moment. In meetings with the president and his advisers leading up to March 1985, when NST was set to begin, the refrain was how to get to zero nuclear weapons. President Reagan intervened during the discussion to remind his advisers that his objective was zero nuclear weapons. And, in meetings without the president, Secretary of State Shultz reminded his cabinet member peers (and, sometimes, his subordinates) that the president had set this objective and that Reagan had just been reelected in a landslide.[22] Whether or not Nitze really believed that the goal of zero nuclear weapons was achievable, he agreed with the president in White House meetings. He cited his plan for a phased transition to mutual defenses as the surest path toward achieving that outcome.

ABM Treaty

The initial rounds of NST, which lasted from March 12 until July 16, yielded few tangible results. "Atmosphere thus far has been businesslike—many veterans of earlier negotiations on Soviet side," veteran US negotiator Edward Ifft reported back to Washington. "Few surprises so far in Soviet approach—heavy stress on the need to ban 'space-strike arms,' and on the linkage between this, an INF solution and possible reductions in strategic offensive arms."[23]

Questions about SDI hovered over these negotiations. Did the 1972 ABM Treaty restrict testing of SDI components based on "other physical principles" (i.e., lasers, not intercepting missiles)? More broadly, what exactly did the treaty allow and prohibit? Such questions went unresolved. The third track of the Geneva talks, the DST, was meant to come up with an agreement that would update the treaty or, alternatively, constitute a new one. While it was unlikely that the Soviets would ever agree to replace the ABM Treaty, the fact that DST was happening showed how SDI had become an important bargaining chip. INF and START negotiators aspired to reduce existing missiles; DST conveyed a sense of legitimacy on SDI, an "initiative" that featured no workable system by that point. Another way of putting it is that the first round of NST was successful in that it did not break down over SDI.

A breakthrough on DST was unlikely. Within the Reagan administration, SDI proponents pressed for a "broad interpretation" of the ABM Treaty to allow for research and testing of SDI components. Nitze's riposte was to figure out how the United States could strengthen its position in Geneva with the soundest legal brief. That meant acknowledging potential instances that would violate the ABM Treaty. It also suggested establishing a consistent US interpretation of that agreement and acknowledging that it was not in the long-term US interest to scrap it.

On Monday, June 10, 1985, Nitze sent Shultz what became known as the "Monday Package."[24] In it, he elaborated on his four-part strategic concept and how it could be applied to the NST. The goal remained to achieve a blockbuster agreement that would initiate a transition from strategic offenses to strategic defenses. SDI hardliners within the administration derided Nitze's formulas as recipes for giving away SDI. However, to him, they were the best way to preserve strategic modernization, SDI, and alliances—especially if the Soviets once again walked out in Geneva. And, if they stayed, it was potentially a winning formula for achieving that which Nitze had devoted at least the previous decade and a half: reaching an arms reduction agreement with the Soviets that advanced US national security.

Accompanying Shultz and McFarlane in a meeting with Soviet ambassador Anatoly Dobrynin on June 17, 1985, Nitze reiterated: "if we can agree on fewer offensive forces then our defense requirements would be less." He cited the four-paragraph strategic concept as the way to achieve both. He also agreed with a recent statement by Soviet marshal Sergei Akhromeyev, who averred that the ABM Treaty was "the cornerstone of East/West détente and strategic stability."[25] Confirming the suspicions of Weinberger and his associates—who were not represented in this meeting—Nitze admitted that SDI would need to be scaled down. Also, in that meeting, Shultz proposed to Dobrynin to set up a back channel between the Soviet ambassador and Nitze.[26] Shultz also told Dobrynin that while the president had hoped Gorbachev would visit the United States, he would meet him first in Geneva later that year. A few weeks later, Nitze and Shultz benefited from the departure of longtime Soviet foreign minister Andrei Gromyko, whom Gorbachev replaced in July. In his first encounter with Gromyko's successor, Eduard Shevardnadze, on July 31, 1985, in Helsinki, Shultz kidded that "he had to rely on Ambassador Nitze as an historian" on what happened in the strategic arms limitations talks that took place there sixteen years prior.

As it became known that Reagan would meet Gorbachev in Geneva in November, the president's national security team attempted to reconcile his aspirations for an arms reduction agreement with his support for SDI, which the Soviets opposed and domestic critics claimed was illegal under the terms of an existing treaty. The 1972 ABM Treaty was subject to competing interpretations. Earlier in the year, Secretary of Defense Caspar Weinberger hired former New York assistant district attorney Philip Kunsberg to reassess its terms. Kunsberg concluded that the treaty *did not* ban the development and testing—and, perhaps, deployment—of systems based on "other physical principles" than those known to both sides in 1972.

At an October 4 meeting with National Security Advisor Bud McFarlane, Under Secretary of Defense Fred Iklé, and Assistant Secretary of Defense Perle, Nitze argued that the United States had a solid case to adopt a "broad interpretation" of the ABM Treaty—yet it may have been an imprudent choice at that moment. The prospects of souring US allies on SDI and handing the Soviets a propaganda victory outweighed any potential research benefits. Nitze admitted that he had reversed course since the start of the year. After reading Charles Fitzgerald and Sidney Graybeal's classified history of the SALT I and ABM negotiations, he lifted his objections to the "broad interpretation." This was a rare instance where Nitze ceded ground in an argument. He preserved his status with Reagan as a supporter of SDI and an ambitious arms control reduction agreement.

One month before the Geneva Summit, the internal debate about the ABM Treaty went public. In an October 6, 1985, appearance on NBC's *Meet the Press*, Bud McFarlane suggested that the Reagan administration intended to adopt the "broad interpretation" of the ABM Treaty.[27] Amid handwringing from Democrats, Shultz called on the State Department's legal adviser, Abe Sofaer, to conduct his own review of the ABM Treaty. The upshot of this debate was that on October 11, 1985, President Reagan signed NSDD 192, "The ABM Treaty and the SDI Program," formally stating Nitze's position. On the advice of Secretary of State Shultz, the president decided that, under the terms of the ABM Treaty, the United States had every right to interpret the treaty to allow for research, testing, and deployment of some of the technologies that comprised SDI. However, the administration would nevertheless continue to observe the traditional interpretation in the ongoing negotiations in Geneva and the upcoming summit with Gorbachev.[28]

Nitze had prevailed. As with Edward Teller and the H-bomb in late 1949, he defined the problem—here, the parameters of the ABM Treaty—consulted with experts, mobilized the evidence, and briefed his champion—here, George Shultz (whereas before, Dean Acheson). Nitze's position became that of the administration. His top priority during the second half of 1985 was to preserve support for SDI and the strategic modernization of US forces so that US negotiators could negotiate from a position of strength in Geneva. After his earlier time leading the INF delegation, in which nuclear targets had been limited to Europe, Nitze returned to the fundamental challenge at the heart of the "Nitze Scenario": Soviet forces that could strike the American homeland. "Large MIRVed ICBMs—such as the SS-18—threaten stability, particularly in a crisis" and constitute an existential threat, Nitze wrote in a July 8, 1985, letter to a reader of a *New York Times* profile. "Deployed in high numbers, they offer the means for carrying out a first strike against the other side's retaliatory forces while, when deployed in fixed locations, are at the same time inviting of such an attack."[29] While the United States had put forth "constructive proposals in Geneva designed to produce equitable and verifiable agreements reducing the levels and power of nuclear arms," the Soviets had rejected all of them.[30]

"For the past 15 years he's played a special role in the Nation's search for [sound] arms policy," Reagan said of Nitze, presenting him the Presidential Medal of Freedom a week and a half before the November 1985 Geneva Summit. While in government, Nitze worked to ensure that the US approach was correct, Reagan said. "When he saw things headed in the wrong direction, he worked outside the Government to alert his fellow citizens." Now he was "playing an indispensable role in our efforts to forge a bold and creative arms control policy." By Reagan's measure, Paul Nitze was "consistently shrewd, but never cynical; impressively erudite, yet never pedantic; immensely dignified, yet never stuffy; always hopeful, and yet ever realistic."[31]

Both sought the same objective on the eve of the November 19–20 Geneva summit.

Geneva

"The Fireside Summit turned out to be a media triumph for the President," according to Nitze at the time, yet "on the hard issues of substance on arms control and regional issues the score was zero/zero."[32] Although the two leaders agreed to issue a joint statement that "a nuclear war can never be won and must never be fought," Nitze found little meaning in that. He urged Shultz to go bolder on the specifics. Concerned that Western Europeans were captivated by Mikhail Gorbachev and mindful of his own experience leading the INF talks—where the Soviets had insisted on including the British and French independent nuclear forces in any agreement—Nitze now proposed including these countries in later rounds of the START negotiations. "Britain and France are important countries . . . [and] are entitled to consider their nuclear systems to be their ultimate guarantee of security, as does the USSR, the US, and China;

their nuclear forces today are relatively small in relation to those of the super-powers and smaller as a percentage of US and Soviet totals than they were some years ago," he wrote Shultz on November 26, 1985. "We must recognize, however, that British and French forces will not only grow in numbers as they catch up in MIRVing but also increase in significance as US and USSR forces decline pursuant to an appropriate 50% reduction agreement." Once the United States and Soviet Union reached a ceiling of 4,500 strategic offensive arms, Nitze urged including British, French, and Chinese forces in a final agreement. "Each of these countries has expressed such an interest, in one way or the other; and, most importantly, it would be imprudent for us to go below our proposed force level without participation of the other nuclear powers."[33]

"I read Paul Nitze's memo on next steps with great interest and am com-fortable with most of his recommendations," director of the Policy Planning Staff Peter Rodman wrote Shultz on December 3, 1985. "It is not too soon to begin tackling some of the difficult issues. However, I have serious reserva-tions about his proposals for dealing with the issue of French and British forces. As we all know, there is enormous potential for intra-Alliance tension on this issue and we should consider the risks very carefully before proceeding. Spe-cifically my concerns are that Paul's approach would not work, that even rais-ing it with the French and British at this point would needlessly create suspicion and tension, and that we do not need to propose a solution to this issue *now*."[34] Rodman prevailed in the short term; START remained limited to the United States and the Soviet Union.

Nitze's apprehensions about the allies and Congress were well founded, however. "Gorbymania" took hold in Western Europe while congressional critics of President Reagan's policies fixated on shrinking budget deficits. Throughout the Cold War, Nitze had consistently advocated for higher defense spending, yet there was Congress to contend with. On December 12, 1985, President Reagan signed the Gramm–Rudman–Hollings Balanced Budget Act, which imposed automatic sequesters on US federal spending based on pro-jected deficits for the upcoming fiscal year. Gramm–Rudman, as it was com-monly known, was a potential nightmare for long-term defense spending, the most important component of which was needed to complete the strategic modernization of US forces (above all, the MX missile) and provide for more (but still modest) funding to the SDI. Moreover, by capping overall spending and making it contingent upon quarterly projections, Gramm–Rudman took away the president's latitude to authorize strategic systems to trade off against Soviet forces at the negotiating table—as the United States had done in 1969, when Nitze had played a key outside role in support of Safeguard, in the lead-up to the establishment of the SALT.

Gramm–Rudman resulted from the Reagan administration's refusal to make tradeoffs. The president had insisted that his tax cut would pay for itself through economic growth. The combined stimulus of a tax cut, increased defense spending, and deregulation led to economic recovery, yet the national debt skyrocketed. This was precisely what Nitze had warned against in his appearance on William F. Buckley's *Firing Line* in the summer of 1981. Since at least 1950, he had been convinced that the country could afford to raise taxes to support sufficient military forces. Yet there was no political will for a Republican administration to raise taxes, even to sustain defense spending in the middle of the 1980s.

From Nitze's vantage point, the allure of Gorbachev, a self-professed reformer with a sunny disposition, made cuts to defense even more dangerous. Despite the Soviets having fielded two new missile systems—the SS-24 and SS-25—during the first year of the Gorbachev era, the message from the telegenic Soviet leader called for easing Cold War tensions. Nitze thought this a tremendous opportunity to advance his strategic concept dating back to December 1984. However, this could happen only so long as the US side maintained sufficient funding for defense. The MX missile, which Reagan had branded the "Peacekeeper," remained the closest equivalent system to the gigantic Soviet land-based missiles. Yet the White House fought Congress for every deployment and would fall significantly short of the one hundred missiles it initially sought. Soviet negotiators would never agree to reduce their destabilizing systems in exchange for systems the US Congress was about to cut in the next National Defense Authorization Act.

Experts Group

As Nitze ruminated over the prospect of Gorbachev's outflanking the Reagan administration, the Soviet leader proposed in January 1986 to eliminate all nuclear weapons by the year 2000. On some of the specifics of that ultimate objective, Gorbachev seemed willing to leave out certain of the demands of his predecessors. For example, he dropped "compensation" for independent British and French forces upon which former Soviet foreign minister Andrei Gromyko had insisted accompany any INF deal. "This was a significant departure from the Soviets' previous stance," Nitze later recalled.[35] For six months after Gorbachev's proposal, however, Nitze battled with his counterparts in the Office of the Secretary of Defense over the wording of how the president ought to respond.

Ultimately, Nitze prevailed. "The United States does not possess the numbers of weapons needed to carry out an effective first strike; nor do we have intention of acquiring such a capability," Reagan wrote Gorbachev in a July 25,

1986, letter that reiterated Nitze's strategic concept and included elements of the Monday Package. The letter again laid out the three phases by which the United States and Soviet Union could research and deploy strategic defenses while assuring that the other side was *not seeking* a first-strike capability. During the first five years both sides would limit themselves to research, development, and testing of strategic defenses. While the United States would abide by the ABM Treaty during this first phase, Reagan was prepared to sign a new treaty stipulating that any party that decided to proceed beyond research, development, and testing—in 1991, at the end of the first five years—agreed to "share the benefits of such a system with the other providing there is mutual agreement to eliminate the offensive ballistic missiles of both sides."[36]

Should the two sides fail to reach a sharing arrangement within two years after 1991, either side would be free to deploy ABM systems after giving six months' notice. "I believe you would agree that significant commitments of this type with respect to strategic defenses would make sense only if made in conjunction with the implementation of immediate actions on both sides to begin moving toward our common goal of the total elimination of nuclear weapons," Reagan reiterated. "Toward this goal, I believe we also share the view that the process must begin with radical and stabilizing reductions in the offensive nuclear arsenals of both the United States and Soviet Union."[37]

This was the most ambitious nuclear arms control proposal that the US side had put forward to this point in the Cold War. It harkened back to the Lilienthal–Acheson and Baruch Plans when Nitze had first been in DC. Yet, those earlier plans were less complicated because only one country at the time possessed a handful of atomic weapons. In contrast, the United States and Soviet Union in 1986 kept tens of thousands of nuclear warheads and associated delivery vehicles.

In a July 28, 1986, meeting with Deputy Foreign Minister Alexander Bessmertnykh and a US delegation led by Assistant Secretary of State for Europe and Canadian Affairs Rozanne Ridgway, Nitze stressed that Reagan had attempted to allay Gorbachev's concerns about SDI and the ABM Treaty. Under the "supreme interest clause," Nitze reminded Bessmertnykh, the United States retained the right to withdraw from the ABM Treaty. Far short of that approach, Nitze insisted that what Reagan was proposing was for both sides to confine themselves to that which the ABM Treaty permitted: research, testing, and development. "The purpose of this research is to determine the feasibility of advanced defenses against ballistic missiles," he stated. In response to Bessmertnykh's contention that SDI lay outside the ABM Treaty, Nitze insisted that the president's proposal stayed within the parameters of Article V and Agreed Statement D.[38]

Bessmertnykh acknowledged that negotiations in Geneva needed to go faster. He proposed an "experts meeting" of representatives from both countries, separate from the formal sides, to take place in Moscow and be separate from negotiations in Geneva. Accordingly, on August 11, Nitze led a US delegation to Moscow that included the heads of the arms control teams in Geneva as well as overall head Max Kampelman, Assistant Secretary of Defense Richard Perle, and lead NSC staffer for arms control Robert Linhard.[39] This "experts group" would endure throughout the rest of INF and START. Nitze was thus the de facto overseer of US nuclear arms control delegations for the remainder of the Reagan administration.

At Reykjavik, Iceland, on the weekend of October 11–12, 1986, President Reagan sought to bring General Secretary Gorbachev around to the positions outlined in his July 25 letter. In between their storied encounters, Nitze led a US team of experts in an all-night session with Soviet counterparts on Saturday, October 11. From 8 p.m. until 2 a.m., Nitze and Soviet delegation head Sergei Akhromeyev haggled over START. They neared an agreement on eliminating INF forces in Europe (leaving outstanding the question of SS-20s in Asia). After conferring with Gorbachev, Akhromeyev returned at 3 a.m. "and announced that he was prepared to agree to the central point [Nitze] had been sticking to . . . [W]e must have equal final ceilings, not equal reductions from current unequal levels to unequal ceilings still favoring the Soviet Union." After another three and a half hours of negotiations, Nitze and Akhromeyev agreed that, under the terms of START, they would count gravity bombs and short-range attack missiles on heavy bombers as one warhead.

Later that morning, Reagan and Gorbachev—joined by Shultz and Shevardnadze—haggled over what to include in the ten-year phases and how to define research and testing of SDI. While they did not resolve vital outstanding differences, their positions fell within the parameters of the July 25 letter. In other words, Nitze's proposals were now not only the United States' negotiating positions but the basis of the most dramatic and ambitious conversations on nuclear matters between heads of state during the Cold War. Moreover, his proposals provided specificity for Reagan's aspirations to achieve a world without nuclear weapons. Adrenaline fueled Nitze that weekend. After staying up the whole night, he accompanied Shultz in each of the Sunday meetings—although he was not in the final, unscheduled meeting between the presidents and the secretary of state and foreign minister.

Nitze was gloomy upon his return to Washington. In a conversation with longtime friend Charles Burton Marshall a few days later, he downplayed progress and professed to be deeply skeptical whether any agreement could be achieved with Gorbachev. At a November 6 meeting between Shultz and

FIGURE 11.1. (L–R) Special adviser to the president and Secretary of State on Arms Control Nitze, White House chief of staff Donald Regan, President Reagan, Secretary of State George Shultz, National Security Advisor John Poindexter, and Arms Control and Disarmament Agency director Kenneth Adelman, Reykjavik, October 12, 1986. At the Reykjavik Summit in October 1986, Nitze led the US experts group in a meeting with Soviet counterparts that lasted from 8 p.m. until 6:30 a.m. Photo courtesy of the Ronald Reagan Presidential Library.

Shevardnadze in Vienna, the Soviet delegation—which did not include Akhromeyev, whom Nitze respected—appeared to walk back from Gorbachev's positions embraced in Iceland.[40]

Nitze suspected that the Soviet delegation was attempting to spin the outcome at that summit for political gain, aiming at public opinion in Western Europe or peacenik liberals in the United States. "When we arrived at Reykjavik we found the Soviet delegation differed from previous delegations," Nitze put down on paper while preparing for a talk at SAIS on December 15, 1986. Previously, half the delegation had been KGB (Committee for State Security); at Reykjavik, only a few were KGB. "Their delegation was flooded with people dealing with the media, propaganda, psychological dirty tricks," however. Nitze speculated that their job was to figure out how to convince observers that it was the fault of the United States for rejecting Gorbachev's proposals.[41] Nitze anticipated a replay of the "walk in the park" episode from late 1983, right before NATO's INF deployment. "The Soviets have launched a mammoth propaganda offensive asserting the President agreed to things he did not agree to, putting the blame for the failure of Reykjavik on us, and refusing to discuss anything seriously unless we agree to their position."[42]

Still, Nitze retained a sliver of optimism. He gauged that the Soviets were not succeeding in their efforts to derail the political fortunes of leaders of the Western alliance. Thatcher and Kohl's approval numbers had gone up. So had the president's—that is, until the revelations about Iran-Contra in October 1986. The lesson of all this was the enduring importance of US strength. As happened with Richard Nixon during Watergate, however, a weakened US presidency did not strengthen diplomats' negotiating hand in Geneva.

The Politics of National Security

In early 1987, Gorbachev announced that he would no longer consider an INF agreement contingent upon restrictions to SDI. Meanwhile, the Reagan administration was hobbled by fallout from the Iran-Contra scandal, which led to several investigations, hundreds of hours of congressional hearings, and the tarnishing of multiple cabinet officials. Newly emboldened by taking the Senate in 1986, Democrats there asserted themselves on SDI and the ABM Treaty. For example, Michigan senator Carl Levin had previously demanded to see documents leading up to Reagan's decision that a broad interpretation of the ABM Treaty was justified. Now, Georgia's senator Sam Nunn put himself forward as the defender of the ABM Treaty, couching the interpretation of the treaty in terms of a constitutional matter of Senate prerogative.

From Nitze's perspective, Democratic senators were seeking to dictate to the president what US foreign policy ought to be. As someone with over three decades of experience in the executive branch, he considered that to be deeply misguided. Nitze was simultaneously under siege within the administration from SDI proponents who wanted to build a missile defense system and could not care less about the ABM Treaty. They advocated for an early phased deployment, even as Nitze "found no persuasive evidence that deployment of a worthwhile system could begin by 1994."[43]

On May 11, 1987, director of the Policy Planning Staff Richard Solomon convened a meeting in which all of its former directors—every one of which was still alive—were invited. When it came time to give his own tour d'horizon of US national security, Nitze expressed pessimism. "I believe the strategic nuclear balance is already adverse and that there is little prospect of reversing it, at least within this century," he stated. "The question of conducting policy from the position of military inadequacy is not a unique problem in history."

He sounded like an old man recalling simpler times. "The most basic long-term problem for the United States is that of a partial erosion of the basic values that have held this country, and the west generally, together."[44]

Nitze's assessment was consistent with the gist of two books that would become unexpected best sellers in 1987: Allan Bloom's *Closing of the American Mind* and Paul Kennedy's *The Rise and Fall of the Great Powers*. Themes of disunion and decline filled Nitze's mind—just as they had when he picked up Spengler's *Decline of the West* in the 1930s. He continued to press for a nuclear arms agreement with the Soviets while also working on a memoir that he hoped would counter the works of revisionist historians purporting to draw moral equivalence between the United States and the communist world. On a more personal level, the first half of 1987 was a wrenching time for Nitze, as his wife Phyllis's emphysema worsened. She died on June 29.

Nitze grieved for his wife yet maintained his workload. By the fall of 1987, as the Reagan administration recovered from the lows of Iran-Contra, George Shultz sought to broker an INF accord. Nitze threw himself into the work of resolving outstanding disputes. He again found himself a figure of unwanted media attention. Conservatives pilloried Nitze over SDI, which they accused him of trying to trade away for an arms control deal. They cited meetings with Soviet scientist Evgeny Velikhov at the National Academy of Sciences, a gathering that Nitze hosted on his farm in Maryland in advance of the December 1987 Washington Summit, where Reagan and Gorbachev were slated to sign the INF Treaty.[45] Their insinuation was that Nitze was working directly with Soviet counterparts to thwart the intentions of President Reagan.

Unlike the 1972 Moscow Summit, where President Richard Nixon and National Security Advisor Henry Kissinger arrived even before a final agreement was settled (as explained above), the INF Treaty was ready prior to the December 1987 Washington Summit. The real action—and breakthrough—was at the State Department, where the experts group led by Nitze and Akhromeyev hashed out the basic formula for a START agreement. The clock was ticking on the Reagan administration. "The two leaders had agreed to meet in Moscow sometime in first half of 1988 with the hope that a START agreement would then be ready for signature," as Nitze put it in his memoir.[46] Anything less than that would be failure.

A few days after the Washington Summit concluded, Strobe Talbott wrote a profile of Nitze for *Time*.[47] The piece included a phrase that would become associated with the septuagenarian who played tennis against much younger opponents: "My body does what I tell it." Paul Nitze was unwilling to let someone else tell his story and found the quote unamusing. "I was originally displeased by the text of profile," which seemed "to be incompetent and unprofessional," he wrote Talbott on December 17, and one "built around the sharpest available quotes from my well-known critics." When it came to the quote about his athletic prowess, "Such nonsense could not have crossed my mind." More substantively, he corrected Talbott, saying that Senator Joseph McCarthy had not denounced him as being an associate of the "Red Dean" Dean Acheson, in 1953; McCarthy had in fact denounced Nitze for being a Wall Street operator. "I did not help Kennedy proclaim the 'missile gap' in the [1960] campaign and was not rewarded therefore," Nitze went on to say.

Dash for an Agreement

On January 4, 1988, Nitze met NSC staffer Robert Linhard for lunch at the Metropolitan Club to plot an arms control strategy in the final year of the Reagan administration. Both agreed that most of the outstanding START issues involved verification—although there were also unresolved points related to ALCM and ballistic missile counting, as well as a throw-weight protocol and resolution of whether the Soviet Backfire bomber ought to be included in the treaty. Yet it was also not entirely clear, even by this point in the Reagan administration, what strategic systems Congress was going to fund. "We would need to compare the strategic stability of realistically foreseeable deployments under the assumption that a START agreement along the lines we seek is achieved," Nitze told Linhard, "it could then be compared with what we could anticipate in the event of no agreement."[48]

According to Linhard, Secretary of Defense Frank Carlucci was "determined to kill the Midgetman," the single-RV missile that came closest to Nitze's ideal for strategic stability. He thought if both sides possessed low-value mobile targets, neither one would be tempted to strike first.[49] The other mobile basing concept, the so-called Garrison Rail Mobile, was one Nitze considered to be "an invitation to a surprise attack"; he "could convert the improbability of such an attack into a probability."[50] Nitze lamented Linhard's assertion that the air force and navy remained "irreconcilably opposed" to the US land-based deterrent, that the Office of Secretary of Defense was unable to resolve this interservice conflict, and that the State Department was essentially cut out of the deliberative process.

Nitze was not giving up. Three days after meeting with Linhard, he dictated a draft letter to his publisher asking to delay the completion of his memoir, citing the recent summit and his role in attempting "to nurse the INF Treaty through the Senate, with the hope it will emerge relatively unscathed." That prospect, he wrote, was hardly a "foregone conclusion." "Further than that, the far more difficult job of coming to an agreement on strategic offensive nuclear weapons looms ahead." That prospect was within grasp, and both sides were in a better position than ever before. "Another summit meeting in May or June in which the President and the General Secretary sign an agreement governing strategic offensive weapons will be a fitting cap to my career and to the memoir." That objective, Nitze went on to say, "has been my single-minded pursuit since 1969, not to mention the goal that first took root for me in 1945 when I visited the devasted cities of Hiroshima and Nagasaki."[51]

Nitze assisted Secretary of State Shultz in a series of extraordinary meetings with the Joint Chiefs of Staff in which the secretary attempted to persuade them as well as Secretary of Defense Carlucci of the merits of achieving a START agreement by the end of President Reagan's term. On January 14, 1988, Shultz convened the Joint Chiefs in their conference room, known as "The Tank." According to the chairman of the Joint Chiefs William Crowe, the chiefs were "working frantically, especially on counting rules" as well as sea-launched cruise missiles (SLCMs), yet he doubted they could "make it by May," when Reagan was tentatively scheduled to go to Moscow to meet Gorbachev. Crowe also objected—repeatedly and strongly, according to Linhard, who took notes—to the draft of a defense and space treaty, citing objections from congressional leaders about its ambiguity pertaining to interpretations of the ABM Treaty. Carlucci stated that "he wanted to put long lead money in the budget for a 1990 test that would violate the narrow interpretation." Shultz responded: "we should do what we need to do but should not schedule a test just to challenge the narrow interpretation."[52]

A key point of contention was the matter of SLCM. Nuclear SLCMs were indistinguishable from non-SCLMs unless inspectors were allowed on site, yet the US Navy would never allow Soviets to board US ships or submarines. Although Nitze had been secretary of the navy and was proud of his days there in the 1960s, he had no allegiance to the organization. Contention over SL-CMs hardly seemed worthy of standing in the way of the deal he had sought for at least two decades.

Shultz implored the Joint Chiefs and Secretary of Defense Carlucci "to use the deadline of the summit to get the treaty we want and force the bureaucracy to do the necessary work." He bristled at the idea that the US side would "cave into the pressure of a deadline"—especially since "we have not done so in the past." The fact was that "we need to sign something in Moscow," whether that was START or the nuclear testing treaties that were being negotiated in Geneva separately from NST and were perhaps better candidates. Referring to the 1975 verbal agreement between Ford and Brezhnev, Shultz acknowledged the pitfalls in "Vladivostok-type agreements," yet stated, apparently referring to START, that both sides had "gone two-thirds of the way to the top, and we shouldn't have to start over from the bottom."[53]

With a nod to the Winter Olympics set to begin in Calgary, Canada, that February, President Reagan instructed his national security team to reach a START agreement by the end of his second term in office: "we need to go for the gold."[54] Nitze expressed to memoir coauthor Steve Reardon his sense of opportunity. "We've gotten much done with respect to the START treaty; we've gotten no more than 6,000 warheads; that cuts numbers by about 50 percent on both sides; we've gotten them to agree to cut their heavy RVs by fifty percent down to 1540 from 3080; we've gotten an agreement with them [on] how you count bombers carrying long-range cruise missiles; we've gotten an agreement now with how you count the RVs on ballistic missiles having more than ten RV; we've gotten partially there on getting counting rule on how you count cruise missiles."[55] Most importantly, the agreement promised to cut the throw weight of Soviet missiles by 50 percent and the United States would not have to cut it at all. In other words, the Soviets had put on the table the thing that Nitze had been hoping to get for a decade and a half: a radical reduction in Soviet throw weight.

A key outstanding problem, at least from Nitze's perspective, was how to verify mobile missiles. The US side had proposed banning mobile missiles, yet the Soviets had introduced the SS-24s and SS-25s. Mobile missiles could provide stability—as Nitze had laid out in his January 1976 *Foreign Affairs* article—yet only if both sides had confidence in the numbers that the other side possessed. A second problem, as Nitze explained to Reardon, was SLCMs. A third problem was the challenge of reconciling START with the existing ABM Treaty.

To solve the third problem, Nitze proposed to create a list of permitted and unpermitted definitions of systems that would clarify the ambiguities of the contested portions of the ABM Treaty. Doing so made eminent sense to Nitze, who had enlisted scientist (and future secretary of defense) Ashton Carter to assist him with the technical specifications. "So that's the direction I think we ought to go," he told Reardon, "but the President doesn't want to go down that direction."[56] As to Soviet concerns, he thought they were "less worried about SDI than they used to be. They just want to be sure we don't have anything to deploy within ten years."[57] However, it ought to be possible to allay those concerns, since, according to Nitze, the US side was ten years away from deploying them anyway.

"No, they don't want to cooperate with us, that's one thing that they consider unthinkable," was Nitze's candid opinion of President Reagan's offer to share the benefits of SDI technologies with the Soviets. "They think the President is mad on this idea of a cooperative approach." "But I believe that

Mr. Gorbachev really does want a START agreement, and, as I said, he wants to downplay the difficulties of the connection between space-defense, in other words, SDI, and START," Nitze told Reardon on March 1.[58] He could not see how a presidential candidate in 1988 would come out against ratifying an agreement should Reagan and Gorbachev sign one.

With Nitze by his side, Shultz pressed his case to the NSPG: that START was achievable and that neither he nor anyone else in the administration, had gone soft—they were advocating for the president's agenda. "I wouldn't be the negotiator for Jimmy Carter, because he would want agreement for agreement's sake," Shultz asserted. "But I have no fear that we will go bananas and grab a bad deal off the table under your leadership." With "Ronald Reagan as President," he summed up, "the fact that we are working with a deadline is an advantage, not a problem."[59]

"I don't think we made the right impression at the NSPG, although we tried," Crowe lamented to Shultz at a subsequent meeting between the secretary and the Joint Chiefs on February 17.[60] "There are a host of issues that stand between us and a START Treaty. They're very difficult issues; and we're going to have a very difficult time reaching answers." The objective of the chiefs was "a good Treaty, not a fast Treaty."[61] An arcane discussion followed: on INF, range of ACLMs, and Germany. Nitze, Kampelman, and even Rowny joined Shultz in opposition to the chiefs. Air Force Chief of Staff Larry Welch argued strenuously against the Soviet proposals. The main objection on the part of US military leaders was that the Reagan administration had failed to procure sufficient funding for its strategic modernization program.

Other practicalities of finishing up START crept into the deliberations. "We ought to need to know what facilities of ours need to be monitored," as Carlucci put it. "And we can't wait until the end, because I'm getting beat up by a whole bunch of Congressman who think that plants in their [d]istrict[s] are going to get monitored." "Now no one of us is suggesting we do away with the ABM Treaty," according to Carlucci. "We are prepared to live with it for some time. It's just a matter of what's the time." The mood grew increasingly testy. "I feel like I'm hanging you out on mobiles," Crowe said to Shultz at one point. Shultz responded: "Well, you're hanging me out on mobiles and ALCMs."[62]

Shultz reiterated his stance: "Look, Washington is losing its taste for arms control because it's too damn hard. But they also have no taste for spending more money for defense, and no taste for spending money on ICBMs for us. So we have a chance for getting something we need." He referred back to a conversation with President Nixon—"His idea was to get an INF Treaty out of the way and get a START Treaty and have it negotiated and in-place by September or October, and then make it an issue in the campaign. In that way the guy who gets elected will be for it and have the ratification in the bag."[63] In Geneva in 1988, however, the nuclear and space talks were mired in drawn-out debates over matters of second-order consequences.

Nitze attempted to break the logjam. On March 23, he led the US side in an experts group meeting on verifiability, a topic of considerable complexity. The INF Treaty had eliminated an entire class of weapons. Potential violations of that provision were relatively straightforward to identify—one such missile was too many. It was much harder to verify whether one side had reduced its quantity of a particular type of weapon to some number greater than zero.

In a March 28 interview with Steve Rearden, Nitze outlined the three outstanding obstacles to a START agreement: (1) finalizing terms that were verifiable and supported the US national interest; (2) establishing consensus within the executive branch; and (3) overcoming the Soviets' fundamentally different approach to arms control. "They've got all their problems," he told Rearden, and "they're not interested in the same things we're interested in, such as the stabilizing nature of the agreement." The Soviet interest, according to Nitze, was "in maintaining as much of their current advantage as is possible."[64] That disparity of intentions notwithstanding, Nitze still pressed for a deal.

On April 11, Crowe got to the heart of the matter. There were still 1,200 brackets (or, passages to which both sides had not yet agreed) in the joint draft text of the treaty. Nitze intervened by citing the breakthrough at Reykjavik on the bomber counting rule. He also questioned the Joint Chiefs' math. "I do not understand the sentence in your memorandum wherein you say that to accept the ALCMs plus one counting rule would cost us 1400 weapons," Nitze stated. "If we had 80 ALCM carriers they would count at 11 which equal 880. This would leave us room for 220 bombers not carrying ALCMs. Each one of those could carry a large number of SRAMs [Short-Range Attack Missiles]and gravity bombs."[65] Neither Nitze nor Shultz made headway. In a meeting a few days later, Crowe said there was no way for a deal by May. Encouraged to poll the rest of the chiefs, Shultz received the same answer from them.

Nitze accompanied Reagan and Shultz to the summit in Moscow that commenced the following month. He again led the US experts group in meetings with the Soviets led by Marshal Akhromeyev. They made incremental progress but fell short of a breakthrough along the lines of the counting formula in December 1987.[66] Even after the Moscow Summit, Nitze held out hope for a dash to the finish line. "During the next seven months, we intend to build on the momentum that has been generated for stabilizing strategic arms reductions over the past seven years," he wrote in a *Washington Post* op-ed on June 21. "I believe it is possible to complete a worthwhile START agreement before

President Reagan leaves office in January 1989. The task is immensely difficult, but if there is a real opportunity we should not miss it."[67]

The following month Nitze attended a dinner at Admiral Crowe's house in honor of Akhromeyev. Nitze buttonholed Akhromeyev and pressed him for details about his meeting with the US Joint Chiefs, and whether they had made any headway on START. "I asked him whether he still thought we could reach agreement on all major issues by the end of this administration," Nitze recounted. "He said he thought it possible, but not likely; both sides would have to make major concessions." Nitze relayed this message to Crowe, who responded (skeptically): "what kind of pot are you smoking, Paul?"[68]

Nitze continued working toward a deal as the presidential election neared. On September 23, he led a combined session of the START and DST delegations in Geneva, the result of which was "no basic change in either side's position."[69] On November 15, 1988, a few days after Vice President George Bush defeated Democratic presidential nominee Governor Michael Dukakis, Nitze submitted his letter of resignation to President Reagan. He received no response. "I am told that that portion of the White House staff which in the past has dealt with arms control has been told that none of them will have a job in the new Administration," Nitze wrote Shultz on December 21.[70] He was gloomy and clearly hurt by the inattention he had received from the incoming Bush administration. Yet he still laid out the approach the new team ought to take to preserve the chances for a START agreement.

Paul Nitze never stopped trying to get a strategic arms agreement. He sensed opportunity but feared that Gorbachev and the US bureaucracy would conspire to take it away. He saw within his grasp the goal of his great pursuit from 1969 onward: an arms agreement to reduce the most destabilizing missiles. Nitze could not have asked for a better role. He was the de facto head of the delegations in Geneva and reported directly to the secretary of state and the president, both of whom shared his commitment to getting a deal. Moreover, President Reagan had the most ambition of any US president when it came to reducing nuclear weapons, and he had the most credibility with conservative politicians who were the least disposed to ratify such an agreement.

Part of the problem in finishing START was the failure of the Reagan administration's strategic modernization program. For all its talk about restoring US defenses, the administration had not solved the riddle of upgrading its land-based nuclear deterrent to match those of the Soviet Union. Basing MX remained unsolved by the end of the Reagan administration, and there was zero support for the Midgetman missile—Secretary of Defense Frank Carlucci opposed it, and none of the military services wanted it. In his final letter to

Shultz, Nitze also questioned whether the estimated $200 billion the United States was estimated to spend on the B-2 "stealth bomber" was worth it. In sum, by December 1988, Nitze's efforts to achieve "strategic stability," as laid out in 1976, seemed to have reached a dead end.

Nitze's disappointment notwithstanding, his strategic concept gave substance to Reagan's grand aspirations for a world without nuclear weapons—an objective that Gorbachev shared. Ultimately, the START I agreement that Gorbachev and George H. W. Bush would sign in 1991 was based on the framework that Nitze and the so-called experts group had hammered out in December 1987.

CHAPTER 12

No Retirement, 1989–2004

As is customary for political appointees at the end of a presidential administration, Paul Nitze submitted a letter of resignation on November 15, 1988, one week after George H. W. Bush defeated Michael Dukakis. Having received no response, Nitze wrote memos for the incoming national security team. Incoming secretary of state James Baker offered Nitze the option of staying on as "Ambassador at Large Emeritus for Arms Control Matters."

President Bush and Secretary of State Baker wanted to distinguish themselves from their predecessors, President Ronald Reagan and Secretary of State George Shultz. That meant the end of Nitze's "strategic concept," and any transition from strategic offensives toward strategic defenses, and Reagan's ultimate goal of abolishing nuclear weapons. It also meant the end of Nitze's tenure as special adviser to the president and secretary of state.

When it came to Nitze's efforts to shape national security debates, there was no such thing as retirement. He put forth ideas for US leadership in the world, even after the rapid collapse of Soviet power and the dissolution of the Soviet state. He opposed the Persian Gulf War but could not resist marveling at the potential for precision-guided smart weapons to achieve military objectives. Over time, he came to believe that highly advanced conventional weaponry rendered the US nuclear arsenal unnecessary in achieving its primary objective of enabling risk-taking in moments of crisis. That did not mean that

Washington should be overly eager to wield that might or press its advantages. Nitze opposed NATO expansion and was deeply skeptical of humanitarian interventions in the 1990s. He regarded the primary threat to US national security after the Cold War as emanating not from any one state or group of bad actors but rather from global environmental degradation.

George H. W. Bush Transition

"More fun to make them in the business side," Paul Nitze responded to an interviewer's question about deals in the private sector versus arms negotiations, in the waning days of the Reagan administration. "It's exciting; if it works, you make money; if it doesn't work, it isn't fatal." Public service, to Nitze, was not "really a personal decision"—"one works at these issues because you consider them basically much more important, much more significant; that's why you work at them." Negotiations were "much more painful, time-consuming, worrisome; you don't do it for personal satisfaction." Occasionally, there was some satisfaction; however, "I had much more fun with the Aspen skiing company."[1] Nitze intimated that his time in government might be reaching its end. Yet he wanted to keep working.

On February 4, Nitze received from White House aide Chase Untermeyer a boilerplate memo that stated: "we have begun to review and process your resume and shall contact you if your talents can be utilized."[2] He kept scheduled engagements. On February 6, 1989, he delivered an address at the Nobel Institute in Oslo, Norway, "Security Challenges Facing NATO in the 1990s." In it, he lauded NATO's success upon its fortieth anniversary yet warned of impending danger—namely, the Nitze Scenario whereby US forces remained vulnerable to a surprise Soviet attack. "U.S. fixed, land-based missiles have been vulnerable to Soviet attack for some time now, and the problem is getting worse," he declared. "Successive U.S. Administrations have proposed plans for basing new ICBMs in survivable modes, but these plans have not garnered sustained support." The new administration—in which he ostensibly served—"must resolve this problem, if this part of the U.S. strategic triad is to remain viable." Nitze reiterated the importance of a "robust SDI research program" and cited the importance of "survivability and cost-effectiveness at the margin"—the so-called Nitze Criteria from 1985. The "basic outline of a START treaty has been established," slashing by 50 percent strategic nuclear warheads and reducing Soviet ballistic missile throw-weight to equal ceilings.[3] Nitze hoped for a quick resolution of the final hurdles he had failed to overcome the previous year.

In Oslo, Nitze was lauding Shultz's accomplishments and laying out what he believed the new secretary and the rest of the Bush administration should be doing. He offered six lessons about arms control and overall foreign policy. "The Proper Approach to Linkage" was to pursue good agreements on their own merits—"we were negotiating to do ourselves a favor [not the Soviets a favor] by enhancing our security" with the 1987 INF Treaty, even as Soviet forces remained in Afghanistan. Nitze concluded by offering his thoughts on how to deal with Soviet general secretary Mikhail Gorbachev, who had electrified the world during the UN General Assembly in New York City, in December 1988, by announcing a unilateral reduction of five hundred thousand troops. Gorbachev's talk about "military sufficiency" and embrace of perestroika and glasnost were encouraging signs (though privately, Nitze remained highly skeptical). "But we must always remember to base our security policies on Soviet capabilities and behavior rather than hopes or expressed intentions. And, to date, their military capabilities have not changed substantially." Nitze cited "NATO's capability and will to resist unacceptable Soviet behavior" as a critical incentive in bringing about the hopeful signs coming out of the Kremlin.[4] The takeaway was that nothing had fundamentally changed.

"I have thought further about your proposal that I stay at the Department of State with largely consulting duties and more time to do as I wish," Nitze wrote Baker when he returned. "In some ways, it is an attractive offer. I doubt, however, that it will suit my temperament. I am rarely happy in a job unless I feel fully part of the team." He did not want to be "a fifth wheel" and continued "to wish to render such assistance to an imaginative and effective foreign policy for the United States as I can."[5] "You know my unquestioned loyalty to you," Nitze wrote in a less caustic letter to President Bush, on March 6, yet explained that Baker's offer was not "a job in which I could hope to productive and helpful to your Administration."[6] Nitze exited ungracefully and was nearly crushed to death in a horse-riding accident on March 12, after which doctors performed two surgeries on his hip.

Nitze left the State Department and retreated to Massachusetts Avenue to finish his memoir. Then, on April 10, 1989, Johns Hopkins University announced that it was renaming SAIS the Paul Nitze School of Advanced International Studies. "We felt it was time . . . to express our thanks and respect to a man who has made so much of the history which our students are currently studying," according to the dean of SAIS, George Packard.[7] It undoubtedly helped that Nitze himself had given the school $5 million to pay off the loan for its main building at 1619 Massachusetts Avenue, located across the street from Brookings Institution. It is also a short walk from the other DC think tanks that had become permanent fixtures within the national security community. While this announcement seemed finally to certify Nitze's retirement from government, he banished that prospect by saying: "If anybody wants me to come back, I'd be delighted."[8]

The End of the Cold War

After recovering from his equestrian accident, Nitze hosted Soviet academics and diplomats both at SAIS and at his home at 3120 Woodley Road. These conversations intensified Nitze's conviction that Gorbachev was no savior. Indeed, he "was wholly dedicated to a Leninist approach to policy," a visiting Soviet academic told Nitze. Moreover, Gorbachev "would not permit a multiparty system or control of policy to escape from party hands."[9]

On July 22, 1989, Soviet marshal Sergei Akhromeyev, who had sat across the table from Nitze in the October 1986 all-night meeting in Reykjavik, called on him at the SAIS office. Following his meetings with Chairman of the Joint Chiefs of Staff Colin Powell and National Security Advisor Brent Scowcroft, Akhromeyev provided Nitze a broad tour d'horizon of arms control and the Cold War. Nitze seized on the Conventional Forces in Europe Treaty negotiations, about which he had recently published an op-ed telling the Bush administration what it should be doing.[10] Akhromeyev complained about a lack of empathy on the US side. The Soviet Union was a land power surrounded by vulnerable coasts; the naval forces of the United States and its NATO allies vastly outpowered those of the Soviet Union. A balanced Conventional Forces in Europe Treaty needed to consider naval forces; Akhromeyev was doing all he could to reach such an accord. On harmonizing START with the ABM Treaty, Nitze attempted to revive his proposal from the latter of half of the Reagan administration, to establish lists of "other physical principles" technologies. He could not speak for the present administration's priorities, "but his main concern was that the strategic situation [be] stable for both the U.S. and USSR . . . [so that neither] side be tempted to initiate nuclear war." Both sides needed to press for further reductions beyond the 50 percent cut to which he and Akhromeyev agreed at Reykjavik.[11]

Nitze may have given Akhromeyev the impression that he was in a position to influence the Bush administration on the Conventional Forces in Europe and START. He was not, yet he would never stop trying. Through his assistant Michael Stafford, who had worked for him at the State Department during the second Reagan administration, Nitze kept tabs on developments in and around Foggy Bottom. On October 13, Stafford sent him a "State of Play on NST," based on readouts from several State Department officials following Baker and Shevardnadze's meetings in Jackson Hole, Wyoming. Afterward, Shevardnadze declared that the Soviets were willing to accept a START agreement independent of a deal reiterating the ABM Treaty or a new bargain to restrict testing for missile defense. However, concerns about ALCMs, SLCMs, and mobile ICBMs threatened to derail the completion of a strategic arms agreement. "Given this lack of significant progress in START, nobody was able to explain to me why Scowcroft and Bush are predicting completion, or near-completion, of a treaty by the summit [expected to take place by the end of the year]," Stafford wrote Nitze. "So it remains a mystery."[12] There was nothing mysterious about Nitze's role in this phase of nuclear arms negotiations: he had none for the first time in two decades.

Meanwhile, Nitze remained dubious about the prospects that perestroika could succeed. He took note of a September 16, 1989, article in *The Economist* proposing solutions to the challenges to the Soviet economy, which now faced a "ruble overhang" of some 200 billion rubles.[13] Under Gorbachev's plans to build a consumer sector, these would have to be spent in an economy with a gross domestic product of fewer than one trillion rubles. He typed up an analysis of the problems. "Laws concerning ownership, and on various forms of coops and leasing are to be passed before the end of the year," he wrote. "Some say ten or 15 years may be required before enough goods would be available for a market economy. Others say convertibility is necessary for a proper connection to world markets and that this must come quickly. I have seen no model of how all this might be done."[14] Nitze saw no way to integrate the Soviet Union into the global economy.

On October 23, Nitze received the Burkett Miller Award from the Miller Center at the University of Virginia. Following a ceremony in the Dome Room of the Rotunda hosted by Miller Center director Kenneth Thompson, the realist scholar with whom Nitze had collaborated in the 1950s, Nitze reflected on his career and took questions from the audience. "I would not think it a wise idea to 'marry' Gorbachev," he responded to one of them. "I think he has created a personal dictatorship by the threat of intolerable kinds of force against his opponents. He really is a person who believes in the Gulag Archipelago and is not averse to throwing people in it, and has been throwing them into it from time to time." Gorbachev was not "anything other than a very agile and competent dictator, and I don't see any reason for us to marry him as an individual."[15] The United States had already done such a thing during Nitze's own career in government—"Many in the United States decided that Chiang Kai-shek was the answer to every prayer in the Far East, and we had a committee of one million supporting Chiang Kai-shek. That was a great mistake." So was US support for the shah of Iran. "We certainly shouldn't have married our policy in that part of the world to the Shah."[16] Nitze drew these comparisons between Gorbachev and strongmen on both sides of the Cold War despite the very significant political reforms then taking place in the Soviet Union.

When asked about Eastern Europe, Nitze expressed skepticism that Gorbachev would act differently from previous Soviet leaders. "The Poles and the Hungarians don't want to leave the Warsaw Pact because they are afraid that the Russians will disapprove," he opined, "and there are lots of things the Russians could do if they disapprove other than just reoccupying the countries." He went on to say: "I don't know that they will say it is pursuant to the Brezhnev Doctrine, but I do think it is not beyond the realm of the possible, and neither do the people in Eastern Europe think it is beyond the possibility that the Soviets will use military force against Poland, Hungary, etc., in the event they were to separate themselves militarily and come over to the other side."[17]

Nitze needed to be corrected about all of those things. He greatly underestimated Gorbachev, who declined to respond when East German border guards lifted the gates at checkpoints on November 9, 1989. In the following months, Hungary and Poland, which had already taken bold steps away from the Soviet Union, exited the Warsaw Pact. After decades of warning about Soviet might and how that would encourage its leaders to take risks in moments of crisis, Nitze watched as Moscow's imperium over Eastern Europe collapsed—nearly entirely peacefully.

Soviet intentions did not accord with Nitze's expectations. Yet their capabilities remained. Even after the fall of the Berlin Wall, Nitze continued to wage his struggle against the threat posed by Soviet heavy missiles. He urged the Bush administration to become more ambitious on arms reductions to chip away at Soviet strategic advantages. "The President has now decided on a fast track for START," he wrote General Lee Butler, who directed strategic plans and policy for the Joint Chiefs of Staff, on December 6, 1989. "I am concerned that we are not asking for enough." The current proposals, which remained based on the December 1987 START counting formula of 6,000 warheads, 1,600 ICBMs, and 154 heavy missiles—which Nitze and Akhromeyev had hammered out—"would not assure long-term stability and are bound not to be acceptable in the absence of some U.S. negotiating concessions to the Soviets," he went on to say. To this last point, it was essential to trade away US systems before Congress nixed funding for them—so that Soviet negotiators could say they got something in return. "We need to have enough trading room to end up with a truly stable nuclear situation," Nitze insisted. "Otherwise, there will be no basis for a cooperative long-term relationship between us." The "principal long-term thorn in our side" consisted of the SS-18 Mod 5s, of which the Soviets were building as many as 150. While the Soviets were offering the US side the "equal right" to deploy one class of heavy missile to match that, "we don't want one, and there is zero possibility the Congress will authorize one." In sum: "We generally don't ask for enough from the Soviets because of public pressure for an agreement regardless of the degree it can really add to our long-run security."[18]

In previous moments of rapid political change—whether in 1950, 1968, or other times—Nitze had not reflected much about whether his assumptions were valid. Neither did he do so in late 1989, when peaceful revolutions took hold in Eastern Europe. From the 1970s onward, he had focused on the danger of the Nitze Scenario—that Soviet superiority would lead the United States to back down in a crisis, and confidence in that outcome would embolden leaders inside the Kremlin to take risks abroad. His thinking comprised three main propositions: (1) the Soviets enjoyed nuclear superiority, and that prompted them to take political risks; (2) the United States needed to modernize its forces to restore its strength; and (3) both sides should aspire to reach an agreement that would stabilize offenses and defenses so that neither side would be tempted to use them in the event of a crisis. By his own admission at the start of 1989, the first proposition remained, the objective called for in the second was unfulfilled, and that of the third was going nowhere. Yet none of that mattered in the most spectacular season of the Cold War. Revolutions in Central and Eastern Europe *did not* lead the Kremlin to leverage its strategic advantage to preserve the Soviet outer empire. No crisis ensued. Gorbachev's actions defied Nitze's predictions; and, more broadly, negated his entire theory of nuclear weapons and risk-taking.

Persian Gulf War

No longer was the leader of the Kremlin the United States' number one enemy. A new candidate emerged. When Saddam Hussein invaded Kuwait in August 1990, and the George H. W. Bush administration faced a critical test of the emerging post-Cold War political order, Paul Nitze urged restraint. In his remarks to Congress on September 11, 1990, President Bush set the country on a path toward military confrontation with Saddam in order to get him to withdraw from Kuwait and curtail his aspirations for regional supremacy. For Nitze, the more pressing issue remained: deal with Soviet heavy missiles. On October 25, 1990, Nitze published an op-ed in the *New York Times* advocating ditching START and leapfrogging to START II. (Members of the Bush administration had intimated that START II would be on the horizon once they got START I signed and ratified, and that START II would include a ban on mobile MIRVs.) Nitze now regarded START the same way he had once criticized SALT: it squandered the opportunity to restrain or reduce the most destabilizing Soviet forces, the SS-18s, whose aggregate throw weight vastly exceeded that of anything in the US arsenal. Given the myriad challenges they were dealing with simultaneously, few within the Bush administration paid attention to Nitze.

Nor were they interested in his thoughts on how to deal with Saddam Hussein. On January 6, 1991, Nitze and Stafford published a joint op-ed in the *Washington Post* calling on the Bush administration to avoid an "all-out war" with Saddam.[19] While they agreed that some action against Saddam was necessary—mainly to protect the free flow of oil to the global economy—they considered a full-blown allied ground assault to be dangerous. Nitze and Stafford laid out a series of contingency plans short of that. A stricter embargo and limited air strikes were, they thought, better options than an all-out war. Even were the coalition to achieve a smashing military success against Saddam, they warned that the long-term consequence would be the Middle East in chaos.

Nitze was following his own playbook. Accurate or not, his takeaway from the second Eisenhower administration had been that his public criticism of the New Look had nudged the president and Secretary of State John Foster Dulles to shift course. During the Carter administration, his opposition to the president's policies emboldened senators from both parties to withhold ratification of the SALT II. There was, in this case, no chance the Bush administration would back off in January 1991. Following the Senate's vote to authorize the use of force against Saddam, there was also little chance the legislative branch would employ any means to constrain Bush's actions. To the extent that members of the Bush administration read the *Washington Post* in the days leading up to January 17, when Operation Desert Storm commenced, they would probably have regarded Nitze merely as a nuisance.

The Persian Gulf War was in the event a smashing success for US conventional capabilities. Nitze, ever grumpy, warned of hubris after the ceasefire. From his perspective, Bush and Scowcroft's "New World Order" conjured up memories of NSC-79, his unfinished paper on US war objectives with the Soviet Union (and the prospect of a US-imposed world order) that former secretary of state Dean Acheson had told him was inimical to the nation's values. Talk of a "unipolar moment" filled Nitze with apprehension. NSC-79, "which has remained secret until now, should provide cautionary reading for the Bush administration if any of the four copies still exist in State Department archives," read his *Washington Post* article in March 1991. Nitze now spoke openly about that paper, musing that the United States *could* have invaded and occupied the

Soviet Union in the early 1950s—though at the cost of incredible losses and destruction—and then dictated a post-Cold War order. However, the rest of the world "would gang up on us if we tried to go it alone militarily and impose a Pax Americana. It was not in our interest then and it is not in our interest now."[20]

For Nitze, the more pressing objective for the 1990s was still getting verifiable reductions of Soviet heavy missiles. He downplayed the agreement that Bush and Gorbachev signed on July 31, 1991. On August 9, Michael Stafford, now a fellow at Harvard's Belfer Center, wrote Nitze urging him not to come out publicly against START I, which allowed for 154 deployed heavy ICBMs, a category in which the United States possessed zero. Nitze consequently toned down his approach. He wrote an op-ed in the August 14, 1991, edition of the *New York Times*, stating that START I was "no place to stop." That same month, the Pentagon established the Gulf War Air Power Survey, modeled on the Strategic Bombing Survey and led by SAIS professor Eliot Cohen. While Nitze served on the review committee, he did not play a substantive role.

Paul Nitze was now decidedly on the outside. Independent of anything he advocated, the Bush administration had already broached with the Soviets START II, which would eliminate MIRVs on land-based missiles. And it launched the Presidential Nuclear Initiatives, which scrapped tactical and short-range nuclear weapons, took US nuclear forces off hair-trigger alert, and canceled the long-imperiled Midgetman and rail-based MX Garrison systems. The Presidential Nuclear Initiatives, which President Bush announced in September 1991 and January 1992, were reciprocal steps, not treaties, and required neither congressional approval nor a verification regime.

In an October 13, 1991, profile in the *New York Times*, Nitze expressed his reservations about the Bush administration, which had not sought his advice. He approved of scrapping tactical nuclear weapons, which he had long thought pointless. However, he did not approve of taking B-52s off alert, considering it a declaration that had "all the hallmarks of having been produced by a speechwriter, looking for a political gesture that would ring well here and in Europe, not by someone who sat down first to make an objective analysis of the strategic situation."[21] This critique was unfounded. Assistant Secretary of Defense for International Security Policy Stephen Hadley *had* gathered other national security professionals to make objective analyses of the situation. They had not invited Nitze to participate.

START and the Presidential Nuclear Initiatives notwithstanding, Nitze warned of stark dangers. In the aftermath of a failed coup attempt in Moscow in August 1991, the possibility of the collapse of the Soviet military augured the horrifying prospect of Soviet nuclear weapons falling into the hands of bad actors. That scenario animated the Bush administration to send to Moscow William F. Burns, the retired general who had served under Nitze at the INF negotiations in Geneva in the early 1980s. Once again, Nitze gave the administration no credit for their actions. He also criticized Bush for putting too much faith in Mikhail Gorbachev, comparing him (as he had at the Miller Center) to Chiang Kai-Shek and the shah of Iran. In the glow of post-Cold War victory, it was important—he cautioned—not to become complacent. He reiterated the warnings of NSC-79, insisting that "whenever any one country has risen to a position of power and dominance, others have banded together to try to cut it down to size." It was an extraordinary statement for Nitze to blame the White House for making the United States too strong. In his view, Bush was also complicit in allowing the American people to believe that "all the serious threats to peace and stability have evaporated."

Nitze resented that policy makers within the Bush administration failed to consult him. Observing the outcome of the Persian Gulf War did however lead Nitze to rethink some fundamental assumptions about nuclear weapons. In the May 1992 edition of the *Bulletin of the Atomic Scientists*, he reflected on their role (or lack thereof) in the Persian Gulf War. "Much as we might wish otherwise, nuclear weapons cannot be disinvented; their existence, or potential existence, will continue. Therefore, the primary role of US nuclear arms should continue to be deterrence of nuclear use by others." They should continue to be "an insurance policy to deter any future leader who may control all, or a major portion, of the former Soviet arsenal and may contemplate using it." China was important, too—though "the Chinese strategic arsenal now appears to be smaller than once estimated."[22] US nuclear weapons could also serve to reassure friends and allies. However, Nitze did not see that the US nuclear arsenal would deter "other nuclear weapons states," because there was no assurance that their leaders were rational. The overwhelming US nuclear arsenal had not caused Saddam to back down in late 1990, as the Soviets had done during the Cuban Missile Crisis in October 1962.

This hardly meant that unilateral nuclear disarmament was Nitze's answer to this new reality. US strategic forces needed to remain at least equal in size to that of the former Soviet Union, Nitze maintained, and Washington should "also retain a strategic reserve that would be as large as the strategic arsenals of all other nuclear nations combined."[23] He now endorsed significant reductions toward a minimal deterrent and exhorted US planners to think hard about what that constituted. A minimal deterrent meant relying on counterforce—meaning holding the enemy's strategic forces at risk. In the post-Cold War era, he anticipated a lack of public support for targeting civilian populations—if there ever had been such support. The Persian Gulf War had also demonstrated the capabilities of US so-called smart weapons to dismantle Baghdad's sophisticated C^3+I network.

Nitze thus proposed deep cuts in US and Soviet arsenals, including eliminating MIRVed land-based missiles. In fact, the Bush administration was already pursuing that objective. When President Bush hosted the new Russian leader, Boris Yeltsin, in June 1992, both leaders publicly announced their intention to make swift progress toward a START II agreement that drew upon the infrastructure of START I to make drastic reductions in the most destabilizing nuclear systems. Afterward, Nitze praised this announcement while again shifting the goalpost. "There isn't any need for the Russians to have any nuclear deterrent at all," he said in an interview, since they had no actual enemy to fear. However, "it is necessary for the United States to maintain a worldwide nuclear deterrent" because US policy makers had plenty to worry about.[24] Any rogue actor such as Gaddhafi or Saddam Hussein, in possession of only one nuclear device, could pursue regional hegemony safely in the knowledge that the United States would not risk confronting someone who might use it. The primary relationship between US nuclear strategy and risk-taking had not changed with the end of the Cold War. From Nitze's perspective, the great danger was that the nuclear arsenals of opposing states would lead US leaders to self-deter and avoid confrontation. That reticence would encourage further aggression. Such a prospect updated the Nitze Scenario—that the potential of a surprise Soviet nuclear attack would lead US presidents to self-deter—to fit the post-Cold War era.

Even at age eighty-four, Nitze kept at it. He was intrigued by the independent presidential candidacy of Texas businessman H. Ross Perot. Along with those of Martha Stewart and O. J. Simpson, Nitze's name appeared on campaign literature trumpeting a national committee that rejected the old ways of traditional party politics.[25] Nitze attended a luncheon for Perot in July 1992.[26] Private discussions did not go well. Perot "appalled one early booster, foreign affairs expert Paul Nitze, by apparently writing off Europe in favor of Asia," the Washington Post reported that month.[27] In September, Nitze signed a letter organized by former chairman of the Joint Chiefs William Crowe endorsing the presidential candidacy of the former Democratic governor of Arkansas, William Jefferson Clinton.

Meanwhile, the Bush administration completed START II, which George H. W. Bush and Boris Yeltsin signed in January 1993. START II was set to eliminate all land-based MIRVs—an almost incomprehensible prospect during Nitze's singular focus on a nuclear agreement with the Soviets from 1969 onward. Secretary of State James Baker's hard-charging undersecretary, Reginald Bartholomew, took over Nitze's spot in leading the experts groups with

Sergei Akhromeyev, with special assistant James Timbie as the crafter of solutions to seemingly intractable problems. Nitze had no champions to which he could turn. He had never cultivated senators like Sam Nunn or Jesse Helms, who played critical roles in promoting or thwarting arms agreements. In contrast to his predecessor, Ronald Reagan, Bush was regarded skeptically by conservatives. Yet, they were hardly about to fall in with Nitze, whom they blamed for trying to scuttle the SDI. Ultimately, Bush signed off on "Brilliant Pebbles," a modest program that pleased few hardcore SDI supporters. Nitze's logic of not signing START I to get START II faster would have baffled arms control advocates in the Democratic Party.

In November 1992, the month of the first presidential election in fifty years in which Nitze did not aspire for a high position in national security, he got engaged to Elizabeth Scott Porter ("Leezee"), a businesswoman and socialite. The couple set a date to be married on January 23, 1993, three days after the inauguration of President Bill Clinton and one week after Nitze's birthday. "He asked me if I wanted to marry an 85-year-old man or an 86-year-old man," Porter was quoted as saying, "and I said it didn't matter as long as it was Paul Nitze."[28]

Legacy Building, Rethinking, and Climate Change

Nitze refused to retire from public life. Instead, he set about burnishing his legacy. He had wanted his memoir to be a composite of his experiences in government and his development of a theory of international relations based not only on his observation of power politics but also on the literature he had absorbed since his undergraduate days. As in moments throughout Nitze's career, Henry Kissinger and George Kennan set individual examples that he could not surpass. Both synthesized their experiences in clear and vivid prose while propounding a realist theory of international relations.

In completing his memoir, Nitze had to contend with Strobe Talbott's *Master of the Game: Paul Nitze and the Nuclear Peace*, which came out in 1988. A journalist with *Time Magazine*, Talbott wrote confidently and quickly. It was his third book with Nitze as a main character, and it argued that Nitze opposed deals on the outside only to embrace them when he served within the government. Nitze rejected that characterization. However, Talbott's book preempted many interesting anecdotes and quotes that Nitze had shared in his unclassified yet-unpublished Air Force Oral History sessions, which the journalist had managed to unearth. Lee Blessing's play "Walk in the Woods" opened officially on Broadway, on February 28, 1988, based on Nitze and Kvitsinsky's efforts in the summer of 1982 to reach an INF accord prior to NATO's deployment of Pershing II and ground-launched cruise missiles. It reached London later that year in a production starring Alec Guinness and Edward Hermann. The bar was thus set high for the life of the real Nitze to live up to previous depictions of him.

From Hiroshima to Glasnost came out in the fall of 1989 to decidedly mixed reviews. Writing in the *Washington Post*, historian Robert Beisner stated that the "judiciousness of Nitze surprises and disappoints" and lamented the lack of candor about such moments as Nitze's "most recent history—the daring story of a mid-level bureaucrat trying to outmaneuver [President Ronald] Reagan himself in a design to exchange the vision of an Astrodome strategic defense system for sharp cuts in Soviet offensive missiles."[29] Of course, Nitze was hardly a midlevel bureaucrat, and he was not trying to outmaneuver Ronald Reagan. Yet that was not apparent to Beisner, who recommended that readers consult Strobe Talbott's *The Master of the Game* to compensate for all the things Nitze omitted from his memoir.

Beisner's critique of Nitze was mild compared to that of Harvard professor Stanley Hoffmann. In a scathing review in the November 23, 1989, edition of the *New York Review of Books*, he associated Nitze with the Cold War's "extravagant price: so-called 'limited' wars, subversion, oppression within client nations, the grotesque arms race, and the perverse, seemingly 'rational' calculations of the strategic thinkers. George Kennan, who, like Paul Nitze, was 'present at the creation,' has, in beautiful prose, often ruefully reflected on the tragic waste caused by the cold war. Paul Nitze's drab volume is a record of surfaces." While his life "should be an interesting subject," Nitze's memoirs were "dull and dry."[30] "This is a disappointing memoir of a long, admirable life in public service," Gregory Treverton wrote in the *Los Angeles Times*. "I wish Nitze had taken us beyond tactical skirmishes to help us more in understanding what made him tick."[31]

It is true that Nitze never reflected on the "tragic waste" of the Cold War, which he regarded as a just cause in which Americans could always have contributed more for their security. It is also true that he wanted to say more about what made him tick than space allowed him in his memoir. He set about work on a new book aimed at composing a unifying statement about foreign policy such as he had been attempting to develop ever since the 1930s. In 1993, he published *Tension between Opposites*, which featured chapters profiling the men of action he had observed up close and admired the most: James Forrestal, Will Clayton, George Marshall, Dean Acheson, and George Shultz. The common theme was that each was "striving for harmony" between theoretical and practical concepts. His central metaphor was Heraclitus's "bow and the lyre," which created music out of physical tension—the example Nitze had described in his commencement address at the Groton School in 1953 and the one that applies to much of his thinking about the matters of national security. Forrestal and the others had thought similarly. And it was no accident that these figures, who crafted and implemented key policies, were not themselves politicians. Those politicians Nitze praised—especially Harry Truman and Ronald Reagan—excelled because of their plain-spoken common sense. Nor were they academics; each was a man of action. Nitze concluded the book by proposing a "council of state" for the United States that would define the long-term national interests of the country; it would then be up to the politicians to say what was possible. Kennan had also proposed such a council, yet the idea generated little support among the United States' elected leaders.

Nitze lamented the current absence of the great men as had guided the free world through the 1940s. "Since the collapse of communism in 1989, I've often wondered what response [George] Marshall would have proposed now for the West," Nitze wrote in the *Chicago Tribune* on June 12, 1993, following a recent documentary about the former secretary of state. "No doubt he would have felt an obligation to encourage the democratic movements trying to maintain order in Russia and Eastern Europe," Nitze speculated. Yet he would also acknowledge the distinctions between the two periods. "Our economic situation today is not nearly as robust as it was in the late 1940s and, unlike Russia and the countries of the former Soviet bloc, the delicate European democracies of that time, while crippled, had the resilience to provide the institutional structure necessary to make productive use of massive amounts of American aid. Sadly, 50 years of communist stagnation has made the political and economic recovery of Eastern Europe—and especially Russia—a more difficult and complex problem." The Marshall Plan had been "the right response for that time"; the United States now needed "solutions freshly struck from today's clay, based both on U.S. political interests and on the distinctly American spirit of generous, constructive help that radiated from everything Gen. Marshall touched."[32] Nitze did not lay out what those solutions ought to be. Yet he put stock in the new generation—such was the rationale for the SAIS—to train the next generation of policy makers who would come up with the best solutions.

First, they needed to get their history straight. Nitze and other veterans of the Truman era had long assumed that the declassification and release of documents from the early Cold War would cast them all in a positive light. While this had been the case with Ronald Reagan, who cited the newly declassified NSC-68 on the campaign trail in advance of the 1980 election, the language of that document generally led to *increased* scrutiny of the Truman administration's policies. Revisionist scholars cited the harsh language and terms such as "preponderance of power" to claim that the United States bore as much—if not more—responsibility as the Soviet Union for starting the Cold War. Nitze, who had always been ambivalent toward academia (and had also regarded academics as never accepting him), dismissed revisionists' criticisms out of hand. "Don't ever bother with it, it's pure garbage," Nitze would later grouse to editor Harold Evans while working on his memoir. "It had a lot of influence during the '60s. . . . The opposition to Vietnam fed very heavily on these historians."[33]

In a September 23, 1993, address to the National War College titled "Toward a New National Security Strategy," Nitze held forth on the context of the drafting of NSC-68 and refuted misconceptions about it. For example, he and other members of the Policy Planning Staff had *not* anticipated a shooting war with the Soviet Union in 1954, when they drafted NSC-68 in early 1950: they "recognized that Soviet doctrine was exceedingly flexible . . . [and Soviet leaders] assumed that capitalism would eventually fail and communism prevail but that [the Kremlin] made no attempt to predict when." The other misconception, he thought, was that NSC-68 constituted a sharp departure from previous US policies. According to Nitze, it aligned with NSC-20/4 as well as George Kennan's 1948 strategy statement based on his Mr. X article; the key distinction was that NSC-68 shifted the focus from economic assistance to military capabilities as the means toward "timely and adequate preparation" against Soviet aggression. He closed by exhorting members of the audience to take seriously the ideological component of the Cold War, which he regarded as a conflict about much more than just specific national interests: it was about freedom versus slavery.[34]

Nitze did not have great solutions to the immediate challenges of the post-Cold War order. In an October 7, 1993, breakfast interview with the *Christian Science Monitor*, he stated that "whatever happens in the world is of some degree of interest" to the United States. Yet that did not mean that US presidents needed to intervene everywhere. On Somalia, where eighteen US soldiers had just been killed, Nitze stated: "I guess I, along with everyone else, regret that we ever went in there. . . . But now that we're in, it's a different matter. The question is, how the hell do we get out?" Nitze regarded Yugoslavia differently. He encouraged the Clinton administration to use air power against Serbs, send in tanks to occupy Belgrade, and remove Slobodan Milosevic. "The world would be better off if we could get rid of Milosevic," he declared.[35]

Meanwhile, aspiring men and women of action in and around Washington, DC, were following Nitze's example for how to launch and sustain careers in national security. Professionals who chose national security as a career rotated among think tanks on Massachusetts Avenue, the Kennedy School or Belfer Center at Harvard, and branches of government. They yearned to write the policy memo that would become the Long Telegram or Mr. X article for the post-Cold War era and turn them into the new George Kennan. Few followed Kennan's model of serving twenty years in the foreign service before authoring such documents. Instead, they sought to establish such personal connections that allowed them to pull the levers of influence, just as Nitze had successfully done inside and outside government.

Nitze's own (unofficial) biographer, Strobe Talbott, exemplified this new practice of national security. When *Tension between Opposites* came out, Talbott, friendly with President Bill Clinton since their time as Rhodes scholars at Oxford University, held the portfolio at the State Department covering the former Soviet Union; within a year, he would become deputy secretary of state. "By 1994 he had, in a very real sense, become *Paul Nitze*, which is no small accomplishment," so wrote David Ignatius in the *Washington Post*, in an article, "The Curse of the Merit Class," citing the number of Rhodes scholars and members of the Aspen Strategy Group that populated national security positions in the Clinton administration.[36] Talbott rose very early each morning to write extended briefings ("Strobegrams") for the secretary of state and president. He had undoubtedly absorbed Nitze's practice of achieving proximity to the levers of influence.

Nitze was happy to be married again and pleased that *Tension between Opposites* generated a warmer reception than had *From Hiroshima to Glasnost*. James Chace, who had debated Nitze on *Firing Line* over a decade earlier, called it "an arresting meditation on power." On why Nitze never got a cabinet position, Chace quoted former secretary of defense Clark Clifford: "[Nitze's] ambition and impatient intellect often manifested themselves in irritable peevishness and flashes of unveiled contempt for people whom he felt did not deserve the high government positions they held."[37] As Patrick Glynn put it in *Commentary*, "what is most fascinating is the degree of inwardness that this book shows to have been present in a quintessentially public man." More so than his previous memoir, or Strobe Talbott's *Master of the Game*, "this brief volume gives us a real glimpse of the inner Nitze."[38] *Tension between Opposites* was less likely to be assigned in college or graduate classes on international relations than works by Kissinger or Kennan (on whom Nitze bestowed warm words in the book). Nitze's compensation was that his name was on the nation's most prestigious school devoted to graduate studies in policy-oriented international relations.

Buoyed by the positive reception to *Tensions*, Nitze ruminated on power after the collapse of the Soviet Union. "The Gulf War offered a spectacular demonstration of the potential effectiveness of smart weapons used in a strategic role," Nitze wrote in the *Washington Post* in January 1994, revisiting the points in his earlier *Bulletin of Atomic Scientists* article. They had neutralized Saddam's C^3+I

system. Nuclear weapons had not played a role in reaching the US strategic objectives of overwhelming Iraqi forces and liberating Kuwait. "For the first time we might reasonably contemplate making nuclear weapons largely obsolete for the most practical and fundamental strategic missions," Nitze concluded. While the United States should not consider smart weapons as a panacea to all problems—as many military planners had regarded nuclear weapons during the early years of the Cold War—it was time to rethink those weapons' role during that conflict. "The lessons of the military utility of nuclear weapons must . . . be re-examined and frankly acknowledged," as he put it. "We will never be certain what has deterred the use of nuclear weapons since 1945. We can speculate that the strategic nuclear arsenals in their morbid way did stay the use of these weapons, that mutually assured destruction may have prevented the use of nuclear weapons against other nuclear powers." However, in reality, "using nuclear weapons has never entirely been ruled out, and much of the debate of operational nuclear strategy during the Cold War reflected this reality."[39]

"What inhibited the American use of nuclear weapons was clearly sensitivity to the implications of the destructiveness of such weapons," Nitze said. "And however much U.S. military doctrine asserted otherwise, their use was never an easy option for the United States, and some troublesome governments have known this and exploited it as a weakness in U.S. military posture." During the McNamara era, the aspiration toward flexible response may have led to "a more credible U.S. military presence and deterrence for some situations," yet "it did not improve our strategic deterrent." Moreover, the US nuclear arsenal "was a one-use strategic deterrent" in the conflict with the Soviet Union (and fortunately the country had never found out what happened when deterrence fails). Nonnuclear options in the post-Cold War were more promising. "Developing true strategic conventional weapons offers us a flexible capability that no aggressor can discount safely in a wide range of circumstances."[40]

For Paul Nitze at that moment, it still made sense to "continue to maintain a secure and widely dispersed array of nuclear weapons and their delivery systems until we are assured that the nuclear weapons of others constituted no threat to the United States and its associates." Yet that did not mean the United States should ever use them. There remained a gap between the "destructive power of a first-class strategic arsenal, such as that of Russia, and the ability of American strategic conventional weapons to overcome that gap." Therefore, the objective should be to understand and overcome that gap through technological research and astute strategies and tactics. "The Gulf War suggests that U.S. conventional weapons could offer an adequate deterrent against regional aggression. We must still evaluate whether other powers, such as China and Russia, have come to this conclusion. But the present threat does not come primarily from these nations, but rather from states such as Iraq, North Korea or even Libya." The post-Cold War landscape required "nonstrategic conventional forces to stop aggression as it unfolds" as well as "overwhelming nuclear strategic capability, though not necessarily to use such weapons—even in retaliation—if we can disarm an aggressor with smart non-nuclear strategic weapons." It was essential to preserve US preponderance of power, in other words, even after the Soviet Union had collapsed. That meant both conventional and nuclear superiority. "We must learn not merely to re-act, as eye for eye, or out of anger," Nitze concluded, "but with wisdom and a sense of the great responsibility that comes with great power."[41]

Nitze resumed this theme in a July 17, 1994, op-ed in the *Washington Post* in which he supported funding for the B-2 bomber. He cited this system, a legacy of the late Cold War, as part of a "mix of innovative strategic conventional capabilities, technologies and weapons we will need to back future foreign policy and deter emerging crises." While he had not thought much of it during his years attempting to reach a START agreement, Nitze now viewed the B-2 in a conventional (nonnuclear) role to achieve strategic objectives. He again reiterated that, during the Cold War, "nuclear weapons added little to our practical ability to deter petty aggressors." In the post-Cold War era, the prospect existed of nuclear war between countries over which the United States had little influence. There was also the possibility that more lethal nonnuclear technologies would give smaller states outsized power to do harm. "We need new strategies of deterrence and new technologies to permit the United States the flexibility to prevent escalation, as well as to allow us the power to act quickly to reduce further aggression. At the same time, deterrence strategy must also reflect diminished American capabilities and a shorter reaction time, with a smaller force structure, fewer overseas bases, and a smaller industry to support them." Rather than spending more, "we should spend our shrinking defense budget more wisely, and focus on preserving technology and on the difficulty of retooling."[42]

The B-2 could be used in punitive "Libya-style" raids, Nitze went on to say—in reference to the 1986 air campaign against Mu'ammar Gaddhafi following the bombing of a West Berlin disco. He had crunched the numbers and determined that it was more cost-effective than the F-117 "Stealth Fighter" and other such systems. It was also better than cruise missiles or carrier battle groups, and reached much of the globe even though it was based only at Diego Garcia, Whitman AFB, and Guam. In short, it was part of a potential mix of forces that could replace nuclear weapons as the basis for US deterrence.[43]

The United States needed to think bigger and focus on existential threats now that the Cold War was over, Nitze was sure. The man who had repeatedly warned about the prospect of the United States losing a nuclear war now saw the consequences of global climate change as potentially devastating. "The earth's climate has remained stable for the past 10,000 years, but global warming threatens the stability that fostered the development of modern civilization," he wrote in a June 2, 1997, op-ed in the *Washington Post*. "Rapid warming could render whole forests more vulnerable to the ravages of disease, pests and fires, destroying watersheds. Rising sea levels, flooding, drinking-water shortages and the northward spread of tropical diseases could displace millions of people. The economic and human costs may devastate continents, creating a crisis larger, and possibly more enduring, than any in recorded history."[44] Climate change could cause more wars over diminishing natural resources. To combat it, Nitze cited the precedent of Cold War arms reductions.

President Clinton "should not be swayed by arguments that global agreements would spawn an intrusive international bureaucracy," according to Nitze. "Comparable criticisms were leveled at the arms treaties and dispelled—and the danger from not taking action is just as severe. Those agreements demonstrated that global problems could be solved through international agreement. Their lessons can help us limit and reduce the growing threat from climate change before we find ourselves facing catastrophe."[45] In this conception of US national security, no external enemy lurked—only Americans' own ambitions and irresponsibility.

Moreover, in the effort to save mankind's global habitat, there was nothing to be gained by further nuclear testing. On June 21, 1999, Nitze joined scientist Sidney Drell in calling for the US Senate to ratify the Comprehensive Test Ban Treaty. They cited tests the previous year by India and Pakistan as evidence that the world was headed in the wrong direction and that the United States needed to lead a reversal. "We strongly embrace President Reagan's vision of a world free of nuclear weapons," read the letter.[46] This was not something that Nitze himself had believed when he was actually advising President Reagan. Yet he came to embrace it over the course of the decade that followed the collapse of the Berlin Wall. Precision-guided munitions could be used to deter rogue states and did not require vast sums of money. That was not the case in the early Cold War, when nuclear was the most advanced weaponry.

Nitze's Practice of National Security and the Global War on Terror

Drell and Nitze hoped to leverage their Cold War bona fides to persuade Republican senators to ratify the Comprehensive Test Ban Treaty. They also pressed for ratification of START II, which had never entered into force. Leading national security figures advising Republicans during the 1990s had other priorities than Nitze's at that time—even though they respected his Cold War tenure. On April 29, 1993, as the Clinton administration got underway, the Paul Nitze SAIS appointed Paul Wolfowitz as its fifth dean.

In 1969, Wolfowitz had been an intern for Nitze with the Committee to Maintain a Prudent Defense Policy, and his career followed a similar trajectory to Nitze's thereafter. He worked at ACDA and the Department of Defense during the Ford and Carter administrations, assisted with the Team B report, taught courses at SAIS, and switched his political party affiliation from Democrat to Republican in time to join the Ronald Reagan administration. He directed the State Department's Policy Planning Staff for its first two years and then served as assistant secretary of state for East Asia and then, still later, as ambassador to Indonesia. During the presidency of George H. W. Bush, Wolfowitz held the position of under secretary of defense for policy, which was equivalent to that of assistant secretary of defense for ISA (a job title that remained but had been placed under the authority of the under secretary of defense for policy). Nitze had held that position under Secretary of Defense Robert McNamara and was offered it on three other occasions. Like Nitze, Wolfowitz regarded himself as a principled supporter of US values and interests and above the political party line. He also revered George Shultz, whom he served for six years during the Reagan presidency.

"The profession of [international] theory is facing a crisis," said the outgoing dean, George Packard, upon Wolfowitz's appointment. "None of the political scientists predicted how the Cold War would end. . . . Paul's job is [to help SAIS determine] what is the posture the United States should take, what is the role of mutual forces."[47] Not only would he be helping students, but he would also be doing the same types of things that Nitze himself had done during the Eisenhower era. In addition, Wolfowitz would come to serve on various government commissions. In a profile of SAIS on the school's fiftieth anniversary and the appointment of Wolfowitz, the *Washington Post* noted that much of the Cold War focus on Soviet studies now seemed irrelevant, and that the post-Cold War order would require new thinking about military strategy within academia—even as the focus in most political science and history departments shifted away from the study of high politics. "How do you take a field that settled into a rut and make it mean something in a very different world?" according to SAIS professor Eliot Cohen, who in the previous decade had written extensively about a potential NATO–Warsaw Pact conventional war in Europe—an improbable prospect that now seemed impossible.[48]

Critics called Wolfowitz (and Cohen) a "neoconservative," a nebulous term that initially applied to Democrats (or others on the left) who grew disillusioned with the 1960s counterculture and abandonment of Truman-like foreign policies during the Vietnam era. Some, but not all, were *former* Democrats. Paul Nitze was sometimes cited as a neoconservative, as was George Shultz, whose Fifth Avenue Synagogue Speech in 1984, warned against the United States becoming the "Hamlet of Nations."[49] Neoconservatives assailed the foreign policies of President Clinton yet did not champion the causes that Nitze did by the late 1990s. Nitze, who saw the Cold War as a thing of the past, came to believe that nuclear weapons should eventually be eliminated; he regarded the effects of global climate change as an existential threat. He also disapproved of what he considered a failure of imagination by the Clinton administration. Along with George Kennan, Nitze signed a letter to the president warning that NATO expansion would reify Russians' fears that the United States was attempting to isolate and encircle their country.

In the 1996 presidential election, Wolfowitz advised Donald Rumsfeld, the former secretary of defense who served as the campaign chairman of Republican nominee Robert Dole and had years earlier attempted to torpedo Nitze's nomination to be secretary of the navy. Rumsfeld did not regard US national security challenges in the mid-1990s the same way as Nitze. After Clinton defeated Dole, Rumsfeld chaired the Commission to Assess the Ballistic Missile Threat to the United States, which the Republican Congress had mandated as part of the National Defense Authorization Act for Fiscal Year 1997.[50] The report emanating from that commission warned of a threat "more mature and evolving more rapidly than has been reported in estimates and reports by the Intelligence Community."

This report primarily drew from Nitze's practice of national security—especially during his time out of government, when he worked on the Gaither Report and Team B. So was the "Statement of Principles of the Project for a New American Century," which Wolfowitz, Rumsfeld, former secretary of defense Richard Cheney, and others signed on June 3, 1997.[51] The think tank associated with it—the Project for a New American Century—replicated the type of work engaged in by the CPD. By the mid-1990s, Nitze's views about contemporaneous US national security may no longer have mattered to policy makers. Yet his career inspired those figures who had served in government and were attempting to shift the terms of national security debates while carving out roles for themselves in future presidential administrations. Much of their thinking flowed from the premise of the Nitze Scenario. A rogue state knew that the US leader would not hit back. Acquiring a nuclear weapon could allow them to blackmail US leaders.

In the 2000 presidential election, Democratic nominee Vice President Al Gore sought to dispel any caricature of himself as an environmental radical. He did not claim that global climate change was a national security threat. Wolfowitz occupied a place on the national security team advising Gore's opponent, Republican former Texas governor George W. Bush—the son of the former president. When the younger George Bush traveled to Stanford to receive a key endorsement from George Shultz, Nitze was absent. For Nitze, global climate change *was* a national security threat. The consequences of the industrial revolution for the world of his children and grandchildren were far more concerning than topics such as Saddam Hussein's continued rule over Iraq.

"Americans need to understand that what we are talking about here is a large and long campaign [against terrorism] with substantial risks and sacrifices ahead," according to a *Wall Street Journal* editorial on September 20, 2001, a few days after the attacks of September 11. "The task is large enough it warrants planning on the scale of National Security Memorandum 68, the Cold War planning document drawn up in 1950 by a joint State-Defense committee under the leadership of Paul Nitze."[52] The Cold War—not the 1991 Gulf War or humanitarian interventions during the Clinton era—was "the appropriate analogy to this war on terrorism." The editorial warned of "many battles along the way, and not any one conclusive victory, at least not for a long time." Later that month, Nitze met with his grandson, Nicholas Thompson, who was writing a joint biography about him and Kennan. After lamenting the horrible attacks on the United States, Nitze spoke about literature: "Missiles are boring; Conrad is interesting."[53]

In the 1980s Nitze contributed significantly to Cold War deliberations by staying on and continuing to aspire to negotiate a grand bargain on nuclear arms reductions. In the immediate aftermath of 9/11, however, his career boiled down to having crafted NSC-68. In the mid-1990s he had advocated for the use of "smart bombs," yet the *Wall Street Journal* referred to that approach with scorn: "This war won't be won by bombing from 15,000 feet, the way Kosovo was."[54] With the advent of the global war on terror, the premium was placed on constructing a winning wartime strategy. The United States was again on a "wartime" footing, following a decade of ostensible peace—just as it had been in the summer of 1950 when the country intervened in Korea and President Harry Truman signed off on NSC-68.

Nitze's Last Year

As the United States now intervened in Afghanistan, and President George W. Bush attempted to rally international support against the so-called axis of evil—Iraq, Iran, and North Korea—Paul Nitze remained out of the public spotlight.

Meanwhile, Paul Wolfowitz, who was now deputy secretary of defense, advocated for taking the war on terror to Saddam Hussein. The United States and a
coalition of nations ultimately did this in March 2003. A year later, in April 2004,
Wolfowitz delivered the keynote address at an event honoring Nitze hosted by
the Aspen Institute, the think tank founded in 1949 by Nitze's brother-in-law
Walter Paepcke and which had both a sprawling campus beside the ski resort in
Colorado and a Washington office just outside of Georgetown.

Wolfowitz shared personal memories of his interactions with Nitze. The
central theme, however, was the fundamental importance of NSC-68 and how
it was guiding the Bush administration's global war on terror. Wolfowitz described how he and Secretary of Defense Donald Rumsfeld had lunched with
members of the 9/11 Commission. One of the members asked what they
could do to ensure that their report and its recommendations gained traction
and prevented future attacks. Wolfowitz responded that no one ever read the
Pearl Harbor report that examined the lead-up to December 7, 1941. "What I
told them basically was to write something similar to George Kennan's Long
Telegram or Paul Nitze's NSC-68." Unlike the Pearl Harbor report, Wolfowitz
observed, NSC-68 "is still studied in colleges and universities, including colleges for strategists, like the war colleges of our military or our National Defense University."[55]

"People who haven't read NSC-68 or go to it thinking that it was a blueprint for a military build-up, are usually astonished by how much it resembles
a philosophical treatise," Wolfowitz stated. "Paul [Nitze] argued for military
strength, but he argued most of all that the strength of this country comes
from the character of our society and the values on which we are built." "From
the idea of freedom with responsibility derives the marvelous diversity, the
deep tolerance, the lawfulness of the free society," Wolfowitz said, quoting
from section four of that document. "This is the explanation of the strength
of free men. It constitutes the integrity and the vitality of a free and democratic system. It also explains why the free society tolerates those within it who
would use their freedom to destroy it. By the same token, in relations between
nations the prime reliance of the free society is on the strength and appeal of
its idea, and it feels no compulsion to bring all [other] societies into conformity with it."[56] Wolfowitz did not recognize that many critics regarded the actions of the administration in which he served as trying to bring all societies
into this very conformity.

Paul Wolfowitz professed that NSC-68 established the blueprint for the
struggle between freedom and tyranny that underscored the Bush administration's war on terror. "We recently intercepted a letter being sent by Abu
Musab al-Zarqawi, an al Qaeda associate in Iraq, and a major terrorist mas-

termind in that country, to his colleagues in Afghanistan," Wolfowitz told the audience, describing the man who founded the terrorist organization that became ISIS (so-called Islamic State of Iraq and Syria).

> And that letter gives us an idea about how these people think about the benefits of a free and open society emerging in the heart of the Middle East. "Democracy in Iraq," Zarqawi writes, "is coming. And that will mean," he says, "suffocation for the terrorists." Zarqawi talked disparagingly about Iraqis who "look ahead to a sunny tomorrow, a prosperous future, a carefree life, comfort and favor—how dare they." For Zarqawi, prosperity and happiness were inconsistent with the terrorist mission. "We have told these people," Zarqawi writes, "that safety and victory are incompatible, that the tree of triumph and empowerment cannot grow tall and lofty without blood and defiance of death; that the nation cannot live without the aroma of martyrdom and the perfume of fragrant blood spilled on behalf of God, and that people cannot awaken from their stupor unless talk of martyrdom and martyrs fills their days and nights."[57]

As with Marxist-Leninism and the Soviet Union, according to Wolfowitz, Zarqawi's words demonstrated the long-term plans of enemies of freedom.

"Our struggle against these people will be a struggle perhaps even longer than the Cold War," said Paul Wolfowitz. "It will test our resolve perhaps even more than the conflicts of World War II. Although describing the mind of the Soviets, I think NSC-68 was prescient . . . in helping to understand the threat we face today." Once again Wolfowitz quoted Nitze's strategy statement: "The peace the Soviet Union seeks is the peace of total conformity to their policy. The antipathy of slavery to freedom explains the Iron Curtain, the isolation, the autarchy of a society whose end is absolute power. The existence and persistence of the idea of freedom is a permanent and continuous threat to the foundation of a slave society; and it therefore rejects as intolerable the long-continued existence of freedom in the world." NSC-68 regarded the assault on free institutions as "worldwide." "The idea of freedom is the most contagious idea in history"; however, as NSC-68 also stated, Wolfowitz promised that the United States would win the war on terror "like the previous great challenges the nation has faced, as long as we remain committed, like Paul Nitze, to defending freedom where it seeks to flourish." Nitze was indeed committed to this goal. It is also true that he remained deeply concerned that a rogue state leader would attempt to curtail the United States' freedom of action, just as the Kremlin did once it had reached and surpassed the United States in various nuclear capabilities after the Cuban Missile Crisis. During the last decade of his life, however, Nitze cautioned against waging a global ideological struggle and, as we have noted, regarded global climate change as the existential threat to the values he espoused in NSC-68.

In October 2004, six months after Wolfowitz's testimonial, Secretary of State Colin Powell honored Nitze at the School of Advanced International Relations. "He is an icon to those of us who are in the State Department," according to Powell, who had worked with Nitze during the last two years of the Reagan administration. "It was like having Moses at the table. [He] had 50 years under his belt when I was just trying to figure out how to be National Security Advisor." Powell marveled at the spectacular achievement of the 1987 INF Treaty: "Paul, George Shultz and so many of us worked so very hard."[58]

"Paul Henry Nitze, author of the basic U.S. strategy against the Soviet Union at the start of the Cold War and later a key negotiator of U.S.–Soviet arms accords that helped dismantle the global conflict, died of pneumonia Tuesday at his home in Georgetown," the *Washington Post* reported on October 21, 2004.[59] A memorial for Nitze was held on October 23, 2004, at the National Cathedral in Washington, DC, less than two weeks before the conclusion of the presidential contest between President George W. Bush and Senator John Kerry. Secretary of Defense Donald Rumsfeld and Deputy Secretary of Defense Paul Wolfowitz spoke admiringly. Meanwhile, all the ships in the US fleet lowered their flags to half-mast. A man of action, Paul Nitze, lay at rest. Nevertheless, his practice of national security endures.

Conclusion

"Wise men come and wise men go, but one wise man goes on and on," declared National Security Advisor Condoleezza Rice at the Paul Nitze SAIS on April 29, 2002. "And, Paul, we're very glad for that."[1] Rice was paraphrasing a quotation drawn from one of her mentors, former secretary of state George Shultz, who served during the Ronald Reagan administration. Initially scheduled for September 11, 2001, her speech had been intended to promote the merits of ballistic missile defense. Instead, the revised version dealt nearly entirely with the events of that terrible day as well as the global war on terror that President George W. Bush had commenced in response.[2]

In actuality, the Bush administration had withdrawn from the 1972 ABM Treaty, which Nitze had helped craft. After September 11, 2001, the top US national security priorities were terrorism and the threat that rogue states were perceived to pose to the American way of life. Policy makers in Washington, DC, and elsewhere surely could appreciate that 9/11 mirrored the Nitze Scenario from the Cold War, wherein an adversary might attack some part of the US homeland and threaten to massacre civilians unless the country surrendered. Implicit in that scenario was the perception that fear of another attack would force US leaders to back down from global commitments.

Nitze's ideas about national security directly influenced the George W. Bush administration. They remain vital to the 2020s, as the United States competes with Russia and China, each possessing an enormous nuclear arsenal. The Cold War metaphor is omnipresent in debates about how the United States should approach these countries. So is the search for a new George Kennan and an updated Long Telegram or Mr. X article aimed to address such challenges as Russia, China, or global climate change pose. The problem with focusing on Kennan—and aspiring to be the next Kennan—is that it presumes that someone merely needs to lay out a basic strategy. That is not how the United States and its allies prevailed in the Cold War. It succeeded because of an individual like Nitze—even though Nitze underestimated Mikhail Gorbachev, whom he thought incapable of taking the necessary steps to end the Cold War.

Throughout his long career, Nitze was both correct and wrong about many things. He stayed relevant, however, and his Cold War bona fides allowed him to take risks with the walk in the woods proposal in 1982 and "Strategic Concept" in 1985. His practice of national security tells us far more about the nature of US foreign policy than Kennan or any other writer. In his focus on the matters of war and peace in the nuclear age—whether over Berlin or Cuba or elsewhere—Nitze and those to whom he reported were considering the least terrible options. Outside critics of insiders' choices do well to keep that in mind. Whether for Cold War policy makers or those of the George W. Bush administration—or in the years since—a fair account of history requires empathizing with complexity, imperfect information, and the challenge of taking actions that not all Americans (or anyone else in the world) will embrace.

The Difficulty of Making National Security a Career (Then and Now)

A prerequisite for Nitze's entry into his field and longevity was his status as a white male born to privilege. He grew up comfortably, attended elite institutions, and walked through many open doors. Nevertheless, Nitze worked hard. Through daring, luck, and persistence, he made money in the 1930s when most Americans did not. His investment in a vitamin company during that era paid off handsomely a few decades later. So did his post-World War II investment in Aspen, Colorado, which was possible only because of his very wealthy brother-in-law Walter Paepcke.

Unlike millions of other Americans who served in the Pacific or European theaters, Nitze seldom faced mortal danger during his wartime service. After 1945, he could have chosen an easier way to live. But, instead, he decided to tackle complex problems based on simple questions, which included: How to protect the US homeland and the American way of life? How to ensure that the United States' allies recovered economically while also committing money to defend themselves? How to ensure that Americans' aspirations for peace did not lead them to wish away the threat that the Soviet Union and communism posed to core values? And, perhaps most importantly, how to reduce the danger of nuclear war?

Nitze's wealth allowed him to take political risks that might have led him otherwise to be fired. He was blessed with a robust physical constitution and took advantage of mountain and rural settings to renew his strength. Yet he also worked punishing hours and flew worldwide at the expense of spending time with his wife and children, who seldom appear in this book.

The Difficulty of Acknowledging Tension between Opposites (Then and Now)

Paul Nitze embraced a concept of "tension between opposites" and extolled the merits of holding two opposing ideas simultaneously. He criticized and endorsed presidents from both major political parties, switching his party registration from Democrat to Republican to Democrat, after which he served in multiple Republican administrations. He considered himself as a national security "expert" who could help manage crises and formulate solutions to complex—mostly nonpartisan—problems. Given the polarized state of today's politics, the need for ideological purity would probably prohibit someone like Paul Nitze from serving in high positions in successive Republican and Democratic administrations.

Considering two conflicting viewpoints simultaneously is sound strategic planning. Simply putting certain ideas down on paper does not suffice today, nor did it during the Cold War. After drafting NSC-68 in early 1950, Nitze could have returned to New York and claimed authorship of the United States' basic Cold War strategy. Yet he remained in Washington to keep working on the issues. Now, as then, follow-through is required. Staying on, while at times facing inglorious moments of rejection and failure, is a necessary burden. Then and now, meeting US national security objectives requires resilience and endurance.

The Difficulty of Nuclear Strategy (Then and Now)

Atomic weapons did not exist when Paul Nitze moved to Washington. After their advent in 1945, he seized the opportunity to gain expertise on the role they played in geopolitics. No one could prove or disprove any assertions about this topic. Since no nuclear state has (fortunately) ever used such weapons against another nuclear state, it is unknowable when and how they would. Even with declassified documents, it is impossible to prove or disprove why leaders acted as they did in moments when the use of nuclear weapons seemed plausible. For instance, Soviet leader Nikita Khrushchev ultimately backed down over Berlin in 1961 and then Cuba in 1962. Was it because of US nuclear superiority? That undoubtedly played a factor. However, US nuclear superiority did not prevent him from taking the tremendous risk of placing missiles on Cuba in the first place.

Then and now, it is not a simple matter to define victory and defeat in such crises. Khrushchev failed to achieve his objective of keeping missiles in Cuba. Yet was this a long-term victory for the Americans? Not by Paul Nitze's analysis. The resolution of the Cuban Missile Crisis allowed the Soviets to build up, while the Kennedy and Johnson administrations unilaterally stopped enhancing US forces. A nuclear war between the United States and the Soviet Union in October 1962 would have killed far more Soviets than Americans and not actually ended civilization. Ten years later, that grim calculus had changed. By Nitze's logic, this change in circumstances was a Soviet victory. To proponents of MAD, it was a shared victory. Few within the Nixon administration saw it as a US victory.

During the Cold War, the two nuclear superpowers did not engage in serious arms negotiations until seven years after the Cuban Missile Crisis ended in October 1962. Not until two decades later did they reach agreements to reduce nuclear weapons. Today there are three nuclear superpowers—the United States, Russia, and the People's Republic of China—and no historical precedent for trilateral nuclear arms reductions.

In sum, today's world demands people who are willing to make a career in national security and focus on the types of questions that animated Paul Nitze—especially people who did not come from the same elite background as he did.

Paul Nitze and the United States' Past and Future

The United States never redressed the strategic balance that obsessed Nitze since at least the 1970s. The collapse of Soviet power in Central and Eastern Europe did not lead to a crisis between East and West. Nor did it impair US risk-taking as the new administration set the objective for a post-Cold War geopolitical order. Nitze had always been skeptical that Soviet leader Mikhail Gorbachev was sincere in his stated goals of reforming the Soviet system and pursuing restraint abroad. Just days before the fall of the Berlin Wall, on November 9, 1989, Nitze dismissed any notion that Gorbachev would allow such a thing to occur.

For Paul Nitze, the chief existential threat became global climate change. Policy makers ignored him. Critics of President Clinton's foreign policy would turn to his playbook for assailing a sitting administration by citing "provocative weakness." Only in the aftermath of the September 11, 2001, terrorist attacks did they embrace the spirit of NSC-68 in seeking a foundational document for the global war on terror, equating the terrorist network Al-Qaeda with the Soviet-led totalitarianism that seemed to be marching across the globe in 1950. Nitze was relevant to that cause insofar as his practice of national security had laid out a career path for translating ideas into policy. But these were not the foreign policy priorities he valued toward the end of his life.

"Karl Marx's *Communist Manifesto* impressed me by its nostalgia for the cultural warmth and beauty of the preindustrial-revolution era," Nitze recalled at the end of his memoir. "I have a different but analogous nostalgia—a nostalgia for the warmth and beauty of European and American culture before the tragedy of the First World War as I remember it from my boyhood." Whereas Marx had "wished to lay the foundations for a totally new society to be made possible by the prior elimination of all existing social structures," Nitze attempted "to participate with others in building a new and wider world order in which scope for the further development of the main existing cultural elements would be possible."[3]

Here is an expression of the nonideological pragmatism that drove Nitze's career. He appreciated high culture and wished to be known as someone who did. Yet, when it came to national security problems, he advocated for applying cold logic. "You've got to be both an optimist and very careful," Nitze once stated. "You've got to be like a mountain climber. A mountain climber doesn't take any chances. He is very careful about each step he takes and he isn't a mountain climber unless he prepares for every step with great caution." "You want to keep policy headed in the optimistic, aggressive, forward direction, but you want to go at it with the greatest prudence and careful preparation."[4]

His emphasis on prudence and preparation led Nitze to gain a reputation as someone with an unquenchable thirst for more money to be spent on defense. There is merit to that charge in that he sincerely believed that US strength enhanced global stability. Moreover, he was skeptical that democratically elected governments could plan well over the long term, given the constant pressures of elections, which demanded short-term results. He spent most of his adult life a Democrat yet had no particular loyalty to a political party. Very importantly, he never actually questioned democracy itself.

For Paul Nitze, the nation's past—and that of civilization—contained the core values he sought to defend. "Even though more lives were lost in the Second World War," he recalled, "the impact of the First on the structure of civilization, the disillusionment and brutalization of man and his humanity, were such that the civilized world was never again the same."[5] However, the core values of the United States did not need to be invented anew. Nitze committed to the founding ideals and aspirations of the United States—what the country should be striving for even when it was not living up to them in practice. In the Cold War, the Soviet Union provided a foil to those values, just as Nazi Germany did in World War II.

"The fundamental purpose of the United States is laid down in the Preamble to the Constitution," according to NSC-68. It was "to form a more perfect Union, establish Justice, insure domestic Tranquility, provide for the common defense, promote general Welfare, and secure the Blessings of Liberty to ourselves and our Posterity." What that meant in 1950 and throughout the Cold War was "to assure the integrity and the vitality of our free society, which is founded upon the dignity and worth of the individual."[6] "Three realities emerge as a consequence of this purpose," NSC-68 went on to say: "Our determination to maintain the essential elements of individual freedom, as set forth in the Constitution and Bill of Rights; our determination to create conditions under which our free and democratic system can live and prosper; and our determination to fight if necessary to defend our way of life." Quoting the Declaration of Independence, NSC-68 summed up the fundamental purpose of the nation: "with a firm reliance on the protection of Divine Providence, we mutually pledge to each other our lives, our Fortunes and our sacred Honor."

In his practice of national security, Paul Nitze was dogged in pursuit of these objectives. He helped create the architecture of the US national security state and a system for training future professionals to work in all branches of government. He contributed directly to the most pressing national security dilemma of the Cold War: nuclear confrontation. While Nitze saw himself as failing in most of his pursuits, his overall legacy has profoundly influenced the crafting of the policy during and after the Cold War. He only sometimes lived up to his standards of excellence; even when he did, he was only sometimes correct. Yet he never gave up and lost sight of the United States' foundational aspirations.

NOTES

Introduction

1. Paul H. Nitze, with Ann M. Smith and Steven L. Rearden, *From Hiroshima to Glasnost: At the Center of Decision—A Memoir* (New York: Grove Weidenfeld, 1989), xii.

2. Memorandum from Colby Cooper to Condoleezza Rice, September 11, 2001, National Security Council—Media Communications and Speechwriting, Gina Wolford Files, SAIS Speech, September 11, 2001, George W. Bush Presidential Library, https://www.georgewbushlibrary.gov/research/finding-aids/foia-requests/2014-0508-f-condoleezza-rices-cancelled-speech-johns-hopkins-school-ofadvanced-international-studies

3. Charles Hill, *Grand Strategies: Literature, Statecraft, and World Order* (New Haven, CT: Yale University Press, 2010), 3.

4. S. Nelson Drew, ed., *NSC-68: Forging the Strategy of Containment* (Washington, DC: National Defense University Press, 1994), https://www.files.ethz.ch/isn/139678/1994-09_NSC68_Forging_Strategy.pdf.

5. Bruce Kuklick, *Blind Oracles: Intellectuals and War from Kennan to Kissinger* (Princeton, NJ: Princeton University Press, 2007), 43.

6. Paul H. Nitze, *Tension between Opposites: Reflections on the Practice and Theory of Politics* (New York: Scribner, 1993).

7. Melvyn P. Leffler, *Safeguarding Democratic Capitalism: U.S. Foreign Policy and National Security, 1920–2015* (Princeton, NJ: Princeton University Press, 2017), 318.

8. On the social world of Nitze and his associates in Washington, DC, see Gregg Herken, *The Georgetown Set: Friends and Rivals in Cold War Washington* (New York: Knopf Doubleday, 2015).

9. Securities and Exchange Commission News Digest, January 5, 1966, https://www.sec.gov/news/digest/1966/dig010566.pdf.

10. Nitze, *Tension between Opposites*, 14.

11. Nitze, *Tension between Opposites*, 15.

12. Nitze, *Tension between Opposites*, 15.

13. Nitze, *Tension between Opposites*, 15.

14. Nitze, *Tension between Opposites*, 15.

15. Nitze, *Tension between Opposites*, 17.

16. Nitze, *Tension between Opposites*, 19.

17. Nitze, *Tension between Opposites*, 3.

18. Nitze, *Tension between Opposites*, 3.

19. Nitze, *Tension between Opposites*, 3.

20. Robert Jervis, *The Meaning of the Nuclear Revolution* (Ithaca, NY: Cornell University Press, 1989).

21. Presidential Directive 58, "Continuity of Government/C3I," June 30, 1980, Jimmy Carter Presidential Library, https://www.jimmycarterlibrary.gov/assets/documents/pd58.pdf.

22. Campbell Craig and Fredrik Logevall, *America's Cold War: The Politics of Insecurity*, 2nd ed. (Cambridge, MA: Harvard University Press, 2020), 6.

23. SAIS Talking Points, December 15, 1986, box 161, Paul H. Nitze Papers, Manuscript Division, Library of Congress, Washington, DC (hereafter Nitze Papers).

24. Craig and Logevall, *America's Cold War*, 2.

1. Men of Action

1. Paul H. Nitze, US Air Force Oral History Interview, 1977, 4, box 117, Nitze Papers.

2. Nitze, US Air Force Oral History Interview, 1977, 5, box 117, Nitze Papers.

3. Nitze, US Air Force Oral History Interview, 1977, 21, box 117, Nitze Papers.

4. Nicholas Thompson, *The Hawk and the Dove: Paul Nitze, George Kennan, and the History of the Cold War* (New York: Henry Holt, 2009), 27.

5. Thompson, *Hawk and the Dove*, 27.

6. Nitze, *Hiroshima to Glasnost*, xi.

7. Nitze, *Hiroshima to Glasnost*, xii–xiii.

8. Thompson, *Hawk and the Dove*, 12.

9. Nitze, *Hiroshima to Glasnost*, xii.

10. Nitze, US Air Force Oral History Interview, 1977, 27, box 117, Nitze Papers.

11. Nitze, US Air Force Oral History Interview, 1977, 27, box 117, Nitze Papers.

12. Nitze, US Air Force Oral History Interview, 1977, 27, box 117, Nitze Papers.

13. Nitze, *Hiroshima to Glasnost*, xiii.

14. Nitze, *Hiroshima to Glasnost*, xiii.

15. Thompson, *Hawk and the Dove*, 27.

16. Nitze, US Air Force Oral History Interview, 1977, 13, box 117, Nitze Papers.

17. Nitze, US Air Force Oral History Interview, 1977, 18, box 117, Nitze Papers.

18. Nitze, US Air Force Oral History Interview, 1977, 32, box 117, Nitze Papers.

19. Thompson, *Hawk and the Dove*, 28–29.

20. Thompson, *Hawk and the Dove*, 28–29.

21. Nitze, US Air Force Oral History Interview, 1977, 19, box 117, Nitze Papers.

22. Nitze, US Air Force Oral History Interview, 1977, 20–21, box 117, Nitze Papers.

23. Nitze, US Air Force Oral History Interview, 1977, 22, box 117, Nitze Papers.

24. Nitze, US Air Force Oral History Interview, 1977, 22–23, box 117, Nitze Papers.

25. Nitze, US Air Force Oral History Interview, 1977, 34, box 117, Nitze Papers.

26. Nitze, US Air Force Oral History Interview, 1977, 36, box 117, Nitze Papers.

27. Nitze, US Air Force Oral History Interview, 1977, 39, box 117, Nitze Papers.

28. Nitze, US Air Force Oral History Interview, 1977, 38, box 117, Nitze Papers.

29. "Frederic Winthrop, 72, Founder of Organization to Aid the Deaf," *New York Times*, February 20, 1979, https://www.nytimes.com/1979/02/20/archives/frederic-winthrop-72-founder-of-organization-to-aid-the-deaf.html.

30. Thompson, *Hawk and the Dove*, 29.

31. Nitze, US Air Force Oral History Interview, 1977, 39, box 117, Nitze Papers.

32. Thompson, *Hawk and the Dove*, 32–33.

33. Draft Chapter 1, 1, box II:64, Nitze Papers.

34. Nitze, US Air Force Oral History Interview, 1977, 41, box 117, Nitze Papers.

35. Draft Chapter 1, 1, box II:64, Nitze Papers.

36. Nitze, *Hiroshima to Glasnost*, xvi.

37. Paul H. Nitze, *Tension between Opposites: Reflections on the Practice and Theory of Politics* (New York: Scribner, 1993), 88.

38. Nitze, US Air Force Oral History Interview, 1977, 49, box 117, Nitze Papers.

39. Nitze, *Hiroshima to Glasnost*, xviii.

40. Draft Chapter 1, 14, box II:64, Nitze Papers.

41. Draft Chapter 1, 15, box II:64, Nitze Papers.

42. Draft Chapter 1, 16, box II:64, Nitze Papers.

43. Draft Chapter 1, 1, box II:64, Nitze Papers.

44. Draft Chapter 1, 1, box II:64, Nitze Papers.

45. Draft Chapter 1, 17, box II:64, Nitze Papers.

46. Draft Chapter 1, 17, box II:64, Nitze Papers.

47. Draft Chapter 1, 18, box II:64, Nitze Papers.

48. Draft Chapter 1, 20, box II:64, Nitze Papers.

49. Draft Chapter 1, 19–20, box II:64, Nitze Papers.

50. Nitze, *Hiroshima to Glasnost*, xviii.

51. Nitze, *Hiroshima to Glasnost*, xviii–xix.

52. Caroll Quigley, *Tragedy & Hope* (New York: Macmillan, 1962), 62.

53. Nitze, *Hiroshima to Glasnost*, xix.

54. Draft Chapter 1, 24, box II:64, Nitze Papers.

55. Draft Chapter 1, 25–26, box II:64, Nitze Papers.

56. Nitze, US Air Force Oral History Interview, 1977, 81, box 117, Nitze Papers.

57. Draft Chapter 1, 26–27, box II:64, Nitze Papers.

58. Draft Chapter 1, 27, box II:64, Nitze Papers.

59. Draft Chapter 1, 27–28, box II:64, Nitze Papers.

60. Nitze, US Air Force Oral History Interview, 1977, 82, box 117, Nitze Papers.

61. Nitze, US Air Force Oral History Interview, 1977, 83, box 117, Nitze Papers.

62. Nitze, US Air Force Oral History Interview, 1977, 83–84, box 117, Nitze Papers.

63. Nitze, US Air Force Oral History Interview, 1977, 86, box 117, Nitze Papers.

64. Nitze, *Hiroshima to Glasnost*, xx.

65. Nitze, US Air Force Oral History Interview, 1977, 62–63, box 117, Nitze Papers.

66. Nitze, US Air Force Oral History Interview, 1977, 88–89, box 117, Nitze Papers.

67. Nitze, US Air Force Oral History Interview, 1977, 89, box 117, Nitze Papers.

68. Nitze, US Air Force Oral History Interview, 1977, 89–90, box 117, Nitze Papers.

69. Nitze, US Air Force Oral History Interview, 1977, 92–93, box 117, Nitze Papers.

70. Nitze, US Air Force Oral History Interview, 1977, 94, box 117, Nitze Papers.

71. Nitze, *Hiroshima to Glasnost*, 3–4.

72. Nitze, *Hiroshima to Glasnost*, 7.

73. Nitze, *Hiroshima to Glasnost*. 7.

74. Thompson, *Hawk and the Dove*, 38–40.

75. Thompson, *Hawk and the Dove*, 11.

76. Paul Nitze FBI file, November 4, 1940, 5, https://archive.org/details/PaulNitze/1368656-0_-_File_1_-_Section_1/

77. Nitze FBI file, 49.

78. Nitze FBI file, 45.

79. Nitze, *Hiroshima to Glasnost*, xix.

80. Nitze, US Air Force Oral History Interview, 1977, 106–7, box 117, Nitze Papers.

2. The Levers of Influence

1. Nitze, *Hiroshima to Glasnost*, 13.

2. Minutes of a Meeting in Northeast Harbor, August 17–18, 1987, 2, box II:64, Nitze Papers.

3. David Reynolds, *From Munich to Pearl Harbor: Roosevelt's America and the Origins of the Second World War* (Chicago: Ivan Dee, 2001), 4.

4. Interview with Paul H. Nitze, July 11, 1985, 13, box I:119, Nitze Papers.

5. Interview with Paul H. Nitze, January 30, 1986, 9, box I:119, Nitze Papers.

6. Interview with Paul H. Nitze, July 11, 1985, 13, box I:119, Nitze Papers.

7. See Walter Isaacson and Evan Thomas, *The Wise Men: Six Friends and the World They Made* (New York: Simon & Schuster, 1986).

8. Nitze, *Hiroshima to Glasnost*, 8–9.

9. Nitze, *Hiroshima to Glasnost*, 9.

10. Nitze, *Hiroshima to Glasnost*, 9.

11. See Reynolds, *Munich to Pearl Harbor*.

12. Oral History Interview with Paul H. Nitze, by Richard D. McKinzie, June 11, 1975, 19, Arlington, VA, Harry S. Truman Presidential Library, https://www.trumanlibrary.gov/library/oral-histories/nitzeph1.

13. Draft Post—1939 Chapter, 18, box II:64, Nitze Papers.

14. Oral History Interview with Paul H. Nitze, June 11, 1975, 19.

15. See, for instance, John M. Schuessler, *Deceit on the Road to War: Presidents, Politics, and American Democracy* (Ithaca, NY: Cornell University Press, 2015).

16. Paul H. Nitze, US Air Force Oral History Interview, 1977, 147, box 117, Nitze Papers.

17. See Brendan Simms and Charles Laderman, *Hitler's American Gamble: Pearl Harbor and Germany's March to Global War* (New York: Basic Books, 2021).

18. Oral History Interview with Paul H. Nitze, June 11, 1975, 25.

19. Oral History Interview with Paul H. Nitze, June 11, 1975, 28.

20. Nitze, *Hiroshima to Glasnost*, 18–19.

21. Interview with Paul H. Nitze, June 4, 1985, 25, box I:119, Nitze Papers.

22. Interview with Paul H. Nitze, June 4, 1985, 29, box I:119, Nitze Papers.

23. Nitze, *Hiroshima to Glasnost*, 23.

24. Nitze, *Hiroshima to Glasnost*, 23.

25. Oral History Interview with Paul H. Nitze, by Richard D. McKinzie, June 17, 1975, 63, Arlington, VA, Harry S. Truman Presidential Library, https://www.trumanlibrary.gov/library/oral-histories/nitzeph1.

26. David Callahan, *Dangerous Capabilities: Paul Nitze and the Cold War* (New York: HarperCollins, 1990), 39.

27. Callahan, *Dangerous Capabilities*, 39.

28. Callahan, *Dangerous Capabilities*, 39–40.

29. United States Strategic Bombing Survey (USSBS), *Summary Report (European War)* (Washington, DC: Government Printing Office, 1945), 15.

30. USSBS, *Summary Report (European War)*, 37.

31. Oral History Interview with Paul H. Nitze, June 17, 1975, 84–85.

32. Callaway, *Dangerous Capabilities*, 30–31.

33. Interview with Paul H. Nitze, June 4, 1986, 14, box I:119, Nitze Papers.

34. Paul Nitze, "The Role of Learned Man in Government," in *Paul Nitze on Foreign Policy*, ed. Kenneth Thompson and Steven Reardon (Lanham, MD: University Press of America, 1989), 24.

35. Minutes of a Meeting in Northeast Harbor, 3.

36. Oral History Interview with Paul H. Nitze, June 17, 1975, 87.

37. Robert P. Newman, "Ending the War with Japan: Paul Nitze's 'Early Surrender' Counterfactual," *Pacific Historical Review* 64, no. 2 (May 1995): 172.

38. Callahan, *Dangerous Capabilities*, 47.

39. Oral History Interview with Paul H. Nitze, June 17, 1975, 90.

40. Nitze, *Hiroshima to Glasnost*, 37.

41. Oral History Interview with Paul H. Nitze, June 17, 1975, 99.

42. See John W. Dower, *War without Mercy: Race & Power in the Pacific War* (New York: W. W. Norton, 1986).

43. United States Strategic Bombing Survey (USSBS), *Summary Report (Pacific War)* (Washington, DC: Government Printing Office, 1946), 87.

44. Newman, "Ending the War," 189.

45. USSBS, *Summary Report (Pacific War)*, 52.

46. USSBS, *Summary Report (Pacific War)*, 69.

47. USSBS, *Summary Report (Pacific War)*, 69.

48. USSBS, *Summary Report (Pacific War)*, 69.

49. USSBS, *Summary Report (Pacific War)*, 56.

50. USSBS, *Summary Report (Pacific War)*, 56.

51. USSBS, *Summary Report (Pacific War)*, 111.

52. USSBS, *Summary Report (Pacific War)*, 112.

53. USSBS, *Summary Report (Pacific War)*, 114.

54. USSBS, *Summary Report (Pacific War)*, 116.

55. USSBS, *Summary Report (Pacific War)*, 119.

56. USSBS, *Summary Report (Pacific War)*, 119.

57. USSBS, *Summary Report (Pacific War)*, 120.

58. Nitze, *Hiroshima to Glasnost*, 42.

59. USSBS, *Summary Report (Pacific War)*, 111.

60. Nitze, *Hiroshima to Glasnost*, 43–44.

3. Cold Warrior

1. *Foreign Relations of the United States* (hereafter *FRUS*), 1947, General; The United Nations, volume I, document 459, https://history.state.gov/historicaldocuments/frus1947v01/d459.

2. Nitze, *Hiroshima to Glasnost*, 47.

3. Interview with Paul H. Nitze, March 30, 1982, 4, box I:118, Nitze Papers.

4. Quoted in Richard Crowder, *Aftermath: The Makers of the Postwar World* (London: Bloomsbury, 2015), 179.

5. *FRUS*, 1947, The British Commonwealth; Europe, volume III, document 136, https://history.state.gov/historicaldocuments/frus1947v03/d136.

6. *FRUS*, 1947, The British Commonwealth; Europe, volume III, document 136, https://history.state.gov/historicaldocuments/frus1947v03/d136.

7. See Benn Steil, *The Marshall Plan: Dawn of the Cold War* (New York: Simon & Schuster, 2018).

8. Quoted in Steil, *Marshall Plan*, 232.

9. Nitze, *Hiroshima to Glasnost*.

10. *FRUS*, 1947, The British Commonwealth; Europe, volume III, document 214, https://history.state.gov/historicaldocuments/frus1947v03/d214.

11. Nitze, *Hiroshima to Glasnost*, 53.

12. Paul H. Nitze, US Air Force Oral History Interview, 1981, 441–42, box 117, Nitze Papers.

13. Nitze, *Hiroshima to Glasnost*, 66.

14. *FRUS*, 1948, The Far East; China, volume VIII, document 111, https://history.state.gov/historicaldocuments/frus1948v08/d111.

15. *FRUS*, 1948, General; The United Nations, volume I, part 2, document 60, https://history.state.gov/historicaldocuments/frus1948v01p2/d60.

16. *FRUS*, 1948, General; The United Nations, volume I, part 2, document 60, https://history.state.gov/historicaldocuments/frus1948v01p2/d60.

17. *FRUS*, 1948, General; The United Nations, volume I, part 2, document 61, https://history.state.gov/historicaldocuments/frus1948v01p2/d61.

18. *FRUS*, 1949, National Security Affairs, Foreign Economic Policy, volume I, document 148, https://history.state.gov/historicaldocuments/frus1949v01/d148.

19. *FRUS*, 1949, National Security Affairs, Foreign Economic Policy, volume I, document 148, https://history.state.gov/historicaldocuments/frus1949v01/d148.

20. *FRUS*, 1949, National Security Affairs, Foreign Economic Policy, volume I, document 148, https://history.state.gov/historicaldocuments/frus1949v01/d148.

21. *FRUS*, 1949, National Security Affairs, Foreign Economic Policy, volume I, document 148, https://history.state.gov/historicaldocuments/frus1949v01/d148.

22. *FRUS*, 1949, National Security Affairs, Foreign Economic Policy, volume I, document 212, https://history.state.gov/historicaldocuments/frus1949v01/d212.

23. *FRUS*, 1949, National Security Affairs, Foreign Economic Policy, volume I, document 212, https://history.state.gov/historicaldocuments/frus1949v01/d212.

24. *FRUS*, 1949, National Security Affairs, Foreign Economic Policy, volume I, document 148, https://history.state.gov/historicaldocuments/frus1949v01/d216.

25. Paul H. Nitze, US Air Force Oral History Interview, 1977, 233–34, box 117, Nitze Papers.

26. *FRUS*, 1950, National Security Affairs, Foreign Economic Policy, volume I, document 64, https://history.state.gov/historicaldocuments/frus1950v01/d64.

27. Nitze, *Hiroshima to Glasnost*, 90.

28. *FRUS*, 1949, National Security Affairs, Foreign Economic Policy, volume I, document 220, https://history.state.gov/historicaldocuments/frus1949v01/d220.

29. *FRUS*, 1949, National Security Affairs, Foreign Economic Policy, volume I, document 156, https://history.state.gov/historicaldocuments/frus1949v01/d156.

30. *FRUS*, 1949, National Security Affairs, Foreign Economic Policy, volume I, document 156, https://history.state.gov/historicaldocuments/frus1949v01/d156.

31. *FRUS*, 1949, National Security Affairs, Foreign Economic Policy, volume I, document 224, https://history.state.gov/historicaldocuments/frus1949v01/d224.

32. *FRUS*, 1949, National Security Affairs, Foreign Economic Policy, volume I, document 225, https://history.state.gov/historicaldocuments/frus1949v01/d225.

33. Nitze, *Tension between Opposites*, 139.

4. NSC-68

1. *FRUS*, 1950, National Security Affairs, Foreign Economic Policy, volume I, document 4, https://history.state.gov/historicaldocuments/frus1950v01/d4.

2. *FRUS*, 1950, National Security Affairs, Foreign Economic Policy, volume I, document 160, https://history.state.gov/historicaldocuments/frus1950v01/d160.

3. *FRUS*, 1950, National Security Affairs, Foreign Economic Policy, volume I, document 85, https://history.state.gov/historicaldocuments/frus1950v01/d85.

4. *FRUS*, 1950, National Security Affairs, Foreign Economic Policy, volume I, document 56, https://history.state.gov/historicaldocuments/frus1950v01/d56.

5. *FRUS*, 1950, National Security Affairs, Foreign Economic Policy, volume I, document 57, https://history.state.gov/historicaldocuments/frus1950v01/d57.

6. *FRUS*, 1950, National Security Affairs, Foreign Economic Policy, volume I, document 59, https://history.state.gov/historicaldocuments/frus1950v01/d59.

7. *FRUS*, 1950, National Security Affairs, Foreign Economic Policy, volume I, document 59, https://history.state.gov/historicaldocuments/frus1950v01/d59.

8. On Acheson's speech, which generated little attention at the time, see Robert Beisner, *Dean Acheson: A Life in the Cold War* (New York: Oxford University Press, 2006), 327–29.

9. *FRUS*, 1950, National Security Affairs, Foreign Economic Policy, volume I, document 59, https://history.state.gov/historicaldocuments/frus1950v01/d59; see also documents 64, 65, 69, 70, and 71; https://history.state.gov/historicaldocuments/frus1950v01/d64; https://history.state.gov/historicaldocuments/frus1950v01/d65; https://history.state.gov/historicaldocuments/frus1950v01/d69; https://history.state.gov/historicaldocuments/frus1950v01/d70; https://history.state.gov/historicaldocuments/frus1950v01/d71.

10. On the culmination of the NSC-68 and the showdown between Acheson and Johnson, see Beisner, *Dean Acheson*, 236–51.

11. *FRUS*, 1950, National Security Affairs, Foreign Economic Policy, volume I, document 72, https://history.state.gov/historicaldocuments/frus1950v01/d72.

12. *FRUS*, 1950, National Security Affairs, Foreign Economic Policy, volume I, document 73, https://history.state.gov/historicaldocuments/frus1950v01/d73.

13. Nitze, *Hiroshima to Glasnost*, 95.

14. *FRUS*, 1950, National Security Affairs, Foreign Economic Policy, volume I, document 85, https://history.state.gov/historicaldocuments/frus1950v01/d85.

15. *FRUS*, 1950, National Security Affairs; Foreign Economic Policy, volume I, document 85, https://history.state.gov/historicaldocuments/frus1950v01/d85.

16. *FRUS*, 1950, National Security Affairs; Foreign Economic Policy, volume I, document 85, https://history.state.gov/historicaldocuments/frus1950v01/d85.

17. *FRUS*, 1950, National Security Affairs; Foreign Economic Policy, volume I, document 85, https://history.state.gov/historicaldocuments/frus1950v01/d85.

18. Transcript of Princeton Seminars Discussion, reel 3, track 1, October 10, 1953, National Archives, https://catalog.archives.gov/id/75850809.

19. Interview with Paul H. Nitze, March 30, 1982, 21, box I:118, Nitze Papers. Following Douglas MacArthur's dramatic landing in Inchon in September 1950, he admitted: "My judgment was wrong."

20. Nitze, *Hiroshima to Glasnost*, 104–5.

21. *FRUS*, 1950, Korea, volume VII, document 349, https://history.state.gov/historicaldocuments/frus1950v07/d349; see also document 365, https://history.state.gov/historicaldocuments/frus1950v07/d365.

22. *FRUS*, 1950, National Security Affairs; Foreign Economic Policy, volume I, document 120, https://history.state.gov/historicaldocuments/frus1950v01/d120.

23. Leffler, *A Preponderance of Power: National Security, the Truman Administration, and the Cold War* (Stanford, CA: Stanford University Press, 1992), 371.

24. *FRUS*, 1950, Western Europe, volume III, document 212, https://history.state.gov/historicaldocuments/frus1950v03/d212. See also document 215, https://history.state.gov/historicaldocuments/frus1950v03/d215.

25. Nitze, *Hiroshima to Glasnost*, 109.

26. *FRUS*, 1950, Korea, volume VII, document 745, https://history.state.gov/historicaldocuments/frus1950v07/d745.

27. See David Alan Rosenberg, "The Origins of Overkill: Nuclear Weapons and American Strategy, 1945–1960," *International Security* 7, no. 4 (Spring 1983): 14.

28. *FRUS*, 1952–1954, National Security Affairs, volume II, part 1, document 38, https://history.state.gov/historicaldocuments/frus1952-54v02p1/d38.

29. Nitze, *Hiroshima to Glasnost*, 118–19.

30. Quoted in Leffler, *Preponderance of Power*, 402.

31. *FRUS*, 1952–1952, National Security Affairs, volume II, part 1, document 40, https://history.state.gov/historicaldocuments/frus1952-54v02p1/d40.

32. *FRUS*, 1952–1952, National Security Affairs, volume II, part 1, document 40, https://history.state.gov/historicaldocuments/frus1952-54v02p1/d40.

33. *FRUS*, 1952–1952, National Security Affairs, volume II, part 1, document 40, https://history.state.gov/historicaldocuments/frus1952-54v02p1/d40.

34. *FRUS*, 1952–1954, National Security Affairs, volume II, part 2, document 65, https://history.state.gov/historicaldocuments/frus1952-54v02p2/d65.

35. *Public Papers of the Presidents: Harry S. Truman, 1952–53* (Washington, DC: Government Printing Office, 1966), 366.

36. *FRUS*, 1952–1954, National Security Affairs, volume II, part 2, document 34, https://history.state.gov/historicaldocuments/frus1952-54v02p1/d34.

37. Paul H. Nitze, US Air Force Oral History Interview, 1977, 186–87, box 117, Nitze Papers.

38. *FRUS*, 1952–1954, Eastern Europe; Soviet Union; Eastern Mediterranean, volume VIII, document 542, https://history.state.gov/historicaldocuments/frus1952-54v08/d542.

39. *FRUS*, 1952–1954, Western Europe and Canada, volume VI, part 1, document 273, https://history.state.gov/historicaldocuments/frus1952-54v06p1/d273; *FRUS*, 1952–1954, Indochina, volume XIII, part 1, document 236, https://history.state.gov/historicaldocuments/frus1952-54v13p1/d236; *FRUS*, 1952–1954, National Security Affairs, volume II, part 1, document 61, https://history.state.gov/historicaldocuments/frus1952-54v02p1/d61.

40. *FRUS*, 1952–1954, East Asia and the Pacific, volume XII, part 1, document 99, https://history.state.gov/historicaldocuments/frus1952-54v12p1/d99.

41. Interview with Paul H. Nitze, June 3, 1986, 4, box I:120, Nitze Papers.

5. No Exile

1. "Groton Commencement Address," in *Paul H. Nitze on Foreign Policy*, ed. Kenneth W. Thompson and Steven L. Rearden (Lanham, MD: University Press of America, 1989), 7.

2. "Groton Commencement Address," 9.

3. Tammi Gutner, *The Story of SAIS* (Washington, DC: School of Advanced International Studies, 1987), 4–5.

4. Gutner, *Story of SAIS*, 7.

5. Gutner, *Story of SAIS*, 15.

6. Gutner, *Story of SAIS*, 17.

7. Gutner, *Story of SAIS*, 21–22.

8. Interview with Paul H. Nitze, May 7, 1982, 4, box I:118, Nitze Papers.

9. A version of this speech was published as John Foster Dulles, "Policy for Security and Peace," *Foreign Affairs*, April 1954, 353–64.

10. Paul Nitze, "Critique of Dulles' 'Massive Retaliation' Speech," *Paul H. Nitze on National Security and Arms Control*, ed. Kenneth W. Thompson and Steven L. Rearden (Lanham, MD: University Press of America, 1990), 41.

11. Nitze, "Critique of Dulles' 'Massive Retaliation' Speech," 41.

12. Nitze, "Critique of Dulles' 'Massive Retaliation' Speech," 43.

13. Nitze, "Critique of Dulles' 'Massive Retaliation' Speech," 44.

14. Nitze, "Critique of Dulles' 'Massive Retaliation' Speech," 44.

15. Nitze, "History and Our Democratic Tradition in the Formulation of United States Foreign Policy," in Thompson and Rearden, *Nitze on Foreign Policy*, 150.

16. Nitze, "History and Our Democratic Tradition," 151.

17. Nitze, "History and Our Democratic Tradition," 151.

18. Nitze, "History and Our Democratic Tradition," 152.

19. Interview with Paul H. Nitze, May 28, 1986, 2–3, box I:120, Nitze Papers.

20. Interview with Paul H. Nitze, April 20, 1982, 17, box I:118, Nitze Papers.

21. For a succinct summary of the RAND's work during the period 1949–60, see Andrew Krepinevich and Barry Watts, *The Last Warrior: Andrew Marshall and the Shaping of Modern American Defense Strategy* (New York: Basic Books, 2015), 15–50.

22. Nitze, "Letter to Joseph Alsop on Preventive War," in Thompson and Rearden, *Nitze on National Security*, 49.

23. Nitze, "Letter to Joseph Alsop on Preventive War," in Thompson and Rearden, *Nitze on National Security*, 50.

24. Nitze, "Letter to Joseph Alsop on Preventive War," in Thompson and Rearden, *Nitze on National Security*, 50.

25. *FRUS*, 1955–1957, China, volume II, document 9, https://history.state.gov/historicaldocuments/frus1955-57v02/d9.

26. Interview with Paul H. Nitze, May 28, 1986, 10–11, box I:120, Nitze Papers.

27. Interview with Paul H. Nitze, April 20, 1982, 10–11, box I:118, Nitze Papers.

28. Nitze, *Hiroshima to Glasnost*, 162.

29. Nitze, *Hiroshima to Glasnost*, 162.

30. Nitze, *Hiroshima to Glasnost*, 163–64.

31. Interview with Paul H. Nitze, April 20, 1982, 8, box I:118, Nitze Papers.

32. Interview with Paul H. Nitze, April 20, 1982, 10, box I:118, Nitze Papers.

33. Interview with Paul H. Nitze, April 20, 1982, 22, box I:118, Nitze Papers.

34. Paul Nitze, "Atoms, Strategy and Policy," *Foreign Affairs*, January 1956.

35. Gutner, *Story of SAIS*, 43.

36. *FRUS*, 1955–1957, United Nations and General International Matters, volume XI, document 72, https://history.state.gov/historicaldocuments/frus1955-57v11/d72.

37. See Nitze, "The Effect of New Weapons Systems on Our Alliances," in Thompson and Rearden, *Nitze on Foreign Policy*, 153–66.

38. On the consequences of the Soviet space test, see Yanek Mieczkowski, *Eisenhower's Sputnik Moment: The Race for Space and World Prestige* (Ithaca, NY: Cornell University Press, 2013).

39. *FRUS*, 1955–1957, National Security Policy, volume XIX, document 156, https://history.state.gov/historicaldocuments/frus1955-57v19/d156; see also David Snead, *The Gaither Committee, Eisenhower, and the Cold War* (Columbus: Ohio State University Press, 1999).

40. Nitze, *Hiroshima to Glasnost*, 167.

41. Nitze, *Hiroshima to Glasnost*, 168.

42. "NATO Heads of Government Meeting, Paris, December 1957," box I:118, Nitze Papers.

43. Strobe Talbott, *The Master of the Game: Paul Nitze and the Nuclear Peace* (New York: Vintage Books, 1988).

44. Interview with Paul H. Nitze, February 25, 1986, 34, box I:119, Nitze Papers.

45. Interview with Paul H. Nitze, February 25, 1986, 23, box I:119, Nitze Papers.

46. Nitze, *Hiroshima to Pearl Harbor*, 169.

47. Interview with Paul H. Nitze, February 25, 1986, 25, box I:119, Nitze Papers.

48. Interview with Paul H. Nitze, March 30, 1982, 40, box I:118, Nitze Papers.

49. Paul H. Nitze, US Air Force Oral History Interview, 1981, 423, box I:117, Nitze Papers.

50. Nitze, US Air Force Oral History Interview, 1981, 424, box I:117, Nitze Papers.

51. *FRUS*, 1958–1960, Berlin Crisis, 1959–1960, Germany, Austria, volume IX, document 264, https://history.state.gov/historicaldocuments/frus1958-60v09/d264.

6. Nuclear Crises, 1961–1963

1. Interview with Paul H. Nitze, July 22, 1982, 4, box I:118, Nitze Papers.

2. Nitze, *Hiroshima to Glasnost*, 177.

3. *FRUS*, 1961–1963, volume VIII, National Security Policy, https://history.state.gov/historicaldocuments/frus1961-63v08/d1.

4. Harold Brown, "US National Security: The Next 50 Years," Paul H. Nitze Award Lecture, April 2000, https://www.cna.org/CNA_files/PDF/D0001565.A1.pdf.

5. Paul H. Nitze, US Air Force Oral History Interview, 1977, 296, box I:117, Nitze Papers.

6. Nitze, *Hiroshima to Glasnost*, 180–81.

7. Nitze, US Air Force Oral History Interview, 1981, 302–3, box I:117, Nitze Papers.

8. Nitze, US Air Force Oral History Interview, 1981, 427, box I:117, Nitze Papers.

9. Talbott, *Master of the Game*, 78–79.

10. Talbott, *Master of the Game*, 79.

11. *FRUS*, 1961–1963, volume X, Cuba, January 1961–September 1962, document 24, https://history.state.gov/historicaldocuments/frus1961-63v10/d24.

12. *FRUS*, 1961–1963, volume XXIV, Laos Crisis, document 10, https://history.state.gov/historicaldocuments/frus1961-63v24/d10.

13. *FRUS*, 1961–1963, volume XX, Congo Crisis, document 16, https://history.state.gov/historicaldocuments/frus1961-63v20/d16.

14. *FRUS*, 1961–1963, American Republics; Cuba 1961–1962; Cuban Missile Crisis and Aftermath, volumes X/XI/XII, Microfiche Supplement, document 244, https://history.state.gov/historicaldocuments/frus1961-63v10-12mSupp/d244.

15. *FRUS*, 1961–1963, volume X, Cuba, January 1961–September 1962, document 80, https://history.state.gov/historicaldocuments/frus1961-63v10/d80.

16. Nitze, *Hiroshima to Glasnost*, 184.

17. *FRUS*, 1961–1963, volume X, Cuba, January 1961–September 1962, document 172, https://history.state.gov/historicaldocuments/frus1961-63v10/d172.

18. *FRUS*, 1961–1963, volume X, Cuba, January 1961–September 1962, document 204, https://history.state.gov/historicaldocuments/frus1961-63v10/d204.

19. *FRUS*, 1961–1963, volume X, Cuba, January 1961–September 1962, document 206, https://history.state.gov/historicaldocuments/frus1961-63v10/d206.

20. *FRUS*, 1961–1963, volume XIV, Berlin Crisis, 1961–1963, document 32, https://history.state.gov/historicaldocuments/frus1961-63v14/d32.

21. Thompson, *Hawk and the Dove*, 173.

22. "President John F. Kennedy's Inaugural Address (1961)," National Archives, last reviewed February 8, 2022, https://www.archives.gov/milestone-documents/president-john-f-kennedys-inaugural-address.

23. Nitze, *Hiroshima to Glasnost*, 196.

24. Nitze, *Hiroshima to Glasnost*, 200.

25. *FRUS*, 1961–1963, volume XIV, Berlin Crisis, 1961–1963, document 69, https://history.state.gov/historicaldocuments/frus1961-63v14/d69.

26. *FRUS*, 1961–1963, volume XIV, Berlin Crisis, 1961–1963, document 70, https://history.state.gov/historicaldocuments/frus1961-63v14/d70.

27. *FRUS*, 1961–1963, volume XIV, Berlin Crisis, 1961–1963, document 76, https://history.state.gov/historicaldocuments/frus1961-63v14/d76.

28. Walter S. Poole, *The Joint Chiefs of Staff and National Policy*, vol. VIII, *1961–1964* (Washington, DC: Office of Joint History, 2011), https://www.jcs.mil/Portals/36/Documents/History/Policy/Policy_V008.pdf.

29. On de Gaulle's Cold War maneuvering, see Garret Joseph Martin, *General de Gaulle's Cold War: Challenging American Hegemony, 1963–1968* (New York: Berghahn Books, 2013).

30. *FRUS, 1961–1963*, volume XIV, Berlin Crisis, 1961–1963, document 56, https://history.state.gov/historicaldocuments/frus1961-63v14/d56.

31. *FRUS, 1961–1963*, volume XIV, Berlin Crisis, 1961–1963, document 166, https://history.state.gov/historicaldocuments/frus1961-63v14/d166.

32. Thompson, *Hawk and the Dove*, 177.

33. Thompson, *Hawk and the Dove*, 178.

34. *FRUS, 1961–1963*, volume XIV, Berlin Crisis, 1961–1963, document 173, https://history.state.gov/historicaldocuments/frus1961-63v14/d173.

35. *FRUS, 1961–1963*, volume XIV, Berlin Crisis, 1961–1963, document 185, https://history.state.gov/historicaldocuments/frus1961-63v14/d185.

36. Nitze, *Hiroshima to Glasnost*, 204.

37. See Matthew Kroenig, *The Logic of American Nuclear Strategy* (New York: Oxford University Press, 2018); see also Todd Sechser and Matthew Furhman, *Nuclear Weapons and Coercive Diplomacy* (New York: Cambridge University Press, 2017).

38. See Francis Gavin, *Nuclear Weapons and American Grand Strategy* (Washington, DC: Brookings Institute Press, 2020).

39. Quoted in Talbott, *Master of the Game*, 81.

40. *FRUS, 1961–1963*, volume VII, Arms Control and Disarmament, document 141, https://history.state.gov/historicaldocuments/frus1961-63v07/d141.

41. *FRUS, 1961–1963*, volume VII, Arms Control and Disarmament, document 148, https://history.state.gov/historicaldocuments/frus1961-63v07/d148.

42. *FRUS, 1961–1963*, volume XV, Berlin Crisis, 1962–1963, document 34, https://history.state.gov/historicaldocuments/frus1961-63v15/d34.

43. *FRUS, 1961–1963*, volume VIII, National Security Policy, document 89, https://history.state.gov/historicaldocuments/frus1961-63v08/d89.

44. *FRUS, 1961–1963*, volume VII, Arms Control and Disarmament, document 206, https://history.state.gov/historicaldocuments/frus1961-63v07/d206.

45. *FRUS, 1961–1963*, volume XV, Berlin Crisis, 1962–1963, document 107, https://history.state.gov/historicaldocuments/frus1961-63v15/d107.

46. *FRUS, 1961–1963*, volume XV, Berlin Crisis, 1962–1963, document 107, https://history.state.gov/historicaldocuments/frus1961-63v15/d107.

47. *FRUS, 1961–1963*, volume VIII, National Security Policy, document 103, https://history.state.gov/historicaldocuments/frus1961-63v08/d103.

48. Heiko Henning, "Senator Keating's Source: How West German Intelligence Discovered Soviet Missiles in Cuba," February 21, 2017, Wilson Center, https://www.wilsoncenter.org/blog-post/senator-keatings-source.

49. *FRUS, 1961–1963*, volume X, Cuba, January 1961–September 1962, document 430, https://history.state.gov/historicaldocuments/frus1961-63v10/d430.

50. Thompson, *Hawk and the Dove*, 183–84.

51. *FRUS, 1961–1963*, volume XI, Cuban Missile Crisis and Aftermath, document 31, https://history.state.gov/historicaldocuments/frus1961-63v11/d31.

52. Interview with Paul H. Nitze, April 1, 1986, 21, box I:120, Nitze Papers.

53. Interview with Paul H. Nitze, April 1, 1986, 21–22, box I:120, Nitze Papers.

54. *FRUS*, 1961–1963, American Republics; Cuba 1961–1962; Cuban Missile Crisis and Aftermath, volumes X/XI/XII, Microfiche Supplement, document 334, https://history.state.gov/historicaldocuments/frus1961-63v10-12mSupp/d334.

55. Quoted in Sheldon M. Stern, *Averting "the Final Failure": John F. Kennedy and the Secret Cuban Missile Crisis Meetings* (Palo Alto, CA: Stanford University Press, 2003), 146.

56. See Serhii Plokhy, *Nuclear Folly: A History of the Cuban Missile Crisis* (New York: W. W. Norton, 2021).

57. *FRUS*, 1961–1963, American Republics; Cuba 1961–1962; Cuban Missile Crisis and Aftermath, volumes X/XI/XII, Microfiche Supplement, document 424, https://history.state.gov/historicaldocuments/frus1961-63v10-12mSupp/d424.

58. *FRUS*, 1961–1963, American Republics; Cuba 1961–1962; Cuban Missile Crisis and Aftermath, volumes X/XI/XII, Microfiche Supplement, document 496, https://history.state.gov/historicaldocuments/frus1961-63v10-12mSupp/d496.

59. *FRUS*, 1961–1963, American Republics; Cuba 1961–1962; Cuban Missile Crisis and Aftermath, volumes X/XI/XII, Microfiche Supplement, document 503, https://history.state.gov/historicaldocuments/frus1961-63v10-12mSupp/d503.

60. *FRUS*, 1961–1963, American Republics; Cuba 1961–1962; Cuban Missile Crisis and Aftermath, volumes X/XI/XII, Microfiche Supplement, document 529, https://history.state.gov/historicaldocuments/frus1961-63v10-12mSupp/d529.

61. Nitze, *Hiroshima to Glasnost*, 208.

62. Interview with Paul H. Nitze, April 1, 1986, 20, box I:120, Nitze Papers.

63. Interview with Paul H. Nitze, April 1, 1986, 21, box I:120, Nitze Papers.

64. See Martin Sherwin, *Gambling with Armageddon: Nuclear Roulette from Hiroshima to the Cuban Missile Crisis* (New York: Knopf, 2020).

65. Quoted in Charles Bohlen, *Witness to History 1919–1969* (New York: Norton, 1973), 495.

66. Nitze, US Air Force Oral History Interview, 1981, 489, box 118, Nitze Papers.

7. Preponderance Lost

1. Paul H. Nitze, US Air Force Oral History Interview, 1981, 323, box 118, Nitze Papers.

2. Interview with Paul H. Nitze, December 22, 1982, 14, box I:118, Nitze Papers.

3. Nitze, *Hiroshima to Glasnost*, 262.

4. Thompson, *Hawk and the Dove*, 198.

5. Interview with Paul H. Nitze, December 10, 1982, 5, box I:118, Nitze Papers.

6. Talbott, *Master of the Game*, 89.

7. See James Cameron, *The Double Game: The Demise of America's First Missile Defense System and the Rise of Strategic Arms Limitation* (New York: Oxford University Press, 2017).

8. Nitze, *Hiroshima to Glasnost*, 248.

9. Nitze, *Hiroshima to Glasnost*, 248.

10. *FRUS*, 1961–1963, volume XXII, Northeast Asia, document 177, https://history.state.gov/historicaldocuments/frus1961-63v22/d177.

11. Nitze, *Hiroshima to Glasnost*, 250.

12. Nitze, *Hiroshima to Glasnost*, 252.

13. "Considerations Involved in a Separable First Stage Disarmament Agreement," National Security Files, box 383: Disarmament, 7/63-10/63, box 4, October 1, 1963, https://www.archives.gov/files/research/jfk/releases/2018/docid-32626321.pdf.

14. *FRUS*, 1964–1968, volume X, National Security Policy, document 131, https://history.state.gov/historicaldocuments/frus1964-68v10/d31.

15. *FRUS*, 1964–1968, volume XI, Arms Control and Disarmament, document 64, https://history.state.gov/historicaldocuments/frus1964-68v11/d64.

16. On the "Long 1964," see Frederik Logevall, *Choosing War: The Lost Chance for Peace and the Escalation of War in Vietnam* (Berkeley: University of California Press, 2001).

17. *FRUS*, 1964–1968, volume II, Vietnam, June–December 1965, document 76, https://history.state.gov/historicaldocuments/frus1964-68v03/d76. Biographer Nicholas Thompson points out that, in his own memoir Nitze recorded his prediction for success as 40:60—not 60:40. Thompson, *Hawk and the Dove*, 202.

18. Nitze, US Air Force Oral History Interview, 1981, 355, box 118, Nitze Papers.

19. Nitze, US Air Force Oral History Interview, 1981, 358, box 118, Nitze Papers.

20. Nitze, US Air Force Oral History Interview, 1981, 359–60, box 118, Nitze Papers.

21. Nitze, US Air Force Oral History Interview, 1981, 406, box 118, Nitze Papers.

22. See Francis Gavin, *Nuclear Statecraft: History and Strategy in America's Atomic Age* (Ithaca, NY: Cornell University Press, 2012), 102.

23. Talbott, *Master of the Game*, 94.

24. On the politics of succession within the Kremlin, see Vladislav Zubok, *A Failed Empire: The Soviet Union in the Cold War from Stalin to Gorbachev* (Chapel Hill: University of North Carolina Press, 2009).

25. *FRUS*, 1964–1968, volume XIII, Western Europe Regional, document 271, https://history.state.gov/historicaldocuments/frus1964-68v13/d271.

26. Talbott, *Master of the Game*, 99.

27. *FRUS*, 1964–1968, volume XXIX, part 1, Korea, document 213, https://history.state.gov/historicaldocuments/frus1964-68v29p1/d213. Clifford responded: "May I leave now?"

28. *FRUS*, 1964–1968, volume XXIX, part 1, Korea, document 217, https://history.state.gov/historicaldocuments/frus1964-68v29p1/d217.

29. *FRUS*, 1964–1968, volume XXIX, Part 1, Korea, document 226, https://history.state.gov/historicaldocuments/frus1964-68v29p1/d226.

30. *FRUS*, 1964–1968, volume VI, Vietnam, January–August 1968, document 156, https://history.state.gov/historicaldocuments/frus1964-68v06/d156.

31. *FRUS*, 1964–1968, volume VI, Vietnam, January–August 1968, document 156, https://history.state.gov/historicaldocuments/frus1964-68v06/d156.

32. Quoted in Callaghan, *Dangerous Capabilities*, 321.

33. *FRUS*, 1964–1968, volume XI, Arms Control and Disarmament, document 238, https://history.state.gov/historicaldocuments/frus1964-68v11/d238.

34. *FRUS*, 1964–1968, volume XI, Arms Control and Disarmament, document 242, https://history.state.gov/historicaldocuments/frus1964-68v11/d242.

35. *FRUS*, 1964–1968, volume XI, Arms Control and Disarmament, document 244, https://history.state.gov/historicaldocuments/frus1964-68v11/d244.

36. *FRUS*, 1964–1968, volume XI, Arms Control and Disarmament, document 252, https://history.state.gov/historicaldocuments/frus1964-68v11/d252.

37. *FRUS*, 1964–1968, volume XI, Arms Control and Disarmament, document 273, https://history.state.gov/historicaldocuments/frus1964-68v11/d273.

38. *FRUS*, 1964–1968, volume XI, Arms Control and Disarmament, document 275, https://history.state.gov/historicaldocuments/frus1964-68v11/d275.

39. *FRUS*, 1964–1968, volume XI, Arms Control and Disarmament, document 275, https://history.state.gov/historicaldocuments/frus1964-68v11/d275.

40. *FRUS*, 1964–1968, volume VII, Vietnam, September 1968–January 1969, document 15, https://history.state.gov/historicaldocuments/frus1964-68v07/d15.

41. *FRUS*, 1964–1968, volume VII, Vietnam, September 1968–January 1969, document 180, https://history.state.gov/historicaldocuments/frus1964-68v07/d180.

42. Nitze, *Hiroshima to Glasnost*, 269–70.

43. *FRUS*, 1964–1968, volume XXXIII, Organization and Management of Foreign Policy; United Nations, document 279, https://history.state.gov/historicaldocuments/frus1964-68v33/d279.

8. Negotiating from Weakness, 1969–1975

1. Nitze, *Hiroshima to Glasnost*, 293.

2. Cameron, *Double Game*, 107–24.

3. *FRUS*, 1969–1976, volume XXXIV, National Security Policy, document 25, https://history.state.gov/historicaldocuments/frus1969-76v34/d25.

4. Nitze, *Hiroshima to Glasnost*, 294.

5. Dean Acheson, *Present at the Creation: My Years in the State Department* (New York: W. W. Norton, 1969).

6. Nitze, *Hiroshima to Glasnost*, 299.

7. These personal dynamics are well established in John Newhouse, *Cold Dawn: The Story of SALT* (New York: Holt, Rinehart & Winston, 1973).

8. Callahan, *Dangerous Capabilities*, 329.

9. *FRUS*, 1969–1976, volume XXXII, SALT I, 1969–1972, document 39, https://history.state.gov/historicaldocuments/frus1969-76v32/d39.

10. On Kissinger's extraordinary rise to fame, see Thomas A. Schwartz, *Henry Kissinger and American Power: A Political Biography* (New York: Hill & Wang, 2020).

11. See *FRUS*, 1969–1976, volume II, Organization and Management of US Foreign Policy, 1969–1972, chapter 1, The NSC System, https://history.state.gov/historicaldocuments/frus1969-76v02/ch1.

12. On the US decisions for ICBM basing, see Gretchen Heefner, *The Missile Next Door: The Minuteman in the American Heartland* (Cambridge, MA: Harvard University Press, 2012).

13. *FRUS*, 1969–1976, volume XXXII, SALT I, 1969–1972, document 39, https://history.state.gov/historicaldocuments/frus1969-76v32/d39.

14. *FRUS*, 1969–1976, volume XXXII, SALT I, 1969–1972, document 39, https://history.state.gov/historicaldocuments/frus1969-76v32/d39.

15. See John D. Maurer, *Competitive Arms Control: Nixon, Kissinger, & SALT, 1969–1972* (New Haven, CT: Yale University Press, 2022).

16. Nitze, *Hiroshima to Glasnost*, 300–301.

17. Nitze, *Hiroshima to Glasnost*, 301.

18. Nitze, *Hiroshima to Glasnost*, 301.

19. Nitze, *Hiroshima to Glasnost*, 302.

20. Nitze, *Hiroshima to Glasnost*, 302–3.

21. Nitze, *Hiroshima to Glasnost*, 304.

22. Nitze, *Hiroshima to Glasnost*, 305.

23. *FRUS*, 1969–1976, volume XXXII, SALT I, 1969–1972, document 42, https://history.state.gov/historicaldocuments/frus1969-76v32/d42.

24. *FRUS*, 1969–1976, volume XXXII, SALT I, 1969–1972, document 58, https://history.state.gov/historicaldocuments/frus1969-76v32/d58.

25. *FRUS*, 1969–1976, volume XXXII, SALT I, 1969–1972, document 59, https://history.state.gov/historicaldocuments/frus1969-76v32/d59.

26. *FRUS*, 1969–1976, volume XXXII, SALT I, 1969–1972, document 59, https://history.state.gov/historicaldocuments/frus1969-76v32/d59.

27. *FRUS*, 1969–1976, volume XXXII, SALT I, 1969–1972, document 59, https://history.state.gov/historicaldocuments/frus1969-76v32/d59.

28. Nitze, *Hiroshima to Glasnost*, 307–8.

29. McGeorge Bundy, "To Cap the Volcano," *Foreign Affairs*, October 1969.

30. On domestic opposition to Sentinels being placed in Seattle, Boston, and Chicago, see Cameron, *Double Game*, 104–5.

31. *FRUS*, 1969–1976, volume XXXII, SALT I, 1969–1972, document 85, https://history.state.gov/historicaldocuments/frus1969-76v32/d85.

32. *FRUS*, 1969–1976, volume XXXII, SALT I, 1969–1972, document 170, https://history.state.gov/historicaldocuments/frus1969-76v32/d170.

33. *FRUS*, 1969–1976, volume XXXII, SALT I, 1969–1972, document 202, https://history.state.gov/historicaldocuments/frus1969-76v32/d202.

34. *FRUS*, 1969–1976, volume XXXII, SALT I, 1969–1972, document 281, https://history.state.gov/historicaldocuments/frus1969-76v32/d281.

35. *FRUS*, 1969–1976, volume XXXII, SALT I, 1969–1972, document 328, https://history.state.gov/historicaldocuments/frus1969-76v32/d328.

36. *FRUS*, 1969–1976, volume XXXII, SALT I, 1969–1972, document 322, https://history.state.gov/historicaldocuments/frus1969-76v32/d322.

37. John Finney, "Senate Approves Pact with Soviet on Nuclear Arms," *The New York Times*, September 15, 1972.

38. *FRUS*, 1969–1976, volume XXXIII, SALT II, 1972–1980, document 2, https://history.state.gov/historicaldocuments/frus1969-76v33/d2.

39. On the first "purge" of ACDA, see Michael Krepon, *Winning and Losing the Nuclear Peace: The Rise, Demise, and Revival of Arms Control* (Stanford, CA: Stanford University Press, 2021), 135–36.

40. Nitze, *Hiroshima to Glasnost*, 335.

41. *FRUS*, 1969–1976, volume XXXIII, SALT II, 1972–1980, document 34, https://history.state.gov/historicaldocuments/frus1969-76v33/d34.

42. On the intersection between US–Soviet détente and the Middle East, see Craig Daigle, *The Limits of Détente: The United States, the Soviet Union, and the Arab-Israeli Conflict, 1969–1973* (New Haven, CT: Yale University Press, 2012).

43. See Kroenig, *American Nuclear Strategy*; see also Sechser and Fuhrmann, *Nuclear Weapons*.

44. Nitze, *Hiroshima to Glasnost*, 337.

45. Nitze, *Hiroshima to Glasnost*, 337.

46. Nitze, *Hiroshima to Glasnost*, 338.

47. *FRUS*, 1969–1976, volume XXXIII, SALT II, 1972–1980, document 43, https://history.state.gov/historicaldocuments/frus1969-76v33/d43.

48. *FRUS*, 1969–1976, volume XXXIII, SALT II, 1972–1980, document 45, https://history.state.gov/historicaldocuments/frus1969-76v33/d45.

49. *FRUS*, 1969–1976, volume XXXIII, SALT II, 1972–1980, document 51, https://history.state.gov/historicaldocuments/frus1969-76v33/d51.

50. *FRUS*, 1969–1976, volume XXXIII, SALT II, 1972–1980, document 37, https://history.state.gov/historicaldocuments/frus1969-76v35/d37.

51. *FRUS*, 1969–1976, volume XXXIII, SALT II, 1972–1980, document 64, https://history.state.gov/historicaldocuments/frus1969-76v33/d64.

52. *FRUS*, 1969–1976, volume XXXIII, SALT II, 1972–1980, document 64, https://history.state.gov/historicaldocuments/frus1969-76v33/d64.

53. Nitze, *Hiroshima to Glasnost*, 341.

54. See *FRUS*, 1969–1976, volume XXXVIII, part 1, Foundations of Foreign Policy, 1973–1976, document 37, https://history.state.gov/historicaldocuments/frus1969-76v38p1/d37.

55. Nitze, *Hiroshima to Glasnost*, 342–43.

56. Nitze, *Hiroshima to Glasnost*, 346.

57. Nitze, *Hiroshima to Glasnost*, 347.

58. *FRUS*, 1969–1976, volume XVIII, China 1973–1976, document 82, https://history.state.gov/historicaldocuments/frus1969-76v18/d82.

59. Robert Jervis, "Why Nuclear Superiority Doesn't Matter," *Political Science Quarterly* 94, no. 4 (Winter 1979–1980): 617–33, https://www.jstor.org/stable/2149629.

60. Kissinger background briefing, December 3, 1974, republished in "The Vladivostok Accord," *Survival* 17, no. 4 (1975): 195, https://doi.org/10.1080/00396337508441560.

61. Schwartz, *Henry Kissinger*.

62. Thompson, *Hawk and the Dove*.

9. The Nitze Scenario

1. Paul Nitze, "Assuring Strategic Stability in an Era of Détente," *Foreign Affairs* 54, no. 2 (January 1976): 207.

2. Nitze, "Assuring Strategic Stability," 214.

3. Nitze, "Assuring Strategic Stability," 215.

4. Nitze, "Assuring Strategic Stability," 227.

5. Nitze, "Assuring Strategic Stability," 229.

6. "Collection: Records of the 1976 Campaign Committee to Elect Jimmy Carter," Jimmy Carter Library, last reviewed September 13, 2023, https://www.jimmycarterlibrary.gov/digital_library/campaign/564806/86/76C_564806_86_07.pdf. Even before Jackson made it official, Nitze donated $500 (about $2,400 in 2022 dollars) to the senator's presidential aspirations.

7. Interview with Paul H. Nitze, July 15, 1986, 16, box I:120, Nitze Papers.

8. Interview with Paul H. Nitze, July 15, 1986, 16, box I:120, Nitze Papers.

9. Undated Memorandum, Richard Cheney Files, Box 16, "Carter, Jimmy," Gerald Ford Presidential Library, last reviewed September 13, 2023, https://catalog.archives.gov/id/1561621.

10. Interview with Paul H. Nitze, September 10, 1985, 7, box I:119, Nitze Papers.

11. Jimmy Carter Papers—Pre Presidential, 1976 Presidential Campaign Issues Office—Stuart Eizenstat, box 9, Defense, 7/27/76–87/76, Jimmy Carter Presidential Library.

12. Jimmy Carter Papers—Pre Presidential, 1976 Presidential Campaign Issues Office—Stuart Eizenstat, box 9, Defense, 7/27/76–87/76, Jimmy Carter Presidential Library.

13. Paul C. Warnke, "Apes on a Treadmill," *Foreign Policy*, no. 18 (Spring 1975): 12–29, https://www.jstor.org/stable/pdf/1147960.pdf?seq=1.

14. Jimmy Carter Papers—Pre Presidential, 1976 Presidential Campaign Issues Office—Stuart Eizenstat, box 9, Defense, 7/27/76–87/76, Jimmy Carter Presidential Library.

15. Jimmy Carter Papers—Pre Presidential, 1976 Presidential Campaign Issues Office—Stuart Eizenstat, box 9, Defense, 7/27/76–87/76, Jimmy Carter Presidential Library.

16. Nitze, *Hiroshima to Glasnost*, 349.

17. Nitze, *Hiroshima to Glasnost*, 349.

18. Telnet Message From Nick Macneil to Richard Holbrooke, September 20, 1976, Records of the 1976 Campaign Committee to Elect Jimmy Carter, Container 95, Telnet Messages, last reviewed September 13, 2023.

19. *FRUS*, 1969–1976, volume XXXV, National Security Policy, 1973–1976, document 104, https://history.state.gov/historicaldocuments/frus1969-76v35/d104.

20. *FRUS*, 1969–1976, volume XXXV, National Security Policy, 1973–1976, document 171, https://history.state.gov/historicaldocuments/frus1969-76v35/d171.

21. Undated Memorandum for President-Elect Jimmy Carter, Office of Staff Secretary Series: 1976 Transition Series File, Jimmy Carter Presidential Library, https://www.jimmycarterlibrary.gov/digital_library/sso/148838/1/SSO_148838_001_03.pdf.

22. Edward C. Keefer, *Harold Brown: Offsetting the Soviet Military Challenge 1977–1981* (Washington, DC: Government Printing Office, 2017), 660, fn. 7.

23. Thompson, *Hawk and the Dove*, 264.

24. According to biographer Nicholas Thompson, "Nitze's description of the incident, in his memoirs, is perhaps the most tortured and absurd paragraph he ever wrote." Thompson, *Hawk and the Dove*, 265.

25. Nitze, *Hiroshima to Glasnost*, 355.

26. Interview with Paul H. Nitze, June 24, 1986, 19, box I:120, Nitze Papers.

27. Letter from Paul Nitze to President Jimmy Carter, March 16, 1977, Jimmy Carter Presidential Library, last reviewed September 11, 2023.

28. Letter from Paul Nitze to President Jimmy Carter, March 16, 1977, Jimmy Carter Presidential Library, last reviewed September 11, 2023, https://www.jimmycarterlibrary.gov/sites/default/files/pdf_documents/digital_library/sso/148878/11/SSO_148878_011_09.pdf.

29. Memorandum from Secretary of Defense Harold Brown to President Jimmy Carter, July 8, 1977, Jimmy Carter Presidential Library, last visited September 11, 2023, https://www.jimmycarterlibrary.gov/digital_library/sso/148878/30/SSO_148878_030_04.pdf.

30. Memorandum From National Security Advisor Zbigniew Brzezinski to President Jimmy Carter, August 5, 1977, Jimmy Carter Presidential Library, last visited October 19, 2023, https://www.jimmycarterlibrary.gov/digital_library/sso/148878/36/SSO_148878_036_08.pdf.

31. Jimmy Carter, *White House Diary* (New York: Farrar, Straus and Giroux, 2010), 76.

32. Memorandum For the President, August 19, 1977, Office of Staff Secretary, Presidential Files, 8/22/77 [1], Container 37, Jimmy Carter Presidential Library, last reviewed September 13, 2023, https://www.jimmycarterlibrary.gov/digital_library/sso/148878/37/SSO_148878_037_08.pdf.

33. National Security Affairs, Brzezinski Material, subject file, box 47, Nuclear War Doctrine: Limited Nuclear Options (LNO), Regional Nuclear Options (RNO), 3/77–1/80, 36, Jimmy Carter Presidential Library.

34. See William E. Odom, "The Origins and Design of PD-59: A Memoir," in *Getting MAD: Nuclear Mutual Assured Destruction, Its Origins and Practice*, ed. Henry D. Sokolski (Washington, DC: Strategic Studies Institute, 2004), 175–96.

35. *FRUS*, 1969–1976, volume XXXIII, SALT II, 1972–1980, document 188, https://history.state.gov/historicaldocuments/frus1969-76v33/d188.

36. National Security Affairs, Brzezinski Material, subject file, box 52, SAC and NORAD 8/20–21/78 Brzezinski Trip, 7–9/78, Jimmy Carter Presidential Library.

37. Interview with Paul H. Nitze, March 30, 1982, box I:118, Nitze Papers. The quotation is from Letter, March 24, 1978, PHN Personal File, Kim, Young-shik.

38. "Yale Debate," *Firing Line*, with William F. Buckley, September 19, 1978, 6, Hoover Institution Archives.

39. "Yale Debate," 7.

40. "Yale Debate," 8.

41. National Security Affairs, Brzezinski Office File, Country Chron file, box 124, Weapons Systems, 4–9/78, Jimmy Carter Presidential Library.

42. Stansfield Turner to Paul Nitze, November 20, 1978, box I:160, Strategic Arms Limitations Talks (SALT) Verification, 1978–79, n.d., Nitze Papers.

43. Paul Nitze, "SALT II: The Objectives v.s. The Results," Chicago Council on Foreign Relations, Chicago, December 5, 1978, Committee on the Present Danger, Paul Nitze Office File, Box 75, Hoover Institution Archives.

44. Paul Nitze, "SALT II: The Objectives v.s. The Results," Chicago Council on Foreign Relations, Chicago, December 5, 1978, Committee on the Present Danger, Paul Nitze Office File, Box 75, Hoover Institution Archives..

45. Memorandum of Conversation with Secretary Vance, June 5, 1979, 3, box I:160, Nitze Papers.

46. Memorandum of Conversation with Secretary Vance, June 5, 1979, 5, box I:160, Nitze Papers.

47. "Verification," June 11, 1979, 1, box I:160, Nitze Papers.

48. Paul Nitze, "Will SALT II Do What Is Claimed for It?" July 20, 1979, Commonwealth Club of California Records, https://digitalcollections.hoover.org/objects/1236

/ will-salt-ii-do-what-is-claimed-for-it?ctx=aa01933f-435b-45dc-a537-84b4e422083a
&idx=0.

49. Letter from Paul Nitze to Senator Jacob Javits, September 24, 1979, box I:2, Nitze Papers. Nitze enclosed in his letter to Senator Javits his reply to Senator Church.

50. Kiron Skinner, Annelise Anderson, and Martin Anderson, eds., *Reagan, In His
Own Hand: The Writings of Ronald Reagan That Reveal His Revolutionary Vision for America* (New York: Touchstone, 2001), 111–12.

51. Skinner, Anderson, and Anderson, eds., *Reagan, In His Own Hand*, 111–12.

52. Ronald Reagan, "Peace: Restoring the Margin of Safety," August 18, 1980, Ronald Reagan Presidential Library and Museum, https://www.reaganlibrary.gov/archives
/speech/peace-restoring-margin-safety.

53. Ronald Reagan, "Peace: Restoring the Margin of Safety," August 18, 1980, Ronald Reagan Presidential Library and Museum, https://www.reaganlibrary.gov/archives
/speech/peace-restoring-margin-safety.

54. Jervis, "Why Nuclear Superiority Doesn't Matter."

10. A Walk in the Woods, 1981–1984

1. "The Debate on American Security," June 12, 1981, *Firing Line* broadcast records,
Hoover Institution Library & Archives, https://digitalcollections.hoover.org/objects
/6642/the-debate-on-american-security.

2. "Debate on American Security."

3. "Debate on American Security."

4. "Debate on American Security."

5. "Debate on American Security."

6. Paul H. Nitze, US Air Force Oral History Interview, 1981, 490–91, box 118, Nitze Papers.

7. *FRUS*, 1981–1988, volume III, Soviet Union, January 1981–January 1983, document 39, https://history.state.gov/historicaldocuments/frus1981-88v03/d39.

8. Paul H. Nitze, US Air Force Oral History Interview, 1981, 419–20, box 118, Nitze Papers.

9. Talbott, *Master of the Game*, 168.

10. Interview with Thomas Graham Jr., May 15, 2001, Association for Diplomatic
Studies and Training, Foreign Affairs Oral History Project, https://adst.org/OH%20
TOCs/Graham-Thomas.pdf.

11. On the importance of the relationship between Reagan and Nakasone, see William Inboden, *The Peacemaker: Ronald Reagan, the Cold War, and the World on the Brink*
(New York: Penguin, 2022).

12. *FRUS*, 1981–1988, volume III, Soviet Union, January 1981–January 1983, document 89, https://history.state.gov/historicaldocuments/frus1981-88v03/d89.

13. *FRUS*, 1981–1988, volume III, Soviet Union, January 1981–January 1983, document 92, https://history.state.gov/historicaldocuments/frus1981-88v03/d92.

14. *FRUS*, 1981–1988, volume III, Soviet Union, January 1981–January 1983, document 92, https://history.state.gov/historicaldocuments/frus1981-88v03/d92.

15. Ronald Reagan, "Remarks to Members of the National Press Club on Arms Reduction and Nuclear Weapons," November 18, 1981, Ronald Reagan Presidential Li-

brary, https://www.reaganlibrary.gov/archives/speech/remarks-members-national
-press-club-arms-reduction-and-nuclear-weapons.

16. *FRUS*, 1981–1988, volume III, Soviet Union, January 1981–January 1983, document 104, https://history.state.gov/historicaldocuments/frus1981-88v03/d104.

17. *FRUS*, 1981–1988, volume III, Soviet Union, January 1981–January 1983, document 104, https://history.state.gov/historicaldocuments/frus1981-88v03/d104.

18. *FRUS*, 1981–1988, volume III, Soviet Union, January 1981–January 1983, document 104, https://history.state.gov/historicaldocuments/frus1981-88v03/d104.

19. *FRUS*, 1981–1988, volume III, Soviet Union, January 1981–January 1983, document 104, https://history.state.gov/historicaldocuments/frus1981-88v03/d104.

20. *FRUS*, 1981–1988, volume III, Soviet Union, January 1981–January 1983, document 118, https://history.state.gov/historicaldocuments/frus1981-88v03/d118.

21. Reagan Diary, January 7, 1982, in Douglas Brinkley, ed., *The Reagan Diaries*, vol. 1, *January 1981–October 1985* (New York: HarperCollins, 2007), 99.

22. Thomas Graham Jr. and Damien J. LaVera, *Cornerstones of Security: Arms Control Treaties in the Nuclear Era* (Seattle: University of Washington Press, 2011), 513.

23. *FRUS*, 1981–1988, volume III, Soviet Union, January 1981–January 1983, document 153, https://history.state.gov/historicaldocuments/frus1981-88v03/d153.

24. David Shribman, "How the Call for Shift in Nuclear Strategy Evolved," *New York Times*, April 9, 1982, https://www.nytimes.com/1982/04/09/world/how-the-call
-for-shift-in-nuclear-strategy-evolved.html.

25. See Thomas Rid, *Active Measures: The Secret History of Disinformation and Political Warfare* (New York: Farrar, Straus and Giroux, 2020).

26. Paul Montgomery, "Throngs Fill Manhattan to Protest Nuclear Weapons," *New York Times*, June 13, 1982, https://www.nytimes.com/1982/06/13/world/throngs-fill
-manhattan-to-protest-nuclear-weapons.html; see also Stephanie L. Freeman, *Dreams for a Decade: International Nuclear Abolitionism and the End of the Cold War* (Philadelphia: University of Pennsylvania Press, 2023).

27. Nitze, *Hiroshima to Glasnost*, 374–75.

28. Nitze, *Hiroshima to Glasnost*, 378.

29. Undated Paper, box 119, Nitze Papers.

30. Nitze, *Hiroshima to Glasnost*, 386.

31. Memorandum from Richard Boverie to Robert "Bud" McFarlane, July 29, 1982, 1, box 119, Nitze Papers.

32. *FRUS*, 1981–1988, volume III, Soviet Union, January 1981–January 1983, document 211, https://history.state.gov/historicaldocuments/frus1981-88v03/d211.

33. *FRUS*, 1981–1988, volume III, Soviet Union, January 1981–January 1983, document 242, https://history.state.gov/historicaldocuments/frus1981-88v03/d242.

34. Interview with Paul H. Nitze, December 10, 1982, 10, box I:118, Nitze Papers.

35. Interview with Paul H. Nitze, December 10, 1982, 10, box I:118, Nitze Papers.

36. Interview with Paul H. Nitze, December 10, 1982, 10, box I:118, Nitze Papers.

37. Bernard Gwertzman, "U.S. Aide Reached Arms Agreement Later Ruled Out," *New York Times*, January 16, 1983, https://www.nytimes.com/1983/01/16/us/us-aide
-reached-arms-agreement-later-ruled-out.html.

38. Bernard Gwertzman, "U.S. Aide Reached Arms Agreement Later Ruled Out," *New York Times*, January 16, 1983, https://www.nytimes.com/1983/01/16/us/us-aide -reached-arms-agreement-later-ruled-out.html.

39. Reagan Diary, January 21, 1983, in Brinkley, ed., *The Reagan Diaries*, vol. I, 191.

40. Reagan Diary, February 11, 1983, in Brinkley, ed., *The Reagan Diaries*, vol. I, 196.

41. Ronald Reagan, "Address to the Nation on Defense and National Security," March 23, 1983, Ronald Reagan Presidential Library, https://www.reaganlibrary.gov /archives/speech/address-nation-defense-and-national-security.

42. Reagan, "Address to the Nation."

43. Public Papers: Reagan, 1983, Book I (Washington: Government Printing Office, 1984), 474.

44. "Report of the President's Commission on Strategic Forces," April 6, 1983, Ha-thiTrust, http://web.mit.edu/chemistry/deutch/policy/1983-ReportPresCommStra tegic.pdf.

45. Paul Nitze, "Assuring Strategic Stability in an Era of Détente," *Foreign Affairs* 54, no. 2 (January 1976): 214.

46. Correspondence with Gregg Herken, box II:2, General Correspondence, 1984 He-Hy, Nitze Papers.

47. Correspondence with Gregg Herken, box II:2, General Correspondence, 1984 He-Hy, Nitze Papers.

48. Reagan Diary, May 12, 1983, in Brinkley, ed., *The Reagan Diaries*, vol. I, 225.

49. Nitze, *Hiroshima to Glasnost*, 390.

50. For Nitze's statement, see *Documents on Disarmament, 1983* (Washington: United States Arms Control and Disarmament Agency, 1986), 1000–1001.

51. *The MacNeil/Lehrer NewsHour*, December 8, 1983, American Archive of Public Broadcasting, https://americanarchive.org/catalog/cpb-aacip_507-0p0wp9tm76.

52. Reagan Diary, January 17, 1984, in Brinkley, ed., *The Reagan Diaries*, vol. I, 309.

53. *FRUS*, 1981–1988, volume XI, START I, document 87, https://history.state.gov /historicaldocuments/frus1981-88v11/d87.

54. McFarlane's summary of Nitze's proposal is laid out in *FRUS*, 1981–1988, vol-ume XI, START I, document 88, https://history.state.gov/historicaldocuments /frus1981-88v11/d88.

55. *FRUS*, 1981–1988, volume XI, START I, document 89, https://history.state.gov /historicaldocuments/frus1981-88v11/d89.

56. Minutes of a National Security Planning Group Meeting, March 27, 1984, last reviewed September 13, 2023, https://www.thereaganfiles.com/19840327-nsc-104 -arms-contr.pdf.

57. *FRUS*, 1981–1988, volume XI, START I, document 96, https://history.state.gov /historicaldocuments/frus1981-88v11/d96.

58. Nitze, *Hiroshima to Glasnost*, 402.

59. *FRUS*, 1981–1988, volume XI, START I, document 97, https://history.state.gov /historicaldocuments/frus1981-88v11/d97.

60. Minutes of a National Security Planning Group Meeting, September 18, 1984, last reviewed September 13, 2023, https://www.thereaganfiles.com/19840918-nspg-96 -arms-contr.pdf.

61. Bernard Gwertzman, "Books of the Times: Arms and Reagan," *New York Times,* September 29, 1984, https://archive.nytimes.com/www.nytimes.com/books/98/12/06/specials/talbott-gambits.html.

62. Strobe Talbott, *Deadly Gambits* (New York: Knopf, 1984).

63. Interview with Paul H. Nitze, April 13, 1983, 17, box I:118, Nitze Papers.

64. Interview with Paul H. Nitze, April 13, 1983, 17, box I:118, Nitze Papers.

11. The Strategic Concept

1. *FRUS*, 1981–1988, volume XI, START I, document 99, https://history.state.gov/historicaldocuments/frus1981-88v11/d99.

2. *FRUS*, 1981–1988, volume XI, START I, document 99, https://history.state.gov/historicaldocuments/frus1981-88v11/d99.

3. *FRUS*, 1981–1988, volume XI, START I, document 99, https://history.state.gov/historicaldocuments/frus1981-88v11/d99.

4. Memorandum from Jack Matlock to Robert McFarlane, Executive Secretariat, NSC Country File, Europe and Soviet Union, USSR (10/15/84–10/23/84), Ronald Reagan Presidential Library.

5. Serge Schmemann, "Soviet Congratulatory Message to Reagan Looks to Better Relations," *The New York Times,* November 8, 1984, A18.

6. George P. Shultz, *Turmoil and Triumph: Diplomacy, Power, and the Victory of the American Deal* (New York: Simon & Schuster, 2010), 495.

7. Letter from President Ronald Reagan to Chairman Konstantin Chernenko, November 16, 1984, last reviewed September 13, 2023, https://www.thereaganfiles.com/19841116.pdf.

8. Shultz, *Turmoil and Triumph,* 489–90.

9. Memorandum From Robert McFarlane to President Reagan, November 18, 1984, Executive Secretariat, NSC Country File, Europe and Soviet Union, USSR (11/16/84–11/25/84), Ronald Reagan Presidential Library.

10. Memorandum From Secretary of State Shultz to President Reagan, December 27, 1984, Sven Kraemer Files, Geneva—NSDD Package, 12/31/1984–01/01/1985 (3), Ronald Reagan Presidential Library.

11. "A Suggestion as to How to Present the Offense–Defense Interaction to Gromyko," Robert McFarlane Files, subject file, Geneva Talks Background Notebook, Ronald Reagan Presidential Library.

12. Memorandum From Secretary of State Shultz to President Reagan, December 27, 1984, with attached paper by Nitze, "A Suggestion as to How to Present the Offense-Defense Interaction to Gromyko," Sven Kraemer Files, Geneva—NSDD Package, 12/31/1984–01/01/1985 (3), Ronald Reagan Presidential Library.

13. Memorandum From Secretary of State Shultz to President Reagan, December 27, 1984, with attached paper by Nitze, "A Suggestion as to How to Present the Offense-Defense Interaction to Gromyko," Sven Kraemer Files, Geneva—NSDD Package, 12/31/1984–01/01/1985 (3), Ronald Reagan Presidential Library.

14. Memorandum From Secretary of State Shultz to President Reagan, December 27, 1984, with attached paper by Nitze, "A Suggestion as to How to Present the

Offense-Defense Interaction to Gromyko," Sven Kraemer Files, Geneva—NSDD Package, 12/31/1984–01/01/1985 (3), Ronald Reagan Presidential Library.

15. Shultz, *Turmoil and Triumph*, 512.

16. Archie Brown, *The Human Factor: Gorbachev, Reagan, and Thatcher, and the End of the Cold War* (New York: Oxford University Press, 2020), 125.

17. For the January 5 telegram and drafting material in its preparation, see "Geneva—Allies & Congress, November 1984–December 1984," box 90718, Ronald Reagan Presidential Library, https://www.reaganlibrary.gov/public/digitallibrary/smof/nsc-defensepolicy/kraemer/90718/40-305-12015482-90718-001-2018.pdf.

18. *FRUS*, 1981–1988, volume IV, Soviet Union, January 1983–March 1985, document 369, https://history.state.gov/historicaldocuments/frus1981-88v04/d369.

19. *FRUS*, 1981–1988, volume IV, Soviet Union, January 1983–March 1985, document 373, https://history.state.gov/historicaldocuments/frus1981-88v04/d373.

20. Paul Nitze, "On the Road to a More Stable Peace," *Department of State Bulletin*, April 1985, 27–29.

21. Callaghan, *Dangerous Capabilities*, 455.

22. *FRUS*, 1981–1988, volume IV, Soviet Union, January 1983–March 1985, document 375, https://history.state.gov/historicaldocuments/frus1981-88v04/d375.

23. *FRUS*, 1981–1988, volume XI, START I, document 109, https://history.state.gov/historicaldocuments/frus1981-88v11/d109.

24. *FRUS*, 1981–1988, volume XI, START I, document 107, https://history.state.gov/historicaldocuments/frus1981-88v11/d107.

25. *FRUS*, 1981–1988, volume V, Soviet Union, March 1985–October 1986, document 43, https://history.state.gov/historicaldocuments/frus1981-88v05/d43.

26. Nitze, *Hiroshima to Glasnost*, 412.

27. Callaghan, *Dangerous Capabilities*, 462–63.

28. NSDD 192, "The ABM Treaty and the SDI Program," October 11, 1985, Ronald Reagan Presidential Library, https://www.reaganlibrary.gov/public/archives/reference/scanned-nsdds/nsdd192.pdf.

29. Letter to Paul Emmanuel, July 8, 1985, Nitze Papers, general correspondence 1985, alphabetical file, E, box 4, folder 9.

30. Letter to Paul Emmanuel, July 8, 1985 Nitze Papers, box 4, folder 9.

31. President Reagan, "Remarks at the Present Ceremony for the Presidential Medal of Freedom," November 7, 1985, Ronald Reagan Presidential Library, https://www.reaganlibrary.gov/archives/speech/remarks-presentation-ceremony-presidential-medal-freedom-0.

32. Memorandum by Paul Nitze, "Facets of the Fireside Summit," December 12, 1985, Nitze Papers, subject file, Geneva Summit, box 161, folder 7.

33. *FRUS*, 1981–1988, volume V, Soviet Union, March 1985–October 1986, document 162, https://history.state.gov/historicaldocuments/frus1981-88v05/d162.

34. *FRUS*, 1981–1988, volume V, Soviet Union, March 1985–October 1986, document 164, https://history.state.gov/historicaldocuments/frus1981-88v05/d164.

35. Nitze, *Hiroshima to Glasnost*, 421.

36. Reagan to Gorbachev, July 25, 1986, Ronald Reagan Presidential Library, http://www.thereaganfiles.com/19860725.pdf.

37. Reagan to Gorbachev, July 25, 1986, Ronald Reagan Presidential Library, http://www.thereaganfiles.com/19860725.pdf.

38. *FRUS*, 1981–1988, volume V, Soviet Union, March 1985–October 1986, document 258, https://history.state.gov/historicaldocuments/frus1981-88v05/d258.

39. *FRUS*, 1981–1988, volume XI, START I, document 142, https://history.state.gov/historicaldocuments/frus1981-88v11/d142.

40. *FRUS*, 1981–1988, volume VI, Soviet Union, October 1986–January 1989, document 6, https://history.state.gov/historicaldocuments/frus1981-88v06/d6.

41. "Talking Points for the School of Advanced International Relations," December 15, 1985, Nitze Papers.

42. "Talking Points for the School of Advanced International Relations," December 15, 1985, Nitze Papers.

43. Nitze, *Hiroshima to Glasnost*, 444.

44. *FRUS*, 1981–1988, volume I, Foundations of Foreign Policy, document 299, https://history.state.gov/historicaldocuments/frus1981-88v01/d299.

45. *FRUS*, 1981–1988, volume XI, START I, document 240, https://history.state.gov/historicaldocuments/frus1981-88v11/d240.

46. Nitze, *Hiroshima to Glasnost*, 452.

47. Strobe Talbott, "Arms and the Man: Paul Nitze," *Time*, December 21, 1987, https://content.time.com/time/subscriber/article/0,33009,966280,00.html.

48. *FRUS*, 1981–1988, volume XI, START I, document 257, https://history.state.gov/historicaldocuments/frus1981-88v11/d257.

49. *FRUS*, 1981–1988, volume XI, START I, document 257, https://history.state.gov/historicaldocuments/frus1981-88v11/d257.

50. *FRUS*, 1981–1988, volume XI, START I, document 257, https://history.state.gov/historicaldocuments/frus1981-88v11/d257.

51. Draft letter to John Herman, January 7, 1988, Nitze Papers.

52. *FRUS*, 1981–1988, volume XI, START I, document 261, https://history.state.gov/historicaldocuments/frus1981-88v11/d261.

53. *FRUS*, 1981–1988, volume XI, START I, document 261, https://history.state.gov/historicaldocuments/frus1981-88v11/d261.

54. *FRUS*, 1981–1988, volume XI, START I, document 268, https://history.state.gov/historicaldocuments/frus1981-88v11/d268.

55. *FRUS*, 1981–1988, volume XI, START I, document 268, https://history.state.gov/historicaldocuments/frus1981-88v11/d268.

56. Interview with Paul Nitze by Stephen Rearden and Ann Smith, March 1, 1988, Nitze Papers, subject file, box 121.

57. Interview with Paul Nitze by Stephen Rearden and Ann Smith, March 1, 1988, Nitze Papers, subject file, box 121.

58. Interview with Paul Nitze by Stephen Rearden and Ann Smith, March 1, 1988, Nitze Papers, subject file, box 121.

59. *FRUS*, 1981–1988, volume XI, START I, document 268, https://history.state.gov/historicaldocuments/frus1981-88v11/d268.

60. *FRUS*, 1981–1988, volume XI, START I, document 270, https://history.state.gov/historicaldocuments/frus1981-88v11/d270.

61. *FRUS*, 1981–1988, volume XI, START I, document 270, https://history.state.gov /historicaldocuments/frus1981-88v11/d270.

62. *FRUS*, 1981–1988, volume XI, START I, document 270, https://history.state.gov /historicaldocuments/frus1981-88v11/d270.

63. *FRUS*, 1981–1988, volume XI, START I, document 270, https://history.state.gov /historicaldocuments/frus1981-88v11/d270.

64. Interview with Paul Nitze by Stephen Rearden, March 28, 1988, Nitze Papers, subject file, box 121.

65. *FRUS*, 1981–1988, volume XI, START I, document 290, https://history.state.gov /historicaldocuments/frus1981-88v11/d290.

66. *FRUS*, 1981–1988, volume XI, START I, document 311, https://history.state.gov /historicaldocuments/frus1981-88v11/d311.

67. Paul H. Nitze, "The Case for Cutting Strategic Arms," *Washington Post*, June 21, 1988, p. A19.

68. *FRUS*, 1981–1988, volume XI, START I, document 314, https://history.state.gov /historicaldocuments/frus1981-88v11/d314.

69. *FRUS*, 1981–1988, volume XI, START I, document 325, https://history.state.gov /historicaldocuments/frus1981-88v11/d325.

70. *FRUS*, 1981–1988, volume XI, START I, document 328, https://history.state.gov /historicaldocuments/frus1981-88v11/d328.

12. No Retirement, 1989–2004

1. Interview with Paul Nitze, December 15, 1988, C-Span, https://www.c-span.org /video/?5607-1/interview-paul-nitze (42:00).

2. Chase Untermeyer to Paul Nitze, February 4, 1989, box II:116, State Department Resignation, Nitze Papers.

3. Paul Nitze, "Security Challenges Facing NATO in the 1990s," February 6, 1989, US Department of State, Bureau of Public Affairs, Washington, DC, https://books .google.com/books?id=W51MAQAAMAAJ&printsec=frontcover&dq=%22paul+h .+nitze%22&hl=en&newbks=1&newbks_redir=0&sa=X&ved=2ahUKEwjA2K _utvnvAhU-MVkFHdvuDXc4HhDoATACegQIAhAC#v=onepage&q=%22paul%20h .%20nitze%22&f=false.

4. Paul Nitze, "Security Challenges Facing NATO in the 1990s," February 6, 1989, US Department of State, Bureau of Public Affairs, Washington, DC, https://books .google.com/books?id=W51MAQAAMAAJ&printsec=frontcover&dq=%22paul+h .+nitze%22&hl=en&newbks=1&newbks_redir=0&sa=X&ved=2ahUKEwjA2K _utvnvAhU-MVkFHdvuDXc4HhDoATACegQIAhAC#v=onepage&q=%22paul%20h .%20nitze%22&f=false.

5. Paul Nitze to James Baker, February 28, 1989, box II:116, State Department Resignation, Nitze Papers.

6. Paul Nitze to George H. W. Bush, March 6, 1989, box II:116, State Department Resignation, Nitze Papers.

7. "Paul Nitze Dies at 97," *JHU Gazette*, October 25, 2004, https://pages.jh.edu /gazette/2004/25oct04/25nitze.html. Nitze had offered $5 million matching grant. In 1960, he had helped Milton Eisenhower raise $4.2 million for a SAIS building at 1740 Massachusetts Avenue.

8. "Paul Nitze Dies at 97," *JHU Gazette*, October 25, 2004, https://pages.jh.edu/gazette/2004/25oct04/25nitze.html. Nitze had offered $5 million matching grant. In 1960, he had helped Milton Eisenhower raise $4.2 million for a SAIS building at 1740 Massachusetts Avenue.

9. Memorandum of Conversation, May 15, 1989, Chase Untermeyer to Paul Nitze, box II:114, Soviet Union Miscellany, Nitze Papers.

10. Memorandum of Conversation, July 22, 1989, Sergei Akhromeyev and Paul Nitze, box II:114, Soviet Union Miscellany, Nitze Papers.

11. Memorandum of Conversation, July 22, 1989, Sergei Akhromeyev and Paul Nitze, box II:114, Soviet Union Miscellany, Nitze Papers.

12. Mike Stafford to Paul Nitze, October 13, 1989, box II:115, Stafford, Michael, Nitze Papers.

13. *The Economist*, September 16, 1989.

14. "Thoughts on Article in *The Economist* of September 16, 1989, 13, 'Wow!'" 1989, box II:114, Nitze Papers.

15. Kenneth Thompson and Steven Rearden, eds., *Paul H. Nitze on the Future* (Lanham, MD: University Press of America, 1991), 19.

16. Thompson and Rearden, *Nitze on the Future*, 20.

17. Thompson and Rearden, *Nitze on the Future*, 20.

18. Memorandum from Paul Nitze to Lee Butler, December 6, 1989, box II:116, subject file, Strategic Arms Reduction Treaty, 1986–1992, Nitze Papers.

19. Paul Nitze and Michael Stafford, "War Whether We Need It or Not? A Blockade—Plus Bombs—Can War," *Washington Post*, January 6, 1991, C1.

20. Jim Hoagland, "Bush's America: Welcome to the Post-Gulf War," *Washington Post*, March 3, 1991, C4.

21. R.W. Apple Jr., "A Cold Warrior Breathes a Little Easier," *New York Times*, October 13, 1991, Section 4, Page 1.

22. Paul Nitze, "Keep Nuclear Insurance," *The Bulletin of the Atomic Scientists*, May 1992, 34–36.

23. Paul Nitze, "Keep Nuclear Insurance," *The Bulletin of the Atomic Scientists*, May 1992, 34–36.

24. Don Oberdorfer, "U.S., Russia Differ on Nuclear Arsenals," *Washington Post*, June 10, 1992, A26.

25. Karen De Witt, "The 1992 Campaign: Undeclared Candidate Perot to Begin Forming a National Advisory Panel," *New York Times*, July 7, 1992, A13.

26. "Perot Throws Lunch for 340 to Gather Ideas for Platform," *Chicago Tribune*, July 8, 1992, 8.

27. Richard Cohen, "The Perot Implosion: No Mourning for America," *Washington Post*, July 19, 1992, C1.

28. Lois Romano, "The Reliable Source," *Washington Post*, November 17, 1992, D03.

29. Robert Beisner, "Of Nuclear Arms and the Man," *Washington Post*, October 22, 1989.

30. Stanley Hoffmann, "The Perfect In-and-Outer," *New York Review of Books*, November 23, 1989.

31. Gregory Treverton, "The Silence of the Master," *Los Angeles Times*, January 7, 1990, 11.

32. Paul Nitze, "The Man Behind the Marshall Plan," *Chicago Tribune*, June 12, 1993, 121.

33. Interview with Paul H. Nitze, October 31, 1985, 24, box I:119, Nitze Papers.

34. Paul Nitze, "The Grand Strategy of NSC-68," in *NSC-68: Forging the Strategy of Containment*, ed. S. Nelson Drew (Washington, DC: National Defense University Press, 1994), https://www.files.ethz.ch/isn/139678/1994-09_NSC68_Forging_Strategy.pdf.

35. "US Face Global Challenges, Nitze Says," *Christian Science Monitor*, October 7, 1993.

36. David Ignatius, "The Curse of the Merit Class," *Washington Post*, February 27, 1994.

37. James Chace, "All the Presidents' Man," *New York Times*, January 2, 1994, https://www.nytimes.com/1994/01/02/books/all-the-presidents-man.html.

38. Patrick Glynn, "Public and Private," *Commentary*, March 1994.

39. Paul Nitze, "Is it Time to Junk our Nukes? The New World Disorder Makes Them Obsolete," *Washington Post*, January 16, 1994.

40. Paul Nitze, "Is it Time to Junk our Nukes? The New World Disorder Makes Them Obsolete," *Washington Post*, January 16, 1994.

41. Paul Nitze, "Is it Time to Junk our Nukes? The New World Disorder Makes Them Obsolete," *Washington Post*, January 16, 1994.

42. Paul Nitze, "To B-2 or not to B-2? The Case for the Supersonic Bomber We Will Need Next Time," *Washington Post*, July 17, 1994.

43. Paul Nitze, "To B-2 or not to B-2? The Case for the Supersonic Bomber We Will Need Next Time," *Washington Post*, July 17, 1994.

44. Paul Nitze, "A Cold-War Solution for a Warming World," *Washington Post*, July 2, 1997, p. A23.

45. Paul Nitze, "A Cold-War Solution for a Warming World," *Washington Post*, July 2, 1997, p. A23.

46. Paul Nitze and Sidney Drell, "This Treaty Must Be Ratified," *Washington Post*, June 21, 1999.

47. Brooke Masters, "At 50, Foreign Policy School Faces Task of Reinterpreting the World," *Washington Post*, April 29, 1993, https://www.washingtonpost.com/archive/politics/1993/04/29/at-50-foreign-policy-school-faces-task-of-reinterpreting-the-world/9a71ef89-b4a3-4217-a47a-5485914924fc.

48. Masters, "At 50," A12.

49. "Shultz Says U.S. Should Use Force Against Terrorism," *New York Times*, October 26, 1984, Section A, Page 1.

50. "Executive Summary of the Report on the Commission to Assess the Ballistic Missile Threat to the United States," July 15, 1998, https://fas.org/irp/threat/bm-threat.htm.

51. Statement of Principles, Project for the New American Century, https://web.archive.org/web/20050205041635/http://www.newamericancentury.org/statementofprinciples.htm, last visited September 18, 2023.

52. "War Aims," *Wall Street Journal*, September 20, 2001, A16.

53. Thompson, The Hawk and the Dove, 317.

54. "War Aims," *Wall Street Journal*, September 20, 2001, A16.

55. "The Legacy of Paul Nitze," April 15, 2004, C-Span, https://www.c-span.org/video/?181376-1/legacy-paul-nitze.

56. "The Legacy of Paul Nitze," April 15, 2004, C-Span, https://www.c-span.org/video/?181376-1/legacy-paul-nitze.

57. "The Legacy of Paul Nitze," April 15, 2004, C-Span, https://www.c-span.org/video/?181376-1/legacy-paul-nitze.

58. "Keynote Address of the 60th Anniversary Dinner of the School of Advanced International Studies, the Johns Hopkins University," October 13, 2004, U.S. Department of State Archive, https://2001-2009.state.gov/secretary/former/powell/remarks/37087.htm.

59. Don Oberdorfer, "Architect of Cold War Had Role in Ending It," *Washington Post*, October 21, 2004, A1.

Conclusion

1. Remarks by National Security Advisor Condoleezza Rice on Terrorism and Foreign Policy, April 29, 2002, https://georgewbush-whitehouse.archives.gov/news/releases/2002/04/text/20020429-9.html.

2. On the differences between the two speeches, see Jeff Nussbaum, *Undelivered: The Never-Heard Speeches That Would Have Rewritten History* (New York: Flatiron Books, 2022).

3. Nitze, *Hiroshima to Glasnost*, 463.

4. Interview with Paul H. Nitze, September 10, 1985, 13, box I:119, Nitze Papers.

5. Nitze, *Hiroshima to Glasnost*, xiii.

6. *FRUS*, 1950, National Security Affairs; Foreign Economy Policy, volume I, document 85, https://history.state.gov/historicaldocuments/frus1950v01/d85.

Bibliography

Archives

Harry S. Truman Presidential Library, Independence, MO
Hoover Institution Archives, Stanford, CA
    Committee on the Present Danger records, 1976–1992
George W. Bush Presidential Library, Dallas, TX
Jimmy Carter Presidential Library, Atlanta, GA
Library of Congress Manuscript Collections, Washington, DC
    Paul H. Nitze Papers, 1922–1998 (Nitze Papers)
Ronald Reagan Presidential Library, Simi Valley, CA

Digital Collections

Foreign Relations of the United States series (FRUS)
    https://history.state.gov/historicaldocuments
Open Vault from WGBH: War and Peace in the Nuclear Age
    https://openvault.wgbh.org/collections/war_peace/interviews
The Reagan Files
    https://www.thereaganfiles.com/

Selected Primary Sources

Acheson, Dean. *Present at the Creation: My Years in the State Department*. Reissue ed. New York: W. W. Norton, 1969.
Bohlen, Charles. *Witness to History, 1929–1969*. New York: Norton, 1973.
Brinkley, David. *The Reagan Diaries*. New York: HarperCollins, 2007.
Carter, Jimmy. *White House Diary*. New York: Farrar, Straus and Giroux, 2010.
Gates, Robert. *From the Shadows: The Ultimate Insider's Story of Five Presidents and How They Won the Cold War*. New York: Simon & Schuster, 1996.
Giltman, Maynard. *The Last Battle of the Cold War: An Inside Account of Negotiating the INF Treaty*. New York: Palgrave Macmillan, 2006.
McFarlane, Robert. *Special Trust*. New York: Cadell & Davies, 1994.
Nitze, Paul. "Assuring Strategic Stability in an Era of Détente." *Foreign Affairs* 54, no. 2 (January 1976): 207–32.
Nitze, Paul. "Atoms, Strategy and Policy," *Foreign Affairs*, January 1956.

Nitze, Paul H. *Tension between Opposites: Reflections on the Practice and Theory of Politics*. New York: Scribner, 1993.

Nitze, Paul, with Ann M. Smith and Steven L. Rearden. *From Hiroshima to Glasnost: At the Center of Decision—A Memoir*. New York: Grove Weidenfeld, 1989.

Shultz, George P. *Turmoil and Triumph: Diplomacy, Power, and the Victory of the American Deal*. New York: Simon & Schuster, 2010.

Skinner, Kiron, Annelise Anderson, and Martin Anderson, eds. *Reagan, In His Own Hand: The Writings of Ronald Reagan That Reveal His Revolutionary Vision for America*. New York: Touchstone, 2001.

Thompson, Kenneth, and Steven Rearden, eds. *Paul H. Nitze on Foreign Policy*. Lanham, MD: University Press of America, 1989.

Thompson, Kenneth, and Steven Rearden, eds. *Paul H. Nitze on National Security and Arms Control*. Lanham, MD: University Press of America, 1990.

Thompson, Kenneth, and Steven Rearden, eds. *Paul H. Nitze on the Future*. Lanham, MD: University Press of America, 1991.

United States Strategic Bombing Survey (USSBS). *Summary Report (European War)*. Washington, DC: Government Printing Office, 1945.

United States Strategic Bombing Survey (USSBS). *Summary Report (Pacific War)*. Washington, DC: Government Printing Office, 1946.

Selected Secondary Sources

Ambrose, Matthew. *The Control Agenda: A History of Strategic Arms Limitations Talks*. Ithaca, NY: Cornell University Press, 2018.

Auten, Brian. *Carter's Conversion: The Hardening of American Defense Policy*. Columbia: University of Missouri Press, 2008.

Beisner, Robert L. *Dean Acheson: A Life in the Cold War*. New York: Oxford University Press, 2009.

Betts, Richard K. *Nuclear Blackmail and Nuclear Balance*. Washington, DC: Brookings Institution Press, 2010.

Bowie, Robert R., and Richard H. Immerman. *Waging Peace: How Eisenhower Shaped an Enduring Cold War Strategy*. New York: Oxford University Press, 2000.

Brown, Archie. *The Human Factor: Gorbachev, Reagan, and Thatcher, and the End of the Cold War*. New York: Oxford University Press, 2020.

Bundy, McGeorge. "To Cap the Volcano." *Foreign Affairs*, October 1969.

Cahn, Anne Hessing. *Killing Détente: The Right Attacks the CIA*. University Park: Pennsylvania State University Press, 1998.

Callahan, David. *Dangerous Capabilities: Paul Nitze and the Cold War*. New York: HarperCollins, 1990.

Cameron, James. *The Double Game: The Demise of America's First Missile Defense System and the Rise of Strategic Arms Limitation*. New York: Oxford University Press, 2017.

Cardwell, Curt. *NSC 68 and the Political Economy of the Early Cold War*. Cambridge: Cambridge University Press, 2011.

Colbourn, Susan. *Euromissiles: The Nuclear Weapons That Nearly Destroyed NATO*. Ithaca, NY: Cornell University Press, 2022.

Costigliola, Frank. *Kennan: A Life between Worlds*. Princeton, NJ: Princeton University Press, 2023.

Craig, Campbell, and Fredrik Logevall. *America's Cold War: The Politics of Insecurity*. 2nd ed. Cambridge, MA: Harvard University Press, 2020.

Craig, Campbell, and Sergey Radchenko. *The Atomic Bomb and the Origins of the Cold War*. New Haven, CT: Yale University Press, 2008.

Crowder, Richard. *Aftermath: The Makers of the Postwar World*. London: Bloomsbury, 2015.

Daigle, Craig. *The Limits of Détente: The United States, the Soviet Union, and the Arab-Israeli Conflict, 1969–1973*. New Haven, CT: Yale University Press, 2012.

Desch, Michael. *Cult of the Irrelevant: The Waning Influence of Social Science on National Security*. Princeton, NJ: Princeton University Press, 2021.

Dobbs, Michael. *One Minute to Midnight: Kennedy, Khrushchev, and Castro on the Brink of Nuclear War*. Repr. ed. New York: Vintage, 2009.

Dower, John W. *War without Mercy: Race & Power in the Pacific War*. New York: W. W. Norton, 1986.

Drell, Sidney D., and George Pratt Shultz. *Implications of the Reykjavik Summit on Its Twentieth Anniversary: Conference Report*. Stanford, CA: Hoover Institution Press, 2007.

Drew, S. Nelson, ed. *NSC-68: Forging the Strategy of Containment*. Washington, DC: National Defense University, 1994.

Dulles, John Foster. "Policy for Security and Peace." *Foreign Affairs*, April 1954

Fischer, Beth. *The Myth of Triumphalism: Rethinking President Reagan's Cold War Legacy*. Lexington: University of Kentucky Press, 2020.

Forrestal, James, and Walter Millis. *The Forrestal Diaries*. Auckland, New Zealand: Pickle Partners, 2015.

Freedman, Lawrence. *The Evolution of Nuclear Strategy*. London: Palgrave Macmillan, 2003.

Freeman, Stephanie L. *Dreams for a Decade: International Nuclear Abolitionism and the End of the Cold War*. Philadelphia: University of Pennsylvania Press, 2023.

Gaddis, John Lewis. *Strategies of Containment: A Critical Appraisal of American National Security Policy during the Cold War*. New York: Oxford University Press, 2005.

Garthoff, Raymond. *Détente and Confrontation: American–Soviet Relations from Nixon to Reagan*. Washington, DC: Brookings Institution Press, 1994.

Gavin, Francis J. *Nuclear Statecraft: History and Strategy in America's Atomic Age*. Ithaca, NY: Cornell University Press, 2012.

Gavin, Francis J. *Nuclear Weapons and American Grand Strategy*. Washington, DC: Brookings Institution Press, 2020.

Gentile, Gian P. *How Effective Is Strategic Bombing? Lessons Learned from World War II to Kosovo*. New York: New York University Press, 2001.

Glaser, Charles L. *Analyzing Strategic Nuclear Policy*. Princeton, NJ: Princeton University Press, 2014.

Gordin, Michael D. *Red Cloud at Dawn: Truman, Stalin, and the End of the Atomic Monopoly*. New York: Farrar, Straus and Giroux, 2009.

Graham, Thomas, Jr. *Disarmament Sketches: Three Decades of Arms Control and International Law*. Seattle: University of Washington Press, 2015.

Graham, Thomas, Jr., and Damien J. LaVera. *Cornerstones of Security: Arms Control Treaties in the Nuclear Era*. Seattle: University of Washington Press, 2011.

Green, Brendan Rittenhouse. *The Revolution That Failed: Nuclear Competition, Arms Control, and the Cold War*. Cambridge: Cambridge University Press, 2020.

Gutner, Tammi. *The Story of SAIS*. Washington, DC: School of Advanced International Studies, 1987.

Halberstam, David. *The Best and the Brightest*. New York: Random House, 2002.

Hasegawa, Tsuyoshi. *The End of the Pacific War: Reappraisals*. Stanford, CA: Stanford University Press, 2007.

Heefner, Gretchen. *The Missile Next Door: The Minuteman in the American Heartland*. Cambridge, MA: Harvard University Press, 2012.

Herken, Gregg. *Brotherhood of the Bomb: The Tangled Lives and Loyalties of Robert Oppenheimer, Ernest Lawrence, and Edward Teller*. New York: Henry Holt, 2013.

Herken, Gregg. *Counsels of War*. New York: Knopf Doubleday, 2015.

Herken, Gregg. *The Georgetown Set: Friends and Rivals in Cold War Washington*. New York: Knopf Doubleday, 2015.

Herken, Gregg. *The Winning Weapon: The Atomic Bomb in the Cold War, 1945–1950*. Princeton, NJ: Princeton University Press, 2016.

Hill, Charles. *Grand Strategies: Literature, Statecraft, and World Order*. New Haven, CT: Yale University Press, 2010.

Hitchcock, William I. *The Age of Eisenhower: America and the World in the 1950s*. New York: Simon & Schuster, 2018.

Hoffman, David. *The Dead Hand: The Untold Story of the Cold War Arms Race and Its Dangerous Legacy*. New York: Random House, 2009.

Hogan, Michael J. *A Cross of Iron: Harry S. Truman and the Origins of the National Security State, 1945–1954*. Cambridge: Cambridge University Press, 2000.

Holloway, David. *Stalin and the Bomb*. New Haven, CT: Yale University Press, 2008.

Hoopes, Townsend, and Douglas Brinkley. *Driven Patriot: The Life and Times of James Forrestal*. Annapolis, MD: Naval Institute Press, 2012.

Hopkins, Michael F. *Dean Acheson and the Obligations of Power*. Lanham, MD: Rowman & Littlefield, 2017.

Hunt, Jonathan R. *The Nuclear Club: How America and the World Policed the Atom from Hiroshima to Vietnam*. Stanford, CA: Stanford University Press, 2022.

Inboden, William. *The Peacemaker: Ronald Reagan, the Cold War, and the World on the Brink*. New York: Penguin, 2022.

Isaacson, Walter, and Evan Thomas. *The Wise Men: Six Friends and the World They Made*. New York: Simon & Schuster, 1997.

Jervis, Robert. *The Meaning of the Nuclear Revolution: Statecraft and the Prospect of Armageddon*. Ithaca, NY: Cornell University Press, 1989.

Jervis, Robert. "Why Nuclear Superiority Doesn't Matter." *Political Science Quarterly* 94, no. 4 (Winter 1979–1980): 617–33. https://www.jstor.org/stable/2149629.

Kaplan, Edward. *To Kill Nations: American Strategy in the Air-Atomic Age and the Rise of Mutually Assured Destruction*. Ithaca, NY: Cornell University Press, 2015.

Kaplan, Fred. *The Bomb: Presidents, Generals, and the Secret History of Nuclear War*. New York: Simon & Schuster, 2021.

Keefer, Edward Coltrin. *Harold Brown: Offsetting the Soviet Military Challenge 1977–1981.* Washington, DC: Government Printing Office, 2017.

Kissinger, Henry. *Nuclear Weapons & Foreign Policy.* New York: W. W. Norton, 1969.

Koch, Susan J. *The Presidential Nuclear Initiatives of 1991–1992.* Fort Belvoir, VA: Defense Technical Information Center, September 1, 2012.

Krepinevich, Andrew, and Barry Watts. *The Last Warrior: Andrew Marshall and the Shaping of Modern American Defense Strategy.* New York: Basic Books, 2015.

Krepon, Michael. *Winning and Losing the Nuclear Peace: The Rise, Demise, and Revival of Arms Control.* Stanford, CA: Stanford University Press, 2021.

Kroenig, Matthew. *The Logic of American Nuclear Strategy: Why Strategic Superiority Matters.* New York: Oxford University Press, 2018.

Kuklick, Bruce. *Blind Oracles: Intellectuals and War from Kennan to Kissinger.* Princeton, NJ: Princeton University Press, 2006.

Lanoszka, Alexander. *Atomic Assurance: The Alliance Politics of Nuclear Proliferation.* Ithaca, NY: Cornell University Press, 2018.

Leffler, Melvyn P. *For the Soul of Mankind: The United States, the Soviet Union, and the Cold War.* New York: Macmillan, 2007.

Leffler, Melvyn P. *A Preponderance of Power: National Security, the Truman Administration, and the Cold War.* Stanford, CA: Stanford University Press, 1992.

Leffler, Melvyn P. *Safeguarding Democratic Capitalism: U.S. Foreign Policy and National Security, 1920–2015.* Princeton, NJ: Princeton University Press, 2017.

Leffler, Melvyn P., and Odd Arne Westad. *The Cambridge History of the Cold War.* Cambridge: Cambridge University Press, 2010.

Lerner, Mitchell B. *The Pueblo Incident: A Spy Ship and the Failure of American Foreign Policy.* Lawrence: University Press of Kansas, 2002.

Lieber, Keir A., and Daryl G. Press. *The Myth of the Nuclear Revolution: Power Politics in the Atomic Age.* Ithaca, NY: Cornell University Press, 2020.

Logevall, Frederik. *Choosing War: The Lost Chance for Peace and the Escalation of War in Vietnam.* Berkeley: University of California Press, 2001.

Martin, Garret Joseph. *General de Gaulle's Cold War: Challenging American Hegemony, 1963–1968.* New York: Berghahn Books, 2013.

Matlock, Jack. *Reagan and Gorbachev: How the Cold War Ended.* New York: Random House, 2004.

Maurer, John D. *Competitive Arms Control: Nixon, Kissinger, and SALT, 1969–1972.* New Haven, CT: Yale University Press, 2022.

May, Ernest R. *American Cold War Strategy: Interpreting NSC 68.* New York: Bedford/St. Martin's, 1993.

McMahon, Robert J. *The Cold War: A Very Short Introduction.* 2nd ed. Oxford: Oxford University Press, 2021.

McMahon, Robert J. *Dean Acheson and the Creation of an American World Order.* Lincoln: University of Nebraska Press, 2009.

Mieczkowski, Yanek. *Eisenhower's Sputnik Moment: The Race for Space and World Prestige.* Ithaca, NY: Cornell University Press, 2013.

Miles, Simon. *Engaging the Evil Empire: Washington, Moscow, and the Beginning of the End of the Cold War.* Ithaca, NY: Cornell University Press, 2020.

Miller, Nicholas L. *Stopping the Bomb: The Sources and Effectiveness of US Nonproliferation Policy.* Ithaca, NY: Cornell University Press, 2018.

Milne, David. *Worldmaking: The Art and Science of American Diplomacy.* New York: Macmillan, 2015.

Moss, Richard A. *Nixon's Back Channel to Moscow: Confidential Diplomacy and Détente.* Lexington: University Press of Kentucky, 2017.

Nau, Henry. *Conservative Internationalism: Armed Diplomacy under Jefferson, Polk, Truman, and Reagan.* Princeton, NJ: Princeton University Press, 2013.

Newhouse, John. *Cold Dawn: The Story of SALT.* New York: Holt, Rinehart & Winston, 1973.

Newman, Robert P. "Ending the War with Japan: Paul Nitze's 'Early Surrender' Counterfactual." *Pacific Historical Review* 64, no. 2 (1995): 167–94.

Nitze, Paul. "The Grand Strategy of NSC-68." In *NSC-68: Forging the Strategy of Containment,* edited by S. Nelson Drew, 7–16. Washington, DC: National Defense University Press, 1994. https://www.files.ethz.ch/isn/139678/1994 -09_NSC68_Forging_Strategy.pdf.

Nussbaum, Jeff. *Undelivered: The Never-Heard Speeches That Would Have Rewritten History.* New York: Flatiron Books, 2022.

Nuti, Leopold, Frederic Bozo, Marie-Pierre Rey, and N Piers Ludlow, eds. *The Euromissiles Crisis and the End of the Cold War.* Washington, DC.: Woodrow Wilson Center Press, 2015.

Odom, William E. "The Origins and Design of PD-59: A Memoir." In *Getting MAD: Nuclear Mutual Assured Destruction, Its Origins and Practice,* edited by Henry D. Sokolski, 175–96. Washington, DC: Strategic Studies Institute, 2004.

Pach, Chester J. *Arming the Free World: The Origins of the United States Military Assistance Program, 1945–1950.* Chapel Hill: University of North Carolina Press, 1991.

Perez, Robert C., and Edward F. Willett. *Clarence Dillon: A Wall Street Enigma.* Seattle, WA: Madison Books, 1995.

Plokhy, Serhii. *Nuclear Folly: A History of the Cuban Missile Crisis.* New York: W. W. Norton, 2021.

Poole, Walter S. *The Joint Chiefs of Staff and National Policy,* vol. VIII, *1961–1964.* Washington, DC: Office of Joint History, 2011.

Preble, Christopher A. *John F. Kennedy and the Missile Gap.* DeKalb: Northern Illinois University Press, 2004.

Quigley, Caroll. *Tragedy & Hope.* New York: Macmillan, 1962.

Rearden, Steven L. *The Evolution of American Strategic Doctrine: Paul H. Nitze and the Soviet Challenge.* New York: Routledge, 2019.

Reynolds, David. *From Munich to Pearl Harbor: Roosevelt's America and the Origins of the Second World War.* Chicago: Ivan R. Dee, 2002.

Rid, Thomas. *Active Measures: The Secret History of Disinformation and Political Warfare.* New York: Farrar, Straus and Giroux, 2020.

Rosenberg, David Alan. "The Origins of Overkill: Nuclear Weapons and American Strategy, 1945–1960." *International Security* 7, no. 4 (1983): 3–71.

Rovner, Joshua. *Fixing the Facts: National Security and the Politics of Intelligence.* Ithaca, NY: Cornell University Press, 2015.

Sarotte, M. E. *Not One Inch: America, Russia, and the Making of Post-Cold War Stalemate.* New Haven, CT: Yale University Press, 2021.

Saunders, Elizabeth N. *Leaders at War: How Presidents Shape Military Interventions.* Ithaca, NY: Cornell University Press, 2014.

Savranskaya, Svetlana, and Thomas S. Blanton. *The Last Superpower Summits: Reagan, Gorbachev and Bush. Conversations That Ended the Cold War.* Budapest: Central European University Press, 2016.

Sayle, Timothy Andrews. *Enduring Alliance: A History of NATO and the Postwar Global Order.* Ithaca, NY: Cornell University Press, 2019.

Schuessler, John M. *Deceit on the Road to War: Presidents, Politics, and American Democracy.* Ithaca, NY: Cornell University Press, 2015.

Schwartz, Thomas A. *Henry Kissinger and American Power: A Political Biography.* New York: Hill & Wang, 2020.

Sechser, Todd, and Matthew Furhman. *Nuclear Weapons and Coercive Diplomacy.* New York: Cambridge University Press, 2017.

Sherwin, Martin J. *Gambling with Armageddon: Nuclear Roulette from Hiroshima to the Cuban Missile Crisis.* New York: Knopf, 2020.

Simms, Brendan, and Charlie Laderman. *Hitler's American Gamble: Pearl Harbor and Germany's March to Global War.* New York: Basic Books, 2021.

Smith, Gaddis. *Dean Acheson.* New York: Cooper Square Publishers, 1972.

Snead, David. *The Gaither Committee, Eisenhower, and the Cold War.* Columbus: Ohio State University Press, 1999.

Sobel, Robert. *The Life and Times of Dillon Read.* New York: Truman Talley Books, 1991.

Spalding, Elizabeth. *The First Cold Warrior: Harry Truman, Containment, and the Remaking of Liberal Internationalism.* Lexington: University Press of Kentucky, 2006.

Spohr, Kristina. *Post Wall, Post Square: How Bush, Gorbachev, Kohl, and Deng Shaped the World after 1989.* New Haven, CT: Yale University Press, 2020.

Steil, Benn. *The Marshall Plan: Dawn of the Cold War.* New York: Simon & Schuster, 2018.

Stern, Sheldon M. *Averting 'The Final Failure': John F. Kennedy and the Secret Cuban Missile Crisis Meetings.* Palo Alto, CA: Stanford University Press, 2003.

Stern, Sheldon M. *The Cuban Missile Crisis in American Memory: Myths versus Reality.* Stanford, CA: Stanford University Press, 2012.

Stern, Sheldon M. *The Week the World Stood Still: Inside the Secret Cuban Missile Crisis.* Stanford, CA: Stanford University Press, 2005.

Stoler, Mark A. *Allies and Adversaries: The Joint Chiefs of Staff, the Grand Alliance, and U.S. Strategy in World War II.* Chapel Hill: University of North Carolina Press, 2004.

Stoler, Mark A. *George C. Marshall: Soldier-Statesman of the American Century.* New York: Simon & Schuster Macmillan, 1989.

Stuart, Douglas. *Creating the National Security State: A History of the Law That Transformed America.* Princeton, NJ: Princeton University Press, 2012.

Stueck, William. *The Korean War: An International History.* Princeton, NJ: Princeton University Press, 1995.

Suri, Jeremi. *Henry Kissinger and the American Century*. Cambridge, MA: Belknap Press, 2009.

Talbott, Strobe. *Deadly Gambits: The Reagan Administration and the Stalemate in Nuclear Arms Control*. New York: Random House, 1984.

Talbott, Strobe. *Endgame: The Inside Story of SALT II*. New York: Harper & Row, 1980.

Talbott, Strobe. *The Master of the Game: Paul Nitze and the Nuclear Peace*. New York: Vintage, 1989.

Taubman, Philip. *In the Nation's Service: The Life and Times of George P. Shultz*. Stanford, CA: Stanford University Press, 2023.

Taubman, William. *Gorbachev: His Life and Times*. New York: W. W. Norton, 2017.

Terriff, Terry. *The Nixon Administration and the Making of U.S. Nuclear Strategy*. Ithaca, NY: Cornell University Press, 1995.

Thompson, Jenny, and Sherry Thompson. *The Kremlinologist: Llewellyn E Thompson, America's Man in Cold War Moscow*. Baltimore, MD: Johns Hopkins University Press, 2018.

Thompson, John A. *A Sense of Power: The Roots of America's Global Role*. Ithaca, NY: Cornell University Press, 2015.

Thompson, Nicholas. *The Hawk and the Dove: Paul Nitze, George Kennan, and the History of the Cold War*. New York: Henry Holt, 2009.

Trachtenberg, Marc. *A Constructed Peace: The Making of the European Settlement, 1945–1963*. Princeton, NJ: Princeton University Press, 2020.

Trachtenberg, Marc. *History and Strategy*. Princeton, NJ: Princeton University Press, 1991.

Warnke, Paul C. "Apes on a Treadmill." *Foreign Policy*, no. 18 (1975): 12–29.

Weisman, Alan. *Prince of Darkness, Richard Perle: The Kingdom, the Power and the End of Empire in America*. New York: Sterling Publishing, 2007.

Wellerstein, Alex. *Restricted Data: The History of Nuclear Secrecy in the United States*. Chicago: University of Chicago Press, 2021.

Wells, Samuel. *Fearing the Worst: How Korea Transformed the Cold War*. New York: Columbia University Press, 2019.

Westad, Odd Arne. *The Cold War: A World History*. New York: Basic Books, 2017.

Westad, Odd Arne. *The Global Cold War: Third World Interventions and the Making of Our Times*. Cambridge: Cambridge University Press, 2007.

Wilson, James Graham. *The Triumph of Improvisation: Gorbachev's Adaptability, Reagan's Engagement, and the End of the Cold War*. Ithaca, NY: Cornell University Press, 2014.

Wolfe, Thomas W. *The SALT Experience*. Cambridge, MA: Ballinger, 1979.

Young, Ken, and Warner Roller Schilling. *Super Bomb: Organizational Conflict and the Development of the Hydrogen Bomb*. Ithaca, NY: Cornell University Press, 2019.

Zaloga, Steven J. *The Kremlin's Nuclear Sword: The Rise and Fall of Russia's Strategic Nuclear Forces, 1945–2000*. Washington, DC: Smithsonian Institution Press, 2002.

Zubok, Vladislav A. *A Failed Empire: The Soviet Union in the Cold War from Stalin to Gorbachev*. Chapel Hill: University of North Carolina Press, 2007.

INDEX

Note: Paul Nitze is simply "Nitze" in subheadings. Italicized page numbers refer to photographs.

"ABM Treaty and the SDI Program" (NSDD-192, 1985), 222
ABM Treaty (Anti-Ballistic Missile Treaty, 1972): congressional approval of, 160, 161, 165–66; drafting of, 157–59; interim agreement, 146; interpretations, 222; signing of, 159–60; Soviet violation, 216; START and, 226–27, 241–42. *See also* NST (Nuclear and Space Arms Talks)
ABMs. *See* missile defense systems
Absolute Weapon (Brodie), 108
academia: Cold War studies, 257; Nitze's views of, 15, 17, 19, 27, 88–89; strategic studies, 92
ACDA (Arms Control and Disarmament Agency), 105, 118, 141, 208
Acheson, Dean: Nitze, association with, 51, 56, 60, 81, 91, 147; strategic policy, 65–66, 90
Acheson-Lilienthal Report (1946), 214, 218, 226
Adenauer, Konrad, 117
Advisory Commission to the Council of National Defense, 29
Afghanistan: Soviet invasion, 14, 171–72, 189, 190; US war on terror, 259, 260–61
Africa, 75, 101, 105, 109
aircraft. *See* bomber aircraft; U-2 spy plane
Air Force Advisory Board, 99–100
air power: national security impacts, 32–33, 34–36, 55, 93; as strategic revolution, 45; in WWII, 41, 42–43, 47
Akhromeyev, Sergei, 221, 227–28, 230, 235–36, 241
Allison, Royal, *154*, 162
Alsop, Joseph, 89–91
Alsop, Stewart, 99
anti-ballistic missile (ABM) launchers. *See* missile defense systems

"Apes on a Treadmill" (Warncke article), 175
aquarator venture, 24
arms control: bargaining without sacrificing, 133, 142–43; congressional approval, 160, 161, 165–66; leverage, 140, 148, 180, 220; moratorium on testing, 117, 150, 151, 154; nuclear crises and, 116–17, 123–25; political will for, 153, 213, 234; qualitative vs. quantitative, 150–51. *See also* specific arms talks and treaties
arms race: evolution of, 93; missile gap, 100, 101; nuclear freeze, 192, 194, 201–2, 211; US inferiority, 116–17, 162, 204
Arnold, Henry (Hap), 38, 41
Asia, US nuclear policy toward, 131–32. *See also* specific countries
Aspen Corporation, 7–8, 188, 239
assured destruction, 132–33. *See also* MAD (mutual assured destruction)
"Assuring Strategic Stability in an Era of Détente" (Nitze article, 1976), 172–74, 175, 183–84, 190, 233
Atlas missiles, 100
atomic bomb, use in Japan, 41–42, 43–44, 45. *See also* nuclear weapons
Atomic Energy Act (1946), 103
Atomic Energy Commission, UN, 58, 214, 218, 226

Bacon, William, 21, 22
Baker, James, 5–6, 238, 240, 242, 248
Ball, George, 122, 178
Barnes, C. Tracy, 109
Baruch Plan (1946), 214, 218, 226
"Basic Strategic Judgments" (Nitze report), 105
"Basic War Aims." *See* NSC-79 (unfinished)
"Basis for Substantive Negotiations" (memorandum, 1962), 124–25

Bay of Pigs invasion (1961), 108–10
Berlin Crisis (1961): development and
    resolution, 110–16; impacts on security
    policy, 116–19; lessons from, 104–5, 125–26
Berlin Task Force, 114, 115, 121
Berlin Wall, 114, 115, 116, 243
Bessmertnykh, Alexander, 226–27
Big Four summit (Geneva, 1955), 93
Bissell, Richard, 92, 109
Black Tom explosion (1916), 28, 29, 79
Blessing, Lee ("Walk in the Woods" play),
    250–51
Bohlen, Charles (Chip), 20, 79, 93–94
bomber aircraft: B-1s, 177, 178, 180; B-2s,
    255; B-52s, 100, 137, 180, 246; Backfires,
    183, 231
Boverie, Richard, 203
Brezhnev, Leonid: policies, 190, 204, 243; US
    and, 166, 197, 199
"Brilliant Pebbles" program, 249
Brodie, Bernard, 92, 108
Brown, Harold, 154, 174–75, 180, 187
Brzezinski, Zbigniew, 174, 178, 181–83, 185
Buckley, William F. (Firing Line), 184,
    193–95, 225, 253
budget. See defense spending
Bulganin, Nikolai, 94
Bulletin of the Atomic Scientists, 247, 253–54
Bullitt, William, 200
Bundy, McGeorge (Mac), 106–9, 119, 156,
    185, 201, 204
Bureau of Economic Warfare, 37–38
Burke, Arleigh, 95, 110
Bush, George H.W. administration, 5, 177,
    237, 238–41, 244–49
Bush, George W., administration, 3, 259–61,
    263–64

Cahill, John T., 29
Carlucci, Frank, 231–32, 234, 236
Carnegie Endowment for Peace, 96, 101
Carnegie Foundation, 84
Carter, Jimmy, 171, 174–77, 180–81, 189,
    285n6
Carter administration: Afghanistan, 189–90;
    arms control policies, 171, 176–80; Nitze's
    role in, 178–79, 180; policy planning,
    174–77; Presidential Directive-58, 13;
    SALT II, 176, 180–83, 189; strategic
    stability and, 172–77, 178–79; Team B
    exercise, 177–78
Casey, William, 148, 193, 204
Castro, Fidel, 108–10, 123, 125

Central Intelligence Agency (CIA), 72, 92,
    144, 167, 193–94
CFR. See Council on Foreign Relations;
    Senate: Committee on Foreign Relations
Chace, James, 253
"Chance for Peace" (Eisenhower speech), 79
Cheney, Richard, 174, 258
Chernenko, Konstantin, 213–14
Chiang Kai-shek, 54, 242
Chicago Council on Foreign Relations,
    185–86
Chicago, Illinois, 16, 17, 22
China (People's Republic of China): civil
    war, 54, 57; offshore island crisis, 101;
    Soviet Union and, 94–95; threat from, 73,
    86, 136, 247; US and, 131–32, 147
Chomsky, Noam, 143, 144
Church, Frank, 167, 187
CIA (Central Intelligence Agency), 72, 92,
    144, 167, 193–94
civil defense network, US, 77
classified information, Nitze's access to,
    91–93, 171, 181–82, 185, 194
Clayton, Will, 35, 50, 51–52
Clifford, Clark, 106, 137, 139, 140, 142–43,
    253
climate change, 6, 239, 255–56, 258–59
Clinton administration, 248, 252, 256,
    257–58, 259
Cold War: in Asia, 134, 138; bipolar era,
    82–83, 108; chess metaphor, 95; free
    world coalition, 87–88; geopolitics and
    ideology, 67, 199; objectives, Nitze's, 11,
    13, 14, 80; objectives, Soviet, 66–67, 86,
    94–95; objectives, US, 72, 74, 193–94;
    reflections on, 253–55; SALT as venue for,
    152; winning the, 90–91, 108, 191;
    winning without war, 62, 70
Cold War, end of: arms negotiation, 241–42,
    243–44; political order, 5, 244–49
command and control (C2), 182, 187–88,
    195–97
Committee on the Present Danger (CPD),
    177–78, 180–82, 188–89
Committee to Maintain a Prudent Defense
    Policy (CMPDP), 147–48
Communist Manifesto (Marx), 267
Comprehensive Test Ban Treaty (CTBT),
    256
Conant, James, 68, 178
Congress, US. See specific committee names
congressional testimonies, Nitze's, 24–25,
    27, 139, 160

"Considerations Involved in a Separable
First Stage Disarmament Agreement"
(long paper, 1963), 132
Constitution, US, 2, 64
Container Corporation of America, 20
containment policy, 74, 86, 105
contingency plans: Berlin, 111–12; Cuba,
119, 123–25; in general, 128; MIRVs and,
156–57
contracting and consulting work, Nitze's,
81, 85, 91–93, 96–97, 103
conventional forces: in Cold War, 80, 255; as
deterrent, 104, 113, 131, 195; Europe,
defense of, 57, 73, 110, 116–17, 241; force
structures, 76, 101, 194; massive
retaliation, 86; in Persian Gulf War, 245,
254; post-Cold War, 254–55; smart
weapons, 6, 238–39; Soviet Union, 97,
201; strategic conventional weapons, 254
Conventional Forces in Europe Treaty, 241
Council on Foreign Relations, 85–86, 97,
101, 164
counterforce strike: damage limitation and,
115, 133; defense against, 140; first strike
vs., 131; minimal deterrent, 247; MIRVs,
149, 156–57; Nitze Scenario, 172, 183;
strategic vulnerability, 13, 187. See also
first-strike capability
Crowley, Leo, 38
Cuba, 108–10, 204
Cuban Missile Crisis (1962): events of,
119–23; impacts of, 14, 121, 129, 136;
lessons from, 11–12, 104–5, 160, 189;
nuclear strategy after, 130–33, 146;
resolution of, 123–26
Czechoslovakia, Soviet invasion of (1968),
142–43

Dam, Kenneth, 209, 213
de Gaulle, Charles, 113, 136
Deadly Gambits (Talbott), 210
Declaration of Independence, 2, 64
Decline of the West (Spengler), 26, 27, 58–59,
230
Defense Department (DOD): Berlin Task
Force, 114, 115, 121; Office of International
Security Affairs (ISA), 79–80, 106–8, 152,
165
defense spending: arms race and, 194, 200,
207; congressional approval, 160, 189;
containment policy, 74, 86; Gramm-
Rudman, 224–25; Korean War and, 72–73;
leverage for negotiations, 201, 225;

massive retaliation, 86, 91; NSC-68 and,
70, 71, 79–80; SALT and, 166, 184–85;
taxes and, 79–80, 86, 111, 173, 225
democracy, 2, 3, 30–31, 53, 91, 267
Democratic Advisory Council, 167–68
Democratic Party, 80, 87–88, 91, 167, 174,
189
Democrats' Advisory Committee on
Foreign and Defense Policy, 97
Department of Defense. *See* Defense
Department (DOD)
Department of State. *See* State Department
(DOS)
Department of Treasury, 105
détente: instability in era of, 184–85;
perception of, 113; Soviet attitude
toward, 94, 163, 172
"Deterrence and Survival in the Nuclear
Age" (Gaither Report, 1957), 98–101
deterrence policy: conventional weapons,
104, 113, 131, 195; massive retaliation
and, 86; NATO and US policy, 112–13,
114–15; in nuclear era, 195–96, 247,
254–55; nuclear weapons, 57–60, 116; in
peacetime, 68; retaliatory capability, 129,
130–31; strength as deterrent, 11–12,
90–91, 116–19, 190, 195; tension between
opposites, 9, 113
Dillon, C. Douglas, 102
Dillon, Clarence, 15, 21, 22–24, 31
Dillon, Read and Co., 22–26, 27–29
diplomacy, 14, 34, 43, 50
Dobrynin, Anatoly: arms negotiations,
199–200, 221; Kissinger back-channel,
153, 157, 160, 166–67; nuclear crises, 115,
123
D'Olier, Franklin, 39, 43
domestic politics: elections, 209, 214,
267–68; geopolitical impacts of, 166–67;
impacts on democracy, 267; NSC-68 and,
66; Soviet *vs.* US, 150, 201–2; treaty
negotiations and, 159–60, 161, 164, 169,
229–31
Draft Act (Selective Service Act, 1940), 29,
35
Draper, William, 25, 29, 35
DST (Defense and Space Talks), 220–21,
232, 236
Dual Track decision (NATO), 190, 197, 211
Dulles, Allen, 92
Dulles, John Foster: career, 77–80, 92;
massive retaliation policy, 85–86, 87;
Nitze, views of, 81, 99–100, 103

early warning systems, 77, 93, 99
Economic Consequences of the Peace (Keynes), 74
Economic Cooperation Administration, 53
Economic Defense Board (Bureau of
    Economic Warfare), 37–38
economic policy, US, 51–53, 55–56. *See also*
    defense spending
"Effect of New Weapons Systems on Our
    Alliances" (Nitze speech), 97
Eisenhower, Dwight D., 78–79, 91, 99–100, 102
Eisenhower administration: Gaither
    Committee, 98–101; New Look, 85–86,
    89, 100; Nitze's role in, 81, 85–88, 91–93,
    95–96; policies, 80, 111; transition period,
    76–79; Vietnam, 89
elections. *See* domestic politics; specific
    presidential administrations
Endgame (Talbott), 210
Enewetak Atoll, 76
Estonia, 157
Europe: conventional defense of, 57, 73, 110,
    116–17, 241; economic restoration of, 6,
    52, 56; independent nuclear arsenals, 113,
    223–24; INF deployment, 201–2; US
    commitment to, 59–60, 73–74, 109, 113,
    211. *See also* NATO (North Atlantic
    Treaty Organization)
Europe, Eastern. *See* Warsaw Pact
ExComm (Executive Committee of the
    National Security Council), 104, 119–25,
    124, 142, 181
Experts Group (INF and START negotia-
    tions), 227–29, *228*, 230, 235, 237, 248–49
extended deterrence, 11–12. *See also* NATO
    (North Atlantic Treaty Organization)

Fair Deal policy, 54
false alarms, MIRVs and, 156
FBI (Federal Bureau of Investigation), 29
Federal Republic of Germany (FRG, West
    Germany), 112–13, 208
Finland, 94
Finletter, Thomas, 85
Firing Line (television program), 184–85,
    193–95, 225, 253
first-strike capability: counterforce *vs.*, 131;
    MIRVs and, 155, 223; opposition to, 201;
    preemptive strike *vs.*, 195; SALT and, 176,
    225–26; Soviet Union, 146–47, 161, 168,
    190; stability and, 12, 173–74, 184;
    survivability, 163, 183. *See also* "Nitze
    Scenario"; nuclear policy, US; preemptive
    strike

Fitzgerald, F. Scott, 3
Ford administration, 166, 174
Foreign Affairs (magazine), 172–74, 175,
    183–84, 190, 201
Foreign Affairs Research Center at SAIS, 106
Foreign Economic Administration, 38
foreign policy discussion group (New York
    City), 85
Foreign Policy Institute (FPI), 92. *See also* SAIS
    (School of Advanced International Studies)
Foreign Policy (magazine), 97, 175
Foreign Service Educational Foundation, 84
Forrestal, James: career, 28, 33–35, 52; death,
    55; N and, 21, 23, 25, 29
Foster, William, 105
FPR (Washington Center of Foreign Policy
    Research), 96–97
"Framework of Theory Useful to the
    Practice of Politics" (Nitze paper), 88
France, 21, 113, 136, 223–24
freedom of action, US, 12, 261
freeze, nuclear, 192, 211. *See also* nuclear
    policy, US
From Hiroshima to Glasnost (Nitze book), 230,
    231–32, 240, 249–53
Fulbright, William, 101, 109

Gaither Report ("Deterrence and Survival in
    the Nuclear Age," 1957), 98–101
Gaither, Rowan, 98
Galosh (Soviet missile defense system), 130,
    151, 157, 158
Garrison Rail Mobile, 231, 246
Gates, Thomas, 105–6
General Theory (Keynes), 26, 92
Geneva Summit (1985), 221–22, 223–25
Geneva talks: aims, evolution of, 216;
    central concept, 215, 225–26; DST, 218,
    220–21, 232, 236; resumption of, 213–14,
    217–18; strategic concept, 215–16, 221
Germany, 17, 21, 26–27, 32, 39–41
Germany, West (FRG, Federal Republic of
    Germany), 112–13, 208
Gilpatrick, Roswell (Ros), 18, 106, 128, 133
Glassboro, New Jersey, summit, 136
Goethe, Johann Wolfgang von, 8
Goldwater, Barry, 165
Goodpaster, Andrew, 102–3
Gorbachev, Mikhail: impressions of, 217,
    223, 224; INF treaty rejection, 229; Nitze's
    views of, 212, 225, 241, 242–43;
    perestroika and glasnost, 13, 240
Gore, Al, 258–59

government contractor work, Nitze's, 81, 85, 91–93, 96–97, 103
Gramm-Rudman-Hollings Balanced Budget Act (1985), 224–25
grand package. *See* strategic concept (Nitze Criteria)
Great Depression, 15, 22–24
Gromyko, Andrei, 198, 221
Groton School, 1953 speech, 9, 40, 82–83
Gulf War (1990–91), 244–49

Haig, Alexander, 159, 196, 197, 198, 200
Halberstam, David, 135
Hammarskjöld, Dag, 50, 71
Harmel Report (1967), 137
Harriman, Averell, 167
Harvard University, 19–20, 27
heavy bombers, 100, 227
heavy missiles. *See* SS-18 "Satan" missiles (Soviet Union)
Helms, Richard, 144
Helsinki. *See* names of specific arms limitation talks
hemispheric defense, 33, 34–35, 36
Henderson, Loy, 50
Heraclitus (philosopher), 8–9, 82, 250
Herter, Christian, 81, 83–84, 100, 101, 105–6
High Frontier (lobby group), 214–15, 220
Hilken, Henry (grandfather), 19
Hilken, Paul (uncle), 28, 29, 79
Hiroshima. *See* Japan
"History and Our Democratic Tradition in the Formulation of the United States Foreign Policy" (Nitze speech), 87–88
history of strategic arms competition (ONA paper), 10
Hitler, Adolph, 26, 37
Hoover, Herbert, 30
Hotchkiss School (Connecticut), 18–19
House of Representatives, US: Pike Committee, 166–67; Un-American Activities Committee, 54
Humphrey, Hubert, 105
Hussein, Saddam, 244–45, 259
hydrogen bomb, 56–62, 65, 71, 76. *See also* nuclear weapons

ICBMs (intercontinental ballistic missiles): arms race, 93; arms talks, 141, 153, 183, 239, 243, 246; basing of, 239; budget issues, 164, 194, 234; MIRV issue, 207, 223; Soviet capabilities, 99, 100, 146, 150, 172; survivability, 239. *See also* throw weight

ideological struggles, Nitze's caution about, 67, 261
"'Impossible' Job of Secretary of State" (Nitze article), 97
India, 123
INF (Intermediate-Range Nuclear Forces) Treaty (1987), 5, 206, 230
INF talks: criteria for limits, 199, 235; European independent forces, 200–201; leadership of, 198, 200, 202, 208–9; no first-use, 200–201; suspension of, 207–11; throw weight reductions, 199–200; zero option, 198–99, 203, 206. *See also* Experts Group (INF and START negotiations); strategic concept (Nitze Criteria)
Institute for Strategic Studies (UK), 116
intelligence community, 151, 166–67
intelligence estimates, 72, 118–19, 142, 151–52
interagency working group on defense policy, Nitze's, 118–19
intercontinental ballistic missiles. *See* ICBMs (intercontinental ballistic missiles)
Interim Agreement. *See* SALT I (Interim Agreement, 1972)
interim INF (Intermediate-Range Nuclear Force) Treaty, 5, 206. *See also* INF talks
Iran, 75–76, 242–43
Iran-Contra scandal, 212, 229–30
IRBMs (intermediate-range ballistic missiles): arms talks, 5, 157, 192, 199, 204, 209; budget issues, 179; in Europe, 190, 206
ISA (Defense Department, Office of International Security Affairs), 79–80, 106–8, 152, 165

Jackson, Henry (Scoop), 148, 160–62, 169, 174, 182–83
Japan, 11, 32, 41–46, 198
Javitz, Jacob, 187
Jervis, Robert, 12, 131, 168, 190
Johns Hopkins University. *See* SAIS (School of Advanced International Studies)
Johnson, Lyndon B. (LBJ), 128, 137, 139
Johnson administration: "Daisy Ad," 165; Nitze's role in, 127–29, 130, 134, 137, 143–44; policy priorities, 133; San Antonio formula, 138; Vietnam task force, 135, 136
Johnson, Alexis, 120, 125, 164
Johnson, Louis, 55–56, 66, 69
Joint Chiefs of Staff (JCS): on arms control, 151–52, 205, 232, 234–36; budget, 71; on force requirements, 132–33

Joint Strategic Bomber Study (Team B exercise), 177–78
Joint Strategic Target Selection Board, 41
Jupiter missiles, 121–23, 125, 202

Kampelman, Max, 218, 227, 234
Keating, Frank, 119
Kennan, George: career, 54–56, 60, 65, 70; Nitze, shared stance, 14; retirement, 62; Vietnam opposition, 135
Kennedy, John F. (JFK), 102, 105, 110–11, 123, 128
Kennedy administration: Berlin Crisis response, 116–19; cabinet selection, 106; CMC response, 119–23, 124; Nitze's role in, 105–6, 125
Kennedy, Paul (Rise and Fall of the Great Powers), 230
Kennedy, Robert F., 104, 119, 120, 123, 139
Keynes, John Maynard, 26, 74, 92
Khrushchev, Nikita: 1961 Vienna Summit, 110–11; domestic politics, 94–95, 136; letter to JFK, 123; US, confrontations with, 110, 116
Kido, 43, 44
Kissinger, Henry A.: career, 149–50; Dobrynin back-channel, 153, 157, 160, 166–67; Nitze, rivalry with, 97–98, 164, 168, 185
Knox, Frank, 33, 37
Knudsen, William S., 38
Korea, North, 137–38
Korean War (1950–1953), 64, 72–73, 79, 85–86
Kosygin, Alexei, 136, 142–43
Kunsberg, Philip, 222
Kvitsinsky, Yuli, 192, 198, 199, 202–5

Laird, Melvin, 148, 162
Landon, Truman, 69
Landsdale, Edward, 109
Larocque, Eugene, 184
Lawrence, Ernest, 68
LeMay, Curtis, 108, 122
Lenin, Vladimir, 86
Leningrad, Russia, 94–95
lessons learned: on clear statement of threats, 100; from CMC and Berlin Crisis, 125–26, 127–28, 144, 160; from Korean War, 85–86; on preparedness, 12–13; from SALT I, 210; from WWII, 41, 45–48
levers of influence, Nitze and: early interest in, 15, 17, 19; ideas about, 31, 32, 89; proximity to power, 81–82, 100–101, 103, 106

Lilienthal-Acheson Report (1946), 214, 218, 226
Lilienthal, David, 58
Limited Test Ban Treaty (1963), 141, 155
limited war, 74, 108, 115, 116, 250
Linhard, Robert, 227, 231
linkage, 153, 209–10, 240
Lippmann, Walter, 122
logic-driven rationality, Nitze and: logic chains, 3, 29–30, 44, 90, 202; policy making, 59, 130, 219–20; problem-solving and, 50–51, 52, 73, 222; USSBS reports, 42, 43–44, 47; writing style, 97–98. See also Nitze, Paul, character traits
"Long Telegram" (Kennan), 55, 260
Lovett, Robert, 68, 106, 148

MacArthur, Douglas, 42–43, 47, 72, 73
MAD (mutual assured destruction): central tenet, 131; Nitze's rejection of, 12, 148; SDI and, 216–17; US acceptance of, 160, 161
Manhattan Project, 58
Mao Zedong, 57, 73
Marshall, Andrew, 10, 169
Marshall, Charles Burton, 85, 152
Marshall, George, 35–36, 51–52, 53–54
Marshall Plan (Economic Recovery Act, 1948), 51–52, 53, 113
Marx, Karl (Communist Manifesto), 267
Marxism-Leninism, 67, 143, 241
Massachusetts Institute of Technology (MIT), 93
massive retaliation, 85–86, 87, 91, 97, 111
Master of the Game (Talbott), 249–50, 253
McCarthy, Eugene, 139
McCarthy, Joseph, 66, 79, 84, 231
McCone, John, 120
McFarlane, Robert (Bud), 209, 213–14, 217, 221–22
McGovern, George, 184
McNamara, Robert: career, 115, 137, 147; on Cuba, 109, 124; on deterrence, 130–31; Nitze's work with, 106, 107–8; on peace in nuclear age, 126
Menshikov, Mikhail, 112
Midgetman missiles, 206–8, 231, 236–37, 246. See also Minuteman missiles
militarization. See outer space, militarization of
military-industrial complex, 14
military spending. See defense spending
Millikan, Max, 17, 92

Minuteman missiles: limitation of, 132–33, 142–43, 150–51, 186–87; MIRVs and, 130, 156; production, 12, 180; silos, 136, 140, 161; vulnerability of, 151, 172, 173, 185. *See also* Midgetman missiles

mir, meaning of, 94

MIRVs (multiple independent reentry vehicles): cost-benefit of, 200; problems with, 156–57, 164; restrictions on, 163, 165; US and, 149–51, 155–56

missile defense systems: area *vs.* point defense, 130, 140; problem of, 156–59. *See also* Galosh (Soviet missile defense system); Sentinel (US missile defense system); Talinn (Soviet missile defense system)

Missile Experimental (MX, Peacekeeper), 161, 185, 186, 205, 206–7, 236

missile gap, Soviet-US, 100, 101

Missile X, road-mobile system, 105–6

MIT (Massachusetts Institute of Technology), 93

modernization, strategic, 160–61, 171, 178, 187, 206

"Monday Package" (Nitze criteria), 10–11, 218–20, 226–27

moratorium on testing, 117, 150, 151, 154

Morgenthau, Hans, 88–89

Mosaddegh, Mohammad, 75

Moscow, Russia, 93–95, 152, 157–58, 159–60, 227

Moscow Summit (1972), 159–60, 230

Moscow Summit (1988), 232–35

Moses, Robert, 25, 40

"Mr. X" (Kennan article), 55

Multilateral Force (NATO), 125

Munich Conference (1938), 32–33

Mutual Defense Assistance Act (MDAA, 1949), 56

mutual destruction. *See* MAD (mutual assured destruction)

MX missile (Peacekeeper), 161, 185, 186, 205, 206–7, 236

Nagasaki. *See* Japan

National Defense Authorization Act (1997), 258

national emergencies, US, 74, 112

National Press Club, 198

National Security Study Directive 6–83 (NSSD 6–83, 1983), 207

National Security Act (1947), 48, 52–53, 56, 65

National Security Action Memorandum-109 (NSAM-109, 1961), 114–16

National Security Commission, Special Committee, 58

National Security Council. *See* ExComm (Executive Committee of the National Security Council)

National Security Council Reports (NSCR): NSC-20/4, 54–56, 70; NSC-79, 64, 79, 80, 90; NSC-135/3, 75; NSC-141, 75–76. *See also* NSC-68 (1950)

National Security Decision Directive (NSDD): NSDD-160, 218–19; NSDD-192, 222

National Security Decision Memorandum (NSDM): NSDM-148, 213; NSDM-242, 183

National Security Planning Group (NSPG), 209–10, 215, 219, 234

national security policy: definition, 7; policymaking, 65–66, 107–8, 167–68; politics of, 229–31, 264; security risks in general, 87–88; shortcomings of, 75, 77

National War College, 6, 252

NATO (North Atlantic Treaty Organization): alliance deterioration, 136–37, 142–43; Dual Track decision, 190, 197, 211; expansion of, 239, 258; extended deterrence, 112–13; founding of, 56; FRG membership, 112–13; independent nuclear arsenals, 113, 223–24; Multilateral Force, 125; US commitment to, 73, 114–15, 121, 211. *See also* Europe

Navy, Office of the Secretary, 128–29, *129*

Nazis, 26–27, 34, 40

negotiations. *See* arms control; names of specific tracks or treaties

New Deal policy, 24

New Look policy, 85–86, 89, 100, 245

New START (2011), 5

"New World Order," 5, 245

New York City: Council on Foreign Relations, 85–86, 101; foreign policy discussion group, 85; Wall Street, 22–26, 27, 50, 51, 68

New York Herald Tribune, 122

newspapers and journals, 99, 135, 152, 168, 180. *See also* specific publication titles

9/11 Commission, 260

9/11 terror attacks, 1, 4, 259, 263, 267

1976 *Foreign Affairs* article on strategic stability, 172–74, 183–84, 190

Nitze, Anina Sophia Hilken (mother), 16, 17–18

Nitze, Charles (grandfather), 16
"Nitze Criteria" for strategic defense. *See* strategic concept (Nitze Criteria)
Nitze, Elizabeth Hilken (sister), 16, 18
Nitze, Paul: academia, views of, 15, 17, 19, 88–89; childhood, 16–18; death, 6, 262; denunciations against, 29, 79, 128, 231; dinner party incident, 28, 29, 30; economics, gravitation toward, 19, 20–26; education, 18–20; expertise, 10–13, 170, 181–82, 200; on ideological struggles, 67, 261; on interim agreements, 149, 153, 202, 210, 213; Kissinger, rivalry with, 97–98, 164, 168, 185; legacy, 5, 14, 48, 62–63, 103, 264–68; marriage, 24, 249; memoir, 230, 231–32, 240, 249–53; original idea, goal of, 27; patriotism, 30, 35–36, 178–79; policy objectives, 11, 13, 14; politics, views on, 37, 97; on public service, 239; security clearances, 91–93, 181–82, 185, 194; *Tension between Opposites* (book), 7, 8–9, 253; tension between opposites (concept), 82–83, 113, 167, 265; theory of international politics, 7, 8, 9, 35, 81; wealth, 7, 25, 63, 264–65; worldview formation, 15, 30–31, 36–37, 53. *See also* levers of influence, Nitze and; Nitze, Paul, career moves; Nitze, Paul, character traits; "Nitze Scenario"; strategic concept (Nitze Criteria); titles of specific documents and publications
Nitze, Paul, career moves: overview, 2–3, 4–8, 10–13, 14, 103, 259; Wall Street, 22–28; move to Washington, DC, 28–30; S/P deputy director, 56; S/P director, 60, 61; NSC-68, drafting of, 65–69; ISA nomination, 79–80; SAIS, 81–82, 84–85; contracting and consulting, 91–93, 96–97, 98–101, 181–82, 190; ISA, policy and diplomacy, 106–8, 114–15, 125; ExComm, 104, 120–24; secretary of navy, 127, 128, 134; deputy secretary of defense, 136, 143–44; SALT delegation, 148, 149, 165–66; Democratic Advisory Council, 168–69; INF talks, 192–93, 198; arms negotiations, 212, 217, 227, 238; retirement, 238–41
Nitze, Paul, character traits: action orientation, 38–40, 82, 212, 250–51; ambition, 95, 253; appetite for risk, 26, 217; argumentative tendency, 29; competition, 53; confidence, 18, 23, 47; decisiveness, 22, 38, 40, 53; efficiency, 38,

40–41; Kissinger, compared with, 97; political acumen, 54; problem-solving, 49–51, 128; self-view, 53, 100, 189; stubborn convictions, 20, 43–44. *See also* logic-driven rationality, Nitze and
Nitze, Phyllis Pratt (wife), 24, 83, 230
"Nitze Scenario": central issue, 223, 239, 244; legacy of, 258; preemptive strike, 3, 195–96; Soviet first-strike, 3–4, 183, 185; strategic stability, 172–76, 204
Nitze, William (father), 16–17, 18
Nixon, Richard, 148, 153, 155, 159
Nixon administration: attitudes toward Soviets, 151; détente strategy, 146; Nitze's resignation, 165–66; Nitze's role in, 146, 147–48, 149, 159–60; power dynamics of, 149–50; reelection campaign, 159–60, 161, 162–63; Vietnam, 148, 153, 155, 159, 167; Watergate scandal, 163–66, 167
Nobel Institute (Norway), 239–40
nonproliferation, nuclear, 105, 118, 133
Norstad, Lauris, 113, 114
North Atlantic Council, 151
North Atlantic Treaty Organization. *See* NATO (North Atlantic Treaty Organization)
NPT. *See* Nuclear Non-Proliferation Treaty (NPT, 1968)
NSAM-109 (1961), 114–16
NSC-20/4 (1948), 54–56, 70
NSC-68 (1950): content of, 65, 69–72, 128, 268; defense spending, 70, 71, 79–80, 178; drafting of, 2, 64, 65–69; Korean War, 64, 72–73; speech about, 6, 252; war on terror, 260–61. *See also* State Department, Policy Planning Staff (S/P)
NSC-79 (unfinished), 64, 79, 80, 90, 245, 247
NSC-135/3 (1952), 75
NSC-141 (1953), 75–76
NSC (National Security Council): Principals Committee, 116–19. *See also* ExComm (Executive Committee of the National Security Council)
NSDD-160 (1985), 218–19
NSDM-148 (1984), 213
NSDM-242 (1974), 183
NSPG (National Security Planning Group), 215
NSSD 6–83 (1983), 207
NST (Nuclear and Space Arms Talks): DST, 218, 220–21, 232, 236; "Monday Package," 218–20; obstacles, 235; zero option, 220

nuclear balance. *See* arms control; MAD (mutual assured destruction); strategic stability
nuclear crises, 11, 101, 104. *See also* Berlin Crisis (1961); Cuban Missile Crisis (1962)
nuclear disarmament. *See* arms control
Nuclear Non-Proliferation Treaty (NPT, 1968), 133, 140, 141, 161
nuclear policy, US: toward arms talks, 101, 140–43; toward Asia, 131–32; capabilities *vs.* commitments, 99; critiques of, Nitze's, 168–69; difficulty of, 265–66; initial debates on, 59–60; methodology for crafting, 219–20; minimal deterrent, 247–48; "no cities" plan, 130–31; peace in nuclear age, 126, 132; post-Cold War, 247–49; Soviet policy *vs.*, 11; theory *vs.* practice, 89–91; unilateral freeze debate, 192, 211. *See also* first-strike capability; preemptive strike
nuclear superiority. *See* strategic superiority, US
nuclear "theology," 11, 150
nuclear war, limited *vs.* total, 11, 152, 157–58, 172–73, 175–76
nuclear weapons: effects of, 41–42, 43–44, 45, 57; elimination of, 101–2, 216–17, 225, 226; geopolitical impacts, 10–13, 76, 81, 151, 163; hydrogen bomb, 56–62, 65, 71, 76; as leverage, 140, 148, 180, 220; role after Cold War, 6, 247; theater nuclear forces, 197–98. *See also* strategic superiority
Nuclear Weapons and Foreign Policy (Kissinger), 97, 98

Odom, William, 182, 183, 185
Office of Net Assessment (ONA), 10
Office of the Coordinator of Inter-American Affairs (OCIAA), 29, 34–36
Offshore Islands Crisis (China-Taiwan, 1958), 101
oil industry, 25
on-site inspections. *See* verification
Operation Zapata (Bay of Pigs invasion), 108–10
Oppenheimer, Robert, 58–59, 68
Osgood, Robert, 96
outer space, militarization of, 209, 213. *See also* NST (Nuclear and Space Arms Talks)
Outer Space Treaty (1967), 141

Paepcke, Walter (brother-in-law), 18, 20, 260, 264
Pan American Airways, 34

parity. *See* strategic stability
Partial Test Ban Treaty (1963), 125
Paul Nitze and Company (New York), 27
Paul Nitze School of Advanced International Studies, 240, 253. *See also* SAIS (School of Advanced International Studies)
Pax Americana, 74, 90, 91, 246
peace movements, 137, 143, 201–2
Peacekeeper (MX missile), 161, 185, 186, 205, 206–7, 236
Pearl Harbor, Japanese attack on (1941): lessons from, 36–37, 44–45, 47–48, 59, 125–26; Nitze's recollections, 36, 42
Pecora, Ferdinand, 24–25
Pentagon, protest at, 137, 143
Perera, Guido, 38
Perle, Richard, 148, 198, 212, 227
Pershing II missiles, 197–98, 202, 206, 208
Persian Gulf War (1990–91), 244–49
Philadelphia World Affairs Council (speech, 1985), 219–20
photographic intelligence, 92, 119, 159
"Plan Dog" (memorandum), 33
Poland, 28, 72, 193–94, 196–97, 200, 243
Polaris submarines, 100, 142, 178
"Policy for Planning the Employment of Nuclear Weapons" (NSDM-242, 1974), 183
Policy Planning Staff. *See* State Department, Policy Planning Staff (S/P)
"Poodle Blanket" (NSAM-109, 1961), 114–16
Porter, Elizabeth Scott (wife), 249
Potsdam Conference (1945), 40
Powell, Colin, 262
Pratt, Ruth, 24, 30
preemptive strike: counterforce capability, 131, 151; first-strike *vs.*, 195; Nitze Scenario, 3, 195–96; option of, 115, 156–57, 181; strategic balance, 129. *See also* first-strike capability; nuclear policy, US
"Preparing for Negotiations with the Soviet Union" (NSDD-160, 1985), 218–19
Present at the Creation (Lovett), 148
Presidential Directive 58 (1980), 13
Presidential Medal of Freedom, 223
President's Commission on Strategic Forces, 205–6
preventive war, 89–91
Project for a New American Century, 258
Project Lamplight, 93
Project Nobska, 95–96

RAND Corporation, 90, 92

Reagan, Ronald: assassination attempt, 196–97; letter to Gorbachev, 225–26, 227; N as link to Truman, 188–90, 205, 211; Nitze's alignment with, 10–11, 189

Reagan administration: arms buildup, 204, 210–11; Nitze's role in, 192–93, 212, 213–14; SDI, 205–8, 229–30; strategic forces commission, 205–6. *See also* INF talks

"Recent Soviet Moves" (Nitze study), 66

"Red Team" exercise, 152

"Report by the Committee on Nuclear Proliferation" (1965), 133

Republic of China (Taiwan), 91

Republican Party, 30, 53, 61, 80, 257

research and development. *See* technology

retaliation. *See* counterforce strike; second-strike capability

Revlon, 25

Reykjavik Summit (1986): agreements, 235, 241; Experts Group, 227, *228;* "Monday Package," 11; reflections on, 14, 227–29

Rice, Condoleezza, 1, 263

Richardson, Elliot, 163

Rise and Fall of the Great Powers (Kennedy), 230

risk-taking behavior: Soviet Union, 146–47, 162, 164, 171–72, 173; strength as deterrent, 13, 67–68, 108, 110–11, 120–21

RISOP (Red Integrated Strategic Offensive Plan), 188

Roberts, Chalmers, 99

Rockefeller Foundation, 96

Rockefeller, Nelson, 29, 35, 36

Roosevelt, Franklin D. (FDR), 20, 30, 40

Roosevelt administration: hemispheric defense, 34–35; national security approach, 32–33; New Deal, 24; war and defense preparation, 28–29, 33, 36

Rostow, Eugene, 189, 197–98, 200, 202–4

Rostow, Walt, 107, 109, 141

Rowny, Edward, 219

Rumsfeld, Donald, 6, 128, 258, 260, 262

Rusk, Dean, 96, 106, 115, 118–19, 142

S/P. *See* State Department, Policy Planning Staff (S/P)

Safeguard (US missile defense system), 147–48, 150, 153, 157, 224

SAIS (School of Advanced International Studies): Foreign Affairs Research Center, 106; Foreign Policy Institute, 92; founding and mission, 6, 81, 83–85; Nitze's instruction at, 88–89, 96; proximity to power, 100–101, 103; S/P, parallels with, 81, 85, 92, 96; Washington Center of Foreign Policy Research, 96–97

SALT (Strategic Arms Limitation Talks): early stages, 149–50, 153–54; failure to stop Soviet activity, 162, 164, 173, 213; INF and, 199; Kissinger-Dobrynin back channel, 153, 157, 159; leverage, 133, 192; MIRV ban, 163; Nixon's goals for, 153, 155; Soviet position, 158; SS-9 missiles and, 151–52, 153; survivability, 159, 163; undersea testing, 140, 141, 164; US delegation, 148, *154;* US goals for, 140–43, 152–54, 155; Verification Panel, 155, 158, 160, 162, 163–64; Vienna Option, 157

SALT I (Interim Agreement, 1972): congressional approval of, 160, 161–62, 165–66; imperfections of, 159–61; Jackson Amendment, 162, 163, 169; Nitze's opposition to, 146, 149, 182

SALT II Treaty (1979): opposition to, 162–63, 180, 183, 184–86, 199; original objectives, 161–62, 186; signing and ratification, 180–83, 186–88; Watergate scandal and, 164

San Antonio formula, 138

Savage, Carlton, 77

SBSC. *See* Strategic Bombing Survey (USSBS)

Schelling, Thomas, 11, 114, 121

Schlesinger, Arthur, Jr., 89–91, 164

Scowcroft, Brent, 165, 205, 241, 242, 245

Scowcroft Commission, 206–7

SDI (strategic defense initiative): arms talks and, 205–8, 216, 229; criteria for, 219–20; as destabilizing, 217; importance of, 239; Nitze's formulas for, 214, 221–22

second-strike capability, 99, 129, 142, 168

Securities Act (1933), 24

"Security Challenges Facing NATO in the 1990s" (Nitze speech), 239–40

security dilemma, model of, 68

security studies (academic field), 90

Selective Service Act (Draft Act, 1940), 29, 35

Senate, US: Church Committee, 166–67; Committee on Banking and Currency, 24–25; Committee on Foreign Relations, 99–100, 139, 153; Subcommittee on African Affairs, 105

Senior Arms Control Policy Group, 209

Sentinel (US missile defense system), 136, 147
September 11 terrorist attacks (2001), 1, 4,
259, 263, 267
Shevardnadze, Eduard, 221
Shultz, George: arms talks, 209, 222, 223–24,
227–30, 235–37; Dobrynin and, 221;
Gromyko and, 214, 218; JCS meetings,
232; Nitze, bond with, 208, 211–12, 215,
257; role, Reagan administration, 205,
217, 219
Sino-Soviet cooperation, 94–95
SIOP (Single Integrated Operations Plan),
113, 188
SLBMs (submarine-launched ballistic
missiles), 100, 164, 168, 180, 187
Smith, Gerard, 151, 157, 158, 159, 162
Sorokin, Pitirim, 27
Souers, Sidney, 52, 65
Soviet Union: atomic pursuit, 56, 67;
buildup, analysis, 12–13, 133; civil defense
system, 94, 158, 172, 176; collapse of, 5,
238, 244–49; coup attempt, 246–47; loss,
capacity for, 152, 157–58; political system,
150; Supreme Soviet, 94–95; threat
analysis of, 14, 243–44; treaty noncompli-
ance, 215. *See also* Cold War, end of;
Moscow, Russia
space, 209, 213. *See also* NST (Nuclear and
Space Arms Talks)
Speer, Albert, 40–41
Spengler, Oswald *(Decline of the West)*, 26,
27, 58–59, 230
Sputnik I and II, 98
SS Lutzo, 19
SS-9 missiles (Soviet Union), 136, 151–52, 153
SS-20 missiles (Soviet Union), 197–98
SS-18 "Satan" missiles (Soviet Union):
capabilities, 146–47, 168, 169, 190–91;
psychological consequences, 172; US
focus on, 182, 244
stability. *See* strategic stability
Stages of Economic Growth (Rostow), 107
Stalin, Joseph, 40, 79, 92
Star Wars (defense system). *See* SDI
(strategic defense initiative)
Star Wars (movie), 7–8, 188
Stark, Harold, 33
START (Strategic Arms Reduction Talks):
basic formula, 230; Nitze's advocacy for,
216, 235–36, 239; obstacles, 231–36,
241–42; ratification, 5, 245, 246. *See also*
Experts Group (INF and START
negotiations)

START I, 6, 246
START II (1993), 248–49, 256–57
State Department (DOS), Nitze's early
career, 34, 49–53, 66
State Department, Policy Planning Staff
(S/P): deputy director, 56–60; director,
10, 60–63, 78; SDI infighting, 229–30. *See
also* NSC-68 (1950)
Stevenson, Adlai, 75–77, 85, 91, 96
Stimson, Henry, 33, 36, 38
Strategic Air Survey for the Pacific, 59. *See
also* Strategic Bombing Survey (USSBS)
strategic arms competition. *See* arms race
Strategic Arms Reduction Talks. *See* START
(Strategic Arms Reduction Talks)
Strategic Bombing Survey (USSBS):
conclusions, 43–46, 59, 76, 98; creation of,
38–39; Germany, 39–41; Japan, 11, 41–46;
Pacific campaign, 108, 128
strategic concept (Nitze Criteria): central
goals, 212–13, 216–17; concerns over, 224;
end of, 238; Gorbachev and, 225–27;
Midgetman missiles, 231; as negotiating
position, 223, 227–29
strategic forces. *See* nuclear weapons
strategic policy. *See* nuclear policy, US
strategic stability: CMC as turning point,
126; importance of, 160, 172–77, 179;
logic of, 12; 1976 article on, 183–84;
nuclear balance and, 10, 129, 159, 175;
post-Soviet, 247–48
strategic superiority, US: after Cold War,
247; credibility of, 11–12; decline of, 12,
110–11, 125–26, 173, 190–91; geopolitical
stability, 76, 90–91, 108, 126, 129–32, 144;
net assessment on, 193; parity, 152; Soviet
buildup, 12–13, 133
strategic triad, 100, 239. *See also* heavy
bombers; ICBMs (intercontinental
ballistic missiles); submarine-launched
ballistic missiles (SLBMs)
strength. *See* deterrence policy; strategic
superiority, US
"Study on Eliminating the Threat Posed by
Ballistic Missiles" (NSSD 6–83, 1983), 207
submarine-launched ballistic missiles
(SLBMs), 100, 164, 168, 180, 187
submarines, nuclear, 95–96, 128–29, 150. *See
also* Polaris submarines
Summary Report (Pacific War), 43–46, 76, 98.
See also Strategic Bombing Survey
(USSBS)
Supreme Soviet, 94–95

survivability: of C2, 182, 186, 196–97; as deterrence, 99, 175–76, 195; nuclear submarines, 128–29
Sweden, 50, 71
Symington, Stuart, 53

Taiwan (Republic of China), 91, 101
Talbott, Strobe, 210, 230–31, 249–50, 253
Talinn (Soviet missile defense system), 157
Taylor, Maxwell, *124*, 131
Team B exercise, 177–78
technology: Nitze's study of, 56, 58–59; role in national defense, 48, 93, 95–96
Teller, Edward, 58
tension between opposites (concept), 82–83, 113, 167, 265
Tension between Opposites (Nitze book), 7, 8–9, 253
terrorism. *See* September 11 terrorist attacks (2001); war on terror
Thatcher, Margaret, 217
theater nuclear forces, 197–98
theory of international politics, Nitze's, 7, 8, 9, 35, 81
think tanks, 81, 92, 96, 241–42
Thompson, Kenneth, 242
Thompson, Llewellyn E. (Tommy), 59–60, 72
Thompson, Nicholas (grandson, biographer), 124, 170, 178, 259
303 Committee, 144
throw weight: criterion for control, 141, 162, 164, 178; INF talks and, 199–200; trends in Soviet-US ratios, 173; Vladivostok formula, 166
Thurmond, Strom, 128
Timbie, James, 210
"To Cap the Volcano" (Bundy article), 156
Treasury Department, 105
Treaty Banning Nuclear Weapon Tests in the Atmosphere, Outer Space, and Under Water (1963), 125
Trinity Test (1945), 58
Truman, Harry S., 5, 75, 80, 167
Truman administration, 83, 88; aid to free peoples, 50, 74; budget policies, 55; Cold War policy, 50, 74, 188–89; Fair Deal, 54; hydrogen bomb, 10, 56–62, 65, 71, 76; Marshall Plan, 53, 54; NSC-68 approval, 64
Tsongas, Paul, 210–11
Turkey, 121–23, 125, 202

U-2 spy plane, 92, 119, 123, 124
UN (United Nations): Atomic Energy Commission, 58, 214, 218, 226; Charter, 55; 1960 conference on disarmament, 101–2; police force, 96
Undersea Long-Range Missile System (ULMS) and ULMS II, 164
undersea nuclear testing, 140, 141
United Kingdom (UK), 50, 56–57, 113, 223–24
United Nations. *See* UN (United Nations)
"United States Objectives and Programs for National Security." *See* NSC-68 (1950)
United States (US). *See* Central Intelligence Agency (CIA); Defense Department (DOD); FBI (Federal Bureau of Investigation); House of Representatives, US; Senate, US; State Department (DOS); Treasury Department
Ural Mountains, 198, 204, 208
"US Policy on Military Actions in a Berlin Conflict" (NSAM-109, 1961), 114–16
USS Pueblo incident (1968), 137–38
USSBS. *See* Strategic Bombing Survey (USSBS)
USSR (Union of Soviet Socialist Republics). *See* Soviet Union

Vance, Cyrus, 180, 186–87
verification: as criterion for control, 141; inspections, 123, 141; mobile missiles, 183, 233; monitoring *vs.*, 187; obstacles, 231, 235; proliferation problem, 118; technicalities of, 169, 185, 223; test limitations, 110
Verification Panel, 155, 158, 160, 162, 163–64. *See also* SALT (Strategic Arms Limitation Talks)
Vienna Option (1970), 157. *See also* SALT (Strategic Arms Limitation Talks)
Vienna Summit, Kennedy-Khrushchev (1961), 110–11
Vienna talks, 158, 210, 228
Vietnam War (1954–1975), 89, 134–35, 138–39, 143, 148, 159
Vladivostok formula (1974), 166, 183
Vladivostok Summit (1975), 182–83

Wagenfuhr, Rolf, 40
walk in the woods, Nitze-Kvitsinsky (1982), 192, 202–5, 211. *See also* INF (Intermediate-Range Nuclear Forces) Treaty (1987)

Wall Street (New York City), 22–26, 27, 50, 51, 68
Wallace, Henry, 34
"war aims" paper (NSC-79), 64, 79, 80, 90, 245, 247
war on terror, 256–59, 260–61, 263, 267. *See also* September 11 terrorist attacks (2001)
Warnke, Paul, 174, 178
Warsaw Pact, 124, 201, 215, 243, 257. *See also* Czechoslovakia, Soviet invasion of (1968); Poland
Washington Ambassadorial Group, 114–15
Washington Center of Foreign Policy Research (FPR), 96–97
Washington, DC, Nitze's early career, 28–29, 32–33
Washington Post, Gaither Report in, 99
Washington Summit (1987), 230
Watergate scandal (1972), 163–66, 167
Webb, James, 59
Weinberger, Caspar, 198, 212, 214–15, 221–22

Western Europe. *See* Europe
"Why Nuclear Superiority Doesn't Matter" (Jervis article), 190
Wiesner, Jerome, 93
Wilson, Charles, 79
Winthrop, Frederick (Freddie), Jr., 20
Wohlsetter, Albert, 100, 140, 148
Wolfers, Arnold, 96, 100
Wolfowitz, Paul, 148, 257–58, 259, 260–61
World Bank, 137, 147
World War I (WWI), 1, 17, 183–84
World War II (WWII), 33–38, 41, 62–63. *See also* Strategic Bombing Survey (USSBS)
World War III (WWIII), 70, 91

Yale Political Union, debate at, 184–85
Yasuhiro Nakasone, 198
Yom Kippur War (1973), 163

zero option. *See* INF talks
Zumwalt, Elmo (Bud), 132–33, 168, 177, 181, 188